TRUMPET PEALS.

𝔄 Collection of 𝔗imely and 𝔈loquent 𝔈xtracts

FROM THE SERMONS OF THE

REV. T. DE WITT TALMAGE, D.D.

INCLUDING DEMOSTHENEAN PHILIPPICS AGAINST INGERSOLLIAN INFIDELITY,
DARWINIAN EVOLUTION, GAMBLING, STOCK-GAMBLING, THEATRICALS,
CORRUPT LITERATURE AND OTHER EVILS AND PERILS, WITH
SPECIAL APPEALS TO YOUNG MEN AND GOSPEL PEALS
FOR ALL.

COLLATED AND CLASSIFIED

BY THE

REV. L. C. LOCKWOOD.

(WITH THE CONSENT OF DR TALMAGE.).

NEW YORK.
BROMFIELD & COMPANY,
658 BROADWAY

DRUMMOND & NEU,
Electrotypers,

CONTENTS.

CHAPTER IV.

CHAPTER V.

CHAPTER VI.

CHAPTER VII.

CHAPTER VIII.

CHAPTER IX.

CHAPTER X.

CHAPTER XI.

CHAPTER XII.

CHAPTER XIII.

CHAPTER XIV.

CHAPTER XV.

CHAPTER XVI.

CHAPTER XVII.

PREFACE.

DR. TALMAGE needs no introduction, and his Trumpet Peals speak for themselves. The Editor is not a Voice in the Wilderness, proclaiming a coming man, but he can point to one who has already come, and made the world brighter and better for his coming. The collation of some of his thought-gems has been a labor of love that has had its own reward. But the treasure-trove is too good to keep, and he feels like relieving himself of some of the embarrassment of riches by making others as rich as himself. And let each recipient sound aloud the Trumpet Peals, till their echoes reverberate from the Gate of Commerce to the Golden Gate.

If Dr. Talmage is a son of thunder, the thunderbolts are followed by a cloud-burst of refreshing showers of blessing. If he is trumpet-tongued, the trumpet has no uncertain sound, but calls men to battle for the right. If he wields a Damascus blade, sharper than a two-edged sword, it is to cut asunder the bands of wickedness. If he is a second Demosthenes, he utters no second-hand Philippics, but bids us march against modern vices and conquer or die. If he has already won great victories, these but nerve him to win greater. If two tabernacles burn down, he shouts, " None of these things move me," and spurs on a willing people to build one greater than before, after the pattern of the splendid engraving with which this work is embellished.

Nor is Dr. Talmage simply a Reformer, for he wins some of his most signal triumphs on the Gospel field. And with the old Constantinean battle-cry, " In Hoc Signo Vinces "— " By this Sign Conquer," and the motto, " *Via Crucis, via*

Lucis,"—"The Way of the Cross is a Way of Light," he marshals his host at the foot of the Cross, and by the way of Gethsemane leads them up to the glory-height of Olivet, and then up "heaven's infinite steepness" to the glory-height above, and within the pearly gate lays his trophies down at Jesus' feet   Then sound the Trumpet Peals and swell "the consecrated host of God's elect," multiplying the Talmagean trophies by the million, and bringing many sons and daughters unto glory, to shout the loud hallelujahs, and on the Sea of Glass to sing the Song of Moses and the Lamb!

L. C. LOCKWOOD.

WOODHAVEN, L I, January, 1890.

TRUMPET PEALS.

CHAPTER I.

The Great First Cause.

.

"In the beginning God." A beginning must have a Beginner, and that Beginner is God. An effect must have a cause, and the Great First Cause is God —EDITOR

GOD IN CREATION.

The poet of Uz calls us to the laying of the foundation of the great temple of a world. The corner-stone was a block of light, and the trowel was of celestial crystal. All about and on the embankments of cloud stood the angelic choristers unrolling their librettos of overture, and other worlds clapped shining cymbals while the ceremony went on, and God, the architect, by stroke of light after stroke of light, dedicated this great cathedral of a world, with mountains for pillars, and sky for frescoed ceiling, and flowering fields for floor, and sunrise and midnight aurora for upholstery. "Who laid the corner-stone thereof, when the morning stars sang together?"

The whole universe was a complete cadence, an unbroken dithyramb, a musical portfolio. The great sheet of immensity had been spread out, and written on it were the stars, the smaller of them minims, the larger of them sustained notes. The meteors marked the staccato passages, the whole heavens a gamut with all sounds, intonations and modulations, the space between the worlds a musical interval, trembling of stellar light a quaver, the thunder a base clef, the wind among the trees a treble clef. Such the first "music of the spheres."

WHO MADE THE STARS?

Napoleon was on a ship's deck bound for Egypt. It was a bright starry night, and as he paced the deck, thinking of the great affairs of the State and of battle, he heard two men on the deck in conversation about God; one saying there was a God, and the other saying there was no God. Napoleon stopped and looked up at the starry heavens and then turned to these men and said, "Gentlemen, I heard one of you say there is no God, if there is no God, will you please to tell me who made all those stars?"

A GOD! A GOD!

Galileo in prison for his advanced notions of things was asked why he persisted in believing in God, and he pointed down to a broken straw on the floor of his dungeon, and said · "Sirs, if I had no other reason to believe the wisdom and the goodness of God, I would argue them from that straw on the floor of this dungeon." Behold the wisdom of God in the construction of the seeds from which all the growths of spring-time come forth—seeds so wonderfully constructed that they keep their vitality for hundreds and thousands of years. Grains of corn found in the cerements of the Egyptian mummies buried thousands of years ago, planted now, come up as luxuriantly and easily as grains of corn that grew last year planted this spring-time.

After the fire in London in 1666, the Sisimbrium Iris, seeds of which must have been planted hundreds and hundreds of years before that, grew all over the ruins of the fire. Could the universities of the earth explain the mysteries of one rutabaga seed? Could they girdle the mysteries of one grain of corn? Oh, the shining firmament in one drop of dew! Oh, the untravelled continents of mystery in a crystal of snow! Oh, the gorgeous upholstery in one tuft of mountain moss! Oh, the triumphal arch in one tree-branch! All nature cries, "A God!"

Where is the loom in which He wove the curtains of the morning? Where is *the vat of beauty* out of which He dipped the crimson and the gold and the saffron and the blue and the green and the red? Where are the moulds in which He ran out the Alps and the Pyrenees? Where is the harp that gave the warble to the lark, and the sweet call to the robin, and the carol to the canary, and the chirp to the grasshopper? Oh, the God in an atom!

THE PLEIADES AND ORION.

"The heavens declare the glory of God, and the firmament showeth His handiwork." They mirror their Maker.—EDITOR.

"Seek Him that maketh the Seven Stars and Orion."—AMOS 5 : 8.

A country farmer wrote these words: Amos of Tekoa. He ploughed the earth and threshed the grain with a new threshing-machine, as formerly the cattle trod out the grain. He gathered the fruit of the sycamore tree, and scarified it with an iron comb just before it was getting ripe, as it was necessary and customary in that way to take from it the bitterness. He was the son of a poor shepherd; but before the rustic the Philistines, and Syrians, and Phœnicians, and Moabites, and Ammonites, and Edomites, and Israelites trembled.

THE PEASANT ASTRONOMER.

Moses was a law-giver, Daniel was a prince, Isaiah a courtier, and David a king; but Amos was a peasant; and, as might be supposed, nearly all his parallelisms are pastoral, his prophecy full of the odor of new-mown hay, the rattle of locusts, the rumble of carts with sheaves, and the roar of wild beasts devouring the flock, while the shepherd came out in their defence. He watched the herds by day, and by night inhabited a booth made out of bushes, so that through these branches he could see the stars all night long, and was more familiar with them than we who have tight roofs to

our houses and hardly ever see the stars except among the
tall brick chimneys of the great towns.   But at seasons of
the year when the herds were in special danger he would
stay out in the open field all through the darkness, his only
shelter the curtain of the night, heaven, with the stellar embroideries and silvered tassels of lunar light.

What a life of solitude, all alone with his herds!   Poor
Amos! and at twelve o'clock at night, hark to the wolf's
bark, and the lion's roar, and the bear's growl, and the owl's
te-whit-te-whos, and the serpent's hiss as he unwittingly steps
too near while moving through the thickets !   So Amos, like
other herdsmen, got the habit of studying the map of the
heavens, because it was so much of the time spread out before him.   He noticed some stars advancing, and others
receding.   He associated their dawn and setting with certain
seasons of the year.   He had a poetic nature, and he read
night by night, and month by month, and year by year *the
poem of the constellations*, divinely rhythmic.

TWO ROSETTES OF STARS

especially attracted his attention while seated on the ground
or lying on his back under the open scroll of the midnight
heavens—the Pleiades, or Seven Stars, and Orion.   The
former group this rustic prophet associated with the spring,
as it rises about the first of May.   The latter he associated
with the winter, as it comes to the meridian in January.
The Pleiades, or Seven Stars, connected with all sweetness
and joy ; Orion the herald of the tempest.   No wonder that
Amos, having heard these two anthems of the stars, put
down the stout rough staff of the herdsman, and took into
his brown hand and cut and knotted fingers the pen of a
prophet, and advised the recreant people of his time to return to God, saying : " Seek Him that maketh the Seven
Stars and Orion."   This command, which Amos gave 785
years B C , is just as appropriate for us.

WHAT THE STARS TEACH.

In the first place, Amos saw, as we must see, that the God who made the Pleiades and Orion must be the God of order. It was not so much a star here and a star there that impressed the inspired herdsman, but seven in one group, and seven in the other group. He saw that night after night, season after season, and decade after decade, they had kept step of light, each one in its own place, a sisterhood never clashing and never contesting precedence. From the time Hesiod called the Pleiades the "Seven Daughters of Atlas" and Virgil wrote in his Æneid of "Stormy Orion" until now they have observed the order established for their coming and going; order written not in manuscript that may be pigeon-holed, but with the hand of the Almighty on the dome of the sky, so that all nations may read it. Order. Persistent order. Sublime order. Omnipotent order.

What a sedative to you and me, to whom communities and nations sometimes seem going pell-mell, and the world ruled by some fiend at hap-hazard, and in all directions mal-administration ! The God who keeps seven worlds in right circuit for six thousand years can certainly keep all the affairs of individuals, nations, and continents in adjustment. We better not fret, for the peasant's argument was right. If God can take care of the seven worlds of the Pleiades, and the four chief worlds of Orion, He can probably take care of the one world we inhabit. Think for your consolation that, as a part of His care, there are two hundred stars in the Pleiades, and that in what is called the sword of Orion there is a nebula computed to be two trillion two hundred thousand billions of times larger than the sun, the wheel of the constellations turning in the wheel of galaxies for thousands of years without the breaking of a cog, or the slipping of a band, or the snap of an axle; and for your placidity and comfort I charge you, "Seek Him that maketh the Seven Stars and Orion."

THE GOD OF LIGHT.

Again, Amos saw, as we must see, that the God who made these two groups of stars was the God of light. Not satisfied with making one star or two or three stars, He makes seven; and having finished that group of worlds, makes another group, group after group. To the Pleiades He adds Orion. It seems that God likes light so well that He keeps making it. Only one being in the universe knows the statistics of solar, lunar, stellar, and meteoric creations, and that is the Creator Himself. And they have all been lovingly christened, each one a name as distinct as the names of your children. "He telleth the number of the stars; He calleth them all by their names." The seven Pleiades had names given to them, and they are Alcyone, Merope, Celæno, Electra, Sterope, Taygete, and Maia.

But think of the billions and trillions of daughters of starry light that God calls by name as they sweep by Him with beaming brow and lustrous robe. So fond is God of light, natural light, moral light, spiritual light. Again and again is light harnessed for symbolization—Christ, the bright and morning star; evangelization, the daybreak; the redemption of nations, Sun of Righteousness rising with healing in His wings. Oh, with so many sorrows and sins and perplexities, if you want light of comfort, light of pardon, light of goodness, in earnest prayer through Christ, "Seek Him that maketh the Seven Stars and Orion."

THE IMMUTABLE.

Again, Amos saw, as we must see, that the God who made these two archipelagoes of stars must be an unchanging God. There had been no change in the stellar appearance in this herdsman's lifetime, and his father, a shepherd, reported to him that there had been no change in his lifetime. And these two clusters hang over the celestial arbor now just as they were the first night that they shone on Edenic bowers; the same as when the Egyptians built the

Pyramids, from the top of which to watch them ; the same as when the Chaldeans calculated the eclipses; the same as when Elihu, according to the book of Job, went out to study the aurora borealis, the same under Ptolemaic system and Copernican system; the same from Calisthenes to Pythagoras, and from Pythagoras to Herschel. Surely, a changeless God must have fashioned the Pleiades and Orion! Oh what an anodyne amid the ups and downs of life, and the flux and reflux of the tides of prosperity, to know that we have a changeless God, the same yesterday, to-day, and forever!

CHAIN OF EVENTS.

All events are linked together. You who are aged can look back and group together a thousand things in your life that once seemed isolated. One undivided chain of events reached from the Garden of Eden to the Cross of Calvary, and thus up to heaven.

There is a relation between the smallest insect that hums in the summer air and the archangel on his throne. God can trace a direct ancestral line from the blue-jay, that last spring built its nest in a tree behind the house, to some one of that flock of birds which, when Noah hoisted the ark's window, with a whirl and dash of bright wings, went out to sing over Mount Ararat. The tulips that bloomed this summer in the flower-bed were nursed by last winter's snow-flakes. The farthest star on one'side the universe could not look to the farthest star on the other side and say, " You are no relation to me ; " for, from that bright orb, a voice of light would ring across the heavens, responding, " Yes, yes ; we are sisters."

Sir Sidney Smith in prison was playing lawn tennis in the yard, and the ball flew over the wall. Another ball, containing letters, was thrown back, and so communication was opened with the outside world, and Sidney Smith escaped in time to defeat Bonaparte's Egyptian expedition. What a small accident, connected with what vast results ! Sir Rob-

ert Peel, from a pattern he drew on the back of a pewter
dinner-plate, got suggestions of that which led to the important invention by which calico is printed. Nothing in
God's universe swings at loose ends. Accidents are only
God's way of turning a leaf in the book of His eternal decrees. From our cradle to our grave there is a path all
marked out. Each event in life is connected with every
other event in life. Our loss may be the most direct road
to our gain. *Our defeats and victories are twin brothers.*
The whole direction of life was changed by something which
at the time seemed a trifle, while some occurrence, which
seemed tremendous, affected it but little.

God's plans are magnificent beyond all comprehension.
He moulds us, turns and directs us, and we know it not.
Thousands of years are to Him but as the flight of a shuttle.
The most terrific occurrence does not make God tremble,
and the most triumphant achievement does not lift Him into
rapture. That one great thought of God goes on through
the centuries, and nations rise and fall, and eras pass, and
the world itself changes, but God still keeps the undivided
mastery, linking event to event and century to century. To
God they are all one event, one history, one plan, one development, one system. " Great and marvellous are thy works,
Lord God Almighty!"

Lord Hastings was beheaded one year after he had
caused the death of the Queen's children, in the very month,
the very day, the very hour, and the very moment. There
is *wonderful precision in the Divine judgments.* The universe
is only one thought of God Those things which seem frag-
mentary and isolated are only different parts of that one
great thought.

TRUSTING GOD.

I stood on the beach, looking off upon the sea; and
there was a strong wind blowing : and noticing that some of
the vessels were going one way, and other vessels were going
another way, I said to myself, " How is it that the same

wind sends one vessel in one direction and another vessel in another direction?" and I found out, by looking, that it was the difference in the way they had the sails set. And so does trouble come on this world. Some men it drives into the harbor of heaven, and other men it drives on the rocks. It depends upon the way they have their sails set. All the Atlantic and Pacific oceans of surging sorrow cannot sink a soul that has asked for God's pilotage. The difficulty is that, when we have misfortunes of any kind, we put them in God's hand, and they stay there a little while ; and then we go and get them again and bring them back.

A vessel comes in from a foreign port. As it comes near the harbor, it sees a pilot floating about. It hails the pilot. The pilot comes on board and says: "Now, captain, you have had a stormy passage. Go down and sleep, and I will take the vessel into New York harbor." After a while the captain begins to think : "Am I right in trusting this vessel to that pilot? I guess I'll go up and see." So he comes to the pilot and says : "Don't you see that rock? Don't you see those headlands? You will wreck the ship. Let me lay hold the helm for a while for myself, and then I'll trust to you." The pilot becomes angry and says, "I will either take care of this ship or not. If you want to, I will get into my yawl and go ashore or back to my boat." Now, we say to the Lord, "O God, take my life, take my all, in Thy keeping! Be Thou my Guide ; be Thou my Pilot." We go along for a little while, and suddenly wake up and say, " Things are going all wrong. O Lord, we are driving on these rocks, and Thou art going to let us be shipwrecked." God says: " You go and rest ; I will take charge of this vessel, and take it into the harbor." It is God's business to comfort, and it is our business to be comforted.

A little child went with her father, a sea captain, to sea, and when the first storm came the little child was very much frightened, and in the night rushed out of the cabin and said, " Where is father ? where is father?" Then they told her, " Father is on deck, guiding the vessel and watching the storm." The little child immediately returned to her berth and said, " It's all right, for father's on deck."

Oh, ye who are tossed and driven in this world, up by the mountains and down by the valleys, and at your wit's end, I want you to know the Lord God is guiding the ship. Your Father is on deck. He will bring you through the darkness into the harbor. Trust in the Lord.

CHAPTER II.

Evolution: Anti-God, Anti-Bible, Anti-Science, Anti-Common-Sense.

"O Timothy, keep that which is committed to thy trust, avoiding oppositions of science falsely so called."—i TIM 6 : 20.

Science and revelation are *the bass and the soprano of the same tune*. The whole world will yet acknowledge the complete harmony. But between what God describes as science falsely so called and revelation, there is an uncompromising war, and one or the other must go under.

THE CREED OF EVOLUTIONISTS.

The air is filled with social and platform and pulpit talk about evolution, and it is high time that the people who have not time to make investigation for themselves understand that evolution in the first place is up and down, out and out infidelity, in the second place, it is contrary to the facts of science; and in the third place, that it is brutalizing in its tendencies.

I want you to understand that Thomas Paine and Hume and Voltaire no more thoroughly disbelieved the Holy Scriptures than do all the leading scientists who believe in evolution

I put upon the witness stand the leading evolutionists— Ernst Heckel, John Stuart Mill, Huxley, Tyndall, Darwin, Spencer. On the witness stand, ye men of science, living and dead, answer these questions: Do you believe in a God? No. And so say they all. Do you believe the Bible story of Adam and Eve in the Garden of Eden? No. Do you believe the miracles of the Old and New Testaments? No. Do you believe that Jesus Christ died to save the nations?

No. Do you believe in the regenerating power of the Holy Ghost? No. Do you believe that human supplication directed heavenward ever makes any difference? No.

Herbert Spencer, in the only address he made in this country, in his very first sentence ascribes his physical ailments to fate, and the authorized report of that address begins the word fate with a big "F." Professor Heckel, in the very first page of his two great volumes, sneers at the Bible as a so-called revelation. Tyndall, in his famous prayer test, defied the whole of Christendom to show that human supplication made any difference in the result of things. John Stuart Mill wrote elaborately against Christianity, and, to show that his rejection of it was complete, ordered this epitaph for his tombstone: "Most unhappy." Huxley said that at the first reading of Darwin's book he was convinced of the fact that teleology, by which he means Christianity, had received its death-blow at the hand of Mr. Darwin. All the leading scientists who believe in evolution, without one exception the world over, are infidel.

EVOLUTION IS INFIDELITY.

I put opposite to each other the Bible account of how the human race started and the evolutionist account as to how the human race started. Bible account: "God said, let us make man in our image. God created man in his own image; male and female created He them," He breathed into him the breath of life, the whole story setting forth the idea that it was not a perfect kangaroo, or a perfect orang outang, but a perfect man. That is the Bible account. The evolutionist account: Away back in the ages there were four or five primal germs, or seminal spores, from which all the living creatures have been evolved. Go away back, and there you find a vegetable stuff that might be called a mushroom. This mushroom by innate force develops a tadpole, the tadpole by innate force develops a polywog, the polywog develops a fish, the fish by natural force develops into a reptile, the reptile develops into a quadruped, the quadruped develops into a baboon, the baboon develops into a man.

Darwin says that the human hand is only a fish's fin developed. He says that the human lungs are only a swim-bladder showing that we once floated or were amphibious. He says the human ear could once have been moved by force of will, just as a horse lifts its ear at a frightful object. He says the human race were originally web-footed. From primal germ to tadpole, from tadpole to fish, from fish to reptile, from reptile to wolf, from wolf to chimpanzee, and from chimpanzee to man. Now, if anybody says that the Bible account of the starting of the human race and the evolutionist account of the starting of the human race are the same accounts, he makes an appalling misrepresentation.

Prefer, if you will, Darwin's " Origin of the Species" to the Book of Genesis, but know you are an infidel. As for myself, as Herbert Spencer was not present at the creation, and the Lord Almighty was present, I prefer to take the divine account as to what really occurred on that occasion. To show that this evolution is only an attempt to eject God and to postpone Him and to put Him clear out of reach, I ask *a question or two.* The baboon made the man, and the wolf made the baboon, and the reptile made the quadruped, and the fish made the reptile, and the tadpole made the fish, and the primal germ made the tadpole. Who made the primal germ? Most of the evolutionists say, " We don't know " Others say it made itself. Others say it was spon-taneous generation. There is not one of them who will fairly and openly and frankly and emphatically say, " God made it."

The nearest to a direct answer is that made by Herbert Spencer in which he says it was made by the great " unknow-able mystery." But here comes Huxley, with a pail of protoplasm, to explain the thing. The protoplasm, he says, is primal life, giving quality with which the race away back in the ages was started. With this protoplasm he proposes to explain everything. Dear Mr. Huxley, who made the protoplasm?

AN INCONSISTENT THEORY.

To show you that evolution is infidel, I place the Bible account of how the brute creation was started opposite to the evolutionist's account of the way the brute creation was started. Bible account: You know the Bible tells how that the birds were made at one time, and the cattle made at another time, and the fish made at another time, and that each brought forth after its kind. Evolutionist's account: From four or five primal germs, or seminal spores, all the living creatures evolved. Hundreds of thousands of species of insects, of reptiles, of beasts, of fish, from four germs—a statement flatly contradicting not only the Bible, but the very A B C of science. A species never develops into anything but its own species. In all the ages and in all the world there has never been an exception to it. The shark never comes of a whale, nor the pigeon of a vulture, nor the butterfly of a wasp. Species never cross over. If there be an attempt at it, it is hybrid, and hybrid is always sterile and has no descendants.

Agassiz says that he found in a reef of Florida the re-remains of insects thirty thousand years old—not three but thirty thousand years old—and that they were just like the insects now. There has been no change. All the facts of ornithology and zoology and ichthyology and conchology, but an echo of Genesis first and twenty-first—"every winged fowl after his kind." Every creature after its kind. When common observation and science corroborate the Bible, I will not stultify myself by surrendering to the elaborated guesses of evolutionists.

THE ORIGIN OF WORLDS.

To show that evolution is infidel I place also the Bible account of how worlds were made opposite the evolutionist account of how worlds were made. Bible account: God made two great lights—the one to rule the day, the other to rule the night. He made the stars also. Evolutionist account. Away back in the ages, there was a fire mist or star dust, and this fire mist cooled off into granite, and then this granite by earthquake and by storm and by light was shaped into mountains and valleys and seas, and so what was originally fire mist became what we call the earth.

Who made the fire mist? Who set the fire mist to world-making? Who cooled off the fire mist into granite? You have pushed God some sixty or seventy million miles from the earth, but He is too near yet for the health of evolution. For a great while the evolutionists boasted that they had found the very stuff out of which this world and all worlds were made. They lifted the telescope and they saw it, the very material out of which worlds made themselves. Nebula of simple gas. They laughed in triumph because they had found *the factory where the worlds were manufactured*, and there was no God anywhere around the factory! But in an unlucky hour for infidel evolutionists the spectroscopes of Fraunhofer and Kirchoff were invented, by which they saw into that nebula and found it was not a simple gas, but was a compound, and hence had to be supplied from some other source, and that implied a God; and away went their theory shattered into everlasting demolition.

So these infidel evolutionists go wandering up and down guessing through the universe. Anything to push back Jehovah from His empire and make the one Book which is His great communication to the soul of the human race appear obsolete and a derision. But I am glad to know that while some of these scientists have gone into evolution, there are more that do not believe it. Among them, the man who by most is considered the greatest scientist we ever had this side the water—Agassiz. A name that makes every intelligent man the earth over uncover.

Agassiz says: "The manner in which the evolution theory in zoology is treated would lead those who are not special zoologists to suppose that observations have been made by which it can be inferred that there is in nature such a thing as change among organized beings actually taking place. There is no such thing on record. It is shifting

the ground of observation from one field of observation to
another to make this statement ; and when the assertions go
so far as to exclude from the domain of science those who
will not be dragged into this mire of mere assertion, then it
is time to protest."

JUMPING OVERBOARD.

With equal vehemence against this doctrine of evolution
Hugh Miller, Faraday, Brewster, Dana, Dawson, and hundreds of scientists in this country and other countries have
made protest. I know that the few men who have adopted
the theory make more noise than the thousands who have
rejected it. The Bothnia of the Cunard Line took five hundred passengers safely from New York to Liverpool. Not
one of the five hundred made any excitement. But after
we had been four days out, one morning we found on deck
a man's hat, coat, vest and boots, implying that some one
had jumped overboard. Forthwith we all began to talk
about that one man. There was more talk about that one
man overboard than all the five hundred passengers that
rode on in safety. "Why did he jump overboard?" " I
wonder when he jumped overboard?" " I wonder if when
he jumped overboard he would like to have jumped back
again?" " I wonder if a fish caught him, or whether he
went clear down to the bottom of the sea?" And for three
or four days afterwards we talked about that poor man.

Here is the glorious and magnificent theory that God by
His omnipotent power made man, by His omnipotent power
made the brute creation, and by His omnipotent power
made all worlds, and five thousand scientists have taken passage on board that magnificent theory, but ten or fifteen
have jumped overboard. They make more talk than all the
five thousand that did not jump. I am politely asked to
jump with them. Thank you, gentlemen, I am very much
obliged to you. I think I shall stick to the old Cunarder.
If you want to jump overboard, jump, and test for yourselves whether your hand was really a fish's fin, and whether

you were web-footed originally, and whether your lungs were a swim-bladder. And as in every experiment there must be a division of labor, some who experiment and some who observe, you make the experiment and I will observe!

ONE OF THE TENETS.

There is one tenet of evolution which it is demanded we adopt, that which Darwin calls " Natural Selection," and that which Wallace calls the " *Survival of the Fittest.*" By this they mean that the human race and the brute creation are all the time improving because the weak die and the strong live. Those who do not die survive because they are the fittest. They say'the breed of sheep and cattle and dogs and men is all the time naturally improving. No need of God or Bible or religion, but just natural progress.

You see the race started with " spontaneous generation," and then it goes right on until Darwin can take us up with his " natural selection," and Wallace can take us up with his " survial of the fittest," and so we go right on up forever. Beautiful! But do the fittest survive? Garfield dead in September—Guiteau surviving until the following June. " Survival of the fittest?" Ah! no. The martyrs, religious and political, dying for their principles, their bloody perse-cutors living on to old age. " Survival of the fittest?" Five hundred thousand brave Northern men marching out to meet five hundred thousand brave Southern men, and die on the battle-field for a principle. Hundreds of thousands of them went down into the grave trenches. We stayed at home in comfortable quarters. Did they die because they were not as fit to live as we who survived? Ah! no ; not the "sur-vival of the fittest." Ellsworth and Nathaniel Lyon falling on the Northern side. Albert Sidney Johnston and Stone-wall Jackson falling on the Southern side. Did they fall be-cause they were not as fit to live as the soldiers and the gen-erals who came back in safety? No. Bitten with the frosts of the second death be the tongue that dares utter it! It is not the " survival of the fittest."

How has it been in the families of the world? How was it with the child physically the strongest, intellectually the brightest, in disposition the kindest? Did that child die because it was not as fit to live as those of your family that survived? Not "the survival of the fittest." In all communities some of the noblest, grandest men dying in youth, or in mid life, while some of the meanest and most contemptible live on to old age. Not the " survival of the fittest."

NO NATURAL PROGRESS.

But to show you that this doctrine is antagonistic to the Bible and to common-sense I have only to prove to you that there has been *no natural progress*. Vast improvement from another source, but, mind you, no natural progress. Where, where is the fine horse in any of our parks whose picture of eye and mane and nostril and neck and haunches are worthy of being compared to *Job's picture of a horse* as he, thousands of years ago, heard it paw and neigh and champ its bit for the battle? Pigeons of to-day not so wise as the carrier pigeons of five hundred years ago—pigeons that carried the mails from army to army and from city to city; one of them flung into the sky at Rome or Venice landing without ship or rail train in London.

And *as to the human race,* so far as mere natural progress is concerned, it started with men ten feet high, now the average is about five feet six inches. It started with men living two hundred, four hundred, eight hundred, nine hundred years, and now thirty years is more than the average of human life. Mighty progress we have made, haven't we? I went into the cathedral at York, England, and the best artists in England had just been painting a window in that cathedral, and right beside it was a window painted four hundred years ago, and there is not a man on earth but would say that the modern painting of the window by the best artists of England is not worthy of being compared with the painting of four hundred years ago right beside it. Vast improvement, as I shall show you in a minute or two, but no natural evolution.

EVOLUTION DOWNWARD.

I tell you, my friends, that natural evolution is not upward, but is always downward. Hear Christ's account of it. Fifteenth Matthew and nineteenth verse : " Out of the heart proceed evil thoughts, murders, adulteries, fornications, thefts, false witness, blasphemies." This is *what Christ said of Evolution.* Give natural evolution full swing in our world and it will evolve into two hemispheres of crime, two hemi-, spheres of penitentiary, two hemispheres of lazaretto, two hemispheres of brothel. New Yorks Tombs ; Moyamensing Prison, Philadelphia ; Seven Dials, London ; and Cowgate, Edinburgh; only festering carbuncles on the face and neck of natural evolution. See what the Bible says about the heart, and then what evolution says about the heart. Evolution says, " better and better and better gets the heart by natural improvement." The Bible says : " The heart is deceitful above all things, and desperately wicked. Who can know it ?" When you can evolve fragrance from malodor, and oratorio from a buzz-saw, and fall pippins from a basket of decayed crab apples, then you can by natural evolution from the human heart develop goodness. Ah ! my friends, evolution is always downward ; never upward.

BIBLE EVOLUTION.

I am not a pessimist, but an optimist. I do not believe everything is going to destruction ; I believe everything is going on to redemption But it will not be through the infidel doctrine of evolution, but through our glorious Christianity, which has effected all the good that has ever been wrought and which is yet to reconstruct all the nations.

Away with your rotten, deceptive, infidel, and blasphemous evolution, and give us the Bible, salvation through Jesus Christ our Lord.

"Salvation ! let the echo fly
The spacious earth around,
Till all the armies of the sky
Conspire to raise the sound."

MODERN EVOLUTIONISTS.

Oh, it makes me sick to see these literary fops going along with a copy of Darwin under one arm and a case of transfixed grasshoppers and butterflies under the other arm, telling about the "survival of the fittest," and Huxley's protoplasm, and the nebular hypothesis.

As near as I can tell, evolutionists seem to think that God at the start had not made up His mind as to exactly what He would make, and so He has been changing it all through the ages.

Evolution is one great mystery, it hatches out fifty mysteries, and the fifty hatch out a thousand, and the thousand hatch out a million. Why, my brother, not admit the one great mystery of God, and have that settle all the other mysteries? I can more easily appreciate the fact that God by one stroke of his omnipotence could make man than I could realize how out of five millions of ages He could have evolved one, putting on a little here and a little there. It would have been just as great a miracle for God to have turned an orang-outang into a man as to make a man out and out—the one job just as big as the other.

It seems to me we had better let God have a little place in our world somewhere. It seems to me if we cannot have Him make all creatures, we had better have Him make two or three. There ought to be some place where He could stay without interfering with the evolutionists. "No," says Darwin. And so for years he is trying to make fan-tailed pigeons into some other kind of pigeon, or to have them go into something that is not a pigeon—turning them into quail, or barnyard fowl, or brownthresher. But pigeon it is. And others have tried with the ox and the dog and the horse, but they stayed in their species. If they attempt to cross over, it is a hybrid, and a hybrid is always sterile and goes into extinction. There has been *only one successful attempt* to pass over from speechless animal to the articulation of man, and that was the attempt which Balaam witnessed in the beast that he rode; but an angel of the Lord, with drawn sword, soon stopped that long-eared evolutionist.

But, says some one, "if we cannot have God make a man, let us have Him make a horse." "Oh no!" says Huxley, in his great lectures in New York several years ago. No, he does not want any God around the premises. God did not make the horse. The horse came of the pliohippus, and the pliohippus came from the protohippus, and the protohippus from the mio-hippus, and the mio-hippus came from the meshohippus, and the meshohippus came from the orohippus, and so away back, all the living creatures, we trace it in a line until we get to the moneron; and no evidence of divine intermeddling with the creation until you get to the moneron; and that, Huxley says, is of so low a form of life that the probability is, it just made itself or was the result of spontaneous generation. What a narrow escape from the necessity of having a God!

I tell you plainly that if your father was a muskrat and your mother an oppossum, and your great aunt a kangaroo, and the toads and the snapping-turtles were your illustrious predecessors, my father was God. I know it. I feel it. It thrills through me with an emphasis and an ecstasy which all your arguments drawn from anthropology and biology and zoology and morology and paleontology and all other ologies can never shake.

SONS OF A GORILLA OR SONS OF GOD?

"Professing themselves to be wise, they became fools, and changed the glory of the uncorruptible God into an image made like to corruptible man, and to birds, and to four-footed beasts, and creeping things."—ROM. 1: 22, 23.

A full-length portrait of an evolutionist who substitutes the bestial origin for the divine origin. Sons of a gorilla, or sons of God? is the great question of this day, and every intelligent man and woman must be able to give an intelligent answer.

In the first chapter of Genesis, we find that God, without

any consultation, created the light, created the trees, created the fish, created the fowl, but when He was about to make man He called a convention of divinity, as though to imply that all the powers of Godhead were to be enlisted in the achievement. " Let us make man." Put *a whole ton of em phasis* on that word " us." " Let *us* make man." *All to show the pre-eminence of man over the brute and the absurdity of evolution.*

THE MISSING LINK.

Evolutionists are trying to impress people with the idea that there is *an ancestral line* leading from the primal germ on up through the serpent, and on up through the quadruped, and on up through the gorilla to man. They admit that there is " a missing link," as they call it: but there is not a missing link—it is a whole chain gone. Between the physical construction of the highest animal and the physical construction of the lowest man, there is a chasm as wide as the Atlantic Ocean.

Evolutionists tell us that somewhere in central Africa, or in Borneo, there is a creature half-way between the brute and the man, and that that creature is the highest step in the animal ascent and the lowest step in the human creation. But what are the facts? The brain of the largest gorilla that was ever found is thirty cubic inches, while the brain of the most ignorant man that was ever found is seventy. Vast difference between thirty and seventy. It needs a bridge of forty arches to span that gulf.

Beside that, there is a difference between the gorilla and the man—*a difference of blood globule*, a difference of nerve, a difference of muscle, a difference of bone, a difference of sinew.

Beside that, if a pair of apes had a man for descendant, why would not all the apes have the same kind of descendants? Can it be that that one favored pair only was honored with human progeny? Beside that, evolution says that as one species rises to another species, the old type dies off.

Then how is it that there are whole kingdoms of chimpanzee and gorilla and baboon?

EVOLUTION OF A BIRD'S WING.

The evolutionists have come together and have tried to explain *a bird's wing.* Their theory has always been that a faculty of an animal while being developed must always be useful and always beneficial, but the wing of a bird, in the thousands of years it was being developed, so far from being any help must have been a hindrance until it could be brought into practical use away on down in the ages. Must there not have been an intelligent will somewhere that formed that wonderful flying instrument, so that a bird five hundred times heavier than the air can mount it and put gravitation under claw and beak? That wonderful mechanical instrument, the wing, with between twenty and thirty different apparati curiously constructed,—does it not imply a divine intelligence?—does it not imply a direct act of some outside being? All the evolutionists in the world cannot explain a bird's wing, or an insect's wing.

THE RATTLESNAKE.

So they are confounded by the rattle of the rattlesnake. Ages before that reptile had any enemies, this warning weapon was created. Why was it created? When the reptile far back in the ages had no enemies, why this warning weapon? There must have been a divine intelligence foreseeing and knowing that in the ages to come that reptile would have enemies and then this warning weapon would be brought into use You see evolution at every step is a contradiction or a monstrosity. At every stage of animal life as well as at every stage of human life, there is evidence of direct action of divine will.

Beside that, it is very evident from another fact that we are an *entirely different creation,* and that there is no kinship. The animal in a few hours or months comes to full strength and can take care of itself. The human race for the first one, two, three, five, ten years is in complete helplessness. The chick just come out of its shell begins to pick up its own food. The dog, the wolf, the lion, soon earn their own livelihood and act for their own defence. The human race does not come to development until twenty or thirty years of age, and by that time the animals that were born the same year the man was born—the vast majority of them have died of old age. This shows there is no kinship, there is no similarity. If we had been born of the beast, we would have had the beast's strength at the start, or it would have had our weakness. Not only different but opposite.

EVOLUTION A GUESS.

Darwin admits that the dovecote pigeon has not changed in thousands of years. It is demonstrated over and over again that the lizard on the lowest formation of rocks was just as complete as the lizard now. It is shown that the ganoid, the first fish, was just as complete as the sturgeon, another name for the same fish now. Darwin's entire system is a guess, and Huxley, and John Stuart Mill, and Tyndall, and especially Professor Heckel, come to help him in the guess, and guess about the brute, and guess about man, and guess about worlds, but as to having one solid foot of ground to stand on, they never have had it and never will have it.

THE INWARD TESTIMONY.

I put in opposition to these evolutionist theories the *inward consciousness* that we have no consanguinity with the dog that fawns at our feet, or the spider that crawls on the wall, or the fish that flops in the frying-pan, or the crow that swoops on the field carcass, or the swine that wallows in the mire. Everybody sees the outrage it would be to put beside the Bible record that Abraham begat Isaac, and Isaac begat Jacob, and Jacob begat Judah, the record that the microscopic animalcule begat the tadpole, and the tadpole begat the polliwog, and the polliwog begat the serpent, and the serpent begat the quadruped, and the quadruped begat the baboon, and the baboon begat man.

A STRANGE GENEALOGY!

The evolutionists tell us that the apes were originally fond of climbing the trees, but after a while they lost their prehensile power, and therefore could not climb with any facility, and hence they surrendered monkeydom and set up in business as men. Failures as apes, successes as men. According to the evolutionists a man is a bankrupt monkey. I pity the person who in every nerve and muscle and bone and mental faculty and spiritual experience does not realize that he is higher in origin and has had a grander ancestry than the beasts which perish. However degraded men and women may be, and though they may have foundered on the rocks of crime and sin, and though we shudder as we pass them, nevertheless there is something within us that tells us they belong to the same great brotherhood and sisterhood of our race, and our sympathies are aroused in regard to them. But gazing upon the swiftest gazelle, or upon the tropical bird of most flamboyant wing, or upon the curve of grandest courser's neck, we feel there is no consanguinity. The grandest, the highest, the noblest of them ten thousand fathoms below what we are conscious of being.

It is not that we are stronger than they, for the lion with one stroke of his paw could put us into the dust. It is not that we have better eyesight, for the eagle can descry a mole a mile away. It is not that we are fleeter of foot, for a roebuck in a flash is out of sight, just seeming to touch the earth as he goes. Many of the animal creation surpassing us in fleetness of foot and in keenness of nostril and in strength of limb ; but notwithstanding all that, there is something within us that tells us we are of celestial pedigree. Not of the mollusk, not of the rhizopod, not of the primal germ, but of the living and omnipotent God. Lineage of the skies. Genealogy of Heaven.

THE JURY DISAGREE.

Evolutionists say that science is overcoming religion in our day. They look through the spectacles of the infidel scientists and they say, "It is impossible that this book be true; people are finding it out; the Bible has got to go overboard." Science is going to throw it overboard. Do you believe that the Bible account of the origin of life will be overthrown by infidel scientists who have fifty different theories about the origin of life? If they should come up in solid phalanx, all agreeing on one sentiment and one theory, perhaps Christianity might be damaged, but there are not so many differences of opinion inside the church as outside the church.

The fact is that some naturalists, just as soon as they find out the difference between the feelers of a wasp and the horns of a beetle, begin to patronize the Almighty; while Agassiz, glorious Agassiz, who never made any pretension to being a Christian, puts both his feet on the doctrine of evolution, and says: "I see that many of the naturalists of our day are adopting facts which do not bear observation, or have not passed under observation." These men warring with each other—Darwin warring against Lamarck, Wallace warring against Cope, even Herschel denouncing Ferguson. They do not agree about anything. They do not agree on embryology, do not agree on the gradation of the species.

What do they agree on? Herschel writes a whole chapter on the errors of astronomy. La Place declares that the moon was not put in the right place. He says if it had been put four times farther from the earth than it is now, there would be more harmony in the universe; but Lionville comes up just in time to prove that the moon was put in the right place. How many colors woven into the light? Seven, says Isaac Newton. Three, says David Brewster. How high is the *Aurora borealis?* Two and a half miles, says Lias. How far is the sun from the earth? Seventy-six million miles, says Lacaille. Eighty-two million miles, says

Humboldt. Ninety million miles, says Henderson. One hundred and four million miles, says Mayer. Only a little difference of twenty-eight million miles! All split up among themselves—not agreeing on anything.

Here these infidel scientists have empanelled themselves as a jury to decide this trial between evolution, the plaintiff, and Christianity, the defendant, and after being out for centuries they come in to render their verdict. Gentlemen of the jury, have you agreed on a verdict? No, no. Then go back for another five hundred years and deliberate and agree on something. There is not a poor miserable wretch in the Tombs Court to-morrow that could be condemned by a jury that did not agree on the verdict, and yet you expect us to give up our glorious Christianity to please these men, who cannot agree on anything.

[The Editor adds By the disagreement of the jury, the plaintiff, Evolution, loses the case.]

SPECIES TO REMAIN DISTINCT.

I believe that God made the world as He wanted to have it, and that the happiness of all the species will depend upon their staying in the species where they were created.

Once upon a time there was in a natural amphitheatre of the forest a convention of animals, and a gorilla from western Africa came in with his club and pounded "Order!" Then he sat down in a chair of twisted forest roots. The delegation of birds came in and took their position in the galleries of the hills and the tree-tops. And a delegation of reptiles came in, and they took their position in the pit of the valley. And the tiers of rocks were occupied by the delegation of intermediate animals; and there was a great aquarium and a canal leading into it through which came the monsters of the deep to join the great convention. And on one table of rock there were four or five primal germs under a glass case, and in a cup on another table of rock there was a quantity of protoplasm.

Then this gorilla of the African forest, with his club,

pounded again," Order ! order '" and then he cried out : " Oh,
you great throng of beasts and birds and reptiles and insects,
I have called you together to *propose that we move up* into
the human race, and be beasts no longer; too long already
have we been hunted and caged and harnessed ; we shall
stand it no longer " At that speech the whole convention
broke out in roars of enthusiasm like as though there were
many menageries being fed by their keepers, and it did seem
as if the whole convention would march right up and take
possession of the earth and the human race.

But *an old lion* arose, his mane white with many years,
and he uttered his voice ; and when that old lion uttered his
voice, all the other beasts of the forest were still, and he said :
" Peace, brothers and sisters of the forest. I think we have
been placed in the spheres for which we were intended ; I
think our Creator knew the place that was good for us."

He could proceed no further, for the whole convention
broke out in an uproar like the House of Commons when the
Irish question comes up, or the American Congress the night
of adjournment, and the reptiles hissed with indignation at
the lionine Gambetta, and the frogs croaked their contempt,
and the bears growled their contempt, and the panthers
snarled their disgust, and the insects buzzed and buzzed with
excitement, and though the gorilla of the African forest, with
his club, pounded, " Order, order !" there was no order ; and
there was a thrusting out of adderine sting, and a swinging
of elephantine tusk, and a stroke of beak, and a swing of claw,
until it seemed as if the convention would be massacred.

Just at that moment appeared Agassiz and Audubon and
Silliman, and Moses And Agassiz cried out, " Oh, you
beasts of the forests, I have studied your ancestral records and
found you always have been beasts, and you always will be
beasts ; be contented to be beasts "

And Audubon aimed his gun at a bald-headed eagle,
which dropped from the gallery, and as it dropped struck a
serpent that was winding around one of the pillars to get up
higher. Silliman threw a rock of the tertiary formation at
the mammals, and Moses thundered, " Every beast after its

kind, every bird after its kind, every fish after its kind."
And, lo ! *the parliament of wild beasts was prorogued* and
went home to their constituents, and the bat flew out into
the night, and the lizard slunk under the rocks, and the gorilla went back to the jungle, and a hungry wolf passing out
ate up the primal germs, and a clumsy buffalo upset the protoplasm, and the lion went to his lair, and the eagle went to
his eyrie, and the whale went to his palace of crystal and
coral, and there was peace—peace in the air, peace in the
waters, peace in the fields. Man in his place, the beasts of
the earth in their places.

EVOLUTION BRUTALIZING.

But, my friends, evolution is not only infidel and atheistic
and absurd; it is *brutalizing in its tendencies.* If there is
anything in the world that will make a man bestial in his
habits, it is the idea that he was descended from the beast.
Why, according to the idea of these evolutionists, we are
only a superior kind of cattle, a sort of Alderney among other
herds. To be sure, we browse on better pasture, and we
have better stall and better accommodations, but then we
are only Southdowns among the great flocks of sheep.
Born of a beast, to die like a beast; for the evolutionists
have no idea of a future world. They say the mind is only
a superior part of the body. They say our thoughts are only
molecular formation. They say, when the body dies, the
whole nature dies. The slab of the sepulchre is not a mile-
stone on a journey upward, but a wall shutting us into eternal nothingness. We all die alike—the cow, the horse, the
sheep, the man, the reptile. Annihilation is the heaven of
the evolutionist. From such a stenchful and damnable doctrine, turn away. Compare that idea of your origin—an idea
filled with the chatter of apes, and the hiss of serpents, and
the croak of frogs—to an idea in one or two stanzas which I
shall read to you from an old book of more than Demos-
thenic, or Homeric, or Dantesque power: "What is man,
that thou art mindful of him ? and the son of man, that thou

visitest him? Thou hast made him a little lower than the angels, and hast crowned him with glory and honor. Thou madest him to have dominion over the works of thy hand; thou hast put all things under his feet. All sheep and oxen, yea, and the beasts of the field; the fowl of the air, and the fish of the sea, and whatsoever passeth through the paths of the seas. O Lord, our Lord, how excellent is Thy name in all the earth!"

DESTINY ABOVE ORIGIN.

How do you like that origin? The lion the monarch of the field, the eagle the monarch of the air, behemoth the monarch of the deep, but man monarch of all. Ah! my friends, I have to say to you that I am not so anxious to know what was my origin, as to know what will be my destiny. I do not care so much where I came from as where I am going to. I am not so interested in who was my ancestry ten million years ago, as I am to know where I will be ten million years from now. I am not so much interested in the preface to my cradle, as I am interested in the appendix to my grave. I do not care so much about protoplasm as I do about eternasm. The "was" is overwhelmed with the "to be." But on this question, *Evolution* is as comfortless as *Hindoo Brahminism.*

"Where shall I go?" said a dying Hindoo to the Brahmin priest to whom he had given his money to have his soul saved. "Where shall I go after I die?" asked the dying Hindoo. "Well," said the Brahminic priest, "you will go into a holy quadruped." "But where shall I go after that?" said the dying Hindoo. "Well," said the Brahminic priest, "then you will go into a bird." "But" said the dying Hindoo, "where shall I go then?" "Then you will go into a beautiful flower." Then the dying Hindoo threw up his arms and said, "But where shall I go *last of all?*" This glorious Bible answers 'the Hindoo's question, answers my question, answers your question—not where shall I go to-day? not where shall I go to-morrow? or where shall I go next year? but where shall I go last of all?

And here comes in the evolution I believe in : not natural evolution, but gracious and divine and heavenly evolution —evolution out of sin into holiness, out of grief into gladness, out of mortality into immortality, out of earth into heaven ! That is the evolution I believe in.

Evolution from *evolvere*, to unroll! Unrolling of attributes, unrolling of rewards, unrolling of experience, unrolling of angelic companionship, unrolling of divine glory, unrolling of providential obscurities, unrolling of doxologies, unrolling of rainbow to canopy the throne, unrolling of a new heaven and a new earth in which to dwell righteousness. Oh, the thought overwhelms me! I have not the physical endurance to consider it.

Monarchs on earth of all lower orders of creation, and then lifted to be hierarchs in Heaven. Masterpiece of God's wisdom and goodness, our humanity ; masterpiece of divine grace, our enthronement. I put one foot on Darwin's " Origin of the Species," and I put the other foot on Spencer's " Biology," and then holding in one hand the books of Moses I see our genesis, and holding in the other hand the book Revelation, I see our celestial arrival. For all wars I prescribe the Bethlehem chant of the angels. For all sepulchres I prescribe the archangel's trumpet. For all the earthly griefs I prescribe the hand that wipes away all tears from all eyes. Not an evolution from beast to man, but an *evolution from contestant to conqueror*, and from the struggle with wild beasts in the arena of the amphitheatre, to a soft, high, blissful seat in the King's galleries.

EVOLUTION NO NOVELTY.

What is remarkable about this thing is, it is all the time developing its dishonesty. In our day it is ascribing this evolution to Herbert Spencer and Charles Darwin. It is a dishonesty. Evolution was known and advocated hundreds of years before these gentlemen began to be evolved. The Phœnicians thousands of years ago declared that the human race wobbled out of the mud. *Democritus*, who lived 460

years before Christ—remember that—knew this doctrine of
evolution when he said: " Everything is composed of atoms,
or infinitely small elements, each with a definite quality,
form, and movement, whose inevitable union and separation
shape all different things and forms, laws and effects, and
dissolve them again for new combinations.   The gods themselves and the human mind originated from such atoms.
There are no casualties.   Everything is necessary and determined by the nature of the atoms, which have certain mutual
affinities, attractions, and repulsions." *Anaximander* centuries ago declared that the human race started at the place
where the sea saturated the earth. *Lucretius* developed, long
centuries ago, in his poems, the doctrine of evolution.

It is an old heathen corpse set up in a morgue.   Charles
Darwin and Herbert Spencer are trying to galvanize it.
They drag this old putrefaction of three thousand years
around the earth, boasting that it is their originality; and so
wonderful is the infatuation that at the Delmonico dinner
given in honor of Herbert Spencer, there were those who
ascribed to him this great originality of evolution.   There
the banqueters sat around the table in honor of Herbert
Spencer, chewing beef, turkey, and roast pig, which, according to their doctrine of evolution, made them eating their
own relations !

There is only one thing *worse than English snobbery*, and
that is American snobbery.   I like democracy and I like
aristocracy ; but there is one kind of ocracy in this country
that excites my contempt, and that is what Charles Kingsley, after he had witnessed it himself, called snobocracy.
Now I say it is a gigantic dishonesty when they ascribe this
old heathen doctrine of evolution to any modern gentleman.

People are also becoming dissatisfied with philosophy and
science as a matter of comfort. They say it does not amount
to anything when you have a dead child in the house. They
tell you when they were sick and the door of the future
seemed opening, the only comfort they could find was in
the Gospel.   People are having demonstrated all over the
land that science and philosophy cannot solace the trouble

and woes of the world, and they want some other religion, and they are taking Christianity, the only sympathetic religion that ever came into the world.

You just take your scientific consolation into that room where a mother has lost her child. Try in that case your splendid doctrine of the "*survival of the fittest.*" Tell her that child died because it was not worth as much as the other children. That is your "survival of the fittest." Just try your transcendentalism and your philosophy and your science on that widowed soul, and tell her it was a geological necessity that her companion should be taken away from her, just as in the course of the world's history the megatherium had to pass out of existence; and then you go on in your scientific consolation until you get to the sublime fact that fifty million years from now we ourselves may be scientific specimens on a geological shelf, petrified specimens of an extinct human race. And after you have got all through with your consolation, if the poor afflicted soul is not crazed by it, I will send forth from this church the plainest Christian we have, and with one half-hour of prayer and reading of Scripture promises, the tears will be wiped away, and the house from floor to cupola will be flooded with the calmness of an Indian summer sunset. There is where I see the triumph of Christianity. People are dissatisfied with everything else. They want God. They want Jesus Christ.

EVOLUTION FOR A WRECK.

What is that in the offing? A ship gone on the rocks at Cape Hatteras. The hulk is breaking up, crew and passengers are drowning. The storm is in full blast and the barometer is still sinking. What does that ship want? Development. Develop her broken masts. Develop her broken rudder. Develop her drowning crew. Develop her freezing passengers. Develop the whole ship. That is all it wants. Development. O! I make a mistake. What that ship wants is a lifeboat from the shore. Leap into it, you men of the life-station. Pull away to the wreck. Steady there! Bring the women and children first to the shore. Now the stout men. Wrap them up in flannels, kindle a crackling and roaring fire until the frozen limbs are thawed out, and between their chattering teeth you can pour restoration.

Well, my friends, *our world is on the rocks.* God launched it well enough, but through mis-pilotage and the storms of six thousand years it has gone into the breakers. What does this old ship of a world want? Development! Enough old evolution in the hulk to evolve another mast and another rudder, to evolve all the passengers and evolve the ship out of the breakers. Development! Ah! no, my friends, what this old shipwreck of a world wants is a lifeboat from the shore. And it is coming. Cheer, my lads, cheer. It is coming from the shining shore of heaven, taking the crests of ten waves with one sweep of the shining paddles. *Christ is in the lifeboat.* Many wounds on hands and feet and side and brow, showing He has been long engaged in the work of rescue, but yet mighty to save—to save one, to save all, to save forever. My Lord and my God, get us into the lifeboat! Give us God, Christ, and the Bible.

CHAPTER III.

Ingersollian Infidelity Confuted.

"The fool hath said in his heart, There is no God."—PSALM 53 1

No one but a fool would say so, and he would not say it with his head, for it does not require any especial brain to see a design in all things, and hence a designer. But the heart, the wicked heart, the proud heart, is hurt at such a pure and overtowering existence.

Were there any prospect of success, and an army were organized to dethrone God, or drive Him off the edges of existence, the first division of the army would be made up of infidels, and Mr. Robert Ingersoll, the champion blasphemer of America, would be the colonel of one of the regiments. When the world slew Jesus Christ, it showed what it would do with the eternal God if it could get its hands on Him.

Prove a benevolent God and you prove a Bible. You cannot think of a good God not giving a revelation to His children. Atheism and infidelity are twin brothers.

BIG BUSINESS ON SMALL CAPITAL.

The war against the Bible and against God is no new thing. Mr. Ingersoll is only dealing in the second-hand furniture of Paine, and Volney, and Hobbes, and Voltaire, and Colenso, save when he quotes from himself, and the most of his lectures are about one thing It does not make any difference whether he calls it the Mistakes of Moses, or Skulls, or the Liberty of Man, woman, and child, or no name at all, it is the same lecture. There never was a man who carried on so large a business on such a small capital, and that borrowed capital.

He picks up one bone from Adam's skeleton, and he runs with that bone through all his lectures, and it happens to be a rib, and the rib that was said to be the nucleus for the womanly creation , and he sharpens that rib, and he flourishes it, and he gnaws on it, and gnaws on it, and he holds on to it, as my greyhound for six months used to spend all his spare time in gnawing on a bleached and juice-less bone when he had plenty of good food offered him. Coming suddenly on him in the morning, I would find him gnawing that bone, though the day before I had thrown it over the fence, and he would keep on gnawing it, and look up to me as much as to say : "Sir, you don't know how much I am dependent for happiness upon this bone; I am an infidel." People coming late to Mr. Ingersoll's lecture inquire of the janitor whether he has got to Adam's rib yet.

I must, at the risk of spoiling Mr Ingersoll's favorite joke and raising a snarl, snatch from him his favorite bone, while I tell you that there was

NO ABSURDITY IN WOMAN'S CREATION.

The word translated "rib" is a general word meaning side. Stupendous ignorance on the part of Mr. Ingersoll that he does not know that the word here translated "rib" simply means side. That man, without knowing a word or a letter of Hebrew, proposes to expound Genesis. As well might a man expound Sophocles, not knowing a word of Greek or Horace, not knowing a word of Latin or Richter, not knowing a word of German or William Shakespeare, not knowing a word of English. From his side ! How any man who has a good wife can find derision in the nearness and the solemnity of the relation there suggested, I cannot un-derstand.

I will not quote Matthew Henry's over-quoted theory about woman's being taken from the left side, and near the door of the heart. I think she was taken from the right side and under the right arm, suggestive that he was to fight her battles for her, and be her unfailing defence, and strike down her assailants, and avenge her honor. That is what fills a man with indignation unbounded, and makes him livid with rage, when you say anything against his wife. You may abuse him, you may cheat him, you may defraud him, you may assault him, and he will forgive you ; but you say any-thing against his wife, and you better stand out of the reach of the right arm.   From his side !   From his side, that they might walk the path of life together.   From his side, that when she steps in the deep wave of trouble he may hold her up. From his side, that when they stand by the little grave he may say to her, " Don't cry, we'll get our darling back again in the resurrection."   From his side,—his equal, his joy, his pride, his exultation, his care,'his angelic ministry. To him the best being in all the earth.   From his side !   Oh, the tenderness, and the pathos, and the beauty, and the sub-limity of the Mosaic account !

MAKING MOUTHS.

" They have set their mouth against the heavens."—PSALM 73 : 9.

This is a full-length portrait of a blasphemer. As a wolf howls at the sky, or a dog bays at the moon, so the blas-phemer is represented as making mouths at the heavens ; and on the night when the wolf shall frighten away the sky, and the dog shall stop the moon, that night will the blas-phemer drive away the God of the Bible.

[The laugh returned. See Psalm 2 : 4.—ED.]

FOOTPRINTS OF DEITY.

An Arab guide was leading a French infidel across a des-ert, and ever and anon the Arab guide would get down in the sand and pray to the Lord. It disgusted the French in-fidel, and after a while as the Arab got up from one of his prayers the infidel said : " How do you know there is any God ?" and the Arab guide said : " How do I know that a man and a camel passed along by our tent last night ? I know

it by the footprint in the sand. And you want to know how
I know whether there is any God. Look at that sunset. Is
that the footstep of a man?" And by the same process you
and I have come to understand that this is the footstep of a
God.

BLASPHEMOUS PROGRAMME.

It seems from what *we have heard* that Bible religion is
a huge blunder; that the Mosaic account of the creation is
an absurdity large enough to throw all nations into rollicking guffaw; that Adam and Eve never existed; that the
ancient flood and Noah's Ark were impossibilities; that there
never was a miracle; that the Bible is the friend of cruelty,
of murder, of polygamy, of obscenity, of adultery, of all forms
of base crime; that the Christian religion is woman's tyrant
and man's stultification; that the Bible from lid to lid is a
fable, an obscenity, a cruelty, a humbug, a sham, a lie; that
the martyrs who died for its truth were miserable dupes;
that the Church of Jesus Christ is properly gazetted as a
fool; that it is something to bring a blush to the cheek of
every patriot that John Adams, the father of American independence, declared " the Bible is the best book in all the
world;" and that iron, lion-hearted Andrew Jackson turned
into a snivelling coward when he said, " That book, sir, is the
rock on which our republic rests;" and that Daniel Webster
abdicated the throne of his intellectual power and resigned
his logic, and, from being the great expounder of the Constitution and the great lawyer of his age, turned into an idiot
when he said: " My heart assures and reassures me that the
Gospel of Jesus Christ must be a divine reality. From the
time that, at my mother's feet or on my father's knee, I first
learned to lisp verses from the sacred writings, they have been
my daily study and vigilant contemplation, and if there is
anything in my style or thought to be commended, the credit
is due to my kind parents, in instilling into my mind an early
love of the Scriptures;" and that *William H. Seward*, the
diplomatist of the century, only showed his puerility when

he declared, " The whole hope of human progress is suspended on the ever-growing influences of the Bible ;" and that it is wisest for us to take that Book from the throne in the affections of uncounted multitudes, and put it under our feet to be trampled upon by hatred and hissing contempt ; and that your old father was hoodwinked and cajoled and cheated and befooled when he leaned on this as a staff after his hair grew gray and his hands were tremulous and his steps shortened as he came up to the verge of the grave ; and that your mother sat with a pack of lies on her lap while reading of the better country, and of the ending of all her aches and pains, and reunion, not only with those of you who stood around her, but with the children she had buried with infinite heartache, so that she could read no more until she took off her spectacles and wiped from them the heavy mist of many tears.

Alas! that for forty and fifty years they should have walked under this delusion, and had it under their pillow when they lay a-dying in the back room, and asked that some words from the vile page might be cut upon the tombstone under the shadow of the old country meeting-house where they sleep this morning waiting for a resurrection that will never come. This Book, having deceived them, and having deceived the mighty intellects of the past, must not be allowed to deceive our larger, mightier, vaster, more stupendous intellects.

Well, we will give it a trial. I empannel you as a jury to render your verdict in this case. And I ask you to affirm that you will well and truly try this issue of traverse joined between Infidelity, the plaintiff, and Christianity, the defendant, so help you God.

ROBERT INGERSOLL'S TESTIMONY.

The jury empannelled, call *your first witness.* Robert G. Ingersoll! " Here !" Swear the witness But how are you to swear the witness ? I know of only two ways of taking an oath in a court-room. The one is by kissing the Bible,

and the other is by lifting the hand. I cannot ask him to
swear by the Bible, because he considers that a pack of lies,
and therefore it could give no solemnity to his oath. I cannot ask him to lift the hand, for that seems to imply the existence of a God, and that is a fact in dispute. So I swear
him by the rings of Saturn, and the spots on the sun, and
the caverns in the moon, and the Milky Way, and the nebular hypothesis, that he will tell the truth, the whole truth,
and nothing but the truth in this case between Infidelity, the
plaintiff, and Christianity, the defendant.

Let me say that I know nothing of the private character
of that person, neither do I want to know. I have no taste
for exploring private character. I shall deal with him as a
public teacher.

You say: Why answer the champion blasphemer of America? Am I afraid that Christianity will be overborne by his
scoffing harlequinade? Oh no. Do you know how near
he has come to stopping Christianity? I will tell you how
near he has come to impeding the progress of Christianity
in the world. About as much as one snowflake on the track
will impede the half-past three o'clock Chicago lightning express train. Perhaps not so much as that. It is more like
a Switzerland insect floating through the air impeding an
Alpine avalanche.

Within ten years Mr. Ingersoll has done his most conspicuous stopping of Christianity, and he has stopped it at
the following rate. In the first fifty years of this century
there were three million people who professed the faith of
Christ. In the last ten years there have been three million
people connecting themselves by profession with the Church
of Christ. In other words, the last ten years have accomplished as much as the first fifty years of this century.

My fear is not that he will arrest Christianity. I answer
his charges *for the benefit of individuals.* There are young
men who through his teachings have given up their religion
and soon after gave up their morals. Ingersoll's teachings
triumphant would fill all the penitentiaries and the gam-
bling-hells and houses of shame on the continent —on the

planet. No divine system of morals, and in twenty years we would have a hell on earth eclipsing in abomination the hell that Mr. Ingersoll has so much laughed at.

My fear is not that Christianity in general shall be impeded, but I want to persuade these young men to get aboard the train instead of throwing themselves across the track.

So let the trial come on. The jury has been empanelled. The first witness has been called.

MR. INGERSOLL'S CHARGES.

Now, my friends, it is a principle settled in all courtrooms, and among all intelligent people, "*false in part, false in all.*" If a witness is found to be making a misrepresentation on the stand, it does not make any difference what he testifies to afterward ; it all goes overboard. The judge, the jury, every common-sense man says " false in part, false in all." Now, if I can show you, and I will show you, the Lord helping me, that Mr. Ingersoll makes misrepresenta tions in one respect, or two respects, or three respects, I demand that, as intelligent men and as fair-minded women, you throw overboard his entire testimony. If he misrepresent in one thing, he will misrepresent all the way through. " False in one, false in all."

IS THIS BOOK TRUE?

In the first place, he raises a roystering laugh against the Bible by saying : " Is this book true ? The gentleman who wrote it said that the world was made out of nothing. I cannot imagine *nothing* being made into *something.*" In nearly all his lectures he begins with that gigantic misrepresentation.

Refer to your memory that you may see it is *an Ingersol-lian misstatement*—a misstatement from stem to stern, and from cutwater to taffrail, and from the top of the mainmast down to the barnacles on the bottom. If he had taken some obscure passage, he would not have been so soon found out; but he has taken the most conspicuous, the most memorable, the most magnificent passage, all geological and astronomical discovery only adding to its grandeur. "In the beginning."

There you can roll in ten million years if you want to. There is no particular date given—no contest between science and revelation. Though the world may have been in process of creation for millions of years, suddenly and quickly, and in one week, it may have been fitted up for *man's residence.* There is as much difference between Mr. Ingersoll's statement and the truth as between nothing and omnipotence.

CREATION OF LIGHT.

I take a step further in the impeachment of this witness. He swoops upon the third and fourth verses of the same chapter in caricature and says: "Ha, ha! the Bible represents that light was created on Monday, and the sun was not created until Thursday. Just think of it! a book declaring that light was created three days before the sun shone!" Here Mr. Ingersoll shows his geological and chemical and astronomical ignorance. If Mr. Ingersoll had asked any schoolboy on his way home from one of our high schools: "My lad, can there be any light without the shining of the sun?" the lad would have said: "Yes, sir; *heat and electricity emit light* independent of the sun. Beside that, when the earth was in process of condensation, it was surrounded by thick vapors and the discharge of many volcanoes in the primary period, and all this obscuration may have hindered the light of the sun from falling on the earth until that Thursday morning."

Mr. Ingersoll has only to go to one of our high schools to learn there are ten thousand sources of light besides the light of the sun. But whether wilful or ignorant misrepresentation, either or both will impeach Robert G. Ingersoll as incompetent to give testimony in this case between Infidelity and Christianity.

THE FIRMAMENT.

Mr. Ingersoll goes on to say that when Moses spoke of God as creating the firmament, he showed his ignorance, for he thereby implied that the heaven, the sky, was a solid affair, and he knew nothing about evaporation. Wise Ingersoll! Ignorant Moses! But Noah Webster, and indeed all the lexicographers, agree in saying that the word firmament used in the Bible, instead of meaning a solidity, means an expanse—instead of representing a metallic roof, it means a stretching out and an extension.

Mr. Ingersoll goes on laughing at the statement, and says that the stars are represented by Moses as being fastened to this solid roof, and that he shows he knew nothing about astronomy because all reference made to other worlds is in five words: " He made the stars also.' And Mr. Ingersoll says therefore, it is evident that Moses was very ignorant and thought the other worlds were very small or a mere nothing, while this world was very great, when they are so much larger than this. " He made the stars also." My friends, Moses did not write Genesis because he wanted to teach us astronomy any more than he wanted to teach us botany, or chemistry, or anatomy, or physiology, or any other modern science. His only idea was to give us the origin and the outfit of the world.

Had the book gone into all these particulars, all the other sciences, fifty thousand volumes would not have contained the record, and sacred literature would have been cumbrous and unmanageable.

But we see again and again indicated in this book that these Bible writers, instead of being ignoramuses, as Mr. Ingersoll represents them, really knew a great deal more than many people who in this time deride them. Ages, thousands of years, passed along before the world found out the law of condensation and evaporation; but Job knew it. He described the process when he said: " He maketh small the drops of water ; they pour out according to the vapor there-

of." In other words, it took the world thousands of years
to find out what Job knew thousands of years before. For
thousands of years people thought that the light of the sun
came straight to our earth, and the law of refraction or the
bending of the rays to the earth, is comparatively a modern
discovery; but Job knew it. He says of the sunlight: "It
is turned as clay to the seal." The world struggling thousands of years to find out what Job knew at the start. "It
is turned as clay to the seal."

Astronomers thought that they made a great discovery
when they found out that the world, instead of being station-
ary, was in motion; but Isaiah knew it, and thousands of years
before had spoken of the orbit of the earth, the circle of the
earth, indicating that it had a path through the heavens.
For thousands of years it was thought that the earth was
built on some solid foundation. Isaiah knew better: "He
hangeth the earth upon nothing." Long before Maury discovered the revolution of the wind-currents, and the law of
the trade winds, the Bible describes it: "The wind goeth
toward the south, and turneth about unto the north; it
whirleth about continually, and the wind returneth again
according to his circuits." So that while we called General
Myer "Old Probabilities," Job was *the first "Old Probabilities."* He described the currents of the air which, after
struggling and struggling and struggling for thousands of
years, were found out by philosophers.

Ages passed along before the world knew anything about
physiology; but Solomon speaks of the spinal cord as the
silver cord; and thousands of years before Harvey found out
the circulation of the blood, Solomon described it under a
figure as the pitcher at the fountain, the pitcher carrying the
crimson liquid up through the temple of the body. James
Watt thought he was making a wonderful invention when
he applied steam to the rail-carriage; but thousands of years
before, the prophet Nahum had described the lightning express train at night, and the jamming of the car-coupling:
"The chariots shall rage in the streets, they shall jostle one
against another in the broad ways; they shall seem like

torches, they shall run like the lightnings." Professor Morse thought that he was making a wonderful invention when he found out the magnetic telegraph; but Job describes electrical communication thousands of years before, when he says: "Canst thou send lightnings, that they may go and say unto thee, Here we are?"

By the Leyden jar, the voltaic pile, the magnetic battery, the microscope, the telescope, and all philosophic apparatus toiling on and on and on until at last, at last, Silliman and Agassiz and Joseph Henry and Dr. Draper have actually caught up to antiquated Job and old Moses! Yet Mr. Ingersoll says they were ignorant. Moses knew nothing about astronomy and thought the sky was just a solid roof and that the stars were mere adornments hung up against it, because he says, " He made the stars also!"

THE BIBLE UNSCIENTIFIC.

Mr. Ingersoll and his coadjutors vehemently charge the Bible with being an unscientific book. But who are those that say there is a collision between science and revelation? Well, Herbert Spencer, Tyndall, Darwin, Ingersoll. They say there is a discord between science and revelation; but I will bring you names of men who have found a perfect accord between science and revelation—men as much higher in intellectual character above those whom I have mentioned as the Alps and Mount Washington and the Himalayas are higher than Ridgewood Water-works: Herschel, Kepler, Leibnitz, Ross, Isaac Newton. My friends, we are in respectable company when we believe in the Word of God—very respectable company.

Did you ever hear General Mitchell or Dr. Doremus lecture on the harmony between Science and Revelation? Science is a boy, Revelation a man. The boy thinks he knows more than the man, and asks many unanswered questions.

In the temple of Nature there are *two orchestras*—the orchestra of revelation, and the orchestra of science. The orchestra of revelation has all the musical instruments full strung, and it is ready for the burst of eternal accord. The orchestra of science is only just stringing the instruments. If you will only wait long enough, you will find that it is as in the old German cathedrals where they have an organ at one end of the building, and an organ at the other end of the building, both responding to each other, and making mighty music. So it will be in the temple of the universe : the orchestra of revelation and the orchestra of science will respond to each other after a while, and it will be found that the roar of the ocean is only the magnificent bass of the temple voices, and that the earth is only the pedals of a great organ of which the heavens are the key-board.

There is no contest between genuine science and revelation. The same God who by the hand of prophet wrote on parchment, by the hand of the storm wrote on the rock. The best telescopes and microscopes and electric batteries and philosophical apparatus belong to Christian universities. Who gave us magnetic telegraphy? *Professor Morse*, a Christian. Who swung the lightnings under the sea, cabling the continents together? *Cyrus W. Field*, the Christian.

James Y Simpson, of Edinburgh, as eminent for piety as for science, on week-days in the University lectures on profoundest scientific subjects, and on Sabbaths preaches the Gospel of Jesus Christ.

THE DELUGE.

I take a step further in impeaching this witness against the Bible. He sharpens all his witticisms to destroy our belief in the ancient Deluge and Noah's Ark. He says that from the account there, it must have rained eight hundred feet of water each day in order that it might be fifteen cubits above the hills. He says that the Ark could not have been large enough to contain "two of every sort," for there would have been hundreds of thousands and hundreds of thousands of creatures! He says that these creatures would have came from all lands and all zones! He says there was only one small window in the Ark and that would not have given fresh air to keep the animals inside the Ark from suffocation ! Then he winds up that part of the story by saying that the Ark finally landed on a mountain seventeen thousand feet high.

He says he does not believe the story. *Neither do I. There is no such story in the Bible.* I will tell you what the Bible story is.

Why did the Deluge come ? It came for the purpose of destroying the outrageous inhabitants of the then thinly populated earth, nearly all the population probably very near the Ark before it was launched. What would have been the use of submerging North and South America, or Europe, or Africa, when they were not inhabited?

God speaks after the manner of men when He says every-thing went under. And Mr. Ingersoll most grossly misrep-resents when he says that, in order to have that depth of water, it must have rained eight hundred feet every day. The Bible distinctly declares that the most of the flood rose instead of falling. Before the account where it says " the windows of heaven were opened," it says "all the fountains of the great deep were broken up." All geologists agree in saying that there are caverns in the earth filled with water, and they rushed forth, and all the lakes and rivers forsook their beds.

What am I to think, and what are you to think, of a man who, ignoring this earthquake spoken of in the Bible as pre-ceding the falling of the rain, and for the purpose of making a laugh at the Bible, will say it must have rained over eight hundred feet every day?—taking the last half instead of the first half. The fountains of the great deep were broken up, and then the windows of heaven were opened.

THE SIZE OF THE ARK.

Instead of being a mud-scow, as some of these infidels would have us understand, it was a magnificent ship, nearly as large as our Great Eastern, three times the size of an ordi-nary man-of-war.

Well, the animal creation going into this ark were the animals from that region, where alone inhabitants were to be found; and they went in two and two of all flesh.

Two or three years ago I was on a steamer on the river Tay, and I came to Perth, Scotland. I got off and saw *the most wonderful agricultural show* that I had ever witnessed. There were horses and cattle such as Rosa Bonheur never sketched, and there were dogs such as the loving pencil of Edwin Landseer never portrayed, and there were sheep and fowl and creatures of all sorts. Suppose that "two and two" of all the creatures of that agricultural show were put upon the Tay steamer to be transported to Dundee, and the next day I should be writing home to America and giving an account of the occurrence, I would have used the same general phraseology that is used in regard to the embarkation of the brute creation in the ark—I would have said that they went in two and two of every sort. I would not have meant six hundred thousand. A common-sense man myself, I would suppose that the people who read the letter were common-sense people.

"But how could you get them into the ark?" says Mr. Ingersoll, with a great sneer. "How could they be induced to go into the ark? He would have to pick them out and drive them in, and coax them in." Could not the same God who gave instinct to the animal inspire that instinct to seek for shelter from the storm? However, nothing more than ordinary animal instinct was necessary. Have you never been in the country when an August thunder-storm was coming up, and heard the cattle moan at the bars to get in, and seen the affrighted fowl go upon the perch at noonday, and heard the affrighted dog and cat calling at the door, supplicating entrance? And are you surprised that, in that age of the world, when there were fewer places of shelter for dumb beasts, at the muttering and rumbling and flashing and quaking and darkening of an approaching deluge, the animal creation came moaning and bleating to the sloping embankment reaching up to the ancient *Great Eastern*, and passed in? I have owned horses and cattle and sheep and dogs, but I never had a horse or a cow or a sheep or a dog that was *so stupid it did not know enough to come in when it rained!*

Yet Mr. Ingersoll cannot understand how they could get in. It is amazing to him. And then, that one window in the ark which afforded such poor ventilation to the creatures there assembled—that small window in the ark which excites so much mirthfulness on the part of the great infidel. If he had known as much Hebrew as you could put on your little-finger nail, he would have known that that word translated "window" there means *window-course,* a whole range of lights. This ignorant infidel does not know a window-pane from twenty windows.

So, if there is any criticism of the ark, there seems to be too much window for such a long storm. This infidel says that during the long storm the window must have been kept shut and hence no air. There are people who, all the way from Liverpool to Barnegat Lighthouse, and for two weeks, were kept under deck, the hatches battened down because of the storm. Some of you, in the old-time sailing-vessels, were kept nearly a month with the hatches down because of some long storm.

LANDING OF THE ARK.

Mr. Ingersoll says that the ark landed on a mountain seventeen thousand feet high, and that of course, as soon as the animals came forth, they would all be frozen in the ice! Here comes in Mr. Ingersoll's *geographical ignorance.* He does not seem to know that Ararat is not merely the name for a mountain, but for a *hilly district,* and that it may have been a hill twenty feet high, or a hundred feet, or two hundred feet high on which the ark alighted. But in order to raise a laugh against the Holy Scriptures, Mr. Ingersoll lifts the ark seventeen thousand feet high, showing an ignorance of just that altitude!

The flood that Ingersoll describes is not Noah's flood; it is *Ingersoll's flood* of hatred against God. It is not Noah's ark that Ingersoll describes ; it is Ingersoll's ark, with a whole flock of hooting owls of the midnight of Infidelity, whole nests of viperine and adderine venom against God, whole lairs of panthers which with spotted claw, if they could, would maul the eternal God to pieces. And there is only one small window in that ark and it opens into the blackness of darkness described by the words, "having the understanding darkened, being alienated from the life of God through the ignorance that is in them."

We are not entirely dependent on the Bible for the story of the flood. All ages and all literatures have traditions— broken traditions, indistinct traditions, but still traditions. The traditions of the Chaldeans say that in the time when Xysuthrus was king, there was a great flood, and he put his family and his friends in a large vessel and all outside of them were destroyed, and after a while the birds went forth and they came back and their wings were tinged with mud. Lucian and Ovid, celebrated writers who had never seen the Bible, described a flood in the time of Deucalion. He took his friends into a boat, and the animals came running to him in pairs. And so all lands, all ages, and all literatures seem to have a broken and indistinct tradition of a calamity which Moses, here incorporating Noah's account, so grandly, so beautifully, so accurately, so solemnly records.

Gentlemen of the jury, I have impeached Robert G. Ingersoll for having misrepresented once, twice, thrice, and I demand that you put into execution the principle of every court-room, and throw overboard his entire testimony. "False in part, false in all." And my prayer is that the God who created the world, not out of nothing, but out of his own omnipotence, may create us anew in Christ Jesus ; and that the God who made light three days before the sun shone may kindle in our souls a light that will burn on long after the sun has expired ; and that the God who ordered the ark built and kept open more than one hundred years, that the antediluvians might enter it for shelter, may graciously incline us to accept the invitation which rolls in music from the throne, saying, "Come thou and all thy house into the ark."

THE JEWS IN EGYPT.

Mr. Ingersoll also says the Bible lies because when the Jews went into Egypt there were seventy of them; they stayed there two hundred and fifteen years, and there were three millions; and he says according to that calculation there must have been sixty-eight children in each of the households. It seems a very funny thing to him   The fact is, instead of being there in Egypt two hundred and fifteen years, according to Mr. Ingersoll's statement, the Bible plainly declares they were there *four hundred and thirty years*, and the population of three millions was just the ordinary increase in all lands and in all ages. For the purpose of making his audience laugh, Mr. Ingersoll cuts off two hundred and fifteen years, in order that he may make that story about the enormous and improbable and impossible increase. In order that he may appear smart, he cuts off from the Jewish nation twice as much history as transpired between the Declaration of American Independence, in 1776, and 1882. He says it   is two hundred and fifteen years according to the Bible, when the Bible twice declares it was four hundred and thirty. Now I say that a man who will do that, will do anything but be honest about the Word of God.

THE ANOINTING-OIL.

The blasphemer also laughs at the anointing-oil used in setting apart Aaron to his office, and he jeers at the judgments of God for the misuse of the anointing-oil in olden time. Now, my friends, it is very easy to scoff at anything which is used as a symbol. I do not belong to the Order of Masons, nor have I ever seen the ceremony, but when the Order of Masons puts anointing-oil on the corner-stone of a new building, no good man would laugh at it. Any man would know that it is a symbol of dedication and consecration; anybody would know that is a prayer; just as in one case it might be a prayer of the lips, in the other case it is a prayer of the right hand—as much as to say: "Let this be a prosperous building, let this be a consecrated building."

A man might just as well laugh at the water used in holy rite in the church; whether sprinkled from the font, or standing in the baptistery, it is simply a farce unless it be a symbol; and if a symbol, then every earnest man, whether Christian or unbeliever, sees it to be beautifully significant. A man's immortal nature must be awfully atwist who can find anything to laugh at either in the water of baptism, or in the anointing-oil on the corner-stone of a new building, or in the oil of the ancient sanctuary used in consecration. A man can laugh at anything if he wants to. *He might laugh at the screws on his child's coffin.*

THE SUN AND MOON STOOD STILL.

Mr. Ingersoll finds great cause for caricature in the Bible statement that in Joshua's time the sun and moon stood still to allow him to complete his victory. He declares that an impossibility. If a man have brain and strength enough to make a clock, can he not start it and stop it? and start it again and stop it again? If a machinist have strength and brain enough to make a corn-thresher, can he not start it and stop it? and start it again and stop it again? If God have strength and wisdom to make the clock of the universe, the great machinery of the worlds, has He not strength enough and wisdom enough to start it and stop it? and start it again and stop it again? or stop one wheel, or stop twenty wheels, or stop all the wheels? Is the clock stronger than the clockmaker? Does the corn-thresher know more than the machinist? Is the universe mightier than its God?

Mr. Ingersoll finds great cause of glee in the fact that the Bible states that the moon stopped as well as the sun. If you have never seen the moon in the daytime, it is because you have not been a very diligent observer of the heavens. Beside that, it was not necessary for the world literally to stop. By unusual refraction of the sun's rays the day might have been prolonged. So that, while the earth continued on its path in the heavens, it figuratively stopped. You must remember that these Bible authors used the vernacular of their own day, just as you and I say the sun went down. The sun never goes down. We simply describe what appears to the human eye.

Now, I say, if God can start a world, and swing a world, He could stop one or two of them without a great deal of exertion, or He could by unusual refraction of the sun's rays, continue the illumination.

Mr. Ingersoll goes into great scoff and jeer at that battle which Joshua fought, as though it were an insignificant battle, and was not worthy to have the day prolonged Why, sirs, what Yorktown was for Revolutionary times, and what Gettysburg was in our civil contest, and what Sedan was in the Franco-German war, and what Waterloo was in Napoleonic destiny—that was this battle of Joshua against the five allied armies of Gibeon. It was a battle that changed the entire course of history. It was a battle to Joshua as important as though a battle now should occur in which England and the United States and France and Germany and Italy and Turkey and Russia should fight for victory or annihilation. However much any other world, solar, lunar, or stellar, might be hastened in its errand of light, it would be excusable if it lingered in the heavens for a little while and put down its sheaf of beams, and gazed on such an Armageddon.

A celebrated eye-doctor in Boston recently declared that right after an eclipse of the sun he had an unusual number of cases of diseases of the eye to treat; and he accounted for it by the fact that so many people were, through smoked glass, looking at the sun in eclipse. So it seems that the sun that stood above Gibeon damaged the eyes of Mr. Ingersoll, because he looks at it through a glass smoked with the fires of his own hatred against Christianity and against God. Under this explanation, instead of being sceptical about this sublime passage of the Bible, you will when you

read it feel more like going down on your knees before God
as you read, " Sun, stand thou still above Gibeon, and thou
moon in the valley of Ajalon."

JONAH AND THE WHALE.

Mr. Ingersoll finds great cause of caricature in the Bible
statement that a whale swallowed Jonah and ejected him
upon the dry ground in three days. If Mr. Ingersoll would
go to the museum at Nantucket, Massachusetts, he would
find the skeleton of a whale large enough to swallow a
man I said to the janitor while I was standing in the
museum, " Why, it does not seem from the looks of this
skeleton that that story in the Book of Jonah is so very improbable, does it ?" " O, no," he replied, " it does not."
There is a cavity in the mouth of the common whale large
enough for a man to live in. There have been sharks found
again and again with an entire human body in them.

Beside that, if Mr Ingersoll and the other scoffers at the
Bible would only read this Book of Jonah a little more carefully, they would find that it says nothing about a whale. It
says, "the Lord prepared a great fish ;" and there are scientists who tell us that there were sea monsters in other
days that make the modern whale seem very insignificant.
I know in one place in the New Testament it speaks of the
whale as appearing in the occurrence I had just mentioned ;
but the word may just as well be translated " sea monster "
—any kind of *a sea monster*

Procopius says that in the year 582 a sea monster was slain
which had for fifty years destroyed ships. I suppose this
sea monster that took care of Jonah may have been one of
the great sea monsters that could have easily taken down a
prophet, and he could have lived there three days if he had
kept in motion so as to keep the gastric juices from taking
hold of him and destroying him—a sea monster large enough
to take down Mr. Ingersoll and all his blasphemy, and at
the end of three days *it would be as sick* as the historic
whale which regurgitated Jonah !

Beside that, my friends, there is one word which explains the whole thing. It says, " *the Lord prepared* a great fish." If a ship carpenter prepare a vessel to carry Texan beeve- to Glasgow, I suppose it can carry Texan beeves, if a ship carpenter prepare a vessel to carry coal to one of the north- ern ports, I suppose it can carry coal ; if a ship carpenter pre- pare a vessel to carry passengers to Liverpool, I suppose it can carry passengers to Liverpool ; and if the Lord prepared a fish to carry one passenger, I suppose it could carry a pas- senger and the ventilation have been all right.

Did not a meteor run on evangelistic errand on the first Christmas night, and designate the rough cradle of our Lord ? Did not the stars in their courses fight against Sis- era ? Was it merely coincidental that before the destruc- tion of Jerusalem the moon was eclipsed for twelve consecu- tive nights ? Did it merely happen so that a new star ap- peared in constellation Cassiopeia, and then disappeared just before King Charles IX. of France, who was responsible for St. Bartholomew massacre, died ? Was it without sig- nificance that in the days of the Roman Emperor Justinian war and famine were preceded by the dimness of the sun, which for nearly a year gave no more light than the moon, although there were no clouds to obscure it ?

INCREDULITY REBUTTED.

In the days of George Stephenson, the perfector of the locomotive engine, the scientists proved conclusively that a railway train could never be driven by steam-power success- fully without peril ; but the rushing express trains from Liv- erpool to Edinburgh, and from Edinburgh to London, have made all the nation witnesses of the splendid achievement. Machinists and navigators proved conclusively that a steamer could never cross the Atlantic Ocean ; but no sooner had they successfully proved the impossibility of such an under- taking than the work was done, and the passengers on the Cunard and the Inman and the National and the White Star lines are witnesses. There went up a guffaw of wise laughter at Professor Morse's proposition to make the lightning of heaven his errand boy, and it was proved conclusively that the thing could never be done; but now all the news of the wide world, by Associated Press, put in your hands every morning and night, has made all nations witnesses.

So in the time of Christ it was proved conclusively that it was impossible for Him to rise from the dead. It was shown logically that when a man was dead, he was dead, and the heart and the liver and the lungs having ceased to perform their offices, the limbs would be rigid beyond all power of friction or arousal. They showed it to be an absolute absurdity that the dead Christ should ever get up alive; but no sooner had they proved this than the dead Christ arose, and the disciples beheld Him, heard His voice, and talked with Him, and they took the witness stand, to prove that to be true which the wiseacres of the day had proved to be impossible; the record of the experiment and of the testimony is in the text: " Him hath God raised from the dead, whereof we are witnesses."

" There is no God," says the skeptic, " for I have never seen him with my physical eyesight. Your Bible is a pack of contradictions There never was a miracle. Lazarus was not raised from the dead, and the water was never turned into wine. Your religion is an imposition on the credulity of the ages." You are in one respect like Lord Nelson, when a signal was lifted that he wished to disregard and he put his sea-glass to his blind eye and said : " I really do not see the signal." Oh, my hearer, put this field-glass of the Gospel no longer to your blind eye, and say I cannot see, but put it to your other eye, the eye of faith, and you will see Christ and _He is all you need to see._

[The EDITOR here quotes the old adage · " None are so blind as those who will not see "]

GRAVEN IMAGES.

Mr. Ingersoll also runs his head against the tables of stone and tries to break off one of the ten commandments. He says when the Bible declares we must not make any graven image, it prohibits art and it killed all art in Palestine. He says that a commandment which is opposed to art cannot be a good commandment, it must be a bad commandment. Now, every man of common-sense knows that when the commandment prohibits the making of graven images, it is the making of them for purposes of worship, and that it does not forbid painting and sculpture, which are the regalement of elevated taste.

Let us see: Is the Bible opposed to art? Just look over and find that God sent two sculptors, Bezaleel and Aholiab, to ornament the ancient temple. If God were opposed to art, if the Bible were hostile to sculpture, would Bezaleel and Aholiab have been ordained of high Heaven to ornament that ancient building? Is the Bible antagonistic to painting? Go through all the picture-galleries of the world, and find that the great subjects of the painters are Bible subjects. Blot out all the Bible subjects from the art galleries of the world, and you blot out the best part of the galleries at Naples, and at Florence, and at Rome, and at Paris, and at Edinburgh, and of all the private picture galleries of the world; and you tear down St. Paul's, and Westminster Abbey, and the cathedrals of Cologne and Milan, and you destroy the Vatican.

Is the Bible opposed to the art of painting, as Mr. Ingersoll over and over again declares? What were the subjects of Raphael's great paintings? The Transfiguration, The Miraculous Draught of Fishes, The Charge to Peter, The Holy Family, The Massacre of the Innocents, Moses at the Burning Bush, The Nativity; Michael, The Archangel, and four or five exquisite Madonnas.

What were Paul Veronese's great pictures? Queen of Sheba, The Marriage in Cana, Magdalen Washing the Feet of Christ, The Holy Family. Who has not heard of Da Vinci's Last Supper? Who has not heard of Turner's Pools of Solomon? Who has not heard of Rubens' Scourging of Jesus? Who has not heard of Doré on everything from the creation to the last conflagration? The mightiest paintings ever made are on Bible subjects and yet Mr. Ingersoll dares to stand in the presence of an American audience and tell them that the Bible is antagonistic to art—never a ghastlier or more outrageous misrepresentation since the world stood. The very best paintings, the very grandest art, born at the altars of our God.

THE BIBLE A CRUEL BOOK.

Mr. Ingersoll and his coadjutors with great vehemence declare that the Bible is *a cruel book*. They read the story of the extermination of the Canaanites, and of all the ancient wars, and of the history of David and Joshua, and they come to the conslusion that the Bible is in favor of laceration and manslaughter and massacre. Now, a bad book will produce a bad result, a cruel book will produce a cruel result.

Where does the cruelty crop out? At what time did you notice that the teachings of this Holy Bible created cruelty in the heart and the life of George Peabody, of Miss Dix, of Florence Nightingale, of John Howard, of John Frederick Oberlin, of Abbott Lawrence? Have you not, on the contrary, noticed that all the institutions of mercy were established or, being established,were chiefly supported by the friends of this Book? When you can make the rose-leaf stab like a bayonet, and when you can manufacture icicles out of the south wind, and when you can poison your tongue with honey gotten from blossoming buckwheat,then you can get cruelty out of the Bible. That charge of Mr. Ingersoll and his coadjutors falls flat in the presence of every honest man.

A MASS OF CONTRADICTIONS.

Mr. Ingersoll and his coadjutors also say the Bible is a mass of contradictions, and they put prophet against prophet, evangelist against evangelist, apostle against apostle, and they say if this be true, how then can that be true? Mr. Mill, who was a friend of the Bible, said he had discovered thirty thousand different readings of the Scriptures, and yet *not one important difference*—not one important difference out of thirty thousand—only the difference that you might expect from the fact that the book came down from generation to generation and was copied by a great many hands. And yet I put before you this fact to-day, that all the Bible-writers agree in the *four great doctrines* of the Bible.

What are those four great doctrines? God—good, kind, patient, just, loving, Omnipotent. Man—a lost sinner. Two destinies—one for believers, the other for unbelievers, all who accept Christ reaching that home, and only those de stroyed who destroy themselves; only those who turn their back upon Christ and come to the precipice and jump off, for God never pushes a man off, he jumps off Now, in these four great doctrines all the Bible-writers agree. Mozart, Beethoven, Handel, Haydn never wrote more harmonious music than you will find in this perfect harmony in the Word of God, the harmony in providence and in grace.

You must remember also that the authors of the Bible came from different lands, from different ages, and from different centuries They had no communication with each other, they did not have an idea as to what was the chief design of the Bible, and yet their writings, gotten up from all these different lands, and from all these different ages, and all these different centuries, coming together make a perfect harmony in the opinion of the very best scholars of this country and of England. Is not that a most remarkable fact?

It is as though some great cathedral were to be built and a hundred workmen were to be employed on it, and they were in many lands, and in different centuries, and these workmen had no communication with each other in regard to the grand design of the building, and yet all their fragments of work brought together, it is a perfect architectural triumph, although the man who built a pillar knew nothing of the man who built the dome, and the man who built the doorway knew nothing of the man who lifted the arch · yet a complete accord, a complete architecture, and a complete triumph.

IMPOSITION ON CREDULITY.

Mr. Ingersoll and his coadjutors go on to say that the Bible is made up of a lot of manuscripts, one picked up here and another there, and another from some other place, and that the whole thing is an imposition on the credulity of the human race. I must reply to that charge.

The Bible is made up of the Old Testament and the New Testament. Let us take the New Testament first. Why do I believe it? Why do I take it to my heart? It is because it can be traced back to the divine heart.

Jerome and Eusebius in the fourth century, and Origen in the second century, and other writers in the third and fourth centuries gave a list of the New-Testament writers just exactly corresponding with our list, showing that the same New Testament which we have they had in the fourth century, and the third century, and the second century, and the first century. But where did they get the New Testament? They got it from Irenæus. Where did Irenæus get it? He got it from Polycarp. Where did Polycarp get it? He got it from St. John, who was the personal associate of the Lord Jesus Christ. My grandfather gave a book to my father, my father gave it to me, I give it to my child. Is there any difficulty in tracing this line?

On Communion Day I will start the chalice at that end of the aisle, and the chalice will pass along to the other end of this aisle. Will it be difficult to trace the line of that holy chalice? No difficulty at all. This one will say, " I gave it to that one," and this one will say, " I gave it to that one " But it will not be so long a line as this to trace the New Testament. It is easier to get at the fact. But you say : " Although this was handed right down in that way, who knows but they were lying impostors? How can you take their testimony?" *They died for the truth* of that book. Men never die for a lie cheerfully and triumphantly. They were not lying impostors. They died in triumph for the truth of that New Testament.

"But how about the Old Testament? Why do you believe that?" I believe the Old Testament because the prophecies foretold events hundreds and thousands of years ahead, events which afterward took place. How far can you see ahead? Two thousand years? Can you see ahead a hundred years? Can you see ahead five minutes? No, no. Human prophecy amounts to nothing. Here these old prophets stood thousands of years back, and they foretold events which came accurately true far on in the future centuries. Suppose I should stand here this morning and say to you, twenty-five hundred and sixty years from now, three miles and a half from the city of Moscow there will be an advent, and it will be in a certain family, and it will be amid certain surroundings. It would make no impression upon you, because you know I cannot foresee a thousand years, or one year, or one minute, and I cannot tell what is going to transpire in a land that I have never looked at. But that is what these old prophets did.

You must remember that Tyre and Babylon and Nineveh were in full pomp and splendor when these prophecies, these old prophecies, said they would be destroyed. Those cities had architecture that make the houses on Madison Square and Fifth Avenue perfectly insignificant. Yet these old prophets walked right through those magnificent streets and said : "This has all got to come down ; that is all going to be levelled."

Suppose a man should stand up in these cities to-day and say : "The East River will overflow and Brooklyn will be destroyed, and the Hudson River will overflow and New York will be destroyed ; and then there will be a great earthquake and the two rivers will forsake their beds, and there will be harvests of wheat and corn where these cities now stand, and Fulton Street and Broadway will be pasture for cattle." Such a man would be sent to Bloomingdale Insane-Asylum. Yet the old prophets did that very thing. Where is Babylon to-day? You go and walk over the ruins of Bab-

ylon and you will not find a leaf or a grass-blade of those
splendid hanging-gardens, and in the summer-time the ground
actually blisters the feet of the traveller. Babylon destroyed
according to the prophecy.

Where is Tyre? In the day of its pomp, the prophet
said : "The fishermen will dry their nets where this city
stands" If you should go to that place to-day, you would
find that literally, the fishermen are drying their nets on
the rocks where the city of Tyre once stood. Tartar, and
Turk, and Saracen, drying their nets on the rocks

Go up Chatham Street and find the fulfilment of a prophecy made thousands of years ago. Why is it the Jew is always distinguishable, whether you see him in New York, or
Brooklyn, or Madras, or Pekin, or Vienna, or Stockholm, or
London, or Paris? The Englishman comes to America, and
after a while he loses his nationality. The American goes
to England, and after a while he loses his nationality. The
Norwegian his, the Russian his, the Italian his, the Spaniard
his, the Jew never. Why? Because this Book provided
thousands of years ago that the Jews should be scattered in
all lands, and that they should be kept *separate, separate,* until
the Lord took them back to Jerusalem. And ye who perse-
cute the Jews had better look out. They are God's people
yet, and *worse calamities than the assassination of a Czar will
come upon Russia* if she does not take her foot off the
Jews. They are God's people, and according to the prophecy made thousands of years ago they are distinguishable,
they are kept *separate,* until the Lord takes them to their
native land.

How could those old prophets foretell that? How could
they know that thousands of years ago? Was it mere human
skill? Could you have seen so far ahead? Could you have
predicted anything like it? Those old prophets stood looking down in the great future, and said a Messiah would be
born, in a certain nation, in a certain tribe, in a certain family, in a certain place, at a certain time, thousands of years
ahead Ages rolled on, ages on ages, and after a while Christ,
the only One who has been called Messiah by any great

number of people—Christ was born, in that very nation predicted, in that very tribe, in that very family, in that very
place, at that very time. Could human skill have predicted it ?
Does not that prove beyond all controversion and beyond
all doubt that those prophets were inspired of the Lord Almighty, looking down in the future and seeing thousands of
years ahead occurrences to take place ?

INDECENCIES.

Mr. Ingersoll picks up the Bible from his lecture-stand,
reads a little, and says, " I cannot read it all—it would not
be proper for me to read it all,"—and then he affects to
blush. He is overcome with modesty and delicacy ' He
dares the clergy to read certain passages in the pulpit, and
dares parents to read certain passages in the family circle.
Now my reply is this : There are parts of the Bible that
were not intended either to be read in the pulpit or family
circle, just as I can go into any physician's office in Brooklyn
or elsewhere and find medical journals on the table or books
in his library which he never has read to his family, yet
good books, pure books, scientific books, without which he
would not be worthy the name of physician. They are to
be read in private.

You must know that there is such a thing as the pathology of disease. You must know that there are parts of the
Bible which are *the anatomy of iniquity*, which are descriptions of the lazar-house of the soul when it is unrestrained ;
and from the reading of those portions in private we arise
with a healthy disgust and horror for sin. The pathology
must come before the pharmacy and the therapeutics.
Every physician knows that. Any man who has the least
smattering of medicine knows that. The pathology, or discussion of disease, before the pharmacy, or the cure of it

From certain portions of the Word of God we go forth
as from a dissecting-room, more intelligent than when we
went in, but in no wise enamored of putrefaction. There is

a Byronic description of sin which allures and destroys, but there is a Bible description of sin which warns and saves.

And yet Mr. Ingersoll and his coadjutors most vehemently charge that this Bible is an impure book. But you all know that an impure book produces impure results. No amount of money could hire you to allow your child to read an unclean book. Now, if this Bible be an impure book, where are the victims? Your father read it—did it make him a bad man? Your mother read it—did it make her a bad woman? Your sister fifteen years in Heaven died in the faith of this Gospel—did it despoil her nature? Some say there are two million copies of the Bible in existence, some say there are three million copies of the Bible. It is impossible to get the accurate statistics; but suppose there are two million copies of the Bible abroad,—this one book read more than any twenty books that the world ever printed, this book abroad for ages, for centuries,—where are the victims? Show me a thousand. Show me five hundred victims of an impure book. Show me a hundred despoiled of the Bible. Show me fifty. Show me ten. Show me two. Show me one! Two hundred million copies of an impure book, and not one victim of the impurity! On the contrary, you know very well that it is where the Bible has the most power that the family institution is most respected.

The Bible is *the friend of all that is pure,* and infidelity is the friend of all that is impure. This much-abused Book is the only fit foundation for the household.

One of the best families I ever knew of, for thirty or forty years, morning and evening, had all the members gathered together, and the servants of the household, and the strangers that happened to be within the gates—twice a day, without leaving out a chapter or a verse, they read this Holy Book, morning by morning, night by night. Not only the older children, but the little child who could just spell her way through the verse while her mother helped her. The father beginning and reading one verse, and then all the members of the family in turn reading a verse. The father maintained his integrity, the mother maintained her integrity, the sons grew up and entered professions and commercial life, adorning every sphere in the life in which they lived, and the daughters went into families where Christ was honored, and all that was good and pure and righteous reigned perpetually. For thirty years that family endured the Scriptures. Not one of them ruined by it.

Now, if you will tell me of a family where the Bible has been read twice a day for thirty years, and the children have been brought up in that habit, and the father went to ruin, and the mother went to ruin, and the sons and daughters were destroyed by it—if you will tell me of one such incident, I will throw away my Bible or I will doubt your veracity. I tell you if a man is shocked with what he calls the indelicacies of the Word of God, he is prurient in his taste and imagination. If a man cannot read the book Solomon's Song without impure suggestion, he is either in his heart, or in his life, a libertine.

The Old-Testament description of wickedness, uncleanliness of all sorts, is purposely and righteously a disgusting account, instead of the Parisian vernacular which makes sin attractive instead of appalling. When those old prophets point you to a lazaretto, you understand it is a lazaretto. No gilding of iniquity. No garlands on a death's head. No pounding away with a silver mallet at iniquity when it needs an iron sledge-hammer.

I can easily understand how people, brooding over the description of uncleanness in the Bible, may get morbid in mind until they are as full of it as the wings and the beak and the nostril and the claw of a buzzard is full of the odors of a carcass ; but what is wanted is not that the Bible be disinfected, but that you, the critic, have your heart and mind washed with carbolic acid !

POLYGAMY.

Mr. Ingersoll says to his audience . " Is there any man here who believes in polygamy ? No. Then you are better than your God : for four thousand years ago He believed in it, and taught it, and upheld it." Does the God of the Bible uphold polygamy? or did He? How many wives did God make for Adam? *He made one wife.* Does not your common-sense tell you when God started the marriage institution He started it as He wanted it to continue? If God had favored polygamy He could have created for Adam five wives, or ten wives, or twenty wives just as easily as He made one. At the very first of the Bible, God shows Himself in favor of monogamy, and antagonistic to polygamy. Genesis 2. 24: "Therefore shall a man leave his father and his mother, and shall cleave unto his wife." Not his *wives*, but his *wife.*

How many wives did God spare for Noah in the ark? Two and two the birds: two and two the cattle: two and two the lions: two and two the human race. If the God of the Bible had favored a multiplicity of wives He would have spared a plurality of wives. When God first launched the human race, He gave Adam one wife. At the second launching of the human race He spares for Noah one wife, for Ham one wife, for Shem one wife, for Japhet one wife. Does that look as though God favored polygamy? In Leviticus 18. 18, God thunders His prohibition of more than one wife.

God permitted polygamy. Yes; just as He permits to-day murder and theft and arson and all kinds of crime. He permits these things, as you well know, but He does not sanction them. Who would dare to say He sanctioned them? Because Presidents Hayes and Garfield permitted, and President Harrison permits, polygamy in Utah, you are not, therefore, to conclude that they patronized it, that they approved it, when on the contrary they denounced it. All the Jews knew that the God of the Bible was against polygamy, for in the four hundred and thirty years of their stay in Egypt there is only one case of polygamy recorded—only one. All the mighty men of the Bible stood aloof from polygamy except those who, falling into the crime, were chastised within an inch of their lives. Adam, Aaron, Noah, Joseph, Joshua, Samuel, monogamists

But you say, " Didn't David and Solomon favor polygamy ?" Yes; and did they not get well punished for it ?
Read the lives of these two men, and you will come to the
conclusion that all the attributes of God's nature were
against their behavior. David suffered for his crimes in
the caverns of Adullam and Masada, in the wilderness of
Maon, in the bereavements of Ziklag. The Bedouins after
him, sickness after him, Absalom after him, Ahithophel after
him, Adonijah after him, the Edomites after him, the Syrians
after him, the Moabites after him, death after him, the Lord
God Almighty after him. The poorest peasant in all the
empire married to the plainest Jewess was happier than the
king after his *liaison* with Bathsheba.

How did Solomon get along with polygamy ? Read his
warnings in Proverbs, read his self-disgust in Ecclesiastes.
He throws up his hands in loathing, and cries out, "Vanity
of vanities, all is vanity." His seven hundred wives nearly
pestered the life out of him. Solomon got well paid for his
crimes—well paid. I repeat that all the mighty men of the
Scriptures were aloof from polygamy save as they were
pounded and flailed, and cut to pieces for their insult to
holy marriage. Yet Mr. Ingersoll, in the face of an audience,
declares the Bible approves of polygamy

If it does, why is it that, in all the lands where the Bible
predominates, polygamy is forbidden ? and in the lands where
there is no Bible, it is favored ? Polygamy all over China, all
over India, all over Africa, all over Persia, all over heathendom save as the missionaries have done their work , while
polygamy does not exist in England and the United States,
except in defiance of law as in Utah, from which the President of the United States and the Congress are about to
eject it The Bible abroad, God-honored monogamy. The
Bible not abroad, God-abhorred polygamy. And yet, Mr.
Ingersoll says the Bible approves of polygamy. I take the
ulcerous and *accursed slander* and hurl it back into his blasphemous teeth. God is against polygamy. The Bible is
against polygamy. All Christendom is against polygamy.
How much Mr. Ingersoll's opinion of the marriage institution

is worth I leave you to judge when I tell you that in one of his lectures he compares an English authoress of blackened reputation with Queen Victoria, to the depreciation of the latter. In other words, rather than Queen Victoria, the purest specimen of Christian womanhood on any throne in all the earth, he prefers an authoress whose life was an offence to the marriage institution, and her example an insult to every pure woman in Christendom.

As for myself I have less admiration for the literary adulteress than I have for her who at nineteen years of age, informed that the crown of England was hers, knelt and asked the Archbishop to pray for the blessing of God on her reign ; and who, rearing her princes and princesses in the faith of the Christian life, finds in her widowhood a consolation in that Gospel which comforted Prince Albert in his dying moments, when with trembling lip in Windsor Castle she sang to him, " Rock of ages, cleft for me." And who, whether in plain dress going out from the castle at Balmoral or Osborne to read the Scripture to the poor in the lane, or carrying some delicacy to tempt the invalid's appetite, or going down to Chiselhurst holds by the hand the banished empress standing by the casket of her dead boy, "the only son of his mother, and she a widow;" or cables to the capital of our nation her anxiety about our wounded chief, and then sits down and writes with her own hand such comfort as only a widowed soul can give a widowed soul—always and everywhere the same good, kind, sympathetic Christian woman, for whom we Americans and Englishmen and Scotchmen, whether in earnest prayer or exhilarant huzza, are ready at all times to exclaim, " God save the Queen !"

WOMAN'S SHAME AND HUMILIATION.

Mr. Ingersoll caricatures and denounces the Bible because, he says, there is not a word in the Old Testament but is woman's shame and humiliation, and then he picks up the Bible and reads a few verses in the New Testament to show that the Bible all the way through is the degradation of woman. Come now, let us see. Come into the picture gallery, the Louvre, the Luxemburg of the Bible, and see which pictures are the more honored. Here is Eve, a perfect woman, as perfect a woman as could be made by a perfect God. Here is Deborah, with her womanly arm hurling a host into the battle. Here is Miriam, leading the Israelitish orchestra on the banks of the Red Sea.

Here is Ruth, putting to shame all *the modern slang about mothers-in-law* as she turns her back on her home and her country, and faces wild beasts and exile and death that she may be with Naomi, her husband's mother; Ruth, the queen of the harvest-fields; Ruth, the grandmother of David; Ruth, the ancestress of Jesus Christ. The story of her virtues and her life-sacrifice, the most beautiful pastoral ever written.

Here is Vashti, defying the bacchanal of a thousand drunken lords; and Esther, willing to throw her life away that she may deliver her people. And here is Dorcas, the sunlight of eternal flame gilding her philanthropic needle; and the woman with perfume in a box made from the hills of alabastron, pouring the holy chrism on the head of Christ, the aroma lingering all down the corridor of the centuries. Here is Lydia, the merchantess of Tyrian purple, immortalized for her Christian behavior.

Oh how the Bible hates women! Who has more worshippers to-day than any being that ever lived on earth, except Jesus Christ? Mary. For what purpose did Christ perform His first miracle upon earth? To relieve the embarrassment of a womanly housekeeper at the falling short of a beverage. Why did Christ break up the silence of the tomb, and tear off the shroud and rip up the rocks? It was to stop the bereavement of the two Bethany sisters. *For whose comfort was Christ most anxious* in the hour of dying excruciation? For a woman, an old woman, a wrinkled-faced woman, a woman who in other days had held Him in her arms, His first friend, His last friend, as it is very apt to be, His mother. All the pathos of the ages compressed into one utterance, " Behold thy mother." Oh how the Bible hates women!

If the Bible is so antagonistic to woman, how do you account for the difference in woman's condition in China and Central Africa, and her condition in England and America? There is no difference except that which the Bible makes. In lands where there is no Bible, she is hitched like a beast of burden to the ploughs, she carries the hod, she submits to indescribable indignities. She must be kept in a private apartment, and if she come forth she must be carefully hooded and religiously veiled, as though it were a shame to be a woman.

Do you know that the very first thing the Bible does when it comes into a new country is to strike off the shackles of woman's serfdom? O woman, where are your chains to-day? Hold up both your arms and let us see your hand-cuffs. Oh, we see the handcuffs: they are bracelets of gold, bestowed by husbandly or fatherly or brotherly or sisterly or loverly affection. Loosen the warm robe from your neck, O woman, and let us see the yoke of your bondage. Oh! I find the yoke is a carcanet of silver, or a string of corneli-ans, or a cluster of pearls that must gall you very much. How bad you must all have it?

Since you put the Bible on your stand in the sitting-room, has the Bible been to you, O woman, a curse or a blessing? Why is it that a woman when she is troubled will go to her worst enemy, the Bible? Why do you not go for comfort to some of the great infidel books, Spinoza's Ethics, or Hume's Natural History of Religion, or Paine's Age of Reason, or Dedro's dramas, or any one of the two hundred and sixty volumes of Voltaire? No, the silly, deluded woman persists in hanging about the Bible verses, "Let not your heart be troubled," "All things work together for good," "Weeping may endure for a night," "I am the resurrec-tion," "Peace, be still." Why do more women read the Bible than men? Because while the Bible is a good book for a man, it is a better book for a woman, and it has done her more good and more kindness, and brought her more grace. The Bible is a friend of man; it is a better friend to woman.

Just read some of the cruel injunctions this Bible gives in regard to woman. See how the Scriptures maltreat her case. "Honor thy mother;" "Husbands, love your wives even as Christ loved the church and gave himself for it;" "Let them"—that is, the male converts—"let them learn first to show piety at home," "She hath done what she could."

Ah! you know there is not a person in all the house to-day but knows that the Bible is woman's emancipation, woman's eulogy, woman's joy, woman's heaven;—and yet Mr. Ingersoll stands in the presence of an audience and declares that the Bible is woman's shame, woman's degradation, woman's enemy, and one thousand idiots clap their hands in commendation!

COUNTER-CHARGES AGAINST INGERSOLLISM.

The plaintiff, Infidelity, has not made out its case against the Bible, the defendant ; and I might in the court of your reason move for *a nonsuit*, but I will rather turn the tables upon him and bring him to the bar. And I here and now charge him with Jehoiakim's folly. "When Jehudi had read three or four leaves, he cut it with the penknife."—JEREMIAH 36 23.

There sits Jehoiakim in the winter-house, his feet to the fire, which is blazing and crackling on the hearth. His private secretary, Jehudi, is reading to him from a scroll containing God's word to Jeremiah. Jehoiakim is displeased at the message, gets very red in the face, jumps up and snatches the scroll from the hand of his private secretary, takes out his penknife, and cuts and slashes it all to pieces.

Jehoiakim was under the impression that if he destroyed the scroll he would destroy the prophecy. Ah! no. Jeremiah immediately takes another scroll and the prophecy is redictated. The fact is that all the penknifes ever made at

Sheffield and in all the cutleries of the world cannot successfully destroy the Scriptures.

THE MODERN JEHOIAKIM.

We have *a Jehoiakim in our day*, Mr. Ingersoll, the repre-
sentative of the infidelity of the hour, who proposes with his
penknife to hack the Word of God to pieces. With that
penknife he tries to stab Moses, and to stab Joshua, and to
stab all the prophets and apostles, and evangelists, and to
stab Christ, and to stab the God of the Bible; but while he
is cutting to pieces his own copy of the Bible—for I suppose
he has only one copy of this dangerous book in his house,
and that carefully guarded and locked up so none of his
friends may be poisoned by it—there are innumerable copies of the Bible being distributed.

No book, secular or religious, ever multiplied with such
speed and into such vastness as the Word of God,—Disraeli's
" Endymion," Macaulay's " History of England," Shakespeare's tragedies, having very small and limited reading,
and very small and limited sale and distribution as compared
with this Book; which, after for centuries being bombarded
by thousands of Ingersolls, to-day has abroad over three
hundred millions of copies. Where one Bible dies ten thousand Bibles are born. Cut away, then, with your infidel pen-
knives.

Mr. Ingersoll, with his knife-blade, proposes to cut the
Bible to pieces in ridicule. Now, I like fun; no man was
ever built with a keener appreciation of it. There is health
in laughter instead of harm—physical health, mental health,
moral health, spiritual health—*provided you laugh at the right
thing*

But there is a laughter which is deathful, there is a laughter which has the rebound of despair. It is not healthful to
giggle about God, or chuckle about eternity, or smirk about
the things of the immortal soul. What caused the accident
some time ago on the Hudson River Railroad? It was an
intoxicated man who for a joke pulled the string of the air-

brake and stopped the train at the most dangerous point of the journey. But the lightning train, not knowing there was any impediment in the way, came down, crushing out of the mangled victims the immortal souls that went speeding in stantly to God and judgment. *It was only a joke.*

And so Mr. Ingersoll is chiefly anxious to stop the long train of the Bible, and the long train of the churches, and the long train of Christian influences, while coming down upon us are death, judgment, and eternity, coming a thousand miles a minute, coming with more force than all the avalanches that ever slipped from the Alps, coming with more strength than all the lightning express trains than ever whistled, or shrieked, or thundered across the continent. Stop! says Mr. Ingersoll, it is only a joke. It is a spectacle which almost splits him with laughter. It is a subject which, though agonizing the nations, throws him into uproars of laughter; and the theme of his funniest lecture is the most stupendous question that was ever asked—" What must I do to be saved?"

INFIDELITY AND SUICIDE.

There is recorded in the Acts of the Apostles the story of a would-be suicide arrested in his deadly attempt. He was a sheriff, and according to the Roman law a bailiff himself must suffer the punishment due an escaped prisoner; and if the prisoner breaking jail was sentenced to be endungeoned for three or four years, then the sheriff must be endungeoned for three or four years; and if the prisoner breaking jail was to have suffered capital punishment, then the sheriff must suffer capital punishment. The sheriff had received especial charge to keep a sharp lookout for Paul and Silas. The government had not had confidence in bolts and bars to keep safe these two clergymen, about whom there seemed to be something strange and supernatural.

Sure enough, by miraculous power, they are free, and the sheriff, waking out of a sound sleep, and supposing these ministers have run away, and knowing that they were to die for preaching Christ, and realizing that he must therefore die, rather than go under the executioner's axe on the morrow and suffer public disgrace, resolves to precipitate his own decease. But before the sharp, keen, glittering dagger of the sheriff could strike his heart one of the loosened prisoners arrests the blade by the command, "Do thyself no harm." In olden time, and where Christianity had not interfered with it, suicide was considered honorable and a sign of courage. Demosthenes poisoned himself when told that Alexander's ambassador had demanded the surrender of the Athenian orators. Isocrates killed himself rather than surrender to Philip of Macedon. Cato, rather than submit to Julius Cæsar, took his own life, and after three times his wounds had been dressed tore them open and perished. Mithridates killed himself rather than submit to Pompey, the conqueror. Hannibal destroyed his life by poison from his ring, considering life unbearable. Lycurgus a suicide, Brutus a suicide. After the disaster of Moscow, Napoleon always carried with him a preparation of opium, and one night his servant heard the ex-emperor arise, put something in a glass and drink it, and soon after the groans aroused all the attendants, and it was only through utmost medical skill he was resuscitated from the stupor of the opiate.

Times have changed, and yet the American conscience needs to be toned up on the subject of suicide. God gave you a special trust in your life. He made you the custodian of your life as He made you the custodian of no other life. He gave you as weapons with which to defend it two arms to strike back assailants, two eyes to watch for invasion, and a natural love of life

To show how God in the Bible looked upon this crime, I point you to

THE ROGUES' PICTURE-GALLERY

in some parts of the Bible, the pictures of the people who have committed this unnatural crime. Here is the headless trunk of Saul on the walls of Bethshan. Here is the man who chased little David—ten feet in stature chasing four. Here is the man who consulted a clairvoyant, Witch of Endor. Here is a man who, whipped in battle, instead of surrendering his sword with dignity, as many a man has done, asks his servant to slay him ; and when the servant declines, then the king plants the hilt of the sword in the earth, the sharp point sticking upward, and he throws his body on it and expires, the coward, the suicide. Here is Ahithophel, the Machiavelli of olden times, betraying his best friend David in order that he may become prime minister of Absalom, and joining that fellow in his attempt at parricide. Not getting what he wanted by change of politics, he takes a short cut out of a disgraced life into the suicide's eternity. There he is, the ingrate!

Here is Abimelech, practically a suicide. He is with an army, bombarding a tower, when a woman in the tower takes a grindstone from its place and drops it upon his head, and with what life he has left in his cracked skull he commands his armor-bearer, " Draw thy sword and slay me, lest men say a woman slew me." There is his *post-mortem* photograph in the Book of Samuel. But the hero of this group is Judas Iscariot. Dr. Donne says he was a martyr, and we have in our day apologists for him. And what wonder, in this day when we have a book revealing Aaron Burr as a pattern of virtue, and in this day when we uncover a statue to George Sand as the benefactress of literature, and in this day when there are betrayals of Christ on the part of some of His pretended apostles—a betrayal so black it makes the infamy of Judas Iscariot white! Yet this man by his own hand hung up for the execration of all the ages, Judas Iscariot.

All the good men and women of the Bible left to God the decision of their earthly terminus, and they could have said with Job, who had a right to commit suicide if any man ever had—what with his destroyed property, and his body all aflame with insufferable carbuncles, and everything gone from his home except the chief curse of it, a pestiferous wife, and four garrulous people pelting him with comfortless talk

while he sits on a heap of ashes scratching his scabs with a
piece of broken pottery, yet crying out in triumph, "All the
days of my appointed time will I wait till my change come."
And I therefore table this charge against infidelity as tending to increase suicide and other crimes.

If there be no hereafter, or if that hereafter be blissful
without reference to how we live and how we die, why not
move back the folding-doors between this world and the
next? And when our existence here becomes troublesome,
why not pass right over into Elysium? Put this down
among your most solemn reflections, and consider it after
you go to your homes; there has never been a case of suicide where the operator was not either demented, and therefore irresponsible, or an infidel. I challenge all the ages,
and I challenge the whole universe. There never has been
a case of self-destruction while in full appreciation of his
immortality, and of the fact that that immortality would be
glorious or wretched according as he accepted Jesus Christ
or rejected Him.

You say it is business trouble, or you say it is electrical
currents, or it is this, or it is that, or it is the other thing.
Why not go clear back, my friend, and acknowledge that in
every case it is the abdication of reason or the teaching of
infidelity which practically says: "If you don't like this life
get out of it, and you will land either in annihilation, where
there are no notes to pay, no persecutions to suffer, no gout
to torment, or you will land where there will be everything
glorious, and nothing to pay for it." Infidelity always has
been apologetic for self-immolation. After Tom Paine's
"Age of Reason" was published and widely read, there was
a marked increase of self-slaughter.

A man in London heard Mr. Owen deliver his infidel lecture on Socialism, and went home, sat down, and wrote
these words, "Jesus Christ is one of the weakest characters
in history, and the Bible is the greatest possible deception,"
and then shot himself. David Hume wrote these words: "It
would be no crime for me to divert the Nile or Danube from
its natural bed. Where, then, can be the crime in my di-

verting a few drops of blood from their ordinary channel?"
And having written the essay he loaned it to a friend, the
friend read it, wrote a letter of thanks and admiration, and
shot himself. Appendix to the same book.

Rousseau, Voltaire, Gibbon, Montaigne, under certain
circumstances, were apologetic for self-immolation. Infidelity puts up no bar to people's rushing out from this world
into the next. They teach us it does not make any difference how you live here or go out of this world, you will
land either in an oblivious nowhere or a glorious somewhere.
And Infidelity holds the upper end of the rope for the suicide, and aims the pistol with which a man blows his brains
out, and mixes the strychnine for the last swallow. If Infidelity could carry the day and persuade the majority of
people in this country that it does not make any difference
how you go out of the world you will land safely, the Hudson and the East rivers would be so full of corpses the ferry-
boats would be impeded in their progress, and the crack of
a suicide's pistol would be no more alarming than the rumble of a street car.

I have sometimes heard it discussed whether the great
dramatist was a Christian or not. I do not know; but I
know that he considered appreciation of a future existence
the mightiest hindrance to self-destruction:

> " For who could bear the whips and scorns of time,
>   The oppressor's wrong, the proud man's contumely,
>   The pangs of despis'd love, the law's delay,
>   The insolence of office, and the spurns
>   That patient merit of the unworthy takes,
>   When he himself might his quietus make
>   With a bare bodkin? Who would fardels bear,
>   To grunt and sweat under a weary life,
>   But that the dread of something after death—
>   The undiscovered country, from whose bourn
>   No traveller returns—puzzles the will?"

Would God that the coroners would be brave in rendering the right verdict, and when, in a case of irresponsi-
bility they say " While this man was demented he took his

life," in the other case say " Having read infidel books and attended infidel lectures, which obliterated from this man's mind all appreciation of anything like future retribution, he committed self-slaughter !"

Ah! Infidelity, stand up and take thy sentence! In the presence of God and angels and men, stand up, thou monster, thy lip blasted with blasphemy, thy cheek scarred with lust, thy breath foul with the corruption of the ages! Stand up, Satyr, filthy goat, buzzard of the nations, leper of the centuries! Stand up, thou monster Infidelity! Part man, part panther, part reptile, part dragon, stand up and take thy sentence! Thy hands red with the blood in which thou hast washed, thy feet crimson with the human gore through which thou hast waded, stand up and take thy sentence! Down with thee to the pit and sup on the sobs and groans of families thou hast blasted, and roll on the bed of knives which thou has sharpened for others, and let thy music be the everlasting *miserere* of those whom thou hast damned ! I brand the forehead of Infidelity with all the crimes of self-immolation for the last century on the part of those who had their reason.

Ah! you and I may give our fifty cents or our dollar to hear Mr. Ingersoll's lecture, in which the Bible is caricatured and the Lord Jesus Christ insulted ; but I tell you plainly the time will come when we would give the whole earth, if we owned it, for the cheer of its promises, and the whole universe, if we could, for the smile of His love. How black and terrible is departure from this life without this Gospel. One who had served the world and jeered at Christianity, and pronounced the Bible a cheat and a humbug, in the last hour said : " It is so dark ! it is so dark ! it is so dark."

On the day when the coffin goes out of the front door, and down the front steps, it leaves a house very lonesome if there be no Bible on the stand and no Christ to stand at the desolated hearthstone.

THE MEANNESS OF INFIDELITY.

Mr. Ingersoll demonstrates the meanness of infidelity by satirizing his early home, and leaving the people of this country under the impression that his father at least was a bigot, and a tyrant, and a fool. Now, can you imagine anything meaner than the assailing of a parent's reputation after he is dead and gone? I had a Christian ancestry of elevated type; but suppose my father or mother had been hypocritical and tyrannical, and bigoted, and bad—would it not have been debasing in me to have hooked up the horses to the ploughshare of contempt, and turned up the mounds of their graves?

Far better the conduct of Shem and Japhet, who at their father's inebriation took a mantle and walked backward, and with averted eyes threw it over him to hide the shame. But while Mr. Ingersoll leads his audiences to believe that his father was a tyrant and a bigot, why does he not say something about his mother? All the accounts agree in saying she was a grandly good Christian woman. Why does he not tell us the source of her goodness? Where is the Bible she used to read? Is it still in the family? Why does he not extol her Christian graces? How did religion seem to agree with her? Did the Christian religion make her cross, and sour, and queer, and crabbed? or did it make her kind, and genial, and loving, and patient? Did it give her comfort in the days of trouble? Was she deluded with it to the last? In her dying-hour was it a pest or an encouragement? Amid all the flowers of rhetoric can he not twist one garland for her memory?

Oh, it is insufferably mean, it is accursedly mean, that a man should throw a cloud of obloquy on his early home when there was at least one parent who loved God, kept His commandments, and lived a grandly beautiful and useful life. I stand at the door of the sepulchre of that Christian mother and I cry out for justice from the infidel lecturer. Oh, ungrateful man, you are nothing to the bosom that

nursed you, and the arm that encircled you, and the lips that
prayed for you, and the hands that were blistered for you,
and the shoulders that stooped to carry your burdens. You
do not believe in the Bible, you do not believe in the God
of the Bible : do you believe in your mother?

I do not implead you by John Calvin's God, for you say
he is a fiend ; I do not implead you by John Wesley's God,
for you say he is a fanatic ; I do not implead you by the
God of the Westminster Catechism ; I do not implead you
by your father's God ;—but I implead you by your mother's
God. By the birth-pang that launched you, by the Christian cradle that rocked you, by the solemn hour in which
you were held up in the old country meeting-house while
the minister of religion said, " Robert, I baptize thee in the
name of the Father, and of the Son, and of the Holy Ghost,"
—by that God I implead you to reconsider, and turn and
live.

Mr. Ingersoll also shows the meanness of infidelity by
trying to substitute for the chief consolation of the world
absolutely nothing. You have only to hear him at the edge
of the grave, or at the edge of the coffin, discoursing, to find
out that there is no comfort in infidelity. There is more
good cheer in the hooting of an owl at midnight than in his
discourses at the verge of the grave. You might as well ask
the spirit of eternal darkness to discourse on the brightness
of everlasting day. You know there are millions of people
who get their chief consolation from this Holy Book. Now,
Mr. Ingersoll proposes to take away that consolation. What
do you think of it? What would you think of a crusade of
this sort? Suppose a man should resolve that he would
organize a conspiracy to destroy all the medicines from all
the apothecaries and from all the hospitals of the earth.
The work is done. The medicines are taken and they are
thrown into the river, or the lake, or the sea. A patient
wakes up at midnight in a paroxysm of distress and wants
an anodyne. " Oh," says the nurse, " the anodynes are all
destroyed—we have no drops to give you ; but instead of
that I'll read you a lecture on the absurdities of morphine,

and on the absurdities of all remedies." But the man continues to writhe in pain, and the nurse says : "I'll continue to read you some discourses on anodynes—the cruelties of anodynes, the indecencies of anodynes, the absurdities of anodynes. For your groan I'll give you a laugh."

Here in the hospital is a patient having a gangrened limb amputated. He says, "Oh for ether! Oh for chloroform!" The doctors say, "Why, they are all destroyed ; we don't have any more chloroform or ether, but I have got something a great deal better. I'll read you a lecture on the mistakes of James Y. Simpson, the discoverer of cloroform as an anæsthetic, and upon the mistakes of Doctors Agnew, and Hamilton, and Hosack, and Mott, and Harvey, and Abernethy." "But," says the man, "I must have some anæsthetics." "No," say the doctors, "they are all destroyed ; but we have got something a great deal better." "What is that ?" "Fun." Fun about medicines.

Lie down, all ye patients in Bellevue Hospital, and stop your groaning—all ye broken-hearted of all the cities, and quit your crying ; we have the catholicon at last ! Here is *a dose of wit*, here is a strengthening-plaster of sarcasm, here is a bottle of ribaldry that you are to keep well shaken up and take a spoonful of after each meal ; and if that does not cure you, here is a solution of blasphemy in which you may bathe, and here is a tincture of derision. Tickle the skeleton of death with a repartee ! Make the King of Terrors cackle! For all the agonies of all the ages, a joke !

Millions of people willing with uplifted hand toward heaven to affirm that the Gospel of Jesus Christ is full of consolation for them, and yet Mr. Ingersoll proposes to take it away, giving nothing, absolutely nothing, except fun. Is there any greater height, or depth, or length, or breadth, or immensity of meanness in all God's universe !

Mr. Ingersoll still further demonstrates the meanness of infidelity by trying to substitute for the Bible-explanation of the future world a religion of "don't know." Is there a God ? Don't know ! Is the soul immortal ? Don't know ! If we should meet each other in the future world will we

recognize each other? Don't know! This man proposes
to substitute the religion of "don't know" for *the religion of*
"*I know.*" "I know in whom I have believed." "I know
that my Redeemer liveth." Infidelity proposes to substitute a religion of awful negatives for our religion of glorious
positives showing right before us a world of reunion and
ecstasy, and high companionship, and glorious worship, and
stupendous victory; the mightiest joy of earth not high
enough to reach to the base of the Himalaya of uplifted
splendor awaiting all those who on wing of Christian faith
will soar toward it.

Have you heard of the *conspiracy to put out all the lighthouses* on the coast? Do you know that on a certain night
of next month Eddystone Lighthouse, Bell Rock Light-
house, Skerryvore Lighthouse, Montauk Lighthouse, Hatteras Lighthouse, New London Lighthouse, Barnegat Light-
house, and the 640 lighthouses on the Atlantic and Pacific
coasts are to be extinguished? "Oh," you say, "what will
become of the ships on that night? What will be the fate
of the one million sailors following the sea? What will be
the doom of the millions of passengers? Who will arise to
put down such a conspiracy?" Every man, woman, and
child in America and the world.

But that is only a fable. That is what infidelity is trying
to do—put out all the lighthouses on the coast of eternity,
letting the soul go up the "Narrows" of death with no light,
no comfort, no peace—all that coast covered with the blackness of darkness. Instead of the great lighthouse, a glow-
worm of wit, a fire-fly of jocosity. Which do you like the
better, oh voyager for eternity—the fire-fly or the lighthouse? What a mission Infidelity has started on! The ex-
tinguishment of lighthouses, the breaking up of lifeboats,
the dismissal of all the pilots, the turning of the inscription
on your child's grave into a farce and a lie.

Walter Scott's "Old Mortality," chisel in hand, went
through the land to cut out into plainer letters the half-ob-
literated inscriptions on the tombstones, and it was a beautiful mission. But Mr. Ingersoll is spending his life, and

the men who are like him are spending their lives, with hammer and chisel, trying to cut out from the tombstones of your dead all the story of resurrection and Heaven. He is the iconoclast of every village graveyard, and of every city cemetery, and of Westminster Abbey. Instead of Christian consolation for the dying, a freezing sneer; instead of prayer, a grimace; instead of Paul's triumphant defiance of death, a going out you know not where, to stop you know not when, to do you know not what. That is infidelity— the boast of the CHAMPION ICONOCLAST of America.

NO SUBSTITUTE FOR CHRISTIAN INSTITUTIONS.

To show that infidelity can provide no substitute for what it proposes to destroy, I ask you to mention the names of the merciful and the educational institutions which infidelity founded, and is supporting, and has supported all the way through; institutions pronounced against God and the Christian religion and yet pronounced in behalf of suffering humanity. What are the names of them? Certainly not the United States Christian Commission, or the Sanitary Commission; for Christian George H. Stuart was the president of the one, and Christian Henry W. Bellows was the president of the other. Where are the asylums and merciful institutions founded by Infidelity and supported by Infidelity, pronounced against God and the Bible, and yet doing work for the alleviation of suffering? Infidelity is so very loud in its braggadocio it must have some to mention.

Certainly if you come to speak of educational institutions it is not Yale, it is not Harvard, it is not Princeton, it is not Middletown; it is not Cambridge or Oxford; it is not any institution from which a diploma would not be a disgrace. Do you point to the German universities as exceptions? I have to tell you that all the German universities to-day are under positive Christian influences, except the University of Heidelberg, where the ruffianly students cut and maul and mangle and murder each other as a matter of pride instead

of infamy.   The duello is the chief characteristic of that institution.

There stands Christianity   There stands Infidelity.   Compare what they have done.   Compare their resources.   There
is Christianity, a prayer on her lip , a benediction on her
brow; both hands full of help for all who want help; the
mother of thousands of colleges; the mother of thousands
of asylums for the oppressed, the blind, the sick, the lame,
the imbecile; the mother of missions for the bringing back
of the outcast , the mother of thousands of reformatory institutions for the saving of the lost , the mother of innumerable Sabbath-schools bringing millions of children under a
drill to prepare them for respectability and usefulness, to
say nothing of the great future.   That is Christianity.

IMPEACHMENT OF INFIDELITY.

Here is Infidelity : no prayer on her lips, no benediction
on her brow, both hands clenched—what for ? To fight
Christianity.   That is the entire business, the complete
mission, of Infidelity—to fight Christianity.   Where are her
schools, her colleges, her asylums of mercy ?   Let me throw
you down a whole ream of foolscap paper that you may fill
all of it with the names of her beneficent institutions, the
colleges and the asylums, the institutions of mercy and of
learning, founded by Infidelity and supported alone by Infidelity, pronounced against God and the Christian religion
and yet in favor of making the world better.   "Oh," you
say, "*a ream of paper* is too much for the names of those institutions."   Well, then, I throw you *a quire* of paper.   Fill
it all up now.   I will wait until you get all the names down.
"Oh," you say, "that is too much."   Well, then, I will just
hand you *a sheet* of letter-paper.

"Oh," you say, "that is too much."

Perhaps I better tear out *one leaf* from my hymn-book
and ask you to fill up both sides of it with the names of such
institutions.   "Oh," you say, "that would be too much."

Well, then, suppose you count them on your ten fingers.

"Oh," you say, "not quite so much as that." Well, then, count them on the fingers of one hand. "Oh," you say, "we don't want quite so much room as that." Suppose, men, you halt and count on one finger the name of any institution founded by Infidelity, supported entirely by Infidelity, pronounced against God and the Christian religion, yet toiling to make the world better. Not one! Not one!

Is infidelity so poor, so starveling, so mean, so useless? Get out, you miserable pauper of the universe! Crawl into some rat-hole of everlasting nothingness. Infidelity standing to-day amid the suffering, groaning, dying nations and yet doing absolutely nothing save trying to impede those who are toiling until they fall exhausted into their graves in trying to make the world better. Gather up all the work, all the merciful work, that Infidelity has ever done, add it all together, and there is not so much nobility in it as in the smallest bead of that Sister of Charity who last night went up the dark alley of the town, put a jar of jelly for an invalid appetite on a broken stand, and then knelt on the bare floor, praying the mercy of Christ upon the dying soul.

Infidelity scrapes no lint for the wounded, bakes no bread for the hungry, shakes up no pillow for the sick, rouses no comfort for the bereft, gilds no grave for the dead. While Christ, our Christ, our wounded Christ, our risen Christ, the Christ of this old-fashioned Bible—blessed be His glorious name forever!—our Christ stands this morning pointing to the hospital, or to the asylum, saying: "I was sick and ye gave me a couch, I was lame and ye gave me a crutch, I was blind and ye physicianed my eyes, I was orphaned and ye mothered my soul, I was lost on the mountains and ye brought me home ; inasmuch as ye did it to one of the least of these, ye did it to me."

Oh what a magnificent array of men and women have been made by the religion of the Bible! I cannot call the roll. I call the roll only of a part of one company of a regiment of a battalion of an army of magnificent men and women innumerable: John Howard, John Milton, David Brainard, George Whitefield, Martin Luther, Adoniram

Judson, Alexander Duff, Henry Martyn, William Wilberforce, Richard Cobden, Bishop McIlvaine, James A. Garfield, George Washington, Victoria the Queen; Hannah More, Charlotte Elizabeth, Harriet Newell, Mrs. Sigourney, Florence Nightingale, Lucretia Mott, and ten thousand other men and women, living and dead, standing in the present and in the past, aflame with the transpicuous glories of the Christian religion!

In this trial that has been going on between Infidelity and Christianity, we have only called one witness, and that was Robert G Ingersoll. He testified in behalf of Infidelity. We have shown that his testimony was not worthy of being received. We showed it was founded on ignorance geological, ignorance chemical, ignorance astronomical, ignorance geographical, and ignorance Biblical. Whose testimony will you take—these men, the Ingersolls of earth, who say they have not heard the voice of Christ, have not seen the coronation? or will you take the thousands and tens of thousands of Christians who testify of what they saw with their own eyes and heard with their own ears?

Here is the Gospel of Jesus Christ, an anodyne for all trouble, the mightiest medicine that ever came down to earth. Here is a man who says: "I don't believe in it; there is no power in it." Here are other people who say: "We have found out its power and know its soothing influence, it has cured us." Whose testimony will you take in regard to this healing medicine? "I speak as unto wise men: judge ye what I say."

DOWNFALL OF CHRISTIANITY.

Christianity is the rising sun of our time, and men have tried with the uprolling vapors of scepticism and the smoke of their blasphemy to turn the sun into darkness. Suppose the archangels of malice and horror should be let loose a little while and be allowed to extinguish and destroy the sun in the natural heavens. They would take the oceans from other worlds and pour them on this luminary of the planetary system, and the waters go hissing down amid the ravines and the caverns, and there is explosion after explosion, until there are only a few peaks of fire left in the sun, and these are cooling down and going out, until the vast continents of flame are reduced to a small acreage of fire, and that whitens and cools off until there are only a few coals left, and these are whitening and going out until there is not a spark left in all the mountains of ashes, and the valleys of ashes, and the chasms of ashes. An extinguished sun. A dead sun. A buried sun. Let all worlds wail at the stupendous obsequies. Of course, this withdrawal of the solar light and heat throws our earth into a universal chill, and the tropics become the temperate, and the temperate becomes the Arctic, and there are frozen rivers and frozen lakes and frozen oceans. From the Arctic and Antarctic regions the inhabitants gather in toward the centre and find the equator as the poles. The slain forests are piled up into a great bonfire, and around them gather the shivering villages and cities. The wealth of the coal-mines is hastily poured into the furnaces and stirred into rage of combustion, but soon the bonfires begin to lower, and the furnaces begin to go out, and the nations begin to die Cotopaxi, Vesuvius, Ætna, Stromboli, Californian geysers cease to smoke, and the ice of hail-storms remains unmelted in their craters. All the flowers have breathed their last breath. Ships with sailors frozen at the mast and helmsmen frozen at the wheel, and passengers frozen in the cabin. All nations dying, first at the north and then at the south. Child frosted and dead in the cradle. Octogenarian frosted and dead at the hearth. Workmen with frozen hand on the hammer and frozen foot on the shuttle. Winter from sea to sea. All-congealing winter. Perpetual winter. Globe of frigidity. Hemisphere shackled to hemisphere by chains of ice. Universal Nova Zembla. The earth an ice-floe grinding against other ice-floes. The archangels of malice and horror have done their work, and now they may take their thrones of glacier and look down upon the ruin they have wrought.

What the destruction of the sun in the natural heavens

would be to our physical earth, the destruction of Christianity would be to the moral world. The sun turned into dark
ness.

Infidelity in our time is considered a great joke. There
are people who will gather to hear Christianity caricatured
and to hear Christ assailed with quibble and quirk and misrepresentation and badinage and harlequinade.

A lecturer in Brooklyn Theatre is reported to have
said: "When we compare our God with men, He is not
much of a God. When Christ was here He was forgiving
and half-human ; but now he is God ; and instead of saying,
' Father, forgive them, they know not what they do,' He sends
them to eternal fire. It is wonderful the difference office
makes with some people." "[Laughter]," the reporter says.
The Lord Jesus Christ, who came to carry our sorrows,
maligned in the presence of the city of Brooklyn!

A PUNISHABLE CRIME.

I hold in my hand a book entitled " Religion and the
State," by Rev. Dr. Samuel T. Spear, the ablest ecclesiastical lawyer of our time, and, had he entered the legal profession instead of theology, would long before this have been
upon the bench of the Supreme Court at Washington. In
this book he gives a compilation of authorities upon the
subject of blasphemy.

Now, I say, let the law against blasphemy be erased from
the statute-book, or let it be executed. " Oh," says some
one, " don't you believe in free speech ?"

Yes, I believe in all styles of righteous freedom : free
driving of horses, but no right to run over other people ; free
use of knives, but no right for assassination ; free use of gunpowder, but no right to destroy the lives or the property of
others ; free speech, but no freedom for obscenity or false
speaking or blasphemy. There will after a while arise in
the United States a municipal authority somewhere tall
enough to look over all political considerations and strong
armed enough to execute the law against blasphemy, and

then we shall have no more of the outrageous utterances of last Sabbath night in Brooklyn Theatre, and the carrion stench of leprous infidelity will be fumigated from the atmosphere.

I propose this morning to take Infidelity and Atheism out of the realm of jocularity into one of tragedy, and show you what these men propose, and what, if they are successful, they will accomplish. There are those in all our communities who would like to see the Christian religion overthrown, and who say the world would be better without it. I want to show you what is the end of this road, and what is the terminus of this crusade, and what this world will be when Atheism and Infidelity have triumphed over it, if they can. I say, if they can. I reiterate it, if they can.

DEGRADATION OF WOMANHOOD.

Infidelity would be the complete and unutterable degradation of womanhood. I will prove it by facts and arguments which no honest man will dispute. In all communities and cities and states and nations where the Christian religion has been dominant, woman's condition has been ameliorated and improved, and she is deferred to and honored in a thousand things, and every gentleman takes off his hat before her. You know that while woman may suffer injustices in England and the United States, she has more of her rights in Christendom than she has anywhere else.

Now compare this with woman's condition in lands where Christianity has made little or no advance—in China, in Barbary, in Borneo, in Tartary, in Egypt, in Hindostan. The *Burmese sell their wives* and daughters as so many sheep. The Hindoo bible makes it disgraceful and an outrage for a woman to listen to music, or look out of the window in the absence of her husband, and gives as a lawful ground for divorce a woman's beginning to eat before her husband has finished his meal! What mean those white bundles on the ponds and rivers in China in the morning? Infanticide following infanticide; female children destroyed simply because they are female. Women harnessed to a plough as an ox. Woman veiled and barricaded, and in all styles of cruel seclusion. Her birth a misfortune. Her life a torture. Her death a horror. The missionary of the cross to-day in heathen lands preaches generally to two groups— a group of men who do as they please and sit where they please; the other group women hidden and carefully secluded in a side apartment, where they may hear the voice of the preacher, but may not be seen. No refinement. No liberty. No hope for this life. No hope for the life to come. Ringed nose. Cramped foot. Disfigured face. Embruted soul.

Now, compare those two conditions. How far toward this latter condition that I speak of would woman go if Christian influences were withdrawn and Christianity were destroyed? It is only a question of dynamics. If an object be lifted to a certain point and not fastened there, and the lifting power be withdrawn, how long before that object will fall down to the point from which it started? It will fall down, and it will go still farther than the point from which it started. Christianity has lifted woman up from the very depths of degradation almost to the skies. If that lifting power be withdrawn, she falls clear back to the depth from which she was resurrected, not going any lower because there is no lower depth. And every one must admit that the only salvation of woman from degradation and woe is the Christian religion, and that the only influence that has ever lifted her in the social scale is Christianity,

DEMORALIZATION OF SOCIETY.

If Infidelity triumph and Christianity be overthrown, it means also the general demoralization of society. The one idea in the Bible that atheists and infidels most hate is the idea of retribution. Take away the idea of retribution and punishment from society, and it will begin very soon to disintegrate; and take away from the minds of men the fear of hell, and there are a great many of them who would very soon turn this world into a hell. The majority of those who are indignant against the Bible because of the idea of punishment are men whose lives are bad or whose hearts are impure, and who hate the Bible because of the idea of future punishment, for the same reason that criminals hate the penitentiary. Oh, I have heard this brave talk about people fearing nothing of the consequences of sin in the next world, and I have made up my mind it is *merely a coward's whistling* to keep his courage up. I have seen men flaunt their immoralities in the face of the community, and I have heard them defy the Judgment Day and scoff at the idea of any future consequence of their sin; but when they came to die they shrieked until you could hear them for nearly two blocks, and in the summer night the neighbors got up to put the windows down because they could not endure the horror.

I would not want to see a rail-train with five hundred Christian people on board go down through a drawbridge into a watery grave. I would not want to see five hundred Christian people go into such disaster, but I tell you plainly that I could more easily see that than I could for any protracted time stand and see an infidel die, though his pillow were of eider-down and under a canopy of vermilion. I have never been able to brace up my nerves for such a spectacle. There is something at such a time so indescribable in the countenance! I just looked in upon it for a minute or two, but the clutch of his fist was so diabolic, and the strength of voice was so unnatural, I could not endure it. "There is no hell, there is no hell, there is no hell!" the man had said for sixty years; but that night when I looked into the dying-room of *my infidel neighbor*, there was something on his countenance which seemed to say, "There is, there is, there is, there is!"

The mightiest restraints to-day against theft, against immorality, against libertinism, against crime of all sorts— the mightiest restraints are the retributions of eternity. Men know that they can escape the law, but down in the offender's soul there is the realization of the fact that they cannot escape God. He stands at the end of the road of profligacy, and He will not clear the guilty. Take all idea of retribution and punishment out of the hearts and minds of men, and it would not be long before Brooklyn and New York and Boston and Charleston and Chicago became Sodoms. The only restraints against the evil passions of the world to-day are Bible restraints.

Suppose now these generals of Atheism and Infidelity got the victory, and suppose they marshalled a great army made up of the majority of the world. They are in companies, in regiments, in brigades—the whole army. Forward, march ! ye host of infidels and atheists, banners flying before, banners flying behind, banners inscribed with the words : " No God ! No Christ ! No punishment ! No restraints ! Down with the Bible ! Do as you please !" The sun turned into darkness. Forward, march ! ye great army of infidels and atheists, and first of all attack the churches. Turn them into club-houses. Away with those churches !

Forward, march ! ye great army of infidels and atheists, and next scatter the Sabbath-schools—the Sabbath-schools filled with bright-eyed, bright-cheeked little ones who are singing songs on Sunday afternoon and getting instruction when they ought to be on the street-corners playing marbles, or swearing on the commons. Away with them ! Forward, march ! ye great army of infidels and atheists ; next attack Christian asylums—the institutions of mercy supported by Christian philanthropies Never mind the blind eyes and the deaf ears and the crippled limbs and the weakened intellects. Let paralyzed old age pick up its own food, and orphans fight their own way, and the half-reformed go back to their evil habits. Forward, march ! ye great army of infidels and atheists, and with your battle-axes hew down the cross, and split up the manger of Bethlehem.

On, ye great army of infidels and atheists , now come to the graveyards and the cemeteries of the earth. Pull down the sculpture above Greenwood's gate, for it means the resurrection Tear away at the entrance of Laurel Hill the figure of Old Mortality and the chisel. On, ye great army

of infidels and atheists, into the graveyards and the cemeteries: and where you see " Asleep in Jesus," cut it away;
and where you find a marble story of heaven, blast it; and
where you find over a little child's grave, "Suffer little chil
dren to come unto Me," substitute the words " delusion" and
" sham;" and where you find an angel in marble, strike off the
wing; and when you come to a family vault, chisel on the
door, " Dead once, dead forever."

But on, ye great army of infidels and atheists, on! There
are heights to be taken. Pile hill on hill, Pelian upon Ossa,
and then hoist the ladders against the walls of heaven. On
and on until ye blow up the foundations of jasper and the
gates of pearl. Now charge up the steep. Now aim for the
throne of God.

A world without a Head, a universe without a King! Orphan constellations! Fatherless gallaxies! Anarchy supreme! A dethroned Jehovah! An assassinated God!
Patricide, Regicide, Deicide! That is what they mean.
That is what they will have, if they can, if they can, if they
can!

Civilization hurled back into semi-barbarism, and semi-
barbarism driven back into Hottentot savagery! The wheel
of progress turned the other way and turned toward the
dark ages! The clock of the centuries put back two thousand years! Go back, you Sandwich Islands, from your
schools, and from your colleges, and from your reformed condition, to what you were in 1820, when the missionaries first
came! Call home the five hund ed missionaries from India,
and overthrow their two thousan 1 schools, where they are trying to educate the heathen, and scatter the one hundred and
forty thousand little children that they have gathered out
of barbarism into civilization! Obliterate all the work of
Dr Duff in India, of David Abeel in China, of Dr. King in
Greece, of Judson in Burmah, of David Brainerd amid the
American aborigines, and send home the three thousand
missionaries of the cross who are toiling in foreign lands,
toiling for Christ's sake, toiling themselves into the grave!
Tell these three thousand men of God that they are of no

use! Send home the medical missionaries who are doctor-
ing the bodies as well as the souls of the dying nations! Go
home, London Missionary Society! Go home, American
Board of Foreign Missions! Go home, ye Moravians, and
relinquish back into darkness, and squalor, and filth, and
death the nations whom ye have begun to lift!

Oh, my friends, there has never been such a nefarious
plot on earth as that which Infidelity and Atheism have
planned. We were shocked at the attempt to blow up the
Parliament-houses in London; but if Infidelity and Atheism succeed in their attempt, they would dynamite a world.
Let them have their full way, and this world would be a
habitation with just three rooms: the one a mad-house, another a lazaretto, the other a pandemonium.

I put before you their whole programme from beginning
to close. In the theatre the tragedy comes first and the
farce afterward; but in this infidel drama of death, the farce
comes first and the tragedy afterward. And in the former,
atheists and infidels laugh and mock; but in the latter, God
Himself will laugh and mock. He says so—" I will laugh
at their calamity, and mock when their fear cometh."

From such a chasm of individual, national, world-wide
ruin, stand back. O young men, stand back from that
chasm! You see the practical drift of Infidelity. I want
you to know where that road leads. Stand back from that
chasm of ruin. The time is coming when the infidels and
the atheists who now openly, and out and out, and above
board preach and practice Infidelity and Atheism will be
considered as criminals against society, as they are now
criminals against God. And when they die, the only text in
all the Bible appropriate for the funeral sermon will be Jeremiah 22 : 19—" He shall be buried with the burial of an
ass."

CHRISTIANITY NOT DEAD.

Let us see whether the church of God is in a Bull Run
retreat, muskets, canteens, and haversacks strewing all the

way. The great English historian, Sharon Turner, a man of
vast learning and of great accuracy, not a clergyman but an
attorney as well as a historian, gives this overwhelming
statistic in regard to Christianity and in regard to the
number of Christians in the different centuries. In the
first century, 500,000 Christians; in the second century,
2,000,000 Christians; in the third century, 5,000,000 Christians; in the fourth century, 10,000,000 Christians; in
the fifth century, 15,000,000 Christians; in the sixth century, 20,000,000 Christians; in the seventh century, 24,000,-
000 Christians; in the eighth century, 30,000,000 Christians; in the ninth century, 40,000,000 Christians, in the
tenth century, 50,000,000 Christians; in the eleventh century, 70,000,000 Christians; in the twelfth century, 80,000,-
000 Christians; in the thirteenth century, 75,000,000 Christians; in the fourteenth century, 80,000,000 Christians; in
the fifteenth century, 100,000,000 Christians; in the sixteenth century, 125,000,000 Christians; in the seventeenth
century, 155,000,000 Christians; in the eighteenth century,
200,000,000 Christians—a decadence, as you observe, in only
one century, and more than made up in the following centuries, while it is the usual computation that there will be,
when the record of the nineteenth century is made up, at
least 300,000,000 Christians.

Poor Christianity! what a pity it has no friends   How
lonesome it must be. Who will take it out of the poor-
house? Poor Christianity! Three hundred millions in one
century. In a few weeks of last year 2,500,000 copies of the
New Testament distributed. Why the earth is like an old
castle with twenty gates and a park of artillery ready to
thunder down every gate. Lay aside all Christendom and
see how heathendom is being surrounded and honeycombed
and attacked by this all-conquering Gospel. At the beginning of this century there were only 150 missionaries; now
there are 25,000 missionaries and native helpers and evangelists. At the beginning of this century there were only 50,-
000 heathen converts; now there are 1,650,000 converts from
heathendom. There is not a seacoast on the planet but the

battery of the Gospel is planted and ready to march on, north, south, east, west.

You all know that the chief work of an army is to plant the batteries. It may take many days to plant the batteries. and they may do all the work in ten minutes. These batteries are being planted all along the seacoasts and in all nations. It may take a good while to plant them, and they may do all their work in one day. They will. Nations are to be born in a day. But just come back to Christendom and recognize the fact that during the last ten years as many people have connected themselves with evangelical churches as connected themselves with the churches in the first fifty years of this century. So Christianity is falling back, and the Bible, they say, is becoming an obsolete book!

I go into a court, and wherever I find a judge's bench or a clerk's desk, I find a Bible. Upon what book could there be uttered the solemnity of an oath? What book is apt to be put in the trunk of the young man as he leaves for city life? The Bible. What shall I find in nine out of every ten homes in Brooklyn? The Bible In nine out of every ten homes in Christendom? The Bible. Voltaire wrote the prophecy that the Bible in the nineteenth century would become extinct. The century is almost gone and what do we see? There have been more Bibles published in the latter part of the century than in the former part of the century, and do you think the Bible will become extinct in the next ten years? I have to tell you that the room in which Voltaire wrote that prophecy, not long ago was crowded from floor to ceiling with Bibles for Switzerland.

Suppose the Congress of the United States should pass a law that there should be no more Bibles printed in America, and no more Bibles read. If there are thirty million grown people in the United States there would be thirty million people in an army to put down such a law and defend their right to read the Bible. But suppose the Congress of the United States should make a law against the reading or the publication of any other book, how many people would go out in such a crusade? Could you get thirty million people to go out and risk their lives in the defence of Shakespeare's tragedies, or Gladstone's tracts, or Macaulay's History of England? You know that there are a thousand men who would die in the defence of this book where there is not more than one man who would die in defence of any other book.

Which institution stands nearest the hearts of the people of America to-day? I do not care in what village or in what city, or what neighborhood you go. Which institution is it? Is it the post-office? Is it the hotel? Is it the lecturing hall? Ah! you know it is not. You know that the institution which stands nearest to the hearts of the American people is the Christian church. When the diphtheria sweeps your children off, whom do you send for? The postmaster? the attorney-general? the hotel-keeper? alderman? No, you send for a minister of this Bible religion. And if you have not a room in your house for the obsequies, what building do you solicit? Do you say: "Give me the finest room in the hotel"? Do you say: "Give me that theatre"? Do you say: "Give me a place in that public building where I can lay my dead for a little while until we say a prayer over it"? No; you say: "Give us the house of God." And if there is a song to be sung at the obsequies, what do you want? What does anybody want? The Marseillaise Hymn? God Save the Queen? our own grand national air? No. They want the hymn with which they sang their old Christian mother into her last sleep, or they want sung the Sabbath-school hymn which their little girl sang the last Sabbath afternoon she was out before she got that awful sickness which broke your heart. *I appeal to your common-sense.* You know the most endearing institution on earth is the church of the Lord Jesus Christ. A man is a fool that does not recognize it.

VICTORY FOR GOD.

I know that Mr. Ingersoll and his coadjutors say in their lectures and in their interviews, and in phraseology charged with all venom and abuse and caricature, that Christianity has collapsed, that the Bible is an obsolete book, that the Christian Church is on the retreat. I answer that wholesale charge; No, not *so*, but the *contrary*.

Vast multitudes, I believe, by my arguments have been persuaded that the Bible is a common-sensical book, that it is a reasonable book, that it is an authentic book. Men have told me that while they had been accustomed to receive the New Testament they had disbelieved the Old Testament, until by the blessing of God upon this exposition they have come to believe that the Old Testament is just as true as the New Testament.

A man said to me in Cleveland, Ohio, as he tapped me on the shoulder: " I want to tell you that my son who was at college and who was *a confirmed infidel*, wrote me in a letter which I got this morning, saying that through the arguments you have presented in behalf of the truth of the Bible, he has given up his scepticism and surrendered his heart to God I thought you would like to hear it." I said, " God bless you, that is the best thing I have heard to-night." And so I believe the people are all going to be persuaded that this is God's word.

I was in Boston, and at the place where the most famous infidel church was ever gathered. Music Hall stands just where it did, but the infidel church has perished. " Heaven and earth shall pass away, but God's word shall never pass away." What is that scrolled, clasped, Doré-illustrated volume on the drawing-room centre-table ? What is that defaced, lead-pencilled volume on the clerk's desk in the court-room ? What is that volume put by loving hands into the trunk of the young man as he leaves country life for city life ? What is that book on which all the judges of the Supreme Court of the United States and all our Presidents take their oaths of office ? What is that book of which the world thinks so much that the printing press has multiplied two hundred and fifty million copies ? It is the Book upon which modern infidelity has its hand, and says, " Surrender !" But on it is written " No surrender."

Do I hear you ask, " Have you any nervous anxiety about the overthrow of Christianity?" Oh! no. There never were so many churches of Jesus Christ as there are now, never so many men who believe in the Gospel of the Son of God, never so many institutions of mercy born of Christianity. Have you any fear that people will be laughed out of their religion, and that the modern mode of caricaturing Christianity will destroy it from the hearts of men? Oh! no. A man's religion is a very sacred thing, and it is down in the depths of his soul; and while you may persuade him out of it, or coax him out of it, or argue him out of it, you cannot laugh him out of it.

A thousand voices come up to me, saying, " Do you really think Infidelity will succeed? Has Christianity received its death-blow? and will the Bible become obsolete?" Yes, when the smoke of the city chimney arrests and destroys the noonday sun. Josephus says about the time of the destruction of Jerusalem the sun was turned into darkness, but only the clouds rolled between the sun and the earth. The sun went right on. It is the same sun, the same luminary as when at the beginning it shot out like an electric spark from God's finger, and to-day it is warming the nations, and to-day it is gilding the sea, and to-day it is filling the earth with light. The same old sun, not at all worn out, though its light steps one hundred and ninety million miles a second, though its pulsations are four hundred and fifty trillion undulations in a second. Same sun with beautiful white light made up of the violet and the indigo and the blue and the green and the red and the yellow and the orange—the seven beautiful colors now just as when the solar spectrum first divided them.

At the beginning God said, " Let there be light," and light was, and light is, and light shall be. So Christianity is rolling on, and it is going to warm all nations, and all nations are to bask in its light Men may shut the window-blinds so they cannot see it, or they may smoke the pipe of speculation until they are shadowed under their own vaporing; but the Lord God is a sun! This white light of the Gospel

made up of all the beautiful colors of earth and heaven—
violet plucked from amid the spring grass, and the indigo of
the southern jungles, and the blue of the skies, and the
green of the foliage, and the yellow of the autumnal woods,
and the orange of the southern groves, and the red of the
sunsets. All the beauties of earth and heaven brought out
by this spiritual spectrum. Great Britain is going to take
all Europe for God. The United States are going to take
all America for God. Both of them together will take all
Asia for God. All three of them will take Africa for God.
"Who art thou, oh great mountain? before Zerubbabel thou
shalt become a plain." The mouth of the Lord hath spoken
it. Hallelujah, amen!

Now let us see whether the Bible is a last year's almanac.
You try to insult my common-sense by telling me the Bible
is fading out from the world. It is the most popular book
of the century.

How do I know it? I know it just as I know in regard
to other books. How many volumes of that book are published? Well, you say, five thousand. How many copies of
that book are published? A hundred thousand. Which is
the more popular? Why of course the one that has a hundred thousand circulation. And if this book has more copies
abroad in the world, if there are five times as many Bibles
abroad as any other book, does not that show you that the
most popular book on the planet to-day is the Word of God?

INGERSOLL DEFEATED.

Mr. Ingersoll, years ago, riding in a railcar in Illinois,
said: "What has Christianity ever done?" An old Christian woman said: "*It has done one thing, anyhow;* it has kept
Mr. Ingersoll from being governor of Illinois!" As I stood
in the side room of the opera house at Peoria, Illinois, a
prominent gentleman of that city said: "I can tell you the
secret of that tremendous bitterness against Christianity."
Said I: "What was it?" "Why," said he, "in this very
house there was *a great convention* to nominate a governor,

and when *that champion of infidelity was nominated*, a plain farmer got up and said: ' Mr. Chairman, that nomination must not be made; the Sunday-schools of Illinois will defeat him.' " That ended all prospect of his nomination. The Christian religion mightier to-day than it ever was.

O my friends, the Church of Jesus Christ instead of falling back is on the advance. I am certain it is on the advance. I see the glittering of swords, I hear the tramping of the troops, I hear the thunderings of parks of artillery. O! my God and Saviour, I thank Thee that I have been permitted to see this day—this day of Thy triumph, this day of the confusion of Thine enemies. O! Lord God, take Thy sword from Thy thigh and ride forth to the victory.

I am mightily encouraged because I find among other things that while this Christianity has been bombarded for centuries, infidelity has not destroyed one church, or crippled one minister, or uprooted one verse of one chapter of all the Bible. If that has been their magnificent record for the centuries that are past, what may we expect for the future? The Church all the time getting the victory, and their shot and shell all gone.

And then I find another most encouraging thought in the fact that the secular printing-press and the pulpit seem harnessed in the same team for the proclamation of the Gospel. Every Wall Street banker to-morrow in New York, every State Street banker to-morrow in Boston, every Third Street banker to-morrow in Philadelphia, every banker in the United States, and every merchant will have in his pocket a treatise on Christianity, a call to repentance, ten, twenty, or thirty passages of Scripture in the reports of sermons preached throughout these cities and throughout the land to-day. It will be so in Chicago, so in New Orleans, so in Charleston, so in Boston, so in Philadelphia, so everywhere.

I know the tract societies are doing a grand and glorious work, but I tell you there is no power on earth to-day equal to the fact that the American printing-press is taking up the sermons which are preached to a few hundred or a few thousand people, on Monday morning and Monday evening, in the morning and evening papers, scattering that truth to the millions What a thought it is ! What an encouragement for every Christian man.

That delusion has to-day two hundred million dupes ! It proposes to encircle the earth with its girdle. That which has been called a delusion has already overshadowed the Appalachian range on this side the sea, and it has over-shadowed the Balkan and Caucasian ranges on the other side the sea. It has conquered England and the United States.

This champion delusion, this hoax, this swindle of the ages, as it has been called, has gone forth to conquer the islands of the Pacific, and Melanesia and the Micronesia and Malayan Polynesia have already surrendered to the delu-sion. Yea, it has conquered the Indian archipelago and Borneo, and Sumatra and Celebes and Java have fallen un-der its wiles In the Fiji Islands, where there are 120,000 people, 102,000 have already become the dupes of this Chris-tian religion, and if things go on as they are now going on, and if the influence of this great hallucination of the ages cannot be stopped, it will swallow the globe. The cannibals in South Sea, the Bushmen of Terra del Fuego, the wild men of Australia, putting down the knives of their cruelty, and clothing themselves in decent apparel—all under the power of this delusion. Judson and Doty and Abeel and Camp-bell and Williams, and the three thousand missionaries of the Cross turning their backs on home and civilization and comfort, and going out amid the squalor of heathenism to relieve it, to save it, to help it, toiling until they dropped into their graves, dying with no earthly comfort about them, and going into graves with no appropriate epitaph, when they might have lived in this country, and lived for them-selves, and lived luxuriously, and been at last put into brill iant sepulchre. What a delusion !

WHAT HAS BEEN ACCOMPLISHED?

The delusion has made *a wonderful transformations of human character.*

Lo! the Prototype Captive of this great Christian delusion! There goes Saul of Tarsus, on horseback, at full gallop. Where is he going? To destroy Christians. He wants no better play-spell than to stand and watch the hats and coats of the murderers who are massacring God's children. There goes the same man. This time he is afoot. Where is he going now? Going on the road to Ostia to die for Christ. They tried to whip it out of him, they tried to scare it out of him, they thought they would give him enough of it by putting him into a windowless dungeon, and keeping him on small diet, and denying him a cloak, and condemning him as a criminal, and howling at him through the street; but they could not freeze it out of him, and they could not sweat it out of him, and they could not pound it out of him, so they tried the surgery of the sword, and one summer day in '65 he was decapitated. Perhaps the mightiest intellect of the six thousand years of the world's existence hoodwinked, cheated, cajoled, duped by the Christian religion! I will go down the aisle of any church in Christendom, and I will find on either side that aisle those who were once profligate, pro-fane, unclean of speech, and unclean of action, drunken and lost. But by the power of this delusion of the Christian re-ligion they have been completely transformed, and now they are kind and amiable and genial and loving and useful. Everybody sees the change. Under the power of this great hallucination they have quit their former associates, and whereas they once found their chief delight among those who gambled and swore and raced horses, now they find their chief joy among those who go to prayer-meetings and churches: so complete is the delusion. Yea, their own fami-lies have noticed it—the wife has noticed it, the children have noticed it. The money that went for rum now goes for books and for clothes and for education. He is a new man. All

who know him say there has been a wonderful change. What
is the cause of this change? This great hallucination of the
Christian religion. There is as much difference between what
he is now and what he once was, as between a rose and a
nettle, as between a dove and a vulture, as between day and
night. Tremendous delusion!

Admiral Farragut, one of the most admired men of the
American navy, early became a victim of this Christian delusion, and seated not long before his death, at Long Branch,
he was giving some friends an account of his early life. He
said: " My father went down in behalf of the United States
Government to put an end to Aaron Burr's rebellion. I was
a cabin-boy and went along with him. I could swear like an
old salt. I could gamble in every style of gambling. I knew
all the wickedness there was at that time abroad. One day
my father cleared everybody out of the cabin except myself,
and locked the door. He said: ' David, what are you going
to do? What are you going to be?' ' Well,' I said, ' father,
I am going to follow the sea.' ' Follow the sea! and be a
poor miserable, drunken sailor, kicked and cuffed about the
world and die of a fever in a foreign hospital.'

"' O! no,' I said, ' father, I will not be that, I will tread
the quarter-deck, and command as you do.' ' No, David,'
my father said, ' no, David, a person that has your principles
and your bad habits will never tread the quarter-deck or
command.' My father went out and shut the door after
him, and I said then, ' I will change, I will never swear again,
I will never drink again, I will never gamble again, and, gentlemen, by the help of God I have kept those three vows to
this time. I soon after that became a Christian, and that
decided my fate for time and for eternity.' " *Blessed delusion, that could work such a wonderful transformation of
character!*

THE GREATEST WORK OF THE AGE.

The great works of the great lawyers, the Blackstones,
the Clarendons, the Hales, the Mansfields, the Currans, the

Burkes, the Emmets, the Rufus Choates, the Daniel Web-
sters—all their works, all the English law, all American law,
all Roman law, all the laws of all the nations that are worth
anything, founded on the ten sentences that a venerable
lawyer of olden time recorded in the twentieth chapter of
Exodus: Indorsed by illustrious dupes!

Ah! that is the remarkable thing about this delusion: it
overpowers the strongest intellects. For example: William
Wilberforce, the statesman, Robert Boyle, the philosopher,
Locke, the metaphysician.

Deluded Lawyers.—Lord Cairns, the highest legal authority in England, the ex-adviser of the throne, spending his
vacation in preaching the Gospel of Jesus Christ to the poor
people of Scotland. Frederick T Frelinghuysen, the Secretary of the United States, an old-fashioned evangelical
Christian, an elder in the Reformed Church. John Bright,
a deluded Quaker. Henry Wilson, the Vice-President of
the United States, dying a deluded Methodist or Congrega-
tionalist Earl of Kintore dying a deluded Presbyterian.

Deluded Doctors.—Two hundred and twenty physicians
meeting week by week in London, in the Union Medical
Prayer Circle, to worship God.

Deluded Sceptics.—Thomas Chalmers was once a sceptic,
Robert Hall a sceptic, Robert Newton a sceptic, Christmas
Evans a sceptic. But when once with strong hand they took
hold of the chariot of the Gospel, they rolled it on, and with
what momentum!

Deluded Critics.—Gather the critics, secular and religious,
of this century together, and put a vote to them as to which
is the greatest poem ever written, and by large majority they
will say, "Paradise Lost" Who wrote "Paradise Lost?"
One of the fools who believed in this Bible, John Milton.

Benjamin Franklin surrendered to this delusion, if you
may judge from the letter that he wrote to Thomas Paine
begging him to destroy the "Age of Reason" in manuscript,
and never let it go into type, and writing afterward, in his
old days: "Of this Jesus of Nazareth I have to say that the

system of morals He left, and the religion He has given us, are the best things the world has ever seen or is likely to see."

Patrick Henry, the electric champion of liberty, enslaved by this delusion, so that he says : "The book worth all other books put together is the Bible." *Benjamin Rush*, the leading physiologist and anatomist of his day, the great medical scientist,—what did he say? "The only true and perfect religion is Christianity." *Isaac Newton*, the leading philosopher of his time,—what did he say? That man, surrenderin to this delusion of the Christian religion, crying out : "The sublimest philosophy on earth is the philosophy of the Gospel." *David Brewster*, at the pronunciation of whose name every scientist the world over uncovers his head, David Brewster saying : "Oh, this religion has been a great light to me, a very great light all my days." *President Thiers*, the great French statesman, acknowledging that he prayed when he said : "I invoke the Lord God, in whom I am glad to believe." *David Livingstone*, able to conquer the lion, able to conquer the panther, able to conquer the savage, yet conquered by this delusion, this hallucination, this great swindle of the ages, so when they find him dead they find him on his knees. *William E. Gladstone*, the strongest intellect in England to-day, unable to resist this chimera, this fallacy, this delusion of the Christian religion, goes to the house of God every Sabbath, and often, at the invitation of the rector, reads the prayers to the people.

Oh, if those mighty intellects are overborne by this delusion, what chance is there for you and for me?

Besides that, I have noticed that first-rate infidels cannot be depended on for steadfastness in the proclamation of their sentiments. *Goethe*, a leading sceptic, was so wrought upon by this Christianity that in a weak moment he cried out : "My belief in the Bible has saved me in my literary and moral life." *Rousseau*, one of the most eloquent champions of infidelity, spending his whole life warring against Christianity, cries out : "The majesty of the Scriptures amazes me." *Altemont*, the notorious infidel, one would think he would have been safe against this delusion of the Christian

religion. Oh no! After talking against Christianity all his
days, in his last hours he cried out: "O thou blasphemed
but most indulgent Lord God, hell itself is a refuge if it hide
me from thy frown"

Voltaire, the most talented infidel the world ever saw,
writing two hundred and fifty publications, and the most of
them spiteful against Christianity, himself the most notorious
libertine of the century—one would have thought he could
have been depended upon for steadfastness in the advocacy
of infidelity and in the war against this terrible chimera, this
delusion of the Gospel. But no; in his last hour he asks
for Christian burial, and asks that they give him the sacra-
ment of the Lord Jesus Christ. Why, you cannot depend
upon these first-rate infidels; you cannot depend upon their
power to resist this great delusion of Christianity.

Thomas Paine, the god of modern sceptics, his birthday
celebrated in New York and Boston with great enthusiasm
—Thomas Paine, the paragon of Bible-haters—Thomas
Paine, about whom his brother-infidel William Carver wrote
in a letter, which I have at my house, saying that he drank
a quart of rum a day and was too mean and too dishonest
to pay for it—Thomas Paine, the adored of modern infidelity
—Thomas Paine, who stole another man's wife in England
and brought her to this land—Thomas Paine, who was so
squalid and so loathsome and so drunken and so profligate
and so beastly in his habits, sometimes picked out of the
ditch, sometimes too filthy to be picked out,—Thomas Paine,
one would have thought that he could have been depended
on for steadfastness against this great delusion. But no. In
his dying hour he begs the Lord Jesus Christ for mercy.

Powerful delusion! All-conquering delusion! Earth-
quaking delusion of the Christian religion! Yea, it goes on,
it is so impertinent and it is so overbearing, this chimera of
the Gospel, that having conquered the great picture-galleries
of the world, the old masters and the young masters, it is
not satisfied until it has *conquered the music* of the world.

Look over the programme of a magnificent musical
festival in New York, and see what are the great performances,

and learn that the greatest of all the subjects are religious subjects. Three thousand voices accompanied with a vast number of instruments! "Israel in Egypt " Yes, Beethoven deluded until he wrote the High Mass in D Major Hadyn deluded with this religion until he wrote the "Creation." Handel deluded until he wrote the oratorios of "Jephtha," and "Esther," and "Saul," and "Israel in Egypt," and the "Messiah." Last Friday night, three thousand deluded people singing of a delusion to eight thousand deluded hearers!

Yea, this chimera of the Bible is not satisfied until it goes on and builds itself into the most permanent *architecture*—so it seems as if the world is never to get rid of it. What are some of the finest buildings in the world? St. Paul's, St. Peter's, the churches and cathedrals of all Christendom.

I was impressed in journeying on the other side the sea with the difference the Bible makes in countries. The two nations of Europe that are the most moral to-day, and that have the least crime, are Scotland and Wales. They have by statistics, as you might find, fewer thefts, fewer arsons, fewer murders. What is the reason? A bad book can hardly live in Wales. The Bible crowds it out. I was told by one of the first literary men in Wales. "There is not a bad book in the Welsh language." He said: "Bad books come down from London, but they cannot live here." It is the Bible that is dominant in Wales. And then in Scotland just open your Bible to give out your text, and there is *a rustling all over the house* almost startling to an American. What is it? The people opening their Bibles find the text, looking at the context, picking out the referenced passages, seeing whether you make right quotation. Scotland and Wales, Bible-reading people. That accounts for it. A man, a city, a nation that reads God's Word must be virtuous. That Book is the foe of all wrong-doing. What makes Edinburgh better than Constantinople? The Bible.

I was also impressed in my transatlantic journeys with the wonderful power that Christ holds among the nations. The great name in Europe to-day is not Victoria, not Marquis of Salisbury, not William the Emperor, not Bismarck ; the great name in Europe to-day is Christ. You find the crucifix on gate-post, you find it in the hay-field, you find it at the entrance of the manor, yau find it by the side of the road

The greatest pictures in all the galleries of Italy, Germany, France, England, and Scotland are Bible pictures. The mightiest picture on this planet is Rubens' "Scourging of Christ." Painter's pencil loves to sketch the face of Christ. Sculptor's chisel loves to present the form of Christ. Organs love to roll forth the sorrows of Christ.

The first time you go to London go into the Doré picture-gallery. As I went and sat down before "Christ Descending the Steps of the Prætorium" at the first I was disappointed. I said : "There isn't enough majesty in that countenance, not enough tenderness in that eye ;" but as I sat and looked at the picture it grew upon me until I was overwhelmed with its power, and I staggered with emotion as I went out into the fresh air, and said "Oh, for that Christ I must live, and for that Christ I must be willing to die !" Make that Christ your personal friend, my sister, my brother. You may never go to Milan to see Da Vinci's "Last Supper," but, better than that, you can have Christ come and sup with you. You may never get to Antwerp to see Rubens' "Descent of Christ from the Cross," but you can have Christ come down from the mountain of His suffering into your heart and abide there forever. Oh, you must have him !

A GREAT CHANGE.

You began with thinking that the Christian religion was a stupid farce ; you have come to the conclusion that it is a reality.

There is something the matter with you. All your friends have found out there is a great change. And if some of you would give your experience you would give it in scholarly style, and others giving your experience would give it in broken style, but the one experience would be just as good as the other. Some of you have read everything. You are scientific and you are scholarly, and yet if I should ask you, "What is the most sensible thing you ever did?" you would say, "The most sensible thing I ever did was to give my heart to God."

But there may be others who have not had early advantages, and if they were asked to give their experience, they might give such testimony as the man gave in a prayer meeting when he said : "On my way here to-night, I met a man who asked me where I was going I said, 'I am going to prayer meeting.' He said, 'There are a good many religions and I think the most of them are delusions ; as to the Christian religion, that is only a notion, that is a mere notion, the Christian religion.' I said to him : 'Stranger, you see that tavern over there?' 'Yes,' he said, 'I see it.' 'Do you see me?' 'Yes, of course I see you.' 'Now, the time was, everybody in this town knows, when if I had a quarter of a dollar in my pocket I could not pass that tavern without going in and getting a drink; all the people of Jefferson could not keep me out of that place ; but God has changed my heart, and the Lord Jesus Christ has destroyed my thirst for strong drink, and there is my whole week's wages, and I have no temptation to go in there ;' and, stranger, if this is a notion I want to tell you it is a mighty powerful notion : a notion that has put clothes on my children's back, and it is a notion that has put good food on our table, and it is a notion that has filled my mouth with thanksgiving to God And, stranger, you better go along with me, you might get religion too ; lots of people are getting religion now.'"

Yes, the Bible is right in its effects. I do not care where you put the Bible, it just suits the place. You put it in the hand of a man seriously concerned about his soul. I see people often giving to the serious soul this and that book. It may be very well, but there is no book like the Bible. He reads the commandments and pleads to the indictment, "Guilty." He takes up the Psalms of David and says: "They just describe my feelings." He flies to good works;

Paul starts him out of that by the announcement: "A man is not justified by works." He falls back in his discouragement; the Bible starts him up with the sentences "Remember Lot's wife," "Grieve not the Spirit," "Flee the wrath to come." Then the man in despair begins to cry out: "What shall I do? where shall I go?" and a voice reaches him saying: "Come unto Me all ye that labor and are heavy laden and I will give you rest."

Yea, this delusion of the Christian religion shows itself in the fact that it goes to *those who are in trouble.* Now, it is bad enough to cheat a man when he is well and when he is prosperous; but this religion comes to a man when he is sick, and says: "You will be well again after a while; you are going into a land where there are no coughs and no pleurisies and no consumptions and no languishing; take courage and bear up." Yea, this awful chimera of the Bible comes to the poor and it says to them: "You are on your way to vast estates and to dividends always declarable."

Suppose that there was a great pestilence going over the earth, and hundreds of thousands of men were dying of that pestilence, and some one should find a medicine that cured ten thousand people, would not everybody acknowledge that that must be a good medicine? Why, some one would say: "Do you deny it? There have been ten thousand people cured by it." I simply state the fact that there have been hundreds of thousands of Christian men and women who say they have felt the truthfulness of that Book and its power in their souls. It has cured them of the worst leprosy that ever came down on our earth, namely, the leprosy of sin; and if I can point you to multitudes who say they have felt the power of that cure, are you not reasonable enough to acknowledge the fact that there must be some power in the medicine? Will you take the evidence of millions of patients who have been cured, or will you take the evidence of the sceptic who stands aloof and confesses that he never took the medicine?

A BALM FOR THE WEARY.

Take this Bible and place it in the hands of men in trouble? Is there anybody here in trouble? Ah, I might better ask are there any here who have never been in trouble. Put this Bible in the hands of the troubled. You find that as some of the best berries grow on the sharpest thorns, so some of the sweetest consolations of the Gospel grow on the most stinging affliction. You thought that Death had grasped your child. Oh, no! It was only the heavenly Shepherd taking a lamb out of the cold. Christ bent over you as you held the child in your lap, and putting His arms gently around the little one, said: "Of such is the kingdom of heaven."

BEYOND THE GRAVE.

This delusion of Christianity comes to *the bereft* and talks of reunion before the throne, and of the cessation of all sorrow. And then to show that this delusion will stop at absolutely nothing, it goes to the dying bed and fills the man with anticipations. How much better it would be to have him die without any more hope than swine and rats and snakes. Shovel him under! That is all. Nothing more left of him. He will never know anything again. Shovel him under? The soul is only a superior part of the body, and when the body disintegrates the soul disintegrates. Annihilation, vacancy, everlasting blank, obliteration. Why not present all that beautiful doctrine to the dying, instead of coming with this hoax, this swindle of the Christian religion, and filling the dying man with anticipations of another life, until some in the last hour have clapped their hands, and some have shouted and some have sung, and some have been so overwrought with joy they could only look ecstatic. Palace gates opening, they thought—diamonded coronets flashing—hands beckoning, orchestras sounding. Little children dying actually believing they saw their departed parents, so that although the little children had been so weak and feeble and sick for weeks they could not turn on their dying pillow, at the last, in a paroxysm of rapture uncontrollable they sprang to their feet and shouted: " Mother, catch me, I am coming!"

And to show the immensity of this delusion, this awful swindle of the Gospel of Jesus Christ, I open a hospital and I bring into that hospital the death-beds of a great many Christian people, and I take you by the hand this morning and I walk up and down the wards of that hospital, and I ask a few questions.

I ask, " Dying Stephen, what have you to say ?" " Lord Jesus, receive my spirit." " Dying John Wesley, what have you to say ?" " The best of all is God is with us " " Dying Edward Payson, what have you to say?" " I float in a sea of glory." " Dying John Bradford, what have you to say ?" " If there be any way of going to heaven on horseback, or in a fiery chariot, it is this." " Dying Neander, what have you to say ?" " I am going to sleep now—good-night." " Dying Mrs. Florence Foster, what have you to say ?" " A pilgrim in the valley, but the mountain tops are all agleam from peak to peak." " Dying Alexander Mather, what have you to say ?" " The Lord who has taken care of me fifty years, will not cast me off now ; glory be to God and to the Lamb! Amen, amen, amen, amen !"

" Dying John Powson, after preaching the Gospel so many years, what have you to say ?" " My death-bed is a bed of roses." " Dying Doctor Thomas Scott, what have you to say ?" " This is Heaven begun." " Dying soldier in the last war, what have you to say ?" " Boys, I am going to the front." " Dying telegraph operator on the battlefield of Virginia, what have you to say ?" " The wires are all laid, and the poles are up from Stony Point to headquarters." " Dying Paul, what have you to say ?" " I am now ready to be offered, and the time of my departure is at hand ; I have fought the good fight, I have finished my course, I have kept the faith. O! death, where is thy sting? O! grave, where is thy victory? Thanks be unto God who giveth us the victory through our Lord Jesus Christ."

O! my Lord, my God, what a delusion! What a glorious delusion! Submerge me with it, fill my eyes and ears with it, put it under my dying head for a pillow—this delusion—spread it over me for a canopy, put it underneath me for an outspread wing—roll it over me in ocean surges ten thousand fathoms deep. O! if infidelity, and if atheism, and if annihilation are a reality, and the Christian religion is a delusion, give me the delusion. The strong conclusion of every man and woman must be, that Christianity producing such grand results cannot be a delusion. A lie, a cheat, a swindle, an hallucination cannot launch such a glory of the centuries. Your logic and your common sense convince you that a bad cause cannot produce an illustrious result; out of the womb of such a monster no such angel can be born.

Well, we will soon understand it all. Your life and mine will soon be over. We will soon come to the last bar of the music, to the last act of the tragedy, to the last page of the book—yea, to the last line and to the last word, and to you and to me it will either be midnoon or midnight!

ROUSSEAU'S DREAM.

Rousseau, the infidel, fell asleep amid his sceptical manuscript lying all around the room, and in his dream he entered heaven and heard the song of the worshippers, and it was so sweet he asked an angel what it meant. The angel said, "This is the Paradise of God, and the song you hear is the anthem of the redeemed." Under another roll of the celestial music Rousseau wakened and got up in the midnight and as well as he could wrote down the strains of the music that he had heard in the wonderful tune called the Songs of the Redeemed. God grant that it may not be to you and to me an infidel dream but a glorious reality When we come to the night of death and we lie down to our last sleep, may our ears really be wakened by the canticles of the heavenly temple, and the songs and the anthems and the carols and the doxologies that shall climb the musical ladder of that heavenly gamut.

Colonel Ethan Allen was a famous infidel in his day. His wife was a very consecrated woman. The mother instructed the daughter in the truths of Christianity. The daughter sickened and was about to die, and she said to her father: "Father, shall I take your instruction? or shall I take mother's instruction? I am going to die now; I must have this matter decided." That man, who had been loud in his infidelity, said to his dying daughter: "My dear, you had better take your mother's religion." My advice is the same to you, O! young man; you had better take your mother's religion. You know how it comforted her. You know what she said to you when she was dying. You had better take your mother's religion.

THE BIBLE—THE BOOK OF BOOKS.

The Bible is a great poem. We have in it faultless rhythm, bold imagery, startling antithesis, rapturous lyric, sweet pastoral, instructive narrative and devotional psalm; thoughts expressed in style more solemn than that of Montgomery, more bold than that of Milton, more terrible than that of Dante, more natural than that of Wordsworth, more impassioned than that of Pollok, more tender than that of Cowper, more weird than that of Spenser.

This great poem brings all the gems of the earth into its coronet, weaves the flames of judgment into its garlands, and pours eternal harmonies in its rhythm. Everything this book touches it makes beautiful, from the plain stones of the summer threshing floor to the daughter of Nahor filling the trough for the camels; from the fish pools of Heshbon up to the Psalmist praising God with diapason of storm and whirlwind, and Job's imagery of Orion, Arcturus, and the Pleiades.

Old books go out of date. When they were written they discussed questions which were being discussed; they struck at wrongs which had long ago ceased, or advocated institutions which excite not our interest. Were they books of history, the facts have been gathered from the imperfect mass, better classified and more lucidly presented. Were they books of poetry, they were interlocked with wild my- thologies which have gone up from the face of the earth like mists at sunrise. Were they books of morals, civilization will not sit at the feet of barbarism, neither do we want Sappho, Pythagoras and Tully to teach us morals. What do the masses of the people care now for the pathos of Simonides, or the sarcasm of Menander, or the gracefulness of Philemon, or the wit of Aristophanes? Even the old books we have left, with a few exceptions, have but very little effect upon our times. Books are human; they have a time to be born, they are fondled, they grow in strength, they have a middle life of usefulness, then comes old age, —they totter and they die. Many of the national libraries are merely the cemeteries of dead books. Some of them lived flagitious lives and died deaths of ignominy. Some were virtuous and accomplished a glorious mission. Some went into the ashes through inquisitorial fires. Some found their funeral pile in sacked and plundered cities. Some were neglected and died as foundlings at the door of science. Some expired in the author's study, others in the publisher's hands. Ever and anon there comes into your possession an old book, its author forgotten and its usefulness done, and with leathern lips it seems to say: "I wish I were dead." Monuments have been raised over poets and philanthropists Would that some tall shaft might be erected in honor of the world's buried books! The world's authors would make pilgrimage thereto, and poetry, and literature, and science, and religion would consecrate it with their tears.

Not so with one old book. It started in the world's infancy. It grew under theocracy and monarchy. It with- stood storms of fire. It grew under prophet's mantle and under the fisherman's coat of the apostles; in Rome and Ephesus and Jerusalem and Patmos. Tyranny issued edicts against it, and infidelity put out the tongue, and Mohamme- danism from its mosques hurled its anathemas, but the old

Bible still lived. It crossed the British Channel and was greeted by Wickcliffe and James I. It crossed the Atlantic and struck Plymouth Rock, until, like that of Horeb, it gushed with blessedness. Churches and asylums have gathered all along its way, ringing their bells and stretching out their hands of blessing; and every Sabbath there are ten thousand heralds of the cross with their hands on this open, grand, free, old English Bible.

It will not have accomplished its mission until it has climbed the icy mountains of Greenland; until it has gone over the granite cliffs of China; until it has thrown its glow amid the Australian mines; until it has scattered its gems among the diamond districts of Brazil; and all thrones shall be gathered into one throne, and all crowns by the fires of revolution shall be melted into one crown, and this Book shall at the very gate of heaven have waved in the ransomed empires. Not until then will this glorious Bible have accomplished its mission.

Nine tenths of all the good literature of this age is merely the Bible diluted. Goethe, the admired of all sceptics, had the wall of his house at Weimar covered with religious maps and pictures. Milton's " Paradise Lost" is part of the Bible in blank verse. Tasso's " Jerusalem Delivered " is borrowed from the Bible. Spenser's writings are imitations of the parables. John Bunyan saw in a dream only what St. John had seen before in Apocalyptic vision. Macaulay crowns his most thrilling sentences with Scripture quotations. Thomas Carlyle is only a splendid distortion of Ezekiel; and wandering through the lanes and parks of this imperial domain of Bible truth, I find all the great American, English, German, Spanish, Italian poets, painters, orators and rhetoricians.

Again, the Bible is right in style. I am fascinated with the conciseness yet greatfulness of this Book. Every word is packed full of truth. Every sentence is double barrelled. Every paragraph is like an old banyan-tree with a hundred roots and a hundred branches. It is a great arch; pull out one stone and it all comes down. There has never been a pearl-diver who could gather up one half of the treasures in any verse. John Halsebach, of Vienna, for twenty-one years every Sabbath expounded to his congregations the first chapter of the Book of Isaiah, and yet did not get through with it.

Where is there in the world of poetic description anything like Job's champing, neighing, pawing, lightning-footed, thunder-necked war horse?   Dryden's, Milton's, Cowper's tempests are very tame compared with David's storm that wrecks the mountains of Lebanon and shivers the wilderness of Kadish. Why, it seems as if to the feet of these Bible writers mountains brought all their gems, and the seas all their pearls, and the gardens all their frankincense, and the spring all its blossoms, and the harvests all their wealth, and heaven all its grandeur, and eternity all its stupendous realities ; and that since then poets, and orators, and rhetoricians have been drinking from exhausted fountains, and searching for diamonds in a realm utterly rifled and ransacked.

This Book is the hive of all sweetness. It is the armory of all well-tempered weapons. It is the tower containing the crown jewels of the universe. It is the lamp that kindles all other lights. It is the home of all majesties and splendors. It is the marriage ring that unites the celestial and the terrestrial, while all the clustering white-robed denizens of the sky hovering around rejoice at the nuptials. This Book—it is the wreath into which are twisted all garlands ; it is the song into which are struck all harmonies ; it is the river into which are poured all the great tides of hallelujah ; it is the firmament in which suns and moons and stars and constellations and universes and eternities wheel and blaze and triumph. Where is the young man's soul with any music in it that is not stirred with Jacob's lament, or Nahum's dirge, or Habakkuk's dithyrambic, or Paul's march of the resurrection ?

I am also amazed at the variety of this Book. Mind you, not contradiction or collision, but variety. Just as in the song you have the basso and alto and soprano and tenor—

they are not in collision with each other but come in to make up the harmony. So it is in this Book; there are different parts of this great song of redemption. The prophet comes and takes one part, and the patriarch another part, and the evangelist another part, and the apostles another part, and yet they all come into the grand harmony—" the song of Moses and the Lamb." God prepared the Book for all classes of people. For instance, little children would read the Bible, and God knew that; so He allows Matthew and Luke to write sweet stories about Christ with the doctors of the law, and Christ at the well, and Christ at the cross, so that any little child can understand them. Then God knew that the aged people would want to read the Book, so He allows Solomon to compact a world of wisdom in that Book of Proverbs. God knew that the historian would want to read it, and so He allows Moses to give the plain statement of the Pentateuch. God knew that the poet would want to read it, and so He allows Job to picture the heavens as a curtain, and Isaiah the mountains as weighed in a balance, and the waters as held in the hollow of the Omnipotent hand; and God touched David until in the latter part of the Psalms, he gathers a great choir standing in galleries above each other—beasts and men in the first gallery; above them, hills and mountains; above them, fire and hail and tempest; above them, sun and moon and stars of light; and on the highest gallery arrays the hosts of angels; and then standing before this great choir, reaching from the depths of earth to the heights of heaven, like the leader of a great orchestra, he lifts his hands crying: " Praise the Lord. Let everything that hath breath, praise the Lord;" and all earthly creatures in their song, and mountains with their waving cedars, and tempests in their thunder, and rattling hail, and stars on all their trembling harps of light, and angels on their thrones, respond in magnificent acclaim: " Praise ye the Lord. Let everything that hath breath, praise the Lord."

There are many who would have you believe that the Bible is an outlandish book, and obsolete. It is fresher and

more intense than any book that yesterday came out of the
great publishing houses. " O," you say, "it was made hundreds of years ago, and the learned men of King James
translated it hundreds of years ago." I confute that idea by
telling you it is not five minutes old, when God, by His
blessed Spirit retranslates it into the heart. If, in seeking the
way of life through Scripture study, you implore God's light
to fall upon the page, you will find that these promises are
not one second old, and that they drop straight from the
throne of God into your heart.

There are many people to whom the Bible does not
amount to much. If they merely look at the outside beauty,
it will no more lead them to Christ than Washington's farewell address, the Koran of Mahomet or the Shaster of the
Hindoos. It is the inward light of God's Word you must
get or die. I went up to the church of the Madeleine, in
Paris, and looked at the doors which were the most wonderfully constructed I ever saw, and I could have staid there for
a whole week ; but I had only a little time, and so, having
glanced at the wonderful carving on the doors, I passed in
and looked at the radiant altars, and the sculptured dome.
Alas! that so many stop at the outside door of God's Holy
Word, looking at the rhetorical beauties, instead of going in
and looking at the altars of sacrifice and the dome of God's
mercy and salvation that hovers over every penitent and believing soul!

O my friends, if you merely want to study the laws of
language, do not go to the Bible. It was not made for that.
Take " Howe's Elements of Criticism"—it will be better than
the Bible for that. If you want to study metaphysics, better
than the Bible will be the writings of William Hamilton.
But if you want to know how to have sin pardoned, and at
last to gain the blessedness of Heaven, "Search the Scriptures, for in them ye think ye have eternal life."

I know there are many people who regard the Bible as
merely a collection of genealogical tables and dry facts. That
is because they do not know how to read the book. You
take up the most interesting novel that was ever written,

and if you commence at the four-hundredth page to-day, and to-morrow at the three-hundredth, and the next day at the first page, how much sense or interest would you get from it? Yet that is the very process to which the Bible is subjected every day. An angel from heaven, reading the Bible in that way, could not understand it. The Bible, like all other palaces, has a door by which to enter and a door by which to go out. Genesis is the door to go in and Revelation the door to go out.

The epistles of Paul the Apostle are merely letters written, folded up and sent by couriers to the different churches. Do you read other letters the way you read Paul's letters? Suppose you get a business letter, and you know that in it there are important financial propositions, do you read the last page first and then one line of the third page, and another of the second, and another of the first? No. You begin with "Dear sir" and end with "Yours truly." Now, here is a letter from the throne of God written to our lost world; it is full of magnificent hopes and propositions, and we dip in here and there, and we know nothing about it. Besides that, people read the Bible when they cannot do anything else. It is a dark day, and they do not feel well, and they do not go to business, and after lounging about a bit they pick up the Bible—their mind refuses to enjoy the truth. Or they come home weary from the store or shop, and they feel, if they do not say, it is a dull book. While the Bible is to be read on stormy days and while your head aches, it is also to be read in the sunshine and when your nerves like harp-strings thrum the song of health. While your vision is clear, walk in this paradise of truth, and while your mental appetite is good, pluck these clusters of grace.

O, I am afraid in America we are allowing the good Book to be covered up with other good books! We have our ever-welcome morning and evening newspapers, and we have our good books on all subjects—geological subjects, botanical subjects, physiological subjects, theological subjects—good books, beautiful books, and so many good books that we have not time to read the Bible. O my

friends, it is not a matter of very great importance that you
have a family Bible on the centre-table in your parlor! Better have one pocket New Testament, the passages marked,
the leaves turned down, the binding worn smooth with much
usage, than fifty pictorial family Bibles too handsome to
read! O, let us take a whisk-broom and brush the dust off
our Bibles! Do you want poetry? Go and hear Job describe the war-horse, or David tell how the mountains
skipped like lambs. Do you want logic? Go and hear
Paul reason until your brain aches under the spell of his
mighty intellect. Do you want history? Go and see
Moses put into a few pages stupendous information which
Herodotus, Thucydides, and Prescott never reached after.
And, after all, if you want to find how a nation struck
down by sin can rise to happiness and to heaven, read of
that blood which can wash away the pollution of a world.
There is one passage in the Bible of vast tonnage : "God so
loved the world that He gave His only begotten Son, that
whosoever believeth in Him should not perish, but have everlasting life." O, may God fill this country with Bibles and
help the people to read them!

Palsied be the hand that would take the Bible from the
college and the school. Educate only a man's head and
you make him an infidel. Educate only a man's heart and
you make him a fanatic. Educate them both together, and
you have the noblest work of God. An educated mind without moral principle is a ship without a helm, a rushing rail
train without brakes or reversing rod to control the speed.
Put the Bible in the family. There it lies on the table, an
unlimited power. Polygamy and unscriptural divorce are
prohibited. Parents are kind and faithful, children polite
and obedient. Domestic sorrows lessened by being divided,
joys increased by being multiplied. Oh, father, Oh, mother,
take down that long-neglected Bible, and read it yourselves
and let your children read it!

It may be an old-fashioned gift, but when your daughter
takes the hand of another and goes forth to her new home,
better than the ring of betrothal on her hand, better than

the orange blossoms in her hair, better than the wedding march to which they keep step as they start on the journey of life, will be a well-bound copy of the Holy Scriptures, her name on the fly-leaf with the inscription: "From father and mother on the marriage day." I say let it be well bound, for how many years of joy and sorrow and vicissitude it will have to serve! Let it be well bound.

Put the Bible on the rail train and on ship-board, till all parts of this land and all other lands, shall have its illumination. This hour there rises the yell of heathen worship, and in the face of this day's sun smokes the blood of human sacrifice. Give them the Bible. Unbind that wife from the funeral pyre, for no other sacrifice is needed since the blood of Jesus Christ cleanseth from all sin.

THE STOLEN GRINDSTONES

" Now there was no smith found throughout all the land of Israel: for the Philistines said, Lest the Hebrews make them swords or spears. But all the Israelites went down to the Philistines, to sharpen every man his share, and his coulter, and his axe, and his mattock Yet they had a file for the mattock, and for the coulters, and for the forks, and for the axes, and to sharpen the goads."—I. Samuel, 13 . 19–21.

What a galling subjugation for the Israelites! The Philistines had carried off all the blacksmiths, and torn down all the blacksmiths' shops, and abolished the blacksmiths' trade in the land of Israel. The Philistines would not even allow these parties to work their valuable mines of brass and iron, nor might they make any swords or spears. There were only two swords left in all the land Yea, these Philistines went on until they had taken all the grindstones from the land of Israel, so that if an Israelitish farmer wanted to sharpen his plough or his axe, he had to go over to the garrison of the Philistines to get it done. There was only one sharpening instrument left in the land, and that was a file; the farmers and the mechanics having nothing to whet up the coulter, and the goad, and the pick-axe, save a simple file.

Industry was hindered and work practically disgraced.

The great idea of these Philistines was to keep the Israelites disarmed. They might get iron out of the hills to make swords of, but they would not have any blacksmiths to weld this iron. If they got the iron welded, they would have no grindstones on which to bring the instruments of agriculture or the military weapons up to an edge. Oh, you poor, weaponless Israelites, reduced to a file, how I pity you ! But these Philistines were not for ever to keep their heel on the neck of God's children. Jonathan, on his hands and knees, climbs up a great rock, beyond which were the Philistines ; and his armor-bearer, on his hands and knees, climbs up the same rock, and these two men, with their two swords, hew to pieces the Philistines, the Lord throwing a great terror upon them. So it was then ; so it is now. Two men of God on their knees, mightier than a Philistine host on their feet !

I learn from this subject, that it is dangerous for the Church of God to allow its weapons to stay in the hands of its enemies. These Israelites might again and again have obtained a supply of swords and weapons, as for instance, when they took the spoils of the Ammonites ; but these Israelites seemed content to have no swords, no spears, no blacksmiths, no grindstones, no active iron mines, until it was too late for them to make any resistance. I see the farmers tugging along with their pickaxes and plough, and I say, " Where are you going with those things ?" They say, " Oh, we are going over to the garrison of the Philistines, to get these things sharpened." I say, " You foolish men, why don't you sharpen them at home ?" " Oh," they say, " the blacksmiths' shops are all torn down, and we have nothing left us but a file."

APPEAL TO CHRISTIANS.

So it is in the church of Jesus Christ to-day. We are too willing to give up our weapons to the enemy.

Let us thus take advantage of the world's grindstones.

These Israelites were reduced to a file, and so they went over to the garrison of the Philistines to get their axes, and their goads, and their ploughs sharpened. The Bible dis-

tinctly states it—the text which I read at the beginning of
the service—that they had no other 'instruments now with
which to do this work, and the Israelites did right when they
went over to the Philistines to use their grindstones. My
friends, is it not right for us to employ the world's grindstones? If there be art, if there be logic, if there be business
faculty on the other side, let us go over and employ it, for
Christ's sake. The fact is, we fight with too dull weapons,
and we work with too dull implements We hack and we
maul, when we ought to make a clean stroke. Let us go over
among sharp business men and among sharp literary men, and,
find out what their tact is, and then transfer it to the cause
of Christ. If they have science and art, it will do us good to
rub against it.

In other words, let us employ the world's grindstones.
We will listen to their music, and we will watch their acumen,
and we will use their grindstones, and will borrow their philosophical apparatus to make our experiments, and we will borrow their printing-presses to publish our Bibles, and we will
borrow their rail-trains to carry our Christian literature, and
we will borrow their ships to transport our missionaries. That
was what made Paul such a master in his day. He not only
got all the learning he could get of Doctor Gamaliel, but
afterward, standing on Mars Hill, and in crowded thorough-
fare, quoted their poetry, and grasped their logic, and wielded
their eloquence, and employed their mythology, until Dionysius the Areopagite, learned in the schools of Athens and
Heliopolis, went down under his tremendous powers.

That was what gave *Thomas Chalmers* his power in his
day. He conquered the world's astronomy and compelled it
to ring out the wisdom and greatness of the Lord, until, for
the second time, the morning stars sang together and all the
sons of God shouted for joy. That was what gave to *Jonathan Edwards* his influence in his day. He conquered the
world's metaphysics and forced it into the service of God,
until not only the old meeting-house at Northampton, Massachusetts, but all Christendom, felt thrilled by his Christian
power. Well, now, my friends, we all have tools of Christian

power. Do not let them lose their edges. We want no rusty blades in this fight. We want no coulter that cannot rip up the glebe. We want no axe that cannot fell the trees. We want no goad that cannot start the lazy team. Let us get the very best grindstones we can find, though they be in possession of the Philistines, compelling them to turn the crank while we bear down with all our might on the swift revolving wheel, until all our energies and faculties shall be brought up to a bright, keen, sharp, glittering edge.

LOGIC OF TESTIMONY.

Our weapon in this conflict is faith, not logic; faith, not metaphysics; faith, not profundity; faith, not scholastic exploration. But then, in order to have faith, we must have testimony; and if five hundred men, or one thousand men, or five hundred thousand men, or five million men get up and tell me that they have felt the religion of Jesus Christ a joy, a comfort, a help, an inspiration, I am bound as a fair-minded man to accept their testimony.

The world boasts that it has gobbled up the schools, and the colleges, and the arts, and the sciences, and the literature, and the printing-press Infidelity is making a mighty attempt to get all our weapons in its hand, and then to keep them. You know it is making this boast all the time, and after a while, when the great battle between Sin and Righteousness has opened, if we do not look out we will be as badly off as these Israelites, without any swords to fight with and without any sharpening instruments. I call upon the superintendents of literary institutions to see to it that the men who go into the class-rooms to stand beside the Leyden jars and the electric batteries, and the microscopes and telescopes, be children of God, not Philistines

The Carlylean, Emersonian and Tyndallean thinkers of this day are trying to get all the intellectual weapons in their own grasp. We want scientific Christians to capture the science, and scholastic Christians to capture the scholarship, and philosophic Christians to capture the philosophy,

and lecturing Christians to take back the lecturing platform.   We want to send out against Schenkel and Strauss
and Renan, a Theodore Christlieb, of Bonn, and against the
infidel scientists of the day, a God-worshipping Silliman and
Hitchcock and Agassiz.   We want to capture all the philosophical apparatus, and swing around the telescopes on the
swivel, until through them we can see the morning-star of
the Redeemer, and with mineralogical hammer discover the
Rock of Ages, and amid the flora of all realms find the Rose
of Sharon and the Lily of the Valley.

We want a clergy learned enough to discourse of the
human eye, showing it to be a microscope and telescope in
one instrument, with eight wonderful contrivances, and lids
closing thirty thousand or forty thousand times a day; all
its muscles and nerves and bones showing the infinite skill of
an infinite God, and then winding up with the peroration,
" He that formed the eye, shall He not see ?"   And then we
want to discourse about the human ear, its wonderful integu-
ments, membranes and vibration, and closing with the question, " He that planted the ear, shall He not hear ?"   And
we want some one able to expound the first chapter of
Genesis, bring to it the geology and the astronomy of the
world, until, as Job suggested, " The stones of the field shall
be in league" with the truth, and the stars in their course
shall fight against Sisera.   Oh, Church of God, go out and re-
capture these weapons!

Let men of God go out and take possession of the platform.   Let any printing-presses that have been captured by
the enemy be recaptured for God , and the reporters, and
the type-setters, and the editors, and the publishers swear
allegiance to the Lord God of truth !   Ah! my friend, that
day must come, and if the great body of Christian men have
not the faith, or the courage, or the consecration to do it,
then let some Jonathan on his busy hands and on his praying
knees, climb upon the Rock of Hindrance, and in the name of
the Lord God of Israel slash to pieces those literary Philistines.   If these men will not be converted to God, then they
must be overthrown.

APPEAL TO YOUNG MEN.

Young man, do not be ashamed to be a friend of the Bible. Do not put your thumb in your vest, as young men sometimes do, and swagger about, talking of the glorious light of the nineteenth century, and of there being no need of a Bible. They have the light of nature in India and China and in all the dark places of the earth. Did you ever hear that the light of nature gave them comfort for their trouble? They have lancets to cut and juggernauts to crush, but no comfort. Ah! my friends, you better stop your scepticism.

It is an absorbing question, a practical question, an overwhelming question to you and to me, the authorship of this Holy Bible—whether the Lord God of Heaven and earth, or a pack of dupes, scoundrels, and impostors. We cannot afford to adjourn that question a week or a day or an hour any more than a sea captain can afford to say, "Well, this is a very dark night. I have really lost my bearings; there's a light out there, I don't know whether it's a lighthouse, or a false light on the shore, I don't know what it is; but I'll just go to sleep and in the morning I'll find out." In the morning the vessel might be on the rocks, and the beach strewn with the white faces of the dead crew. The time for that sea captain to find out about the lighthouse is before he goes to sleep.

It is demonstrated to all honest men that it is not so certain that William Cullen Bryant wrote "Thanatopsis," or Longfellow wrote "Hiawatha," as that God, by the hand of prophet and apostle, wrote the Bible.

Science, law, medicine, literature and merchandise, are gradually coming to believe in Christianity, and soon there will be no people who disbelieve in it, except those conspicuous for lack of brain, or men with two families, who do not like the Bible, because it rebukes their swinish propensities.

The time is hastening when there will be no infidels left except libertines, harlots, and murderers.

From the ruins of Babylon and Assyria and Nineveh, and the valleys of the Nile, confirmations have been exhumed proving to all fair-minded men that the Bible is the truest book ever written. The mythologies of Egypt were found to have embodied in them the knowledge of man's expulsion from Paradise, and the sacrifice of a great emancipator. Moses' account of the creation, corroborated by the hammer of Christian geologists; the oldest profane writers like Hiromus, Helanicus, and Berosus, confirming the Bible account of ancient longevity; Tacitus and Pliny confirming the Bible accounts of destroyed Sodom and Gomorrah; Tacitus and Porphyry telling the same story of Christ as Matthew and Luke told; Macrobius telling of the massacre of children in Bethlehem, and Phlegon sketching at the crucifixion.

The Bible intimates that there was a city called Petra, built out of solid rock. Infidelity scoffed at it. "Where is your city of Petra?" Burckhardt and Laborde went forth in their explorations and they came upon that very city. The mountains stand around like giants guarding the tomb where the city is buried. They find a street in that city six miles long, where once flashed imperial pomp and which echoed with the laughter of light-hearted mirth on its way to the theatre. On temples fashioned out of colored stones—some of which have blushed into the crimson of the rose, and some of which have paled into the whiteness of the lily—aye, on column and pediment and entablature and statuary, God writes the truth of that Bible.

The Bible says that Sodom and Gomorrah were destroyed by fire and brimstone. "Absurd," infidels year after year said "it is positively absurd that they could have been destroyed by brimstone. There is nothing in the elements to cause such a shower of death as that." Lieutenant Lynch went out in exploration and came to the Dead Sea, which, by a convulsion of nature, has overflowed the place where the cities once stood. He sank his fathoming line and brought up from the bottom of the Dead Sea great masses of sulphur, remnants of that very tempest that swept Sodom and Gomorrah to ruin. Who was right? The Bible that announced the destruction of those cities or the sceptics who for ages scoffed at it?

The Bible says there was a city called Nineveh, and that it was three days' journey around it, and that it should be destroyed by fire and water. "Absurd," cried out hundreds of voices for many years; "no such city was ever built that it would take three days' journey to go around. Besides, it could not be destroyed by fire and water, they are antago- nistic elements." But Layard, Botta, and Keith go out, and by their explorations they find that city of Nineveh, and they tell us that by their own experiment it is three days' journey around, according to the old estimate of a day's journey, and that it was literally destroyed by fire and water —two antagonistic elements—a part of the city having been inundated by the River Tigris, the brick material in those times being dried clay instead of burned, while in other parts they find the remains of the fire in heaps of charcoal that have been excavated, and in the calcined slabs of gypsum. Who was right the Bible or infidelity?

Moses intimated that they had vineyards in Egypt. "Absurd," cried hundreds of voices; "you can't raise grapes in Egypt; or, if you can, it is a very great exception that you can raise them." But the traveller goes down, and in the underground vaults of Eilithya he finds painted on the wall all the process of tending the vines and treading out the grapes. It is all there, familiarly sketched by people who evidently knew all about it, and saw it all about them every day; and in those underground vaults there are vases still encrusted with the settlings of the wine. You see the vine did grow in Egypt, whether it grows there now or not.

Can you doubt the authenticity of the Scriptures? There is not so much evidence that Walter Scott wrote "The Lady of the Lake;" not so much evidence that Shakespeare wrote "Hamlet;" not so much evidence that John Milton wrote "Paradise Lost," as there is evidence that the Lord God Almighty, by the hands of the prophets, evangelists and apostles, wrote this Book.

Suppose a book now to be written which came in conflict

with a great many things, and was written by bad men or impostors, how long would such a book stand? It would be scouted by everybody. And I say if that Bible had been an imposition; or if it had not been written by the men who said they wrote it; if it had been a mere collection of false-hoods, do you not suppose that it would have been imme-diately rejected by the people? If Job and Isaiah and Jeremiah and Paul and Peter and John were impostors, they would have been scouted by generations and nations. If that Book has come down through fires of centuries without a scar, it is because there is nothing in it destructible.

How near have they come to destroying the Bible? When they began their opposition there were two or three thousand copies of it. Now there are two hundred millions, as far as I can calculate. These Bible truths, notwithstanding all the opposition, have gone into all languages—into the philo-sophic Greek, the flowing Italian, the rugged German, the passionate French, the picturesque Indian, and the exhaust-less Anglo-Saxon. Now, do you not suppose, if that Book had been an imposition and a falsehood, it would have gone down under these ceaseless fires of opposition?

While God wrote the Bible, at the same time He wrote this commentary, that "the statutes of the Lord are right," on leaves of rock and shell, bound in clasps of metal, and lying on mountain tables and in the jewelled vase of the sea. In authenticity and in genuineness the statutes of the Lord are right.

CAVILLING REBUKED.

How foolish in the caviller to allow the technicalities of re-ligion to stop his salvation! I know wise men and great men, competent for all other stations, who are acting a silly and foolish part in regard to the technicalities of religion. They ask us some questions which we cannot answer categorically, and so they burst into a broad guffaw, as though it is of any more interest to us than it ought to be to them. About the Atonement, about God's decrees, about man's destiny, they

ask a great many questions which we cannot answer, and so
they deride us, as though we could not ask them a thousand
questions that they cannot answer, about their eyes, about
their ears, about their finger-nails, about everything. A fool
can ask a question that a wise man cannot answer. O you
cavilling men! O you profound men' O you learned
men, do please admit something. You have a soul? Yes.
Will it live forever? Yes. Where? You say that Jesus
Christ is not a divine Saviour. Who is He? Where will you
go after you leave your law-books and your medical prescriptions and your club-room and your newspaper-office—where
will you go to? Your body will be six feet under ground
Where will your soul be? The black coat will be off, the
shroud on. Those spectacles will be removed from your
vision, for the sod will press your eyelids. Have you any
idea that an earthly almanac describes the years of your lifetime? Of what stuff shall I gather the material for the letters of that word which describes your eternal home? Shall
it be iron chain or amaranthine garland? The air that stirs
the besweated locks of your dying pillow, will it come off a
garden or a desert? Oh, quit the puzzling questions and try
these momentous questions. Quit the small questions and
try these great questions. Instead of discussing whether the
serpent in Eden was figurative or literal, whether the Mediterranean fish did or did not swallow the recreant prophet,
whether this and that, and the other thing is right or wrong,
come and discuss one question : " How shall I get rid of my
sins and win heaven?" *That is the question for you.* Yea, there
have been men who have actually lost their souls because
they thought there was a discrepancy between Moses and Professor Silliman—because they could not understand how
there could be light before the sun rose—the light appearing in verse 3 of Genesis, and the sun appearing not until
verse 16—and because they do not know how the sun could
stand still without upsetting the universe, and because they
had decided upon the theory of natural selection. *A German philosopher* in dying had for his chief sorrow that he had
not devoted his whole life to the study of the dative case.

O, when your immortality is in peril, why quibble? Quit these non-essentials, my dear brother. In the name of God, I ask you in regard to these matters of the immortal soul, that you do not play the fool.

What is that man doing over in Bowling Green, New York? Well, he is going in for a ticket for a transatlantic voyage. He is quarrelling with the clerk about the spots— the red spots on the ticket—and he is quarrelling about the peculiar signature of the president of the steamship company, and he is quarrelling about the manner of the clerk who hands him the ticket. How long has he been standing there? Three weeks. Meanwhile, perhaps, twenty steamers have gone out of port, and I hear the shriek of the steam-tug that could take him to the last vessel that could bear him to his engagement in London. Still he stands in Bowling Green discussing the ticket. What do you say in regard to that man? You say he is a fool. Well, in that very way are many men acting in regard to the matters of the soul. They are cavilling about the Atonement, the red spots on the ticket—about the character of the minister who hands them the ticket—about whether it has a divine or human signa- ture, and meanwhile, all their opportunities for heaven are sailing out of the harbor, and I hear the last tap of the bell announcing their last chance for heaven. Go aboard! Do not waste any more time in higgling and carping and criti- cising and wondering, and, in the presence of an astounded heaven, playing the fool.

The religion of Ralph Waldo Emerson is the philosophy of icicles; the religion of Theodore Parker is a sirocco of the desert, covering up the soul with dry sand; the religion of Renan is the romance of believing nothing; the religion of Thomas Carlyle is only a condensed London fog; the reli- gion of the Huxleys and the Spencers is merely a pedestal on which human philosophy sits shivering in the night of the soul, looking up to the stars, offering no help to the nations that crouch and groan at the base. Tell me where there is one man who has rejected that Gospel for another, who is thoroughly satisfied and helped and contented in his skep-

ticism, and I will take the car to-morrow and ride five hundred miles to see him.

For many things I have admired *Percy Shelley*, the great
English poet, but I deplore the fact that it was a great sweetness to him to dishonor God. The poem "Queen Mab"
has in it the maligning of the Deity. The infidel poet was
impious enough to ask for Rowland Hill's Surrey Chapel
that he might denounce the Christian religion. He was in
great glee against God and the truth. But he visited Italy,
and one day on the Mediterranean with two friends in a
boat, he was coming toward shore when a squall struck the
water. A gentleman standing on shore, through a glass saw
many boats tossed in this squall, but all outrode the terror
except one, that in which Shelley, the infidel poet, and his
two friends were sailing. That never came ashore, but the
bodies of two of the occupants were washed upon the beach,
one of them the poet. A funeral pyre was built on the sea-
shore by some classic friends, and the two bodies were consumed. Poor Shelley! He would have no God while he
lived, and he probably had no God when he died. "The
Lord knoweth the way of the righteous, but the way of the
ungodly shall perish."

You may get all your difficulties settled as Garibaldi, the
magnetic Italian, got his gardens made. When the war between Austria and Sardinia broke out he was living at Caprera,
a very rough and uncultured island home. But he went forth
with his sword to achieve the liberation of Naples and Sicily,
and gave nine million people free government under Victor
Emanuel. Garibaldi, after being absent two years from Caprera, returned, and, when he approached it, he found that
his home had been Edenized by Victor Emanuel as a surprise.
Trimmed shrubbery had taken the place of thorny thickets,
gardens the place of barrenness, and the old rookery in which
he once lived had given way to a pictured mansion where he
lived in comfort the rest of his days. And I tell you if you will
come and enlist under the banner of our Victor Emanuel, and
follow Him through thick and thin, and fight His battles, and
endure His sacrifices, you will find after a while that He has

changed your heart from a jungle of thorny scepticisms into a garden all abloom with luxuriant joy that you have never dreamed of. From a tangled Caprera of sadness into a Paradise of God! Make it your guide in life and your pillow in death.

After the battle of Richmond a dead soldier was found with his hand lying on the open Bible. The summer insects had eaten the flesh from the hand, but the skeleton finger lay on these words: " Yea, though I walk through the valley of the shadow of death, I will fear no evil, for Thou art with me; Thy rod and Thy staff they comfort me." Yes, this Book will become in your last days, when you turn away from all other books, a solace for your soul. Perhaps it was your mother's Bible; perhaps the one given you on your wedding-day, its cover now worn out and its leaf faded with age; but its bright promises will flash upon the opening gates of heaven.

> " How precious is the Book divine,
>   By inspiration given;
> Bright as a lamp its doctrines shine,
>   To guide our souls to heaven.
>
> " This lamp, through all the tedious night
>   Of life, shall guide our way,
> Till we behold the clearer light
>   Of an eternal day."

planks and pry out some of the timbers because the timber
did not come from the right forest! It does not seem to me
a commendable business for the crew to be helping the winds
and storms outside with their axes and saws inside.

Now, this old Gospel ship, what with the roaring of earth and
hell around the stem and stern and mutiny on deck, is having
a very rough voyage, but I have noticed that not one of the
timbers has started, and *the Captain says He will see it through*.
And I have noticed that keelson and counter-timber knee
are built out of Lebanon cedar, and she is going to weather
the gale, but no credit to those who make mutiny on deck.

When I see ministers of religion finding fault with the
Scriptures, it makes me think of a fortress terrifically bombarded, and the men on the ramparts, instead of swabbing
out and loading the guns and helping to fetch up the ammunition from the magazine, are trying with crowbars to pry
out from the wall certain blocks of stone, because they did
not come from the right quarry. O, men on the ramparts,
better fight back and fight down the common enemy, instead
of trying to make breaches in the wall.

WHY EXPURGATION IS WRONG.

While I oppose this expurgation of the Scriptures, I shall
give you my reasons for such opposition. " What !" say some
of the theological evolutionists, whose brains have been
addled by too long brooding over them by Darwin and Spencer, " you don't now really believe all the story of the Garden of Eden, do you?" Yes, as much as I believe all the
roses that were in my garden last summer. " But," say they,
" you don't really believe that the sun and moon stood still?"
Yes, and if I had strength enough to create a sun and moon
I could make them stand still, or cause the refraction of the
sun's rays so it would appear to stand still. " But," they say,
" you don't really believe that the whale swallowed Jonah?"
Yes, and if I were strong enough to make a whale I could
have made very easy ingress for the refractory prophet, leaving to Evolution to eject him, if he were an unworthy tenant!

" But," say they, " you don't really believe that the water was
turned into wine?" Yes, just as easily as water now is often
turned into wine with an admixture of strychnine and logwood! " But," say they, " you don't really believe that
Samson slew a thousand with *the jaw-bone of an ass ?*" Yes,
as I think that the man who in this day assaults the Bible is
wielding the same weapon !

.

EXPURGATION OF THE HEART.

I tell you that a man who does not like this Book, and
who is critical as to its contents, and who is shocked and
outraged with its descriptions, has never been soundly converted. The laying on of the hands of Presbytery, or Epis-
copacy, does not always change a man's heart, and men
sometimes get into the pulpit as well as into the pew, never
having been changed radically by the sovereign grace of
God. Get your heart right and the Bible will be right. The
trouble is men's natures are not brought into harmony with
the Word of God. Ah ! my friends, *expurgation of the heart
is what is wanted*.

You cannot make me believe that the Scriptures, which
this moment lie on the table of the purest and the best men
and women of the age, and which were the dying solace of
your kindred passed into the skies, have in them a taint
which the strongest microscope of honest criticism could
make visible. If men are uncontrollable in their indignation
when the integrity of wife or child is assailed, and judges
and jurors as far as possible excuse violence under such
provocation, what ought to be the overwhelming and long
resounding thunders of condemnation for any man who will
stand in a Christian pulpit and assail the more than virgin
purity of inspiration, the well-beloved daughter of God ?

Expurgate the Bible ! You might as well go to the old
picture galleries in Dresden and in Venice and in Rome and
expurgate the old paintings. Perhaps you could find a foot
of Michael Angelo's " Last Judgment " that might be
improved. Perhaps you could throw more expression

into Raphael's " Madonna." Perhaps you could put more
pathos into Rubens' " Descent from the Cross " Perhaps you could change the crests of the waves in Turner's " Slave Ship." Perhaps you might go into the old galleries of sculpture and change the forms and the posture of
the statues of Phidias and Praxiteles. Such an iconoclast
would very soon find himself in the penitentiary. But it is
worse vandalism when a man proposes to re-fashion these
masterpieces of inspiration and to remodel the moral giants
of this gallery of God.

NO COMPROMISE.

Now, let us divide off. Let those people who do not believe the Bible and who are critical of this and that part of
it, go clear over to the other side. Let them stand behind
the devil's guns. There can be no compromise between infidelity and Christianity. Give us the out-and-out opposition of infidelity rather than the work of these hybrid theo-
logians, these mongrel ecclesiastics, these half-and-half evoluted pulpiteers who believe the Bible and do not believe it,
who accept the miracles and do not accept them, who believe in the inspiration of the Scriptures and do not believe
in the inspiration of the Scriptures—trimming their belief
on one side to suit the scepticism of the world, trimming
their belief on the other side to suit the pride of their own
heart, and feeling that in order to demonstrate their courage they must make the Bible a target and shoot at God.

While I demand that the antagonists of the Bible and
the critics of the Bible go clear over where they belong, on
the devil's side, I ask that all the friends of this good Book
come out openly and above board in behalf of it. That
Book, which was the best inheritance you ever received from
your ancestry, and which will be the best legacy you will
leave to your children when you bid them good-by as you
cross the ferry to the golden city.

There is nothing that so outrages our feelings as to hear
a man talk against this Book. It has been to us so much in

the past, and it shall be to us so much in the future, that you feel like doing oftimes as I saw a man do on the rail-train some time ago when I was on the way to New Orleans. He was all wrapped up with the Bible that he took out of his pocket. After reading awhile, not knowing he was especially noticed, he closed it and *kissed it*, and put it in his pocket. I was not surprised at it, for there are thousands to-day who by the memory of all this Book has been to them in the past, and by the hope and expectation of all it is to be to them in the future, could press it to their soul with a kiss of undying affection.

Young man, do not be ashamed of your Bible. There is not a virtue but it commends, there is not a sorrow but it comforts, there is not a good law on the statute-book of any country but it is founded on these Ten Commandments. There are no braver, grander people in all the earth than the heroes and the heroines which it biographizes.

BETTER ILLUSTRATION THAN DORÉ'S.

I was startled as I saw on the bulletin the announcement of *Gustave Doré's departure.* It said: " Is it possible that that hand has forgotten its cunning?" Of all the works of that great artist, there is nothing so impressive as Doré's illustrated Bible. What scene of Abrahamic faith, or Edenic beauty, of dominion Davidic or Solomonic, of miracle or parable, of nativity, or of crucifixion, or of last judgment, but the thought leaped from the great brain to the skilful pencil, and from the skilful pencil to the canvas immortal. The Louvre, the Luxembourg, the National Gallery of London, compressed within two volumes of Doré's illustrated, Bible. But the Bible will come to *better illustration* than that, my friends, when all the deserts have become gardens, and all the armories have become academies, and all the lakes have become Genesarets with Christ walking them, and all the cities have become Jerusalems with hovering Shekinah; and the two hemispheres shall be clapping cymbals of divine praise, and the round earth a footlight to

Emanuel's throne—that to all lands, all ages, all centuries, and all cycles will be the best specimen of Bible illustrated.

But though thus susceptible of fresh illustration, it is the same old Bible, divinely protected in its present shape. You could as easily, without detection, take from the writings of Shakespeare *Hamlet,* and insert in place thereof Alexander Smith's drama, as at any time during the last fifteen hundred years a man could have made any important change in the Bible without immediate detection. If there had been an element of weakness or of deception, or of disintegration the Book would long ago have fallen to pieces. If there had been one loose brick or cracked casement in this castellated truth, surely the bombardment of eight centuries would have discovered and broken through that imperfection. The fact that the Bible stands intact, notwithstanding all the furious assaults on all sides upon it, is proof to me that it is a miracle, and every miracle is of God.

"But," says some one, "while we admit the Bible is of God, it has not been understood until our time." My answer is, that if the Bible be a letter from God, our Father, to man, His child, is it not strange that that letter should have been written in such a way that it should allow seventy generations to pass away and be buried before the letter could be understood? That would be a very bright father who should write a letter for the guidance and intelligence of his children, not understandable until a thousand years after they were buried and forgotten! While as the years roll on other beauties and excellencies will unfold from the Scriptures, that the Bible is such a dead failure that all the Christian scholars for eighteen hundred years were deceived in regard to vast reaches of its meaning, is a demand upon my credulity so great that if I found myself at all disposed to yield to it I should to-morrow morning apply at Bloomingdale Insane Asylum as unfit to go alone.

THEOLOGICAL FOG.

Thus a great fog has come down upon some of the ministers and some of the churches in the shape of what is called "advanced thought" in Biblical interpretation. These "advanced" ministers and churches deny the full inspiration of the Bible. Genesis is an allegory, and there are many myths in the Bible, and they philosophize and guess and reason and evolute until they land in *a great continent of mud*, from which, I fear, for all eternity they will not be able to extricate themselves.

Who make up this precious group of advanced thinkers to whom God has made especial revelation in our time of that which He tried to make known thousands of years ago and failed to make intelligible? Are they so distinguished for unworldliness, piety, and scholarship that it is to be expected that they would have been chosen to fix up the defective work of Moses and Isaiah and Paul and Christ?

Is it all possible? I wonder on what mountain these modern exegetes were transfigured? I wonder what star pointed down to their birthplace! Was it the north-star, or the evening star, or the Dipper? As they came through and descended to our world did Mars blush or Saturn lose one of its rings? When I find these modern wiseacres attempting to improve upon the work of the Almighty and to interlard it with their wisdom and to suggest prophetic and apostolic errata, I am filled with a disgust insufferable. Advanced thought, which proposes to tell the Lord what He ought to have said thousands of years ago, and would have said if He had been as wise as His nineteenth century critics! I have two wonders in regard to these men. The first one is how the Lord got along without them before they were born. The second wonder is how the Lord will get along without them after they are dead.

"But," say some, "do you really think the Scriptures are inspired thought?" Yes, either as history or as guidance. Gibbon and Josephus and Prescott record in their histories a great many things they did not approve of. When George Bancroft puts upon his brilliant historical page the account of an Indian massacre, does he approve of that massacre? There are scores of things in the Bible which neither God nor inspired men sanctioned.

" But," says some one, " don't you think that the copyists might have made mistakes in transferring the divine words from one manuscript to another?" Yes, no doubt there were such mistakes, but they no more affect the meaning of the Scriptures than the misspelling of a word or the ungrammatical structure of a sentence in a last will and testament affect the validity or the meaning of that will. All the mistakes made by the copyists in the Scriptures do not amount to any more importance than the difference between your spelling in a document the word forty, forty or fourty. This book is the last will and testament of God to our lost world, and it bequeaths everything in the right way, although human hands may have damaged the grammar or made unjustifiable interpolation.

These men who pride themselves in our day on being advanced thinkers in Biblical interpretation will all of them end in atheism, if they live long enough, and I declare here that they are doing more in the different denominations of Christians, and throughout the world, for damaging Christianity and hindering the cause of the world's betterment than five thousand Robert Ingersolls could do. That man who stands inside a castle is far more dangerous if he be an enemy than five thousand enemies outside the castle. Robert G. Ingersoll assails the castle from the outside. These men who pretend to be advanced thinkers in all the denominations are fighting the truth from the inside, and trying to shove back the bolts and swing open the gates.

There is nothing in the Bible that staggers me. There are many things I do not understand—I do not pretend to understand—never shall in this world understand. But that would be a very poor God who could be fully understood by the human. That would be a very small Infinite that can be measured by the finite. You must not expect to weigh the thunderbolts of Omnipotence in an apothecary's balances. Starting with the idea that God can do anything, and that He was present at the beginning, and that He is present now, there is nothing in the Holy Scriptures to arouse scepticism in my heart.

A WHOLE BIBLE FROM LID TO LID.

I am opposed to the expurgation of the Scriptures because the Bible in its present shape has been so *miraculously preserved.* Fifteen hundred years after Herodotus wrote his history, there was only one manuscript copy of it. Twelve hundred years after Plato wrote his book, there was only one manuscript copy of it. God was so careful to have us have the Bible in just the right shape that we have fifty manuscript copies of the New Testament a thousand years old, and many of them fifteen hundred years old—a Book handed down from the time of Christ, or just after the time of Christ, by the hand of such men as Origen in the second century and Tertullian in the third century,—men of different ages who died for their principles. The three best copies of the New Testament manuscript are in the possession of three great churches—the Protestant Church of England, the Greek Church of St. Petersburg, and the Roman Church of Italy.

It is a plain matter of history that *Tischendorf* went to a convent in the peninsula of Sinai and was by ropes lifted over the wall into the convent, that being the only mode of admission, and that he saw there in the waste basket for kindling for the fires, a manuscript of the Holy Scriptures. That night he copied many of the passages of that Bible, but it was not until fifteen years had passed of earnest entreaty and prayer and coaxing and purchase on his part that that copy of the Holy Scriptures was put into the hands of the Emperor of Russia—that one copy so marvellously protected.

Do you not know that *the catalogue of the books* of the Old and New Testaments, as we have it, is the same catalogue that has been coming on down through the ages? Thirty nine books of the Old Testament thousands of years ago.

Thirty-nine now. Twenty-seven books of the New Testament sixteen hundred years ago. Twenty-seven books of the New Testament now. Marcion, for wickedness, was turned out of the Church in the second century, and, in his assault on the Bible and Christianity, he incidentally gives a catalogue of the books of the Bible—that catalogue corresponding exactly with ours—testimony given by the enemy of the Bible and the enemy of Christianity The catalogue now just like the catalogue then. Assaulted and spit on and torn to pieces and burned, yet adhering. The book to-day, in three hundred languages, confronting four fifths of the human race in their own tongue. Three hundred million copies of it in existence. Does not that look as if this Book had been divinely protected, as if God had guarded it all through the centuries? The epidemics which have swept thousands of other books into the sepulchre of forgetfulness, have only brightened the fame of this. There is not one book out of a thousand that lives five years. Any publisher will tell you that. There will not be more than one book out of fifty thousand that will live a century. Yet here is a Book, much of it sixteen hundred years old, and much of it four thousand years old, and with more rebound and resilience and strength in it than when the Book was first put upon parchment or papyrus. This Book was the cradle of all other books, and it will see their graves. Would you not think that an old book like this, some of it forty centuries old, would come along hobbling with age and on crutches? Instead of that, it is more potent than any other book of the time. More copies of it printed in the last ten years than of any other book—Walter Scott's Waverley Novels, Macaulay's "History of England," Disraeli's "Endymion," and all the popular books of the day having no such sale in the last ten years as this old well-worn Book. Do you know what a struggle a book has in order to get through one century or two centuries?

LOST LITERARY TREASURES.

Some old books, during a fire in a seraglio of Constantinople, were thrown into the street. A man without any education picked up one of those books, read it, and did not see the value of it. A scholar looked over his shoulder and saw it was the first and second decades of Livy, and he offered the man a large reward if he would bring the book to his study; but in the excitement of the fire, the two parted, and the first and second decades of Livy were forever lost. Pliny wrote twenty books of history; all lost. The most of Meander's writings lost. Of one hundred and thirty comedies of Plautus, all gone but twenty. Euripides wrote a hundred dramas, all gone but nineteen. Æschylus wrote a hundred dramas, all gone but seven. Varro wrote the laborious biographies of seven hundred Romans, not a fragment left. Quintilian wrote his favorite book on the corruption of eloquence, all lost. Thirty books of Tacitus lost. Dion Cassius wrote eighty books, only twenty remain. Berosus's history all lost.

Nearly all the old books are mummified and are lying in the tombs of old libraries, and perhaps once in twenty years some man comes along and picks up one of them and blows the dust off, and opens it and finds it the book he does not want. But this old Book, much of it forty centuries old, stands to-day more discussed than any other book, and it challenges the admiration of all the good, and the spite, venom, animosity, and hypercriticism of earth and hell.

"Well," says one, "now I am ready to take the New Testament as from the heart of Christ, and I am ready to believe the prophecies. The evidence is beyond all dispute. But you must remember," says my friend, "that the prophecies are only a small part of the old book; you don't expect us to believe all the old book." If you found one of your good, honest letters in an envelope with ten or twenty obscene, cruel, lying, filthy letters, how long would you allow that honest letter to stay here. In a half minute you would

either snatch it out of the envelope, or you destroy the whole
envelope. Now, do you suppose the Lord God would allow
these pure prophecies, these prophecies which you admit must
have come from the hand of God, from divine inspiration, to
be bound up and put in the same envelope with the Book of
Job, and the Book of Psalms, and the Book of Deuteronomy
and the other books, if those books were not good books?

Beside all this, you must remember that the most of the
writers of this book were uneducated men   How can you
account for the fact that when Thomas Babington Macaulay, standing in the House of Parliament in London, wants
to finish off a magnificent sentence, he quotes from the fishermen of Galilee? or, sitting in his house, wanting to finish
one of his great paragraphs of history, he quotes the words
of the fisherman of Galilee? Why is it that those uneducated
men have more influence on modern times than all the
scholars of antiquity? Because they were divinely inspired,
because God stood back of them.

Beside that, you must remember that this book has been
under fire for centuries, and after all the bombardment of
the Ingersolls of all the centuries, they have not knocked
out of this Bible a piece as large as the small end of a sharp
needle. O! how the old book sticks together. Unsanctified
geologists try to pull away the Book of Genesis. They say
they do not believe it ; it cannot be there was light before
the sun shone ; it cannot be all this story about Adam and
Eve ; and they pull at the Book of Genesis, and they have
been pulling a great while, yet where is the Book of Genesis?
Standing just where it stood all the time. There is not a
man on earth who has ever erased it from his Bible.

And so infidels have been trying to pull away the miracles, pulling away at the blasted fig tree, at the turning of the
water into wine, at the raising of Lazarus from the dead.
Can you show me a Bible from which one of these miracles
has been erased?

All the striking at these chapters only drives them deeper
until they are clinched on the other side with the hammers

of eternity. And the book is going to keep right on until the fires of the last day.

WHEN WE CAN DO WITHOUT THE BIBLE.

What will be the use of the Book of Genesis, descriptive of how the world was made, when the world is destroyed? What will be the use of the prophecies when they are all fulfilled? What will be the use of the evangelistic or Pauline description of Jesus Christ when we see Him face to face? What will be the use of His photograph when we have met Him in glory? What will be the use of the Book of Revelation, standing, as you will, with your foot on the glassy sea, and your hand on the ringing harp, and your forehead chapleted with eternal coronation amid the amethystine and twelve-gated glories of heaven? The emerald dashing its green against the beryl, and the beryl dashing its blue against the sapphire, and the sapphire throwing its light on the jacinth, and the jacinth dashing its fire against the chrysoprase, and you and I standing in the chorus of ten thousand sunsets.

But I do not think we will give up the Bible even at that time. I think *we will want the Bible in heaven.* I really think the fires of the last day will not consume the last copy, for when you and I get our dead children out of the dust, we want to show them just the passages, just the promises, which comforted us here in the dark day of interment, and we will want to talk over with Christians who have had trials and struggles, and we will want to show them the promises that especially refreshed us. I think we shall have the Bible in heaven.

O! I want to hear David with his own voice read: "The Lord is my shepherd." I want to hear Paul with his own voice read: "Thanks be unto God that giveth us the victory." I want to hear the archangel play Paul's march of the resurrection with the same trumpet with which he awoke the dead. O! blessed book, good enough for earth, good enough for heaven. Dear old book—book bespattered with

the blood of martyrs who died for its defence—book sprinkled all over with the tears of those who by it were comforted.
Put it in the hand of your children on their birthday. Put
it on the table in the sitting-room when you begin to keep
house. Put it under your head when you die. Dear old
book! I press it to my heart, I press it to my lips. I appeal to your common sense, if a book so divinely guarded
and protected in its present shape, must not be in just the
form that God wants it ; and if it pleases God ought it not
to please us?

NO ADDITIONS MADE.

Not only have all attempts to detract from the Book
failed, but all attempts to add to it. Many attempts were
made to add the apochryphal books to the Old Testament.
The Council of Trent, the Synod of Jerusalem, the Bishops of
Hippo, all decided that the apochryphal books must be
added to the Old Testament. " They must stay in," said
those learned men ; but they stayed out. There is not an intelligent Christian man that to-day will put the Book of
Maccabeus or the Book of Judith beside the Book of Isaiah
or Romans. Then a great many said, " we must have books
added to the New Testament," and there were epistles and
Gospels and apocalypses written and added to the New
Testament, but they have all fallen out. You cannot add
anything. You cannot subtract anything. Divinely protected Book in the present shape. Let no man dare to lay
his hands on it with the intention of detracting from the
Book, or casting out any of these holy pages. Expurgation
means annihilation. Beside that, I am opposed to this expurgation of the Scriptures because if the attempt were successful, *it would be the annihilation of the Bible.* Infidel geologists
would say, " out with the Book of Genesis," infidel astronomers would say, " out with the Book of Joshua ;" people who
do not believe in the atoning sacrifice would say, " out with
the Book of Leviticus ;" people who do not believe in the
miracles would say, " out with all those wonderful stories in the

Old and New Testament;" and some would say, "out with
the Book of Revelation;" and others would say, "out with
the entire Pentateuch," and the work would go on until there
would not be enough of the Bible left to be worth as much
as last year's almanac. The expurgation of the Scriptures
means their annihilation.

GOOD PEOPLE SATISFIED.

I am opposed to this proposed expurgation of the Scriptures for the fact that in proportion as people become self-
sacrificing and good and holy and consecrated, *they like the
Book as it is.* I have yet to find a man or a woman distinguished for self-sacrifice, for consecration to God, for holiness of life, who wants the Bible changed. Many of us have
inherited family Bibles. Those Bibles were in use twenty,
forty, fifty, perhaps a hundred years in the generations.
Take down those family Bibles, and find out if there are any
chapters which have been erased by lead pencil or pen, and
if in any margins you can find the words: "this chapter not
fit to read." There has been plenty of opportunity during
the last half century privately to expurgate the Bible. Do
you know any case of such expurgation? Did not your
grandfather give it to your father, and did not your father
give it to you?

ACHIEVEMENTS OF ORTHODOXY.

Now, I want to show you, as a matter of advocacy for
what I believe to be the right, the splendors of orthodoxy.
Many have supposed that its disciples are people of flat
skulls, and no reading, and behind the age, and the victims of
gullibility. I shall show you that the word orthodoxy stands
for the greatest splendors outside of heaven. Behold the
splendors of its achievements. All the missionaries of the
Gospel the world round are men who believe in an entire
Bible. Call the roll of all the missionaries who are to-day
enduring sacrifices in the ends of the earth for the cause of

religion and the world's betterment, and they all believe in
an entire Bible. Just as soon as a missionary begins to doubt
whether there ever was a Garden of Eden, or whether there
is any such thing as future punishment, he comes right home
from Beyrout or Madras, and goes into the insurance business! All the missionary societies of this day are officered
by orthodox men, and are supported by orthodox churches.

Orthodoxy, beginning with the Sandwich islands, has
captured vast regions of barbarism for civilization, while
heterodoxy has to capture the first square inch. Blatant for
many years in Great Britain and the United States, and
strutting about with a peacockian braggadocia it has yet to
capture the first continent, the first State, the first township,
the first ward, the first space of ground as big as you could
cover with the small end of a sharp pin. Ninety-nine out of
every hundred of the Protestant churches of America were
built by people who believed in an entire Bible. The pulpit
now may preach some other Gospel, but it is *a heterodox gun
on an orthodox carriage.* The foundations of all the churches
that are of very great use in this world to-day were laid by
men who believed the Bible from lid to lid, and if I cannot
take it in that way I will not take it at all; just as if I received a letter that pretended to come from a friend, and
part of it was his and part somebody else's, a sort of literary
mongrelism, I would throw the garbled sheets into the waste
basket.

THE SURE FOUNDATION.

No church of very great influence to-day but was built
by those who believed in an entire Bible. Neither will a
church last long built on a part of the Bible. You have
noticed, I suppose, that as soon as a man begins to give up
the Bible he is apt to preach in some hall, and he has an
audience while he lives, and when he dies the church dies.
If I thought that my church was built on a quarter of a
Bible, or a half of a Bible, or three quarters of a Bible, or
ninety-nine one hundredths of a Bible, I would expect it to

die when I die; but when I know it is built on the entire
Word of God, I know it will last two hundred years after
you and I sleep the last sleep. O the splendors of an orthodoxy which, with ten thousand hands and ten thousand
pulpits and ten thousand Christian churches, is trying to
save the world!

In Music Hall, Boston, for many years stood Theodore
Parker battling orthodoxy, giving it, as some supposed at
that time, its death wound. He was the most fascinating
man I ever heard or ever expect to hear, and I came out
from hearing him thinking, in my boyhood way, "Well,
that's the death of the Church." On that same street, and
not far from being opposite, stood Park Congregational
Church, called by its enemies "Hell-fire Corner." Theodore
Parker died, and his church died with him; or, if it is in
existence, it is so small you cannot see it with the naked
eye. Park Congregational Church still stands on "Hell-fire
Corner," thundering away the magnificent truths of this
glorious orthodoxy just as though Theodore Parker had
never lived. All that Boston, or Brooklyn, or New York, or
the world ever got that is worth having came through the
wide aqueduct of orthodoxy from the throne of God.

Behold the splendors of character built by orthodoxy.
Who had the greatest human intellect the world ever knew?
Paul. In physical stature insignificant; in mind, head, and
shoulders above all the giants of the age. Orthodox from
scalp to heel. Who was the greatest poet the ages ever saw,
acknowledged to be so both by infidels and Christians?
John Milton, seeing more without eyes than anybody else
ever saw with eyes. Orthodox from scalp to heel. Who
was the greatest reformer the world has ever seen? so acknowledged by infidels as well as by Christians. Martin
Luther. Orthodox from scalp to heel.

THE CERTITUDES.

O man, believing in an entire Bible, where did you come
from? Answer: "I descended from a perfect parentage in

Paradise, and Jehovah breathed into my nostrils the breath of life. I am a son of God." O man, believing in a half-and-half Bible—believing in a Bible in spots, where did you come from? Answer. "It is all uncertain; in my ancestral line away back there was an orang-outang and a tadpole and a polywog, and it took millions of years to get me evoluted." O man, believing in a Bible in spots, where are you going to when you quit this world? Answer. "Going into a great to be, so on into the great somewhere, and then I shall pass through on to the great anywhere, and I shall probably arrive in the nowhere." *That is where I thought you would fetch up.* O man, believing in an entire Bible, and believing with all your heart, where are you going to when you leave this world? Answer: "I am going to my Father's house ; I am going into the companionship of my loved ones who have gone before ; I am going to leave all my sins, and I am going to be with God and like God forever and forever." Oh, the glorious certitudes, certainties of orthodoxy!

"Where shall I go?" said a dying Hindoo to the Brahmitic priest to whom he had given money to pray for his salvation. "Where shall I go after I die?" The Brahmitic priest said · "You will first of all go into a holy quadruped." "But," said the dying Hindoo, "where shall I go then?" "Then you shall go into a singing bird." "But," said the dying Hindoo, "where then shall I go?" "Then," said the Brahmitic priest, "you will go into a beautiful flower." The dying Hindoo threw up his arms in an agony of solicitation as he said : "But *where shall I go last of all?*" Thank God this Bible tells the Hindoo, tells you, tells me, not where shall I go to-day, not where shall I go to-morrow, not where shall I go next year, but where shall I go last of all !

CONTRASTED DEATH-BEDS.

Those who deny the Bible, or deny any part of it, never die well. They either go out in darkness or they go out in silence portentous. You may gather up all the biographies

that have come forth since the art of printing was invented,
and I challenge you to show me a triumphant death of a
man who rejected the Scriptures, or rejected any part of
them. Here I make *a great wide avenue.* On the one side
I put the death-beds of those who believe in an entire Bible.
On the other side of that avenue I put the death-beds of
those who reject part of the Bible, or all of the Bible. Now,
take my arm and let us pass through this dividing avenue.
Look off upon the right side. Here are the death-beds on
the right side of this avenue. " Victory through our Lord
Jesus Christ !" " Free grace !" " Glory, glory !" " I am
sweeping through the gates washed in the blood of the
Lamb !" " The chariots are coming !" "I mount, I fly !"
" Wings, wings !" " They are coming for me !" " Peace, be
still !" Alfred Cookman's death-bed, Richard Cecil's death-
bed, Commodore Foote's death-bed. Your father's death-
bed, your mother's death-bed, your sister's death-bed, your
child's death-bed. Ten thousand radiant, songful death-beds
of those who believed an entire Bible.

Now, take my arm and let us go through that avenue,
and look off upon the other side. No smile of hope. No shout
of triumph. No face supernaturally illumined. Those who
reject any part of the Bible never die well. No beckoning
for angels to come. No listening for the celestial escort.
Without any exception they go out of the world because
they are pushed out ; while on the other hand the list of those
who believed in an entire Bible and went out of the world in
triumph is a list so long it seems interminable. O ! is not that
a splendid influence, this orthodoxy, which makes that which
must otherwise be the most dreadful hour of life—the last
hour—positively paradisaical ?

STAND BY THE OLD PATHS.

" Ask for the old paths, walk therein, and ye shall find
rest for your souls " But follow this crusade against any
part of the Bible, and first of all you will give up Genesis,
which is as true as Matthew ; then you will give up all the

historical parts of the Bible , then after a while you will give up the miracles ; then you will find it convenient to give up the Ten Commandments , and then after a while you will wake up in a fountainless, rockless, treeless desert swept by everlasting sirocco.   If you are laughed at, you can afford to be laughed at, for standing by the Bible just as God has given it to you and miraculously preserved it.

Do not jump overboard from the stanch old Great Eastern of old-fashioned orthodoxy until there is something ready to take you up stronger than the fantastic yawl which has painted on the side "Advanced Thought," and which leaks at the prow and leaks at the stern, and has a steel pen for one oar and a glib tongue for the other oar, and now tips over this way and then tips over that way, until you do not know whether the passengers will land in the breakers of despair or on the sinking sand of infidelity and atheism.

I am in full sympathy with the advancements of our time, but this world will never advance a single inch beyond this old Bible.   God was just as capable of dictating the truth to the prophets and apostles as He is capable of dictating the truth to these modern apostles and prophets.   God has not learned anything in a thousand years.   He knew just as much when He gave the first dictation as the last dictation   So I will stick to the old paths.   Naturally a sceptic, and preferring new things to old, I never so much as now felt the truth of the entire Bible, especially as I see into what spectacular imbecility men rush when they try to chop up the Scriptures with the meat-axe of their own preferences, now calling upon philosophy, now calling on the Church, now calling on God, now calling on the devil.   I prefer the thick, warm robe of the old religion—old as God—the robe which has kept so many warm amid the cold pilgrimage of this life and amid the chills of death.   The old robe rather than the thin, uncertain gauze offered us by these wiseacres who *believe the Bible in spots.*

CHAPTER V.

Theory of a Posthumous Opportunity.

[Next in enormity to HIGHER CRITICISM is the fallacious expectation of "A SECOND CHANCE," or a POSTHUMOUS OPPORTUNITY of Salvation ; perhaps the more mischievous device of Satan.—[EDITOR].

" If the tree fall toward the south, or toward the north, in the place where the tree falleth, there it shall be."—ECCLES. 11 : 3.

HERE we have figuratively announced the orthodox doctrine of two destinies Palace and penitentiary. Palace with gates on all sides through which all may enter and live on celestial luxuries world without end, and all for the knocking and the asking. A palace grander than if all the Alhambras and the Versailles and the Windsor castles and the Winter Gardens and the imperial abodes of all the earth were heaved up into one architectural glory. At the other end of the universe a penitentiary where men who want their sins can have them. The first of no use unless you have the last. Brooklyn and New York would be better places to live in with Raymond Street jail and the Tombs and Sing Sing, and all the small-pox hospitals emptied on us than heaven would be if there were no hell.

Thomas Paine and George Whitefield, Jezebel and Mary Lyon, Nero and Charles Wesley, Charles Guiteau and James A. Garfield, John Wilkes Booth and Abraham Lincoln—all in glory together! All the innocent men, women, and children who were massacred, side by side with their murderers. If we are all coming out at the same destiny, without regard to character, then it is true I turn away from such a debauched heaven Against that cauldron of piety and blasphemy, philanthropy and assassination, self-sacrifice and

157

beastliness, I place the two destinies of the Bible forever and forever and forever apart.

PAIN DOES NOT CURE.

Common-sense, as well as revelation, declares that such an expectation is chimerical. You say that the impenitent man having got into the next world and seeing the disaster will, as a result of that disaster, turn, the pain the cause of his reformation. But you can find ten thousand instances in this world of men who have done wrong and distress overtook them suddenly. Did the distress cure them? No, they went right on.

Pain does not correct. Suffering does not reform. Take up the printed reports of the prisons of the United States, and you will find that the vast majority of the incarcerated have been there before, some of them four, five, six times. What is true in one sense is true in all senses, and will forever be so, and yet men are expecting in the next world purgatorial rejuvenation. With a million illustrations all working the other way in this world, people are expecting that distress in the next state will be salvatory, though they know that some men suffer here without any salutary consequence.

AN UNPROPITIOUS BEGINNING.

Furthermore, the prospect of a reformation in the next world is more improbable than a reformation here. In this world the life started with innocence of infancy. In the case supposed the other life will open with all the accumulated bad habits of many years upon him. Surely, it is easier to build a strong ship out of new timber than out of an old hulk that has been ground up in the breakers. If with innocence to start with in this life a man does not become godly, what prospect is there that in the next world, starting with sin, there would be a seraph evoluted? Surely the sculptor has more prospect of making a fine statue out of a block of pure white Parian marble than out of an old black rock seamed and cracked with the storms of a half century. Surely upon a clean, white sheet of paper it is easier to write a deed or a will than upon a sheet of paper all scribbled and blotted and torn from top to bottom. Yet men seem to think that, though the life that began here comparatively perfect turned out badly, the next life will succeed, though it starts with a dead failure.

TIME NO REFORMER.

"But," says some one, "I think we ought to have a chance in the next life, because this life is so short it allows only small opportunity." We hardly have time to turn around between cradle and tomb, the wood of the one almost touching the marble of the other. But do you know what made the ancient deluge a necessity? It was the longevity of the antediluvians. They were worse in the second century of their lifetime than in the first hundred years, and still worse in the third century, and still worse all the way on to seven, eight, and nine hundred years, and the earth had to be washed, and scrubbed, and soaked, and anchored clear out of sight for more than a month before it could be made fit for decent people to live in. Longevity never cures impenitency. All the pictures of Time represent him with a scythe to cut, but I never saw any picture of Time with a case of medicines to heal. Seneca says that Nero for the first five years of his public life was set up for an example of clemency and kindness, but his path all the way descended until at sixty-eight he became a suicide. If eight hundred years did not make antediluvians any better, but only made them worse, the ages of eternity could have no effect except prolongation of depravity.

UNPROPITIOUS SURROUNDINGS.

"But," says one, "in the future state evil surroundings will be withdrawn and elevated influences substituted, and hence expurgation, and sublimation, and glorification." But

the righteous, all their sins forgiven, have passed on into a
beatific state, and consequently the unsaved will be left
alone.   It cannot be expected that Dr. Duff, who exhausted
himself in teaching Hindoos the way to heaven, and Dr.
Abeel, who gave his life in the evangelization of China, and
Adoniram Judson, who toiled for the redemption of Burmah,
should be sent down by some celestial missionary society to
educate those who wasted all their earthly existence.   Evangelistic and missionary efforts are ended.   The entire kingdom of the morally bankrupt by themselves, where are the
salvatory influences to come from ?   Can one speckled and
bad apple in a barrel of diseased apples turn the other apples
good ?   Can those who are themselves down help others up?
Can those who have themselves failed in the business of the
soul pay the debts of spiritual insolvents ?   Can a million
wrongs make one right ?

A LAZARETTO WORLD.

Poneropolis was a city where King Philip of Thracia put
all the bad people of his kingdom.   If any man had opened
a primary school at Poneropolis, I do not think the parents
from other cities would have sent their children there.   Instead of amendment in the other world, all the associations,
now that the good are evolved, will be degenerating and downward.   You would not want to send a man to a cholera or
yellow-fever hospital for his health; and the great lazaretto
of the next world, containing the diseased and plague-struck,
will be a poor place for moral recovery.   If the surroundings
in this world were crowded with temptation, the surroundings
in the next world, after the righteous have passed up and on,
will be a thousand per cent more crowded with temptation.

The Count of Chateaubriand made his little son sleep at
night on the top of a castle turret, where the winds howled
and where spectres were said to haunt the place ; and while
the mother and sisters almost died with fright, the son tells
us that the process gave him nerves that could not tremble
and a courage that never faltered.   But I don't think that

towers of darkness and the spectral world swept by Sirocco and Euroclydon will ever fit one for the land of eternal sunshine. I wonder what is the curriculum of that college of Inferno, where, after proper preparation by the sins of this life, the candidate enters, passing on from Freshman class of depravity to Sophomore of abandonment, and from Sophomore to Junior, and from Junior to Senior, and day of graduation comes, and with diploma signed by Satan, the president, and other professorial demoniacs, attesting that the candidate has been long enough under their drill, he passes up to enter heaven ! Pandemonium a preparative course for heavenly admission ! Ah, my friends, Satan and his cohorts have fitted uncounted multitudes for ruin, but never fitted one soul for happiness.

A DEMORALIZING THEORY.

Furthermore, it would not be safe for this world if men had another chance in the next. If it had been announced that however wickedly a man might act in this world he could fix it up all right in the next, society would be terribly demoralized, and the human race demolished in a few years. The fear that if we are bad and unforgiven here it will not be well for us in the next existence is the chief influence that keeps civilization from rushing back to semi-barbarism, and semi-barbarism from rushing into midnight savagery, and midnight savagery from extinction, for it is the astringent impression of all nations, Christian and heathen, that there is no future chance for those who have wasted this.

Multitudes of men who are kept within bounds would say, "Go to now! Let me get all out of this life there is in it. Come, gluttony, and inebriation, and uncleanness, and revenge, and all sensualities, and wait upon me ! My life may be somewhat shortened in this world by dissoluteness, but that will only make heavenly indulgence on a larger scale the sooner possible. I will overtake the saints at last, and will enter the Heavenly Temple only a little later than those who behaved themselves here. I will on my way

to heaven take a little wider excursion than those who were
on earth pious, and I shall go to heaven *viâ* Gehenna and
viâ Sheol." Another chance in the next world means free
license and wild abandonment in this.

Suppose you were a party in an important case at law,
and you knew from consultation with judges and attorneys
that it would be tried twice, and the first trial would be of
little importance, but that the second would decide everything, for which trial would you make the most preparation,
for which retain the ablest attorneys, for which be most
anxious about the attendance of witnesses? You would put
all the stress upon the second trial, all the anxiety, all the
expenditure, saying, "The first is nothing, the last is everything." Give the race assurance of a second and more important trial in the subsequent life, and all the preparation
for eternity would be *post-mortem*, post-funeral, post-sepul-
chral, and the world with one jerk be pitched off into im-
piety and godlessness.

AN INFIDEL'S PREMONITION.

Voltaire, while rejecting the whole Bible, did not seem
to be so very well persuaded of the non-existence of perdition, for when his friend wrote to him, "I have found out
for sure that there is no hell, Voltaire replied, "I congratu-
late you ; *I am not so fortunate* as you are."

SUFFICIENT CHANCES IN LIFE.

Furthermore, let me ask why a chance should be given
in the next world if we have refused innumerable chances in
this? Suppose you give a banquet, and you invite a vast
number of friends, but one man declines to come, or treats
your invitation with indifference. You in the course of
twenty years give twenty banquets, and the same man is invited to them all, and treats them all in the same obnoxious
way. After a while you remove to another house, larger
and better, and you again invite your friends, but send no

invitation to the man who declined or neglected the other
invitations. Are you to blame? Has he a right to expect
to be invited after all the indignities he has done you? God
in this world has invited us all to the banquet of His grace.
He invited us by His Providence and His Spirit three hundred and sixty-five days of every year since we knew our
right hand from our left. If we declined it every time, or
treated the invitation with indifference, and gave twenty or
forty or fifty years of indignity on our part toward the Ban-
queter, and at last He spreads the banquet in a more luxuriant and kingly place, amid the heavenly gardens, have we
a right to expect Him to invite us again, and have we a right
to blame Him if He does not invite us?

THE GOSPEL SHIP.

If twelve gates of salvation stood open twenty years or
fifty years for our admission, and at the end of that time
they are closed, can we complain of it and say, " These gates
ought to be open again. Give us another chance "? If the
steamer is to sail for Hamburg, and we want to get to Germany by that line, and we read in every evening and every
morning newspaper that it will sail on a certain day, for two
weeks we have that advertisement before our eyes, and then
we go down to the docks fifteen minutes after it has shoved
off into the stream and say : " Come back. Give me another
chance. It is not fair to treat me in this way. Swing up
to the dock again, and throw out the planks, and let me
come on board." Such behavior would invite arrest as a
madman.

And if, after the Gospel ship has lain at anchor before
our eyes for years and years and years, and all the benign
voices of earth and heaven have urged us to get on board,
as she might sail away any moment, and after a while she
sails without us, is it common-sense to expect her to come
back? You might as well go out on the Highlands at Nev-
ersink and call to the Aurania after she has been three days
out, and expect her to return, as to call back an opportunity

for heaven when it once has sped away. All heaven offered
us as a gratuity, and for a lifetime we refuse to take it, and
then rush on the bosses of Jehovah's buckler demanding another chance. There ought to be, there can be, there will
be, no such thing as posthumous opportunity. Thus our
common-sense agrees with my text—" If the tree fall toward
the south or toward the north, in the place where the tree falleth, there it shall be."

You see that this idea lifts this world up from an unimportant way station to a platform of stupendous issues, and
makes all eternity whirl around this hour. But one trial for
which all the preparation must be made in this world, or
never made at all. That piles up all the emphases and all
the climaxes and all the destinies into life here. No other
chance ! O how that augments the value and importance
of this chance.

ALEXANDER'S LIGHT.

Alexander with his army used to surround a city, and
then would lift a great light in token to the people that, if
they surrendered before that light went out, all would be
well ; but if once the light went out, then the battering-rams
would swing against the wall, and demolition and disaster
would follow. Well, all we need to do for our present and
everlasting safety is to make surrender to Christ, the King
and Conquerer, surrender of our hearts, surrender of our
lives, surrender of everything. And He keeps a great light
burning, light of Gospel invitation, light kindled with the
wood of the cross and flaming up against the dark night of
our sin and sorrow. Surrender while that great light continues to burn, for after it goes out, there will be no other
opportunity of making peace with God through our Lord
Jesus Christ Talk of another chance ' Why, this is a supernal chance '

Tell it to all points of the compass. Tell it to night and
day. Tell it to all earth and heaven. Tell it to all centuries, all ages, all millenniums, that we have such a magnifi-

cent chance in this world that we need no other chance in the next.

A DREAM.

I am in the burnished Judgment Hall of the Last Day. A great white throne is lifted, but the Judge has not yet taken it. While we are waiting for His arrival I hear immortal spirits in conversation. "What are you waiting here for?" says a soul that went up from Madagascar to a soul that ascended from America. The latter says: "I came from America, where forty years I heard the Gospel preached and Bible read, and from the prayer I learned in infancy at my mother's knee until my last hour I had Gospel advantage, but for some reason I did not make the Christian choice, and I am here waiting for the Judge to give me a new trial and another chance." "Strange," says the other ; "I had but one Gospel call in Madagascar, and I accepted it, and I do not need another chance."

"Why are you here?" says one who on earth had feeblest intellect to one who had great brain, and silvery tongue, and marvelous influence. The latter responds: "Oh, I knew more than my fellows. I mastered libraries, and had learned titles from colleges, and my name was a synonym for eloquence and power. And yet I neglected my soul, and I am here waiting for a new trial." "Strange," says the one of the feeble earthly capacity: "I knew but little of worldly knowledge, but I knew Christ, and made Him my partner, and I have no need of another chance."

ETERNAL PUNISHMENT.

While I am talking to a young man about his soul he tells me: "I do not become a Christian because I do not believe there is any hell at all."

Ah! don't you? Do all the people, of all beliefs and no belief at all, of good morals and bad morals, go straight to a happy heaven? Do the holy and the debauched have the same destination? At midnight, in a hallway, the owner of a house and a burglar meet each other, and they both fire, and both are wounded, but the burglar died in five minutes and the owner of the house lives a week after. Will the burglar be at the gate of heaven waiting when the house-owner comes in? Will the debauchee and the libertine go right in among the families of heaven? *I wonder if Herod is playing on the banks of the River of Life with the children he massacred.* I wonder if Charles Guiteau and John Wilkes Booth are up there shooting at a mark. I do not now controvert it, although I must say that for such a miserable heaven I have no admiration. But the Bible does not say, "Believe in perdition and be saved." Because all are saved, according to your theory, that ought not to keep you from loving and serving Christ. Do not refuse to come ashore because all the others, according to your theory, are going to get ashore.

You may have a different theory about chemistry, about astronomy, about the atmosphere, from that which others adopt, but you are not therefore hindered from action. Because your theory of light is different from others, you do not refuse to open your eyes. Because your theory of air is different you do not refuse to breathe. Because your theory about the stellar system is different, you do not refuse to acknowledge the North Star. Why should the fact that your theological theories are different, hinder you from acting upon what you know?

HOW FAR IT IS TO HELL.

"Can you tell me how far it is to hell?" said a young man as, one Sunday on horseback, he dashed past a good Christian deacon. At the next turn in the road the horse threw the scoffing rider, and he was dead He wanted to know how far it was to hell, and found out without the deacon's telling him.

So thou art mounted on a swift steed, whose hoofs strike

fire from the pavement as he dashes past, and you cry out:
" How far is it to ruin?"   I answer: " Near—very near!"

> " Perhaps this very day
>   Thy last accepted time may be;
> Oh, should'st thou grieve Him now away,
>   Then hope may never beam on thee!"

Oh, that my Lord God would bring you now to see your
sin and to fly from it; and your duty, and help you to do it,
so that when the last great terror of earth shall spread its
two black wings, and clutch with its bloody talons for thy
soul, it cannot hurt thee, for that thou art safe in the warm
dove-cot of a Saviour's mercy!

> " Come in! come in!
> Eternal glory shalt thou win."

I am talking with one thoughtful about his soul, who has
lately travelled through New England and passed the night
at Andover.   He says to me: " I cannot believe that in this
life the destiny is irrevocably fixed; I think there will be
another opportunity of repentance after death."   I say to
him: My brother, what has that to do with you?   Don't
you realize that the man who waits for another chance after
death when he has a good chance before death is a stark
fool?   Had not you better take the plank that is thrown to
you now and head for shore, rather than wait for a plank
that may by invisible hands be thrown to you after you are
dead?   Do as you please, but as for myself, with pardon for
all my sins offered me now and all the joys of time and eternity offered me now, I instantly take them rather than run
the risk of such other chance as wise men think they can
peel off or twist out of a Scripture passage that has for all
the Christian centuries been interpreted another way.

You admit you are all broken up, one decade of your life
gone by, two decades, three decades, four decades, a half
century, perhaps three quarters of a century gone.   The hour-
hand and the minute-hand of your clock of life are almost

parallel, and soon it will be twelve and your day ended. Clear discouraged are you? I admit it is a sad thing to give all of our lives that are worth anything to sin and the devil, and then at last *make God a present of a first-rate corpse.*

From many a deathbed I have seen the hands thrown up in deploration something like this: "My life has been wasted. I had good mental faculties, and fine social position, and great opportunity, but through worldliness and neglect all has gone to waste save these few remaining hours. I now accept of Christ, and shall enter heaven through His mercy but alas! alas! that when I might have entered the haven of eternal rest with a full cargo, and been greeted by the waving hands of a multitude in whose salvation I had borne a blessed part, I must confess I now enter the harbor of heaven on broken pieces of the ship!"

A VERY STOUT ROPE.

O man astray, God help you! You know that sometimes a rope-maker will take very small threads and wind them together, until after a while they become ship cable. And I am going to take some very small delicate threads and wind them together until they make a very stout rope. I will take all the memories of the marriage day—a thread of laughter, a thread of light, a thread of music, a thread of banqueting, a thread of congratulation, and I twist them together and I have one strand. Then I take a thread of the hour of the first advent in your house, a thread of the darkness that preceded, and a thread of the light that followed; and a thread of the beautiful scarf that little child used to wear when she bounded out at eventide to greet you; and then a thread of the beautiful dress in which you laid her away for the resurrection; and then I twist all these threads together, and I have another strand. Then I take a thread of the scarlet robe of a suffering Christ, and a thread of the white raiment of your loved ones before the throne, and a string of the harp cherubic, and a string of the harp seraphic, and I twist them all together, and I have a third

strand. " Oh," you say, " either strand is enough to hold
fast a world !" No : I will take these strands and I will twist
them together, and one end of that rope I will fasten, not
to the communion table, for it shall be removed ; not to a
pillar of the organ, for that will crumble in the ages; but I
wind it round and round the cross of a sympathizing Christ,
and having fastened one end of the rope to the cross, I
throw the other end to you. Lay hold of it ! Pull for your
life ! Pull for heaven !

CHAPTER VI.

The Plague of Profanity.

Next to denying that there is a God is profaning his Name; and the worst kind of profanity is blasphemy or cursing God. This was " the head and front of the offending" of Job's wife.—EDITOR.

"CURSE God and die!" Job knew right well that swearing would not cure one of the tumors of his agonized body, would not bring back one of his destroyed camels, would not restore one of his dead children. He knew that profanity would only make the pain more unbearable, and the poverty more distressing, and the bereavement more excruciating. But judging from the profanity abroad in our day, you might come to the conclusion that there was some great advantage to be reaped from profanity.

Blasphemy is one of the ten plagues which have smitten our great cities. You hear it in every direction. The drayman swearing at his cart, the sewing girl imprecating the tangled skein, the accountant cursing the long line of troublesome figures. Swearing at the store, swearing on the loft, swearing in the cellar, swearing on the street, swearing in the factory. Children swear. Men swear. Ladies swear! Swearing from the rough calling on the Almighty in the low restaurant, clear up to the reckless "O Lord!" of a glittering drawing-room; and the one is as much blasphemy as the other.

It was no profanity when James A. Garfield, in the Washington depot, cried out, "My God, what does this mean?" But I am speaking now of the triviality and of the recklessness with which the name of God is sometimes abused. The whole land is cursed with it.

A gentleman coming from the Far West sat in the car day after day behind two persons who were indulging in profanity, and he made up his mind that he would make *a record of their profanities,* and at the end of two days several sheets of paper were covered with these imprecations, and at the close of the journey he handed the manuscript to one of the persons in front of him. "Is it possible," said the man, "that we have uttered so many profanities the last few days?" "It is," replied the gentleman. "Then," said the man who had taken the manuscript, "I will never swear again."

But it is a comparatively unimportant thing if a man makes record of our improprieties of speech. The more memorable consideration is that every oath uttered has a record in the book of *God's remembrance!*

IS IT MANLY?

That this habit grows in the community is seen in the fact that young people think it manly to swear. Little children, hardly able to walk straight on the street, yet have enough distinctness of utterance to let you know that they are damning their own souls, or damning the souls of others.

Between sixteen and twenty years of age there is apt to come a time when a young man is as much ashamed of not being able to swear gracefully as he is of the dizziness of his first cigar. There are young men who walk in an atmosphere of imprecation—oaths on their lips, under their tongues, nesting in their shock of hair. They abstain from it in the elegant drawing-room, but the street and the club-house ring with their profanities. They have no regard for God, although they have great respect for the ladies! My young brother, there is no manliness in that. The most ungentlemanly thing a man can do is to swear.

Fathers foster this great crime. There are parents who are very cautious not to swear in the presence of their children; in a moment of sudden anger, they look around to see if the children are present, then they indulge in this habit. Do you not know, O father, that your child is aware of the fact that you swear? He overheard you in the next room, or some one has informed him of your habit. He is practising now.

The crime is also fostered by master-mechanics, boss-carpenters, those who are at the head of men in hat-factories, and in dock-yards, and at the head of great business establishments. When you go down to look at the work of the scaffolding, and you find it is not done right, what do you say? Employers swear, and that makes so many employés swear.

The habit also comes from *infirmity of temper.* There are a good many people who, when they are at peace, have righteousness of speech, but when angered they blaze with imprecation. I knew of a man who excused himself for the habit, saying : " I only swear once in a great while. I must do that just to clear myself out."

The habit comes also from the profuse use of bywords. The transition from a byword to imprecation and profanity is not a very large transition. It is " my stars !" and "mercy on me !" and " good gracious !" and " by George !" and by Jove !" and you go on with that a little while, and then you swear. *The habit is creeping up* into the highest styles of society. Women have no patience with flat and unvarnished profanity. They will order a man out of the parlor for indulging in blasphemy, and yet you will sometimes find them with fairy fan to the lip, and under chandeliers which bring no blush to their cheek, taking on their lips the holiest of names in utter triviality.

Why my friends, the English language is comprehensive and capable of expressing all shades of feeling and every degree of energy, without any profanity—the God-honored Anglo-Saxon in which Milton sang, and John Bunyan dreamed.

This country is pre-eminent for blasphemy. A man travelling in Russia was supposed to be a clergyman. " Why do you take me to be a clergyman ?" said the man. " Oh," said the Russian, " all other Americans swear. Does it not seem to you that the abominations of this earth have gone far enough? Were there ever before so many fists lifted toward God, telling Him to come on if He dare?

BLASPHEMY ABROAD!

What towering profanity! Would it be possible for anyone to calculate the numbers of times that the name of the Almighty God and of Jesus Christ are every day taken irreverently on the lips? So common has blasphemy become, that the public mind and public ear have got used to it, and a blasphemer goes up and down this country in his lectures defying the plain law against blasphemy, and there is not a mayor in America that has backbone enough to interfere with him save one, and that, the mayor of Toronto. Profane swearing is as much forbidden by the law as theft or arson or murder, yet who executes it? Profanity is worse than theft or arson or murder, for these crimes are attacks on humanity—that is, an attack on God.

When the Mohammedan finds a piece of paper he cannot read, he puts it aside very cautiously for fear the name of God may be on it. That is one extreme. We go to the other.

The crime rolls on, up through parlors, up through chandeliers with lights all ablaze, and through the pictured corridors of club-rooms, etc., out through busy exchanges where oath meets oath, and down through all the haunts of sin, mingling with the rattling dice and cracking billiard-balls, and the laughter of her who hath forgotten the covenant of her God; and round the city, and round the continent, and round the earth a seething, boiling surge flings its hot spray into the face of a long-suffering God. And the ship-captain damns his crew, and the merchant damns his clerks, and the master-builder damns his men, and the hack-driver damns his horse; and the traveller damns the stone that bruises his foot, or the mud that soils his shoes, or the defective time-piece that gets him too late to the rail train. I arraign profane swearing and blasphemy, two names for the same thing, as being one of the gigantic crimes of this

land. Do you not know also that the trivial use of God's
name results in perjury?

Make the name of God a foot-ball in the community, and
it has no power when in court-room and in legislative assembly it is employed in solemn adjuration. See the way sometimes they administer the oath: " S'help you God—kiss the
book!" Why is it that so often jurors render unaccountable verdicts, and judges give unaccountable charges, and
useless railroad schemes pass in our State capitals, and there
are most unjust changes made in tariffs—tariff lifted from
one thing and put upon another? May not this be the
why?

May not this also be the reason why smuggling, which is
always a violation of the oath, becomes in some circles a
grand joke? You say to a man: " How is it possible for you
to sell these goods so very cheap? I can't understand it."
" Ah!" he replies, with a twinkle of the eye, " the Custom
House tariff of these goods isn't as much as it might be."

WHAT IS THE CURE?

It is a mighty habit. Men have struggled for years to
get over it. An aged man was in the delirium of a fever.
He had for many years lived a most upright life, and was
honored in all the community, but when he came into the
delirium of this fever he was full of imprecation and profanity, and they could not understand it. After he came
to his right reason he explained it. He said, " When I was
a young man I was very profane. I conquered the habit,
but I had to struggle all through life. You haven't for
forty years heard me say an improper word, but it has been
an awful struggle. *The tiger is chained*, but he is alive yet."

If you would get rid of this habit, I want you, my
friends, to dwell upon the uselessness of it. Did a volley of
oaths ever start a heavy load? Did they ever extirpate
meanness from a customer? Did they ever collect a bad
debt? Did they ever cure a toothache? Did they ever
stop the twinge of the rheumatism? Did they ever help

you forward one step in the right direction? Come now, tell me, ye who have had the most experience in this habit, how much have you made out of it? Five thousand dollars in all your life? No. One thousand? No. One hundred? No. One dollar? No. One cent? No. If the habit be so utterly useless, away with it.

Think too how the habit grows. You start with a small oath, you will come to the large oath. I saw a man die with an oath between his teeth. Voltaire only gradually came to his tremendous imprecation; but the habit grew on him until in the last moment, supposing Christ stood at the bed, he exclaimed, "Crush the wretch! Crush the wretch!"

Remember also, for the cure of this habit, that it arouses God's indignation. Dionysius used to have a cave in which his culprits were incarcerated, and he listened at the top of that cave and he could hear every groan, he could hear every sigh, and he could hear every whisper of those who were imprisoned. He was a tyrant. God is not a tyrant; but He bends over this world and He hears everything— every voice of praise—every voice of imprecation. He hears it all. The oaths seem to die on the air, but *they have eternal echo.* They come back from the ages to come. Listen! listen! God very often shows what He thinks, but for the most part the fatality is hushed up. Families keep them still to avoid the horrible conspicuity. Physicians suppress them through professional confidence. It is a very, very, very long roll that contains the names of those who died with blasphemies on their lips.

A few summers ago, among the Adirondacks, I met the funeral procession of a man who, two days before, had *fallen under a flash of lightning,* while boasting, after a Sunday of work in the fields, that he had cheated God out of one day anyhow, and the man who worked with him on the same Sabbath is still living, but a helpless invalid, under the same flash.

INSTANCES OF AWFUL PUNISHMENT.

There is not a sin in all the catalogue that is so often peremptorily and suddenly punished in this world as the sin of profanity. At New Brunswick, N. J , just before I went there as a student, this occurrence took place in front of the college. On the rail-track a man had uttered a horrid oath. He saw not that the rail-train was coming. The locomotive struck him and instantly dashed his life out. No mystery about it. He cursed God and died. In a cemetery in Sullivan County, in this State, are eight headstones in a line, and all alike, and these are the facts : In 1861 diphtheria raged in the village, and a physician was remarkably successful in curing his patients. So confident did he become that he boasted that no case of diphtheria could stand before him, and finally defied Almighty God to produce a case of diphtheria that he could not cure. His youngest child soon after took the disease and died, and one child after another, until all the eight had died of diphtheria. The blasphemer challenged Almighty God, and God accepted the challenge.

But I come later down and give you a fact that is proved by scores of witnesses. In August of 1886 a man got provoked at the continued drought and the ruin of his crops, and in the presence of his neighbors *he cursed God*, saying that he would cut His heart out if He would come, calling Him a liar and a coward, and flashing a knife. And while he was speaking his lower jaw dropped, smoke issued from mouth and nostrils, and the heat of his body was so intense it drove back those who would come near. Scores of people visited the scene and saw the blasphemer in awful process of expiring.

At Catskill, N. Y., a group of men stood in a blacksmith's shop during a violent thunder-storm. There came a crash of thunder and some of the men trembled. One man said: " Why, I don't see what you are afraid of. I am not afraid to go out in front of the shop and defy the Almighty. I am not afraid of the lightning." And he laid a wager on the subject, and he went out, and he shook his fist at the heavens, crying, "*Strike, if you dare!*" and instantly he fell under a bolt. What destroyed him? Any mystery about it? Oh, no. He cursed God and died.

Years ago, in a Pittsburgh prison, two men were talking about the Bible and Christianity, and one of them, Thompson by name, applied to Jesus Christ a very low and villainous epithet, and as he was uttering it, he fell. A physician was called, but no help could be given. After a day lying with distended pupils and palsied tongue, he passed out of this world.

On the road from Margate to Ramsgate, England, you may find a rough monument with the inscription, "A boy was struck dead here, while in the act of swearing"

In Scotland a club assembled every week for purposes of wickedness, and there was a competition as to which could use the most horrid oath, and the man who succeeded was to be president of the club. The competition went on. A man uttered an oath which confounded all his comrades, and he was made president of the club. His tongue began to swell, and it protruded from the mouth, and he could not draw it in, and he died, and the physicians said: "This is the strangest thing we ever saw: we never saw any account in the books like unto it: we can't understand it." I understand it. He cursed God and died.

Oh, my brother, God will not allow this sin to go unpunished. There are styles of writing with manifold sheets, so that a man writing on one leaf writes clear through ten, fifteen, or twenty sheets, and so every profanity we utter goes right down through the leaves of the book of God's remembrance.

CHAPTER VII.

Lying, Dishonesty, and Fraud.

"A certain man named Ananias, with Sapphira his wife, sold a possession; . . . . and the young men came in, and found her dead, and carrying her forth, buried her by her husband."—Acts 5: 1-10,

A WELL-MATCHED pair, alike in ambition and in falsehood, Ananias and Sapphira. They wanted a reputation for great beneficence, and they sold all their property, pretending to put the entire procéeds in the charity fund while they put much of it in their own pocket. There was no necessity that they give all their property away, but they wanted the reputation of so doing. Ananias first lied about it and dropped down dead. Then Sapphira lied about it and she dropped down dead. The two fatalities a warning to all ages of the danger of sacrificing the truth.

There are thousands of ways of telling a lie. A man's whole life may be a falsehood, and yet never with his lips may he falsify once. There is a way of uttering falsehood by look, by manner as well as by lip. There are persons who are guilty of dishonesty of speech and then afterward say "may be;" call it a white lie, when no lie is that color. The whitest lie ever told was as black as perdition. There are those so given to dishonesty of speech that they do not know when they are lying.

With some it is an acquired sin, and with others it is a natural infirmity. There are those whom you will recognize as born liars. Their whole life, from cradle to grave, is filled up with vice of speech. Misrepresentation and prevarication are as natural to them as the infantile diseases, and are a sort of *moral croup or spiritual scarlatina.* Then there are those who in after life have opportunities of developing this

evil, and they go from deception to deception, and from
class to class, until they are regularly graduated liars.

At times the air in our cities is filled with falsehood, and
lies cluster around the mechanic's hammer, blossom on the
merchant's yardstick, and sometimes sit in the door of
churches. They are called by some, fabrication, and they
are called by some, fiction. You might call them subterfuge
or deceit, or romance, or fable, or misrepresentation, or delusion; but as I know nothing to be gained by covering up a
God-defying sin with a lexicographer's blanket, I shall call
them in plainest vernacular, lies. They may be divided into
agricultural, commercial, mechanical, and social.

AGRICULTURAL FALSEHOODS.

There is something in the presence of natural objects
that has a tendency to make one pure. The trees never
issue false stock. The wheat fields are always honest. Rye
and oats never move out in the night, not paying for the
place they occupy. Corn shocks never make false assign-
ment. Mountain brooks are always current. The gold of
the wheat fields is never counterfeit. But while the tendency of agricultural life is to make one honest, honesty is
not the characteristic of all who come to the city markets
from the country districts. You hear the creaking of the dishonest farm-wagon in almost every street of our great cities,
a farm-wagon in which there is not one honest spoke or one
truthful rivet from tongue to tail-board. Again and again
has domestic economy in our great cities foundered on the
farmer's firkin. When New York and Brooklyn and Cincinnati and Boston sit down and weep over their sins, Westchester and Long Island counties and all the country districts ought to sit down and weep over theirs.

The tendency in all rural districts is to suppose that sins
and transgressions cluster in our great cities; but citizens
and merchants long ago learned that it is not safe to calculate from the character of the apples on the top of the
farmer's barrel what is the character of the apples all the

way down toward the bottom. Many of our citizens and merchants have learned that it is always safe to see the farmer measure the barrel of beets. Milk cans are not always honest.

COMMERCIAL LIES.

There are those who apologize for deviations from the right and for practical deception by saying it is commercial custom. In other words, a lie by multiplication becomes a virtue.

There are large fortunes gathered in which there is not one drop of the sweat of unrequited toil, and not one spark of bad temper flashes from the bronze bracket, and there is not one drop of needlewoman's heart's blood on the crimson plush ; while there are other fortunes about which it may be said that on every door-knob and on every figure of the carpet, and on every wall there is *the mark of dishonor*. What if the hand wrung by toil and blistered until the skin comes off should be placed on the exquisite wall-paper, leaving its mark of blood —four fingers and a thumb ; or, if in the night the man should be aroused from his slumber again and again by his own conscience, getting himself up on elbow and crying out into the darkness, " Who is there ?"

You and I know that there are in commercial life those who are guilty of great dishonesties of speech. A merchant says : " I am selling these goods at less than cost." Is he getting for those goods a price inferior to that which he paid for them ? Then he has spoken the truth. Is he getting more ? Then he lies. A merchant says : " I paid $25 for this article." Is that the price he paid for it ? All right. But suppose he paid for it $23 instead of $25 ? Then he lies.

A man unrolls upon the counter a bale of handkerchiefs. The customer says : " Are these all silk ?" " Yes." " No cotton in them ?" " No cotton in them." Are those handkerchiefs all silk ? Then the merchant told the truth. Is there any cotton in them ? Then he lied. Moreover, he defrauds himself, for this customer coming in from Hempstead, or Yonkers, or Newark, will after a while find out that he has been defrauded, and the next time he comes to town and goes shopping, he will look up at that sign and say: "No, I wont go there, that's the place where I got those handkerchiefs." First, the merchant insulted God, and secondly, he picked his own pocket.

Who would take the responsibility of saying how many falsehoods were yesterday told by hardware men, and clothiers, and lumbermen, and tobacconists, and jewellers, and importers, and shippers, and dealers in furniture, and dealers in coal, and dealers in groceries? Lies about buckles, about saddles, about harness, about shoes, about hats, about coats, about shovels, about tongs, about forks, about chairs, about sofas, about horses, about lands, about everything.

BOTH SIDES THE COUNTER.

But there are just as many falsehoods before the counter as there are behind the counter. A customer comes in and asks: "How much is this article?" "It is five dollars." "I can get that for four somewhere else" Can he get it for four somewhere else, or did he say that just for the purpose of getting it cheap by depreciating the value of the goods? If so, he lied. There are just as many falsehoods before the counter as there are behind the counter.

MECHANICAL LIES.

Some mechanics say they will have the job done in ten days; they do not get it done before thirty. And then when a man becomes irritated and will not stand it any longer, then they go and work for him a day or two and keep the job along; and then some one else gets irritated and outraged and they go and work for that man and get him pacified, and then they go somewhere else. I believe they call that " nursing the job "'

Ah, my friends, how much dishonor such men would

save their souls if they would promise to do only that which they know they can do. "O!" they say, "it's of no importance; everybody expects to be deceived and disappointed." There is a voice of thunder sounding among the saws and the hammers and the shears saying: "All liars shall have their place in the lake that burns with fire and brimstone."

SOCIAL LIES.

How much of society is insincere. You hardly know what to believe. They send their regards; you do not exactly know whether it is an expression of the heart, or an external civility. They ask you to come to their house; you hardly know whether they really want you to come. We are all accustomed to take a discount off what we hear.

"Not at home" very often means too lazy to dress. I read of a lady who said she had told *her last fashionable lie.* There was a knock at her door and she sent word down, "Not at home." That night her husband said to her: Mrs. So-and-so is dead." "Is it possible?" she said. "Yes, and she died in great anguish of mind; she wanted to see you so very much; she had *something very important to disclose* to you in her last hour, and she sent three times to-day, but found you absent every time." Then this woman bethought herself that she had had a bargain with her neighbor that when the long-protracted sickness was about to come to an end, she would appear at her bedside and take the secret that was to be disclosed. And she had said she was " Not at home!"

Social life is struck through with insincerity. Some apologize for the fact that the furnace is out; they have not had any fire in it all winter. They apologize for the fare on their table; they never live any better. They decry their most luxuriant entertainment to win a shower of approval from you. They point at a picture on the wall as a work of one of the old masters. They say it is an heirloom in the family. It hung on the wall of a castle. A duke gave it to their grandfather. People that will lie about nothing else will lie about a picture. On small income we want the world to believe we are affluent, and society to-day is struck through with cheat and counterfeit and sham.

Society is so utterly askew in this matter that you seldom find a seller asking the price that he expects to get; he puts on a higher value than he proposes to receive, knowing that he will have to drop. And if he wants fifty, he asks seventy-five. And if he wants two thousand, he asks twenty-five hundred. To meet this the buyer says, "The fabric is defective; the style of goods is poor; I can get elsewhere a better article at a smaller price. It is out of fashion; it is damaged; it will fade; it will not wear well." After awhile the merchant, from over-persuasion or from desire to dispose of that particular stock of goods, says: "Well, take it at your own price," and the purchaser goes home with a light step, and calls into his private office his confidential friends, and chuckles while he tells how that for half price he got the goods. In other words, he lies, and is proud of it.

SHOPPING LIES.

Thousands of years ago Solomon discovered the tendency of buyers to depreciate goods. "It is naught, saith the buyer: but when he is gone his way, then he boasteth." (Proverbs 20: 14) It may seem to the world a sharp bargain, but the recording angel wrote down in the ponderous tomes of eternity. "Mr. So-and-so, doing business on Fulton Street, or Atlantic Street, or Broadway, or Chestnut Street, or State Street, or Mrs. So-and-so, keeping house on the Heights, or on the Hill, or on Beacon Street, or on Rittenhouse Square, told *one lie.*" And when people tell me at what a ruinously low price they purchased an article, it gives me more dismay than satisfaction. I know it means the bankruptcy and defalcation of men in many departments. The men who toil with the brain need full as much sympathy as those who toil with the hand. All business life is struck through with suspicion, and panics are the result of want of confidence.

May God extirpate from society all social lies and make every man to speak the truth of his neighbor. My friends, let us make our life correspond to what we are. Let us banish all deception from our behavior. Let us remember that the time comes when God will demonstrate before an assembled universe just what we are. The secret will come out. We may hide it while we live, but we cannot hide it when we die.

"O!" says some one, "the deception that I practice is so small it don't amount to anything." Ah! my friends, it does amount to a great deal. You say, "When I deceive it is only about a case of needles, or a box of buttons, or a row of pins." But the article may be so small you can put it in your vest pocket, yet the sin is as big as the pyramids, and the echo of your dishonor will reverberate through the mountains of eternity. There is *no such thing as a small sin.* They are all vast and stupendous, because they will all have to come under inspection in the Day of Judgment.

FRAUD AND DISHONESTY.

No man knows what he will do until he is tempted. There are thousands of men who have kept their integrity merely because they never have been tested. A man was elected treasurer of the State of Maine some years ago. He was distinguished for his honesty, usefulness and uprightness, but before one year had passed he had taken of the public funds for his own private use, and was hurled out of office in disgrace. Distinguished for virtue before. Distinguished for crime after. You can call over the names of men just like that, in whose honesty you had complete confidence, but placed in certain crises of temptation they went overboard.

Never so many temptations to scoundrelism as now. Not a law on the statute-book but has some back door through which a miscreant can escape. Ah! how many deceptions in the fabric of goods; so much plundering in commercial life, that if a man talk about living a life of complete commercial accuracy there are those who ascribe it to greenness and lack of tact   More need of honesty now than ever before, tried honesty, complete honesty, more than in those times when business was a plain affair, and woollens were woollens and silks were silks and men were men.

How many men do you suppose there are in commercial life who could say truthfully, " In all the sales I have ever made I have never overstated the value of goods ; in all the sales I have ever made I have never covered up an imperfection in the fabric ; of all the thousands of dollars I have ever made I have not taken one dishonest farthing" ?

I wish that *the words of George Peabody*, uttered in the hearing of the people of his native town—Danvers, Massachusetts—I wish that those words could be uttered in the hearing of all the young men throughout the land. He said :

" Though Providence has granted me unvaried and universal success in the pursuit of fortune in other lands, I am still in heart the humble boy who left yonder unpretending dwelling.   There is not a youth within the sound of my voice whose early opportunities and advantages are not very much greater than were my own, and I have since achieved *nothing that is impossible* to the most humble boy among you."

George Peabody's success in business was not more remarkable than his integrity and his great-hearted benevolence.   I pray upon you God's protecting and prosperous blessing.   I hope you may all make fortunes for time and fortunes for eternity.

Some day when you come out of your place of business, and you go to the Clearing-house, or the place of custom, or the bank, or your own home, as you come out of your place of business, just look up at the clock of old Trinity and see by the movement of the hands how your life is rapidly going away, and be reminded of the fact that before God's throne of inexorable judgment you must yet give account for what you have done since the day you sold the first yard of cloth or the first pound of sugar.

MONOPOLIES.

The pressure to do wrong is stronger from the fact that in our day the large business houses are swallowing up the smaller, the whales dining on blue-fish and minnows. The large houses undersell the small ones because they can afford it. They can afford to make nothing, or actually lose, on some styles of goods, assured they can make it up on others. So, a great dry-goods house goes outside of its regular line and sells books at cost or less than cost, and that swamps the booksellers; or the dry-goods house sells bric-à-brac at lowest figure, that swamps the small dealer in bric-à-brac. And the same thing goes on in other styles of merchandise, and the consequence is that all along the business streets of all our cities there are merchants of small capital who are in terrific struggle to keep their heads above water. The Cunarders run down the Newfoundland fishing-smacks. This is nothing against the man who has the big store, for every man has as large a store and as great a business as he can manage.

The morals of the Gospel are to be set beside the faith of the Gospel. Mr. Froude, the celebrated English historian, has written of his own country these remarkable words:

" From the great house in the City of London, to the village grocer, the commercial life of England has been saturated with fraud. So deep has it gone that a strictly honest tradesman can hardly hold his ground against competition. You can no longer trust that any article you buy is the thing which it pretends to be. We have false weights, false measures, cheating, and shoddy everywhere. And yet the clergy have seen all this grow up in absolute indifference. Many hundreds of sermons have I heard in England, many a dissertation on the mysteries of the faith, on the divine mission of the clergy, on bishops and justification, and the theory of good works, and verbal inspiration, and the efficacy of the sacraments ; but, during all these thirty wonderful years, never one that I can recollect on common honesty."

Now, that may be an exaggerated statement of things in England, but I am very certain that in all parts of the earth we need to preach the moralities of the Gospel right along beside the faith of the Gospel.

STOLEN GOODS RETURNED.

A missionary in one of the islands of the Pacific preached on dishonesty, and the next morning he looked out of his window, and he saw his yard full of goods of all kinds. He wondered and asked the cause of all this. "Well," said the natives, " our gods that we have been worshipping permit us to steal, but according to what you said yesterday, the God of Heaven and earth will not allow this, so we bring back all these goods, and we ask you to help us in taking them to the places where they belong." If next Sabbath all the ministers in America should preach sermons on the abuse of trust funds, and on the evils of purloining, and the sermons were all blest of God, and regulation were made that all these things should be taken to the city halls, it would not be long before every city hall in America would be crowded from cellar to cupola.

FASCINATIONS OF FRAUD.

Now look abroad and see the fascinations that are thrown around *fraud* and all the different styles of crime.

The question that every man and woman has asked during the last two months has been, Should crime be excused because it is on a large scale? Is iniquity guilty and to be pursued of the law in proportion as it is on a small scale? Shall we have New York Tombs for the man who steals an overcoat from a hat-rack, and all Canada for a man to range in if he have robbed the public of three millions?

O that God would scatter these fascinations, and let us all understand that if I steal from you one dollar I am a thief, and if I steal from you $500,000 I am five hundred thousand times more of a thief! Cultivate old-fashioned honesty. God's Book is full of it. Old-fashioned honesty in *Business* and everything else.

THE DUKE OF WELLINGTON.

I do not suppose there ever was a better specimen of honesty than was found in *the Duke of Wellington.* He marched with his army over the French frontier, and the army was suffering, and he hardly knew how to get along. Plenty of plunder all about, but he commanded none of the plunder to be taken. He writes home these remarkable words : " We are overwhelmed with debts, and I can scarcely stir out of my house on account of public creditors, waiting to demand what is due to them." Yet at that very time the French peasantry were bringing their valuables to him to keep.

A celebrated writer says of the transaction : " Nothing can be grander or more nobly original than this admission. This old soldier, after thirty years' service, this iron man and victorious general, established in an enemy's country at the head of an immense army, is afraid of his creditors ! This is a kind of fear that has seldom troubled conquerors and invaders, and I doubt if the annals of war present anything comparable to its sublime simplicity."

Dr. Livingstone, the famous explorer, was descended from the Highlanders, and he said that one of his ancestors, one of the Highlanders, one day called his family around him. The Highlander was dying ; and with his children around his death-bed, he said : " Now, my lads, I have looked all through our history as far back as I can find it, and I have never found a dishonest man in all the line, and I want you to understand you inherit good blood. You have no excuse for doing wrong. My lads, be honest." Ah ! my friends, be honest before God, be honest before your fellow-men, be honest before your soul.

TRUST FUNDS.

One of the crying sins of this day is *the abuse of trust funds.* Every man during the course of his life, on a larger or smaller scale, has the property of others committed to his keeping. He is so far a safety deposit, he is an administrator, and holds in his hand the interest of the family of a deceased friend. Or, he is an attorney, and through his custody goes the payment from debtor to creditor, or he is the collector for a business house which compensates him for the responsibility ; or he is a treasurer for a charitable institution and he holds alms contributed for the suffering ; or he is an official of the city, or the State, or the nation, and taxes, and subsidies, and salaries, and supplies are in his keeping.

It is as solemn a trust as God can make it. It is concentred and multiplied confidences. On that man depends the support of a bereft household, or the morals of dependants, or the right movement of a thousand wheels of social mechanism. A man may do what he will with his own, but he who abuses trust funds, in that one act commits theft, falsehood, perjury, and becomes in all the intensity of the word a miscreant. How many widows and orphans there are with nothing between them and starvation, but a sewing-machine, or held up out of the vortex of destruction simply by the thread of a needle, and with their own hearts' blood, who a little while ago had, by father and husband, left them a competency. What is the matter? The administrators or the executors have sacrificed it—running risks with it that they would not have dared to encounter in their own private affairs.

How often it is that a man will earn a livelihood by the sweat of his brow, and then die, and within a few months all the estate goes into the stock-gambling rapids of Wall Street.

How often it is that you have known the man to whom trust funds were committed taking them out of the savings-bank and from trust companies, and administrators, turning

old homesteads into hard cash, and then putting the entire
estate in the vortex of speculation. Embezzlement is an
easy word to pronounce, but it has ten thousand ramifications
of horror.

Let me say to those in charge of trust funds: It is a
compliment to you that you have been so intrusted; but I
charge you, in the presence of God and the world, be careful, be as careful of the property of others as you are careful
of your own. Above all, keep your own private account at
the bank separate from your account as trustee of an estate,
or trustee of an institution. That is the point at which
thousands of people make shipwreck. They get the property of others mixed up with their own property, they put it
into investment, and away it all goes, and they cannot return that which they borrowed. Then comes the explosion,
and the money market is shaken, and the press denounces
and the church thunders expulsion.

What a sad thing it would be, if after you are dead your
administrator should find out from the account-books, or
from the lack of vouchers, that you not only were bankrupt in estate, but that you lost your soul.

O! there is such a fearful fascination in this day about
the use of trust-funds. It has got to be popular to take the
funds of others and speculate with them. But O do not
come under the fascination which induces men to employ
trust-funds for purposes of their own speculation.

DEBT.

A debt is a kind of trust-fund, and when incurred with no hope of
payment, is a fraudulent breach of trust.—EDITOR.

Society slaughters a great many young men by the behest, "You must keep up appearances; whatever be your
salary, you must dress as well as others; you must wine and
brandy as many friends, you must smoke as costly cigars,
you must give as expensive entertainments, and you must
live in as fashionable a boarding-house. If you haven't the
money, borrow. If you can't borrow, make a false entry, or

subtract here and there a bill from a bundle of bank-bills; you will only have to make the deception a little while; in a few months, or in a year or two, you can make all right. Nobody will be hurt by it; nobody will be the wiser. You yourself will not be damaged." By that awful process a hundred thousand men have been slaughtered for time and slaughtered for eternity.

Suppose you borrow. There is nothing wrong about borrowing money. There is hardly a man in the house but has sometimes borrowed money. Vast estates have been built on a borrowed dollar. But there are two kinds of borrowed money. Money borrowed for the purpose of starting or keeping up legitimate enterprise and expense, and money borrowed to get that which you can do without. The first is right, the other is wrong. If you have money enough of your own to buy a coat, however plain, and then you borrow money for a dandy's outfit, you have taken the first revolution of the wheel down grade. Borrow for the necessities; that may be well. Borrow for the luxuries; that tips your prospects over in the wrong direction.

The Bible distinctly says the borrower is servant of the lender. It is a bad state of things when you have to go down some other street to escape meeting some one whom you owe. If young men knew what is the despotism of being in debt more of them would keep out of it.

The trouble is, my friends, the people do not understand the ethics of going in debt, and that if you purchase goods with no expectation of paying for them, or go into debt which you cannot meet, you steal just so much money. If I go into a grocer's store, and I buy sugars and coffees and meats, with no capacity to pay for them, and no intention of paying for them, I am more dishonest than if I go into the store, and when the grocer's face is turned the other way I fill my pockets with the articles of merchandise and carry off a ham. In the one case I take the merchant's time, and I take the time of his messenger to transfer the goods to my house, while in the other case I take none of the time of the merchant, and I wait upon myself, and I transfer the goods

without any trouble to him.   In other words, a sneak thief
is not so bad as a man who contracts for debts he never expects to pay.

Now our young men are coming up in this depraved
state of commercial ethics, and I am solicitous about them.
I want to warn them against being slaughtered on the sharp
edges of debt.   You want many things you have not, my
young friends.   You shall have them if you have patience
and honesty and industry.   Certain lines of conduct always
lead out to certain results.   There is a law which controls
even those things that seem hap-hazard.   The most insignificant event you ever heard of is the link between two
eternities—the eternity of the past and the eternity of the
future.   Head the right way, and you will come out at the
right goal.

Bring me a young man and tell me what his physical
health is, and what his mental caliber, and what his habits,
and I will tell you what will be his destiny for this world,
and his destiny for the world to come, and I will not make
five inaccurate prophecies out of five hundred.   All this
makes me solicitous in regard to young men, and I want to
make them nervous in regard to the contraction of unpayable debts.

When a young man wilfully and of choice, having the
comforts of life, goes into the contraction of unpayable
debts, he knows not into what he goes.   The creditors get
after the debtor, the pack of hounds in full cry, and alas! for
the reindeer.   They jingle his door-bell before he gets up in
the morning; they jingle his door-bell after he has gone to
bed at night; they meet him as he comes off his front steps.
They send him a postal-card, or a letter, in the curtest style,
telling him to pay up.   They attach his goods.   They want
cash, or a note at thirty days, or a note on demand.   They
call him a knave.   They say he lies.   They want him disci-
plined at the church.   They want him turned out of the
bank.   They come at him from this side, and from that side,
and from before, and from behind, and from above, and from
beneath, and he is insulted and gibbeted and sued and

dunned and sworn at, until he gets the nervous dyspepsia, gets neuralgia, gets liver complaint, gets heart disease, gets convulsive disorder, gets consumption.

Now he is dead, and you say: "Of course they will let him alone!" Oh, no! Now they are watchful to see whether there are any unnecessary expenses at the obsequies, to see whether there is any useless handle on the casket, to see whether there is any surplus plait on the shroud, to see whether the hearse is costly or cheap, to see whether the flowers sent to the casket have been bought by the family or donated, to see in whose name the deed to the grave is made out. Then they ransack the bereft household, the books, the pictures, the carpets, the chairs, the sofa, the piano, the mattresses, the pillow on which he dies. *Cursed be debt!* For the sake of your own happiness, fos the sake of your good morals, for the sake of your immortal soul, for God's sake, young man, as far as possible, keep out of it!

SWINDLING.

There is not a city or a town that has not suffered from swindling. Where is the court-house, or the city-hall, or the jail, or the post-office, or the hospital, that in the building of it has not had a political job? I want to say here, there ought to be a better style of business introduced into many public places, and there ought to be closer inspection, and there ought to be less opportunity for embezzlement. Lest a man shall take a five-cent piece that does not belong to him, the conductor on the city horse-car must sound his bell at every payment, and we are very cautious about small offences, but give plenty of opportunity for sinners on a large scale to escape. For a boy who steals a loaf of bread from a corner grocer, to keep his mother from starving to death, a prison; but for defrauders who abscond with half a million of dollars, a castle on the Rhine, or, waiting until the offence is forgotten, then a castle on the Hudson.

Another remark needs to be made, and that is, that people

ought not to go into places, into business, or into positions, where the temptation is mightier than their character.

There are men who go into positions full of temptation, considering only the one fact that they are lucrative positions. O! I say to young people, *dishonesty will not pay* in this world or the world to come.

You have no right to run *an unseaworthy craft* into a euroclydon

The devil is not dead. Notwithstanding all the lessons we have learned, people will live beyond their income, and to get means for indulgences they will put their hands in other people's pockets. The forger's pen is not worn out, the burglar's key is not rusty, the perjurer's Bible is not lost.

A speculator comes down from somewhere, takes hold of the money-market of New York, flaunts his abominations in the sight of all the people, defies public morals every day of his life. Young men look up and say, " He was a peddler in one decade, and in the next decade he is one of the monarchs of the stock market. That's the way to do it."

There has been an irresistible impression going abroad among young men that the poorest way to get money is to earn it. The young man of flaunting cravat says to the young man of humble apparel, " What! you only get $1,800 a year? Why, that wouldn't keep me in pin-money. I spend $5000 a year." " Where do you get it?" asks the plain young man. " O! stocks, enterprises, all that sort of thing, you know." The plain young man has hardly enough money to pay his board, has to wear clothes after they are out of fashion, and deny himself all luxuries. After a while he gets tired of his plodding, and he goes to the man who has achieved suddenly large estate, and he says, " Just *show me how it is done.*" And he is shown. He soon learns how, and although he is almost all the time idle now, and has resigned his position in the bank, or the factory, or the store, he has more money than he ever had, trades off his old silver watch for a gold one with a flashing chain, sets his hat a little further over on the side of his head than he ever did, smokes better cigars and more of them. He has his hand in ! Now, if he can escape the penitentiary for three or four years he will get into political circles, and he will get political jobs, and will have something to do with harbors, and pavements, and docks. Now he has got so far along he is safe for perdition.

It is quite a long road sometimes for a man to travel before he gets into the romance of crime. Those are caught who are only in the prosaic stage of it. If the sheriffs and constables would only leave them alone a little while, they would steal as well as anybody. They might not be able to steal a whole railroad, but they could master a load of pig-iron.

Now I always thank God when I find an estate like that go to smash. It is plague-struck, and it blasts the nation. I thank God when it goes into such a wreck it can never be gathered up again.

UNDER THE PRESSURE.

There are hundreds of young men under the pressure, under the fascinations thrown around about commercial iniquity. Thousands of young men have gone down under the pressure ; other thousands have maintained their integrity. God help you ! Let me say to you, my young friend, that you can be a great deal happier in poverty than you ever can be happy in a prosperity which comes from illy gotten gains. "Oh," you say, "I might lose my place. It is easy for you to stand there and talk, but it is no easy thing to get a place when you have lost it. Besides that, I have a widowed mother depending upon my exertions, and you must not be too reckless in giving advice to me." Ah, my young friend, it is always safe to be right, but it is never safe to be wrong. You go home and tell your mother the pressure under which you are in that store, and I know what she will say to you if she is worthy of you. She will say, " My son, come out from there ; Christ has taken care of us all these years, and He will take care of us now; come out of that."

THEIR NAME IS LEGION.

How many dishonesties in the making out of invoices, and in the plastering of false labels, and in the filching of customers of rival houses, and in the making and breaking of contracts. Young men are indoctrinated in the idea that the sooner they get money the better, and the getting of it on a larger scale only proves to them their greater ingenuity. There is a glitter thrown around about all these things. Young men have got to find out that God looks upon sin in a very different light.

An abbot wanted to buy a piece of ground and the owner would not sell it, but the owner finally consented to let it to him until he could raise one crop, and the abbot sowed acorns, *a crop of two hundred years!* And I tell you, young man, that the dishonesties which you plant in your heart and life will seem to be very insignificant, but they will grow up until they will overshadow you with horrible darkness, over-shadow all time and all eternity. It will not be a crop for two hundred years, but a crop for everlasting ages.

I want to show the young men of to-day that fraud will out, that old-fashioned honesty in the long-run pays the most, that *the best way to get a dollar* is to earn it, that there is no hiding-place for those who wrong their fellows.

There is not an honest man, however poor, but is happier than the purse-proud possessor of ill-gotten gains. Such riches, if they do not, according to the Bible figure, take wings and fly toward heaven, will coil like serpents around the heart, to chill and sting it with remorse unutterable. It is not so much what you have, as how you got it. If you want to make the silver and gold of earth bright, you had better wash them with sweat from your own temples. Re-member that financial failure on earth is nothing compared with eternal defalcation. I want all dishonesty, yea, the very appearance of dishonesty to become so loathsome and yield such an insufferable stench that honest young men will take warning.

Let me say in the most emphatic way, O young man, dishonesty will never pay.

A blustering young man arrived at *a hotel in the West*, and he saw a man on the sidewalk, and in a rough way, as no man has a right to address a laborer, said to him : "Carry this trunk upstairs." The man carried the trunk upstairs and came down, and then the young man gave him a quarter of a dollar which was marked, and instead of being twenty-five cents it was worth only twenty cents. Then the young man gave his card to the laborer, and said : "You take this up to Governor Grimes, I want to see him." "Ah!" said the laborer, "*I am Governor Grimes !*" "O!" said the young man, "you—I—excuse me!" Then the governor said : "I was much impressed by the letter you wrote me asking for a certain office in my gift, and I had made up my mind you should have it ; but a young man who will cheat a laborer out of five cents would swindle the government of the State, if he got his hands on it. I don't want you Good-morning, sir." It never pays. Neither in this world nor in the world to come will it pay.

What are you doing with that fraudulent document ? Is that a "*pool ticket*" you have in your pocket? Why, O young man, were you last night practising in copying your employer's signature ! Where were you last night ? Are your habits as good as when you left your father's house? You had a Christian ancestry, perhaps, and you have had too many prayers spent on you to go overboard.

A young man stood behind the counter in New York selling silks to a lady, and he said before the sale was consummated, "I see there is a flaw in that silk." The lady recognized it, and the sale was not consummated. The head man of the firm saw the interview, and he wrote home to the father of the young man living in the country, saying, "Dear sir, come and take your boy : he will never make a merchant." The father came down from the country home in great consternation, as any father would, wondering what

his boy had done. He came into the store, and the merchant said to him, "Why, your son pointed out a flaw in
some silk the other day, and spoiled the sale, and we will
never have that lady, probably, again for a customer, and
your son never will make a merchant." " Is that all?" said
the father. " I am proud of him. I wouldn't for the world
have him another day under your influence. John, get your
hat and come ; let us start."

[The Editor adds, that the young man lost nothing by his honesty,
for that merchant recommended him to a bank, as one who would
neither lie nor cheat for him. And any young man will find in the
end that " honesty is the best policy."]

LOTTERIES.

" Upon My vesture did they cast lots."—MATTHEW 27 : 35.

Christ had been condemned to death and His property
was being disposed of. He had no real estate. He was
born in a stranger's barn, and buried in a borrowed sepulchre.
His personal property was of but little value. His coat
was the only thing to come into consideration. His shoes
had been worn out in the long journey for the world's
redemption. *Who shall have His coat ?* Some one said: " Let
us toss up in a lottery and decide this matter." " I have it!"
said one of the inhuman butchers. " I have it !" " Upon
My vesture did they cast lots." And there, on that spot,
were born all the lotteries the world has seen.

On that spot of cruelty and shame and infamy there was
born *the Royal Havana Lottery.* There was born the famous
New York Lottery, which pretended to have over $722,000 in
cash prizes. There was born the Topeka, Kansas, Laramie
City, Wyoming Territory lotteries. There was born the Louis-
ville lottery, with diamonds, and pearls, and watches by the
bushel. There was born the Georgia lottery, for the East
and the West. There was born the Louisiana Lottery,
sanctioned by influential names. There was born the Ken-

tucky Lottery, for the city school of Frankfort. All the lotteries that have swindled the world were born there. Without any exception, all of them *moral outrages*, whether sanctioned by legislative authority, or antagonized by it, and moral outrages, though respectable people have sometimes damaged their property with them, and blistered their immortal souls for eternity.

One of the sad things about these lotteries is that poor people in their extremity and almost frenzied with their destitution, resort to them, and lose their last dollar, their last fifty cents, their last five cents; for there are lotteries where the drawing occurs every five minutes. In the time of the greatest distress in Italy, $14,000,000 were annually expended by the poorer population in lotteries. The country was flooded with fascinating circulars like this:—

"Agents' prize tickets free of cost. Every ticket a prize. No blanks and a fortune within your reach without cost or risk. Any person can easily sell $10 worth of tickets like the enclosed, monthly, among personal friends, and secure one of the agents' tickets free of cost. Capital prize $5000. Every ticket wins a prize. There are ten thousand prizes, and only ten thousand tickets."

Under the curse of the lottery tens of thousands of people are losing their fortunes and losing their souls. What they call a "wheel of fortune" is a Juggernaut crushing out the life of their immortal nature. In one of the insolvent courts of the country it was found that in one village $200,000 had been expended for lotteries. All the officers of the celebrated United States Bank which failed were found to have expended the embezzled moneys in lottery tickets.

A man won $50,000 in a lottery. He sold his ticket for $42,500, and yet had not enough to pay charges against him for tickets. He owed the brokers $45,000. The editor of a newspaper writes: "My friend was blessed with $20,000 in a lottery, and from that time he began to go astray, and yesterday he asked of me ninepence to pay for a night's lodging."

A man won $20,000 in a lottery. Flattered by his success, he bought another ticket and won still more largely. Another ticket and still more largely. Then, being fairly started on the road to ruin, here and there a loss did not seem to agitate him, and he went on and on until the selectmen of the village pronounced him a vagabond and picked up his children from the street, half starved and almost naked. A hard-working machinist won a thousand dollars in a lottery. He was thrilled with the success, disgusted with his hard work, opened a rum grocery, got debauched in morals and was found dead at the foot of his rum casks.

O ! it would take a pen plucked from the wing of the destroying angel, and dipped in human blood, to describe this lottery business. A suicide was found having in his pocket a card of address showing he was boarding at a grog-shop. Beside that he had three lottery tickets and a leaf from Seneca's Morals arguing in behalf of the righteousness of self-murder. After a lottery in England there were fifty suicides of those who had held unlucky numbers There are people who have lottery tickets in their pockets—tickets which, if they have not wisdom enough to tear up or burn up, will be their *admission tickets at the door of the lost world.* The brazen gate will swing open and they will show their tickets, and they will go in, and they will go down. The wheel of their eternal fortune may turn very slowly, but they will find that the doom of those who reject the teachings of God and imperil their immortal soul is their only prize.

I pray God that you, young man, may never come to the lamentation of *a Boston clerk* who had embezzled $18,000 from his employer, and after it was all spent in this infernal lottery business sat down and wrote these words: " I have for the last seven months gone fast down the broad road. There was a time, and that only a few months since, when I was happy, because I was free from debt and care. The moment of the first steps in my downfall was about the middle of last June, when I took a share in a company— bought lottery tickets whereby I was successful in obtaining a share of one half of *the capital prize*, since which I have gone from myself. I have lived and dragged out a miserable existence for two or three months past. O that the seven or eight months past of my existence could be blotted out. But I must go, and ere this paper is read my spirit has gone to my Maker to give an account of my misdeeds here, and to receive the eternal sentence for self-destruction and abused confidence. Relatives and friends I have from whom I do not wish to part under such circumstances, but necessity compels. O wretch! lottery tickets have been thy ruin. But I cannot add more."

The dismal echo of the ruin of tens of thousands of young men.

GIFT STORES.

Then, there are gift stores which make swindlers by the hundreds. I refer to those stores where, if you buy a watch, or a sewing-machine, or a piano, there is a prize connected with it. It is only a sharp way of getting rid of unsalable goods. Those stores have filled the land with fictitious articles, and covered up our population with brass finger-rings, and despoiled public morals, and have made more swindlers than you can count. The lottery business will stop at no indecency. In Maryland they actually drew for prizes lots in a burying ground!

In the name of God, I arraign all such gift enterprises as having a tendency to make this a nation of swindlers. Men failing in other enterprises go into gift concerts where the attraction is not the music but the packages distributed among the audience, or into a sale of books where the attraction is not the book but the package that goes with the book. So in our time we have known tobacco dealers to advertise that on a certain day in every one of their papers there would be a prize, and whether a man bought the tobacco in Chicago, or Boston, or Charleston, or New Orleans, or New York, he would get a magnificent gratuity. Boys hawking prize pack-

ages through the ears—packages containing no one knows
what until they are opened and found to contain nothing,

Ay, the cause of charity is insulted, and under the name
of gift enterprises the gambling spirit goes on   You remember at the close of the war how we had gift enterprises all
over the country, "the proceeds *for the benefit of the widows
and orphans of soldiers.*"   What did the men engaged in
those enterprises care for the orphans?   They would have
been willing to allow them to freeze on their doorstep.   I
have no faith in a charity which for the purpose of relieving
present distress will open the jaw of a monster which has
taken down so many of the bodies and souls of men.   I believe through these gift enterprises there are thousands of
people being turned into gambling habits.   O, my friends,
do one of two things; be honest, or die!

SNARES.

Yachting and base-ball playing have been the occasion of
putting up excited and extravagant wagers.   That which to
many has been advantageous to body and mind, has been to
others the means of financial and moral loss.   The custom is
pernicious in the extreme, where scores of men in respectable
life give themselves up to betting, now on this boat, now on
that ; now on this ball club, now on that.

BETTING,

that once was chiefly the accompaniment of the race-course,
is fast becoming a national habit, and in some circles any
opinion advanced on finance or politics is accosted with the
interrogation : " How much will you bet on that, sir?"

This custom may make no appeal to slow, lethargic temperaments, but there are in the country tens of thousands of
quick, nervous, sanguine, excitable temperaments, ready to
be acted upon, and their feet will soon take hold on death.
For some months, and perhaps for years, they will linger in

the more polite and elegant circle of gamesters, but, after a while, their pathway will come to the fatal plunge.

OTHER SWINDLING SCHEMES.

There are a good many respectable people who, while they oppose the ordinary lottery, patronize art associations and gift enterprises under the impression that iniquity is not quite so bad if it have a more popular nomenclature, and that there cannot be any very great harm in a ticket which will draw for one Bierstadt's " Yosemite Valley," or Cropsey's " American Autumn." Multitudes who cannot be captivated with the more vulgar forms of gambling or lottery, are captivated by this form.

A few years ago, we saw in all our cities the flaming advertisements of the Crosby Opera House *scheme.* A man in Chicago found an unprofitable building on his hands, and he resolved to make all the nation help him out of that difficulty. Lottery offices were opened in all the great cities. The people rushed in. Philadelphia bought over $30,000 worth of the tickets ; New York bought over $100,000 worth of the tickets. The hour approaches. The trains carry to the city dignified committees to see that the abomination is conducted in a Christian and orderly style. Trains are loaded with great multitudes who come to get their fortunes.

The agony is over. A great number of people have had narrow escape of sudden affluence. Swift horses, foaming and lathered, dash up to the house of the man who holds the successful ticket. The lightnings carry to the four winds of heaven the news, and our enterprising pictorials hasten forward their photographers to take the pictures of the man who had the ticket 58,600. Multitudes of people declared there was foul play, and that if the truth were only known they themselves had won the opera-house. The man who won the opera-house soon died of drunkenness, and the beautiful opera-house which had been raffled away, strange to say, was found at last in the possession of the original owner. A swindle! an insult to God and the American people!

THE TULIP MANIA.

The Hollanders, the most phlegmatic people in the world, had their gambling scene in 1683. It was called *the tulip mania*. It was a speculation in tulips. Properties worth half a million dollars turned into tulips. All the Holland nation either buying or selling tulips. One tulip-root sold for two hundred dollars, another for two thousand.

Excitement rolling on and rolling on until history tells us that one Amsterdam tulip, which was supposed to be the only one of the kind in all the world, actually brought in the markets $1,816,000! That is a matter of history. Of course the crash came, and all Holland went down under it.

MISSISSIPPI SCHEME.

But France must have its gambling expedition, and that was in 1716. John Law's *Mississippi scheme* it was called. The French had heard that this American continent was built out of solid gold, and the project was to take it across the ocean and drop it in France. Excitement beyond anything that had yet been seen in the world. Three hundred thousand applicants for shares. Excitement so great that sometimes the mounted military had to disperse the crowds that had come to get the stocks. Five hundred temporary tents built to accommodate the people until they could have opportunity of interviewing John Law.

A lady of great fashion had her coachman upset her near the place where John Law was passing, in order that she might have an interview with that benevolent and sympathetic gentleman! Stocks went up to two thousand and fifty per cent, until one day suspicion got into the market, and down it all went—John Law's Mississippi scheme—burying its projector and some of the greatest financiers in all France, and was almost as bad as a French revolution.

SOUTH SEA BUBBLE.

Sedate England took its chance in 1720. That was *the South Sea bubble*. They proposed to transfer all the gold of Peru and Mexico and the islands of the sea to England. Five millions' worth of shares were put on the market at three hundred pounds a share. The books open, in a few days it is all taken, and twice the amount subscribed.

Excitement followed excitement, until all kinds of gambling projects came forth under the wing of this South Sea enterprise. There was a large company formed with great capital for *providing funerals* for all parts of the land. Another company with large capital, five million pounds of capital, to develop a wheel in perpetual motion. Another company with a capital of four million pounds, to insure people against loss by servants. Another company with two million five hundred thousand pounds capital to transplant walnut trees from Virginia to England. But of course, when blown to the full capacity, THE BUBBLE BURST!

To cap the climax, a company was formed for " a great undertaking, nobody to know what it is." And lo! six hundred thousand pounds in shares were offered at one hundred pounds a share ; books were opened at 9 o'clock in the morning and closed at 3 o'clock in the afternoon, and the first day it was all subscribed. "A great undertaking, nobody to know what it is." An old magazine of those days describes the scene (*Hunt's Magazine*). It says:

" From morning until evening Change Alley was full to overflowing with one dense moving mass of living beings, composed of the most incongruous materials, and in all things save the mad pursuit wherefor they were employed utterly opposite in their principles and feelings, and far asunder in their stations in life and the professions they follow. Statesmen and clergymen deserted their high stations to enter upon this great theatre of speculation and gambling. Churchmen and Dissenters left their fierce disputes and forgot their wranglings upon church government in the *deep and hazardous game* they were playing for worldly treasures and for riches, which, if gained, were liable to disappear within an hour of their creation.

"Whigs and Tories buried their weapons of political warfare, discarded party animosities, and mingled together in kind and friendly intercourse, each exulting as their stocks advanced in price, and grumbling when fortune frowned upon them. Lawyers, physicians, merchants, and travelling men forsook their employment, neglected their business, disregarded their engagements, to whirl along in the stream and be at last ingulfed in *the wild sea of bankruptcy.*

"Females mixed with the crowd, forgetting the station and employment which nature had fitted them to adorn, and dealt boldly and extensively, and, like those by whom they were surrounded, rose from poverty to wealth, and from that were thrown down to beggary and want, and all in one short week, and perhaps before the evening which terminated the first day of their speculation. Ladies of high rank, regardless of every appearance of dignity, and blinded by the prevailing infatuation, drove to the shops of their milliners and haberdashers, and there met their stock-brokers, whom they regularly employed, and through whom extensive sales were daily negotiated. In the midst of the excitement all distinctions of party, and religion, and circumstances, and character were swallowed up."

MORUS MULTICAULIS.

It was left for our own country to surpass all. We have the highest mountains, and the greatest cataracts, and the longest rivers, and, of course, we had to have the largest swindle. One would have thought that the nation had seen enough in that direction during the *morus multicaulis* excitement, when almost every man had a bunch of crawling silkworms in his house out of which he expected to make a fortune.

OIL FEVER.

But all this excitement was as nothing compared with what took place in 1864, when a man near Titusville, Pa., digging for a well, struck oil. Twelve hundred oil companies call for one billion of stock. Prominent members of churches, as soon as a certain amount of stock was assigned them, saw it was their liberty to become presidents, or secretaries, or members of the board of direction.

Some of these companies never had a foot of ground, never expected to have. Their entire equipment was a map of a region where oil might be, and two phials of grease, crude and clarified. People rushed down from all parts of the country by the first train and put their hard earnings in the gulf.

A young man came down from the oil regions of Pennsylvania utterly demented, having sold his farm at a fabulous price, because it was supposed there might be oil there —coming to a hotel in Philadelphia, at the time I was living there, throwing down a five-thousand-dollar check to pay for his Monday meal and saying he did not care anything about the change! Then he stepped back to the gas-burner to *light his cigar with a thousand-dollar note.* Utterly insane.

The good Christian people said, "This company must all be right, because Elder So-and-so is president of it, and Elder So-and-so is secretary of it, and then there are three or four highly professed Christians in the board of directors. To join this company is almost like joining the church!" They did not know that when a professed Christian goes into stock-gambling he lies like sin!

But alas! for the country; it became a tragedy, and one thousand million dollars were swamped There are families to-day sitting in the shadow of destitution, who but for that great national outrage would have had their cottages and their homesteads.

WARNING TO YOUNG MEN.

I hold up before young men these great swindling schemes that they may see to what length men will go smitten of this passion, and I want to show them how all the best interests of society are against it, and God is against it, and will damn it for time and damn it for eternity.

CHAPTER VIII.

Gambling.

"Aceldama, that is to say, The field of blood."—ACTS 1 : 19.

THE money that Judas gave for surrendering Christ was used to purchase a graveyard. As the money was blood-money, the ground bought by it was called in the Syriac tongue, Aceldama, meaning "The field of blood." Well, there is one word I want to write over every race-course where wagers are staked, and every pool-room, and every gambling saloon, and every table, public or private, where men and women bet for sums of money, large or small, and that is a word incarnadine with the life of innumerable victims—Aceldama. The gambling spirit, which is at all times a stupendous evil, ever and anon sweeps over the country like an epidemic, prostrating uncounted thousands.

The fact that there is not enough moral force to put into the penitentiary the gambling jockeys who belong there, is only a specimen of the power gained by this abomination, which is brazen, sanguinary, transcontinental and hemispheric.

Some of you are engaged in mercantile concerns, as clerks and book-keepers, and your whole life is to be passed in the exciting world of traffic. The sound of busy life stirs you as the drum stirs the fiery war-horse. Others are in the mechanical arts, to hammer and chisel your way through life, and success awaits you. Some are preparing for professional life, and grand opportunities are before you; nay, some of you already have buckled on the armor. But, whatever your age or calling, the subject of gambling about which I speak is pertinent.

"O!" says some one, "that subject has no interest for

me ; that evil never touches me at any point." There is not a man or woman but is touched by it. Years ago a society was formed for the suppression of gambling, and the agent of that society went to a prominent merchant of New York and asked his help. "O!" said the merchant, "I have no interest in that society. Gambling is an evil, but in no-wise touches my business." He did not know that his oldest son, a partner with him in business, was the heaviest player in Hearne's famous gambling establishment.

The agent went to another citizen, who said : " O, that's a very good society, but I don't know why you ask my help. I am well acquainted with all my employés. They have nothing to do with this gambling habit." He did not know that one of his bookkeepers on a thousand a year was losing fifty and a hundred dollars every night just then at the faro table. The agent of that society went to a prominent railroad man, asking for his patronage. "O!" he said, "that society for the suppression of gambling is a good thing for the defence of merchants and manufacturers, but I don't know why you ask help of me, a railroad man." He did not know that two of his conductors were spending three nights of every week at the faro table.

GAMBLING is the great plague of the American nation—a plague that has swept over all our cities and smitten down a vast multitude of those who were once the very best citizens.

And there is not a person in the land but ought to have an interest in the subject.

WHAT IS GAMBLING ?

Gambling is risking something without consideration with the idea of winning more than you hazard. Playing cards is not gambling unless a stake be put up, while on the other hand a man may gamble without cards, without dice, without billiards, without ten-pin alley. It may not be bagatelle, it may not be billiards, it may not be any of the ordinary instruments of gambling. It may be a glass of wine. It may be a hundred shares in a prosperous railroad company. I do

not care what the instruments of the game are, or what the
stakes are that are put up—if you propose to get anything
without paying for it in time, or skill, or money, unless you
get it by inheritance, you get it either by theft or by
gambling.

This is *no new sprite* come forth to curse the nation. It
is a haggard transaction that comes down under a mantle of
curses, staggering through the centuries. Before 1838 the
French government received a revenue from the gaming
tables. In the sixteenth century the English Government,
for the improvement of the harbors, had gambling enacted
at the door of St. Paul's Cathedral. The British Museum
and Westminster Bridge were partially built by gambling.
The Germans used to put themselves and their families up
as prizes, and when they were lost as prizes would allow those
who were physically weaker than themselves to bind them
and take them off. In our day, the House of Commons ad-
journs on Derby Day, to go out and bet on the horses.
What is bad in other lands is bad here, and all through this
land.

A traveller said he travelled one thousand miles on
Western waters, and at every waking moment, from the starting to the closing of his journey, he was in the presence of
gambling. A man, if he is disposed to this vice, will find
something to accommodate him ; if not in the low restaurant
behind the curtain, on the table covered with greasy cards,
or in the steamboat cabin, where the bloated wretch with
rings in his ears winks in an unsuspecting traveller, or in the
elegant parlor, the polished drawing-room, the mirrored and
pictured halls of wealth and beauty. This vice destroys
through unhealthy stimulants.

Look out for any kind of excitement which, after the
gratification of the appetite, hurls the man back into de-
structive reactions. Then the excitement is wicked. Beware
of an agitation which, like a rough musician, in order to call
out the tune, plays so hard he breaks down the instrument.
God never yet made a man strong enough to endure gambling excitements without damage. It is no surprise that

many a man seated at the game has lost and then begun to sweep off imaginary gold from the table. He sat down sane. *He rose a maniac.*

The keepers of gambling saloons school themselves into placidity. They are fat, and round, and rollicking, and obese ; but those who go to play for the sake of winning are thin, and pale, and exhausted, and nervous, and sick, and have the heart-disease, and are liable any moment to drop down dead. That is the character of nine out of ten of the gamblers. You cannot be healthy and practise that vice.

KILLING TO INDUSTRY.

Do you notice that just as soon as a man gets that vice on him he stops his work? How dull is the store, the shop, the factory, the banking-house! Do you not know that this vice has dulled the saw of the carpenter, and cut the band of the factory wheel, and sunk the cargo, and broken the teeth of the farmer's rake, and sent a strange lightning to the battery of the philosopher? What a dull thing is a plough to a farmer, when in one night in the village restaurant he can make or lose the price of a whole harvest! How dull it is for a man to sell tape, and silk, and calico, and nankeen, and weigh sugars, or run up and down a long line of dull figures, when he can in one night make or lose the price of a whole business season!

KILLING TO CHARACTER.

Any trade or occupation that is of use is ennobling. The street sweeper advances the interests of society by the cleanliness effected. The cat pays for the fragments it eats by clearing the house of vermin. The fly that takes the sweetness from the dregs of the cup, compensates by purifying the air and keeping back the pestilence. But the gambler gives only disgrace to the man that he fleeces, despair to his heart, ruin to his business, anguish to his wife, shame to his children, and eternal wasting away to his soul. He pays in tears and blood and agony and darkness and woe.

SHALL GAMBLERS TRIUMPH?

Sennacherib, the Infamous, had taxed and outraged the people until it was time to have him stopped. The Lord proposed to stop him, and not in any mild or complimentary way. God says He will not argue or persuade him, but as a butcher thrusts an iron hook into the nose of an ox and leads it to the slaughter, so He turns back this infamous Sennacherib. "I will put my hook in thy nose, and turn thee back by the way which thou camest."

The gambling evil in our time has taken on imperial airs, and it is a Sennacherib. It has taxed and outraged a multitude of people already to financial and spiritual death. The work is to be stopped. The evil was never so defiant or blatant as to-day. The question, the absorbing question for all classes of people who are interested in the welfare of our cities, is, whether the gamblers shall be triumphant, or whether the officers of the government in all our cities shall be backed by a healthy and vehement public opinion.

Sir Garnet Wolseley prophesied that on the fifteenth of September he should have Arabi Pasha a prisoner and that the Egyptians would be overthrown. With marvellous accuracy the prophecy came true, and on the fifteenth of September the rebellion had practically been overthrown. And though we may not give the date, may we not, in the name of eternal Justice, prophecy that this gigantic evil shall be overthrown?

What all churches, what all reformatory institutions, what all good people now need to do is to rally a vigorous public sentiment on this subject and let the authorities in all our cities know that they will be backed up by all Christian, all decent people, in every effort to put down crime and to elevate virtue.

A SENNACHERIBEAN EVIL.

In Cincinnati, on my way to the depot, I heard *the rat-tling of the dice* of gambling saloons, and then I went out into the country to a large agricultural fair, and in front of the hotel there was a large group of men gambling all day, while their honest neighbors were admiring the fruits of the earth and blessing God for our great prosperity. The evil has rolled over this whole land. This Sennacherib needs to to have an iron hook in his nose until he shall be brought back, until he shall be brought down, until he shall be destroyed, and it shall be demonstrated that honest, Christian sentiment in all our cities is mightier than crime.

Fathers and brothers and sons may well be enlisted in such a discussion, but just as much, wives, mothers, sisters, and daughters need to be enlisted in such a discussion lest their present home be sacrificed, or their intended home blasted. No person can say successfully: " That evil has no relation to me or mine." Before long it may be found out in your own experience that this discussion had for you practical bearing on three worlds—earth, Heaven, and hell. People who have not looked into this matter have no idea of the extent of the evil.

In one year, in New York City, there were seven million dollars sacrificed at the gaming-table. Perhaps some of your friends have been smitten of this sin. Perhaps some of you have been smiten by it. Perhaps there may be a stranger in the house this morning come from some of the hotels. Look out for those agents of iniquity who tarry around about the hotels, and ask you, " Would you like to see the city?" " Yes." " Have you ever seen that splendid building up-town?" " No." Then the villain will undertake to show you what he calls the " lions" and the " elephants," and after a young man, through morbid curiosity or through badness of soul, has seen the " lions" and the " elephants," he will be on enchanted ground. Look out for these men

who move around the hotels with sleek hats—always sleek
hats—and patronizing air, and unaccountable interest about
your welfare and entertainment.   You are a fool if you cannot see through it.   They want your money.

A MERCILESS EVIL.

In Chestnut Street, Philadelphia, when I was living in that
city, a young man went into a gambling-saloon, lost all his
property, then blew his brains out, and before the blood was
washed from the floor by the maid the comrades were
shuffling cards again.   You see, there is more mercy in the
highwayman for the belated traveller on whose body he
heaps the stones, there is more mercy in the frost for the
flower that it kills, there is more mercy in the hurricane that
shivers the steamer on the Long Island coast, than there is
mercy in the heart of a gambler for his victim.

DEEDS OF DARKNESS.

That commercial house that only a little while ago put
out a sign of copartnership will this winter be wrecked on a
gambler's table.   There will be many a money-till that will
spring a leak.

In the third watch of the night pass down the streets
and you hear the click of the dice and the sharp, keen stroke
of the ball on the billiard-table.   At these places merchant
princes dismount, and legislators, tired of making laws, take
a respite in breaking them.   All classes of people are robbed
by this crime—the importer of foreign silks and the dealer
in Chatham Street pocket-handkerchiefs.   The clerks of the
store take a hand after the shutters are put up, and the officers of the court while away their time while the jury is out.

In Baden-Baden, when that city was the greatest of all
gambling places on earth, it was no unusual thing the next
morning, in the woods around about the city, to find the
suspended bodies of suicides.   Whatever be the splendor of
surroundings, there is no excuse for this crime.   The thun-

ders of eternal destruction roll in the deep rumble of that gambling tenpin-alley, and as men come out to join the long procession of sin, all the drums of death beat the dead march of a thousand souls.

A merchant came from the far west. He was largely influential in his own city. Coming to New York he went into an institution of that kind on Park Place, and before morning he had lost all his estate save one dollar, and with that dollar he walked around the room, and then seized upon by this infernal sorcery he again approached the table and was overheard to say as he put his dollar down : "One thousand miles from home and *my last dollar* on a gaming table !" O ! it is merciless.

It is estimated that in this neighborhood of cities there are *three thousand five hundred professed gamblers*. As much as it is your business to sell goods, or doctor the sick, or plead the law, or import goods, or manufacture, or carry on your trade, just so much it is their business to despoil society. In all these cities during these years, how many of the gambling establishments have ever professed to be honest? Nine. These nine professedly honest gambling establishments are only the antechamber to those acknowledged to be fraudulent. There are *the first-class* gambling establishments taking down hundreds of our young men, hundreds of our older men. You go a little out of Broadway, and you go up marble stairs and ring the bell, and a liveried servant comes to the door and introduces you. The walls are lavender tinted. There is a piece of furniture very costly, most exquisite and wonderful, its value so great I cannot compute it. It is the roulette table. Here is the banqueting room. Free drinks, free cigars, free fruits, free everything—sumptuous beyond all parallel. Pictures on the wall of Jephtha's daughter and Dante's "frozen region of hell," a most appropriate picture.

Pass on, and you come to *the second-class* gambling establishments of our cities. You are introduced by a card of some "roper in." Once fairly inside, you must either gamble or fight. Sanded cards, dice loaded with quicksilver, poor drinks mixed with more poor drinks soon help you to get rid of your money to a tune in short meter with no staccato passages! You went in to see. You saw! Does not a panther squatting in the grass know a calf when he sees it? *Wrangle not* in that place for your rights, or your wounded body will be thrown into the street, or your dead body pulled out of the East River.

You pass on and you come to what are ordinarily called *pool rooms.* There is betting on numbers. Betting on two numbers is called a "saddle," betting on three numbers is called a "gig," betting on four numbers is called a "horse," and thousands of men spring into that "saddle," and mount that "gig," and behind that "horse" ride to perdition! The sign says "Exchange." *Wonderfully significant sign—*" Exchange ," for that is where a man gives up his respectability, gives up his money, gives up his morals, gives up his soul, and gets in exchange loss of hope, loss of respectability, loss of decency, loss of family, loss of Heaven. " Exchange !" Infinite exchange. Awful exchange. Everlasting exchange.

FASCINATIONS OF THE GAME.

I have crossed the ocean eight times, and always one of the best rooms has, from morning till late at night, been given up to gambling practices. I heard of many men who went on board with enough money for a European excursion, who landed without enough money to get their baggage up to the hotel or railroad station. To many there is a complete fascination in games of hazard or the risking of money on possibilities. It seems as natural for them to bet as to eat. Indeed the hunger for food is often overpowered with the hunger for wagers, as in the case of Lord Sandwich, a persistent gambler, who not being willing to leave the dice table long enough for the taking of food, invented a preparation of food that he could take without stopping the game; namely, a slice of beef between two slices of bread, which was named after Lord Sandwich.

It is absurd for those of us who have never felt the fascination of the wager to speak slightingly of the temptation. It has slain a multitude of intellectual and moral giants, men and women stronger than you or I. Down under its power went glorious Oliver Goldsmith, and Gibbon the historian, and Charles Fox the statesman ; and in olden times famous senators of the United States, who used to be as regularly at the gambling-house all night, as they were in the halls of legislation by day. Oh, the tragedies of the faro table ! I know persons who began with a slight stake in a lady's parlor, and ended with the suicide's pistol at Monte Carlo. They played with the square pieces of bone with black marks on them, not knowing that Satan was playing for their bones at the same time, and was sure to sweep all the stakes off on his side of the table.

A great many Christian people wonder why it is that men of wealth and men of refinement, and men of education, as fine-looking people as we have in these cities, go down into this evil. Why, my friends, it is easily explained. A great many people are born with a passion for hazard. It is a joy to them to go near a precipice. They climb Jungfrau not for the purpose of seeing the vastness of the landscape, but for the feeling, "what would happen if I should fall off?" There are persons whose blood is filliped and accelerated by skating near an air-hole. There are people who find a joyful feeling in driving within two inches of the edge of a bridge. Do not blame such people. Only blame them for the way in which they develop or put down that passion. "Oh," says one of that temperament, "here are $500; I'll stake them ; I may lose, but I may gain $5000, and *it's excitement anyway.*" Shuffle the cards. Lost ! Heart thumps. Head dizzy. Never mind, it is excitement. So they go on with the play and they go on down. That is the history of thousands of people. And are we to spend our time talking about the sins of the Hittites, Jebusites and Girgashites, and the Ahabs and the Jezebels of the past, when we have these monarchs of iniquity destroying the land?

COVETOUSNESS.

Others are led into this great and absorbing evil through sheer desire of gain. It is especially so with professed gamblers. They always keep cool. They never drink until their brain is unbalanced, or their judgment is overthrown. They see not so much the dice as the dollar beyond the dice. They are as the spider in the web, looking as if dead until the fly passes. There are hundreds of young men who say: "Now, I don't in this office, store or factory, get enough salary; I ought to have a room in a better boarding-house or better hotel; I ought to have better wines; I ought to have finer cigars; I ought, when people banquet me, be able to banquet them, and I am going to endure this no longer. I will with one bright stroke make my fortune. Here goes, right or wrong, principle or no principle, Heaven or hell! Who cares?"

When a young man or an older man resolves to live beyond his means, *Satan has bought him* out and out, and it is only a question of time when the goods shall be delivered. The thing is done. You may plant in his way all the batteries of truth and righteousness, he will press right on. If a man have a thousand dollars of income and he spend twelve hundred, if he have fifteen hundred and spend two thousand, if he have three thousand and spend five thousand, all the powers of darkness say, "Aha! aha! we have him." And they have. The extra five hundred or the extra two thousand or the extra five thousand dollars must be obtained some way.

Here is a young man who says: "There's my friend who came to town with no money at all, and see how he's got on! He went into one of those places and put a certain amount of money on the ace; he has now his hundreds, his thousands, and his tens of thousands, and here I am nothing but a poor clerk." What a dull business this is, adding up this long line of figures in a counting-house. What a dull

business, taking down fifty yards of cloth to sell one rem-
nant. What a dull business this is, my waiting on other
people when I might put a hundred on the ace and take up
a thousand What is the use? It is so insidious, this temptation. Other sins beat the drum, or flaunt the flag, or
gather their recruits with huzza; but this one marches its
pale processions on down, and when they drop into the
grave there is not so much as the sound of the click of dice.

O, how many noble natures have perished under the
power! That grand forehead is licked by a tongue of flame
that shall never be extinguished. Into that heart there are
vulturous beaks plunged which shall never be lifted. Open
the door of that man's soul and see the coil of adders
writhing their indescribable horrors until you turn away and
hide your face and beg God to help you forget it.

The bad thing about all this is that the most of the evil,
the most of the calamity goes unadvertised. The men who
lose money in gambling generally say nothing about it.
They do not want their families to know, they do not want
the Church of God to know, they do not want the world to
know, and so I suppose in ninety cases out of a hundred
when a man loses money in gambling he hushes it up.

Once in a while there is an exception, as where the police
of Boston some years ago broke in upon a gaming establishment and found there some of the first merchants of State
Street, clear down to the Ann Street gambler; as when
Bullock, the cashier of the Georgia Central Railroad, was
found to have purloined $103.000 for gambling purposes, as
when, many years ago, in one of the savings-banks of Brooklyn, a young man was found to have stolen $40,000 to carry
on gaming practices; as when in Wall Street, a man in an
insurance company was found years ago to have stolen
$180,000 to carry on gaming practices. But these are ex
ceptions. The general rule is that in silence the money
leaks out of the merchant's till, or out of the fireproof safe of
the bank into the wallet of the gambler.

ECCLESIASTICAL GAMBLING.

The Church of God has not seemed willing to allow the world to have all the advantage of these games of chance. A church fair opens, and toward the close it is found that some of the more valuable articles are unsalable. Forthwith, the conductors of the enterprise conclude that they will raffle for some of the valuable articles, and, under pretence of anxiety to make their minister a present or please some popular member of the church, fascinating persons are dispatched through the room, pencil in hand, to "solicit shares," or perhaps each draws for his own advantage, and scores of people go home with their trophies, thinking that it is all right, for Christian ladies did the embroidery and Christian men did the raffling, and the proceeds went toward a new communion set. But you may depend on it, that as far as morality is concerned, you might as well have won by the crack of the billiard-ball or the turn of the dice-box. Do you wonder that churches built, lighted, or upholstered by such processes as that come to great financial and spiritual decrepitude? The devil says : "I helped to build that house of worship, and I have as much right there as you have;" and for once the devil is right. We do not read that they had a lottery for building the church at Corinth, or at Antioch, or for getting up an embroidered surplice for St. Paul. All this I style ecclesiastical gambling. More than one man who is destroyed can say that his first step on the wrong road was when he won something at a church fair.

PARLOR CARD-PLAYING.

I will not judge other men's consciences, but I tell you that cards are in my mind so associated with the temporal and eternal damnation of splendid young men, that I should no sooner say to my family, "Come let us have a game of cards," than I would go into a menagerie and say : "Come, let us have *a game of rattlesnakes*," or into a cemetery, and sitting down by a marble slab, say to the grave-diggers: "Come, let us have a game of skulls."

[The Editor adds, that parlor card-playing has often proved a stepping-stone to gambling. A skilful parlor-player in Huntington, L. I., N. Y., took $300 to Princeton College, and soon lost all at the gaming-table, and sent home for more.]

TERRIBLE TALE.

John Borak was sent out as a commercial agent to Bremen and to the United States. After two years had gone by the house which sent him began to suspect there was something wrong. They made investigation and found that he had spent $86,000 in gambling saloons; $29,000 in Lombard Street, London; $10,000 in Fulton Street, New York; $3000 in New Orleans, and other thousands elsewhere. He was caught, tried, condemned, imprisoned; but he broke out of the penitentiary, went into the gambling business, and died a lunatic in an insane asylum. There never was a business strong enough to endure this evil habit.

PERILOUS TO BUSINESS

This crime is getting its lever under many a mercantile house in our cities, and before long down will come the great establishment, crushing reputation, home comfort and immortal souls. How it diverts and sinks capital may be inferred from some authentic statements before us. The ten gaming houses that once were authorized in Paris pass through the banks yearly three hundred and twenty-five millions of francs.

TRAP AND TRICKERY.

The gambling spirit has not stopped for any trap and trickery. Why, in the very shuffling of the cards there are deception and tricks. How often it is that by fraud the player knows what is in his opponent's hand. A skilful gamester has accomplices, and one wink decides the game. The cards are so marked that from the back they may be designated Dice are loaded with platina, and these are put into the game unknown to the honest player, and that is the reason that nine hundred and ninety-nine out of a thousand gamblers, though they may start with wealth, at the end are so poor and miserable and wretched that they would not be allowed to sit on the door-step of the brown-stone front that they once owned.

FOUL PLAY.

In a gaming-house in San Francisco, a young man having just come from the mines deposited a large sum upon the ace, and won twenty-two thousand dollars.   But the tide turns.   Intense anxiety comes upon the countenances of all. Slowly the cards go forth.   Every eye is fixed.   Not a sound is heard until the ace is revealed favorable to the bank. There are shouts of "Foul! Foul!" but the keepers of the table produce their pistols, and the uproar is silenced, and the bank has won ninety-five thousand dollars.   Do you call this a game of chance?   There is no chance about it.

AN ESTATE IN A DICE-BOX.

A young man having suddenly inherited a large property, sits at the hazard tables, and takes up in a dice-box the estate won by a father's lifetime's sweat, and shakes it, and tosses it away.

AN INFERNAL SPELL.

The gambler may be eaten up by the gambler's passion. You only discover it by the greed in his eyes, the hardness of his features, the nervous restlessness, the threadbare coat, and his embarrassed business.   Yet he is on the road to hell, and no preacher's voice, or startling warning, or wife's entreaty, can make him stay for a moment his headlong career.   The infernal spell is on him; a giant is aroused within;

and though you bind him with cables, they would part like thread, and though you fasten him seven times round with chains, they would snap like rusted wire ; and though you pile up in his path heaven-high Bibles, tracts, and sermons, and on the top should set the cross of the Son of God, over them all the gambler would leap like a roe over the rocks, on his way to perdition. "Aceldama, the field of blood!"

Take warning! You are no stronger than tens of thousands who have by this practice been overwhelmed. I have seen the whirling and the foam, and have heard the hissing beneath, and I have seen the mangled wretches writhing one upon another, and they strangled, and they struggled, and they blasphemed, and they cursed God, and they died. The death-stare of eternal despair on their countenances as the waters gurgled over them.

To *the gambler's deathbed* there comes no hope. He will probably die unattended The men who destroyed him will not come and ring the bell and ask how he is. They will not attend the obsequies. Some day his poor body is being carted out to the Potter's Field, and the wretches look out of the window of the gambling saloon, and say; " There goes the old carcass. Dead at last!" Let him down into the grave. Plant no tree there for shade. The eternal glooms that hover over the spot are shadow enough. Visit not that grave in the sunlight, for that would seem like mockery, but in the dismal night, when no stars are out, and spirits of darkness come down horsed on the wind. Then is the time to visit the grave of the gambler. May God save you from the scathing, scalding, blasting, damning influence of the gaming spirit!

AN ENEMY TO THE HOME.

Notice the effect of this crime upon domestic happiness. It has sent its ruthless ploughshare through hundreds of families, until the wife sat in rags, and the daughters were disgraced, and the sons grew up to the same infamous practices, or took a short cut to destruction across the murderer's scaffold. Home has lost all charms for the gambler. How tame are the children's caresses and a wife's devotion to the gambler! How drearily the fire burns on the domestic hearth! There must be louder laughter, and something to win, and something to lose; an excitement to drive the heart faster, fillip the blood and fire the imagination. No home, however bright, can keep back the gamester. The sweet call of love bounds back from his iron soul, and all endearments are consumed in the fire of his passion. The family Bible will go after all other treasures are lost, and if his crown in heaven were put into his hand he would cry: " Here goes; one more game, my boys. On this one throw I stake my crown of heaven."

ANOTHER VICTIM.

A young man in London, on coming of age, received a fortune of one hundred and twenty thousand dollars, and through gambling, in three years, was thrown on his mother for support. An only son went to New Orleans. He was rich, intellectual, and elegant in manners. His parents gave him, on his departure from home, their last blessing. The sharpers got hold of him They flattered him. They lured him to the gaming-table and let him win almost every time for a good while, and patted him on the back and said, "First-rate player." But fully in their grasp they fleeced him, and his thirty thousand dollars were lost. Last of all, he put up his watch and lost that. Then he began to think of his home, and of his old father and mother, and wrote thus :

" *My beloved parents,* you will doubtless feel a momentary joy at the reception of this letter from the child of your bosom, on whom you have lavished all the favors of your declining years. But, ah! alas! cherish it not. I have fallen deep, never to rise. Those gray hairs that I should have honored and protected, I shall bring down in sorrow to the grave. I will not curse my destroyer, but O may God avenge the wrongs and impositions practised upon the unwary in His own way!

This, my dear parents, is the last letter you will ever receive from me. I humbly pray for forgiveness. It is my dying prayer. Long before you have received this letter from me, the cold grave will have closed upon me forever. Life to me is insupportable. I cannot, nay, I will not, suffer the shame of having ruined you. Forget and forgive, is the dying prayer of your unfortunate son."

The old father went to the post-office for the letter. He opened the letter, and after he had read a little way he dropped upon the floor. The people thought he was dead, but they fanned him, and they pushed back the gray locks from his brow, and they found, after a while, that he had only fainted. " I wish he had been dead, for what is life to a father since his son is destroyed." When things go wrong at a gaming-table, they cry "Foul! foul!" Over all the gambling saloons of Brooklyn and New York and the whole earth, I cry, " Foul, foul, infinitely foul!" Beware of the first beginnings! This road is a down-grade, and every instant increases the momentum. Launch not upon this treacherous sea. Split hulks strew the beach. Everlasting storms howl up and down, tossing unwary crafts into the Hell-gate.

CHOICE OF ROAD.

When I go to Chicago I am sometimes perplexed at Buffalo, as I suppose many travellers are, as to whether it is better to take the Lake Shore route or the Michigan Central, equally expeditious and equally safe, getting to their destination at the same time. But suppose that I hear that on one route the track is torn up, the bridges are down, and the switches are unlocked, it will not take me a great while to decide which road to take. Now, here are two roads in the future—the Christian and the unchristian, the safe and the unsafe. Any institution or any association that confuses my ideas in regard to that fact is a bad institution and a bad association. I had prayers before I joined that society, did I have them afterward? I attended the house of God before I connected myself with that union, do I absent myself from religious influences?

Which would you rather have in your hand when you come to die—a pack of cards or a Bible? Which would you rather have pressed to your lips in the closing moment—the cup of Belshazzarean wassail or the chalice of Christian communion? Whom would you rather have for your pall-bearers—the elders of a Christian church or the companions whose conversation was full of slang and innuendo? Whom would you rather have for your eternal companions—those men who spend their evenings betting, gambling, swearing, carousing, and telling vile stories, or your little child, that bright girl whom the Lord took? When the Bridge at Ashtabula broke, and let down the most of the carload of passengers to instant death, Mr. P. P. Bliss was seated on one side of the aisle of the car writing down a Christian song which he was composing, and on the other side a group of men were playing cards. Whose landing-place in eternity would you prefer—that of P. P. Bliss, the Gospel singer, or that of the gambler?

TEN PINS.

Professed gamesters come into the ten-pin alley where there are husbands and fathers, and brothers, and sons, and put down *a thousand dollars in gold eagles.* Let the boy set up the pins at the other end of the alley. Clear the way now. Roll the first. There! it strikes. Down goes respectability. Roll the second. There! it strikes. Down goes the last feeling of humanity. Roll the third There! it strikes Down goes the soul, the immortal soul. It was not so much the pins that fell as the soul, the soul!

RAPID TRANSIT TO PERDITION.

Alas! alas! there are those who have already taken hold on death. They are in the rapids. They try to put back. Then they are hurled over the edge, and they clutch the

side of the boat until their finger-nails, blood-tipped, pierce
the wood, and with pale cheek and agonized stare, and horror lifting the hair from the scalp, they go down into depths
from which no grappling hooks will ever drag them out. O
men! beware if you have begun to tamper with this vice.

THE CAREER OF THE GAMBLER.

Lured by bad company, he finds his way into a place
where honest men ought never to go. He sits down to his
first game, but only for pastime and the desire of being
thought sociable. The players deal out the cards. They
unconsciously play into Satan's hands, who takes all the
tricks and both the players' souls for trumps—he being a
sharper at any game. A slight stake is put up, just to add
interest to the play. Game after game is played. Larger
stakes and still larger. They begin to move nervously on
their chairs. Their brows lower, and eyes flash, until now
they who win and they who lose, fired alike with passion, sit
with set jaws, and compressed lips, and clenched fists, and
eyes like fireballs that seem starting from their sockets to
see the final turn before it comes, if losing, pale with envy
and tremulous with unuttered oaths cast back red-hot upon
the heart, or, if winning, with hysteric laugh—" Ha, ha! I
have it!"

A few years have passed, and he is only the wreck of a
man. Seating himself at the game, ere he throws the first
card, he stakes the last relic of his wife—the marriage-ring
which sealed the solemn vows between them. The game is
lost, and staggering back in exhaustion he dreams. The
bright hours of the past mock his agony, and in his dreams
fiends with eyes of fire and tongues of flame circle about him
with joined hands, to dance and sing their orgies with hell-
ish chorus, chanting · " Hail, brother!" kissing his clammy
forehead until their loathsome locks flowing with serpents,
crawl into his bosom, and sink their sharp fangs and suck up
his life's blood, and coiling around his heart pinch it with
chills and agonies unutterable.

AFFECTIONATE APPEAL.

This is not an abstract subject. I have seen so many go down! There are places where if you go to a cliff and cast a stone, you can hear it far down echo on the rocks. There are other places where the plunge is so great that if you take something and throw it down you may listen and listen and listen, but there comes back no echo of the fall. And this last has been the case in many a moral calamity. Oh, young man, what is your great want? One man says it is higher social position ; another man says it is larger salary ; another man says it is easier work. I do not know what your other wants are, but I will tell you, my brother, what your greatest want is—if you do not already possess it—and that is the grace of God.

There may be those who have fallen under this evil. *You are in a prison.* You feel it. You have tried to get out. You cannot get out. If I should have your personal confidence and talk this matter over, you would say, "I can't get out of that prison." From other habits men seem to get away by the force of natural resolution sometimes ; but from this habit I do not think any man gets away by the force of natural resolution. *You want to get out* of the prison and you rush against the iron bars on one side and you do not escape. And then you soliloquize, and think and think, and then you rush against the other side the cage and against the iron bars, and there is blood on the bars and blood on your soul, and you do not escape. But there is a key that will unlock that door. It is a key of the house of David ; it is a key that Christ wears at His girdle.

O prodigals, it is a poor business for you to be feeding swine when your father stands in the front door straining his eyesight to see the return of the prodigal, and the calf in the paddock is as fat as it ever can be for the celebration, and all the harps of Heaven are strung, and the feet free There are converted gamblers in Heaven. Light from the throne of God flashed upon the green baize of their billiard saloon.

They stopped trying for earthly stakes, and they tried for Heaven and won it.

There is a hand to-day stretched out from Heaven toward the worst man in this audience. It is not a hand clenched as if to strike; it is a hand outspread as though to drop a benediction. Other seas have a shore and may be fathomed, but not so the sea of God's love. Eternity has no plummet to strike the bottom, and immensity has no iron-bound shore to confine it. Its tides are lifted by the great heart of God's compassion. But, alas! for the man who sits down to the last game of life and puts his immortal soul on the ace, and when the kings and queens and knaves and spades have been shuffled and cut and the game is ended, hovering and impending worlds discover that he has lost the game, and the faro of eternal darkness clutches down into its wallet all the blood-stained wagers. Oh, come home to thy God to-day.

STOCK-GAMBLING.

The great business disasters of this country have come from the work of godless speculators and infamous stock-gamblers. The great foe to business in New York and Brooklyn is crime. When the right shall have hurled back the wrong, and shall have purified the commercial code, and shall have thundered down fraudulent establishments, and shall have put into the hands of honest men the keys of business, blessed time for the bargain-makers. I am not talking an abstraction, I am not making a guess. I am telling you God's eternal truth.

WALL STREET.

Across the island of New York, in 1685, a wall made of stone and earth, and cannon-mounted, was built to keep off the savages. Along by that wall a street was laid out, and as the street followed the line of the wall, it was appropriately called Wall Street. It is narrow, it is short, it is un-architectural, and yet its history is unique. Excepting

Lombard Street, London, it is *the mightiest street* on this planet. There the Government of the United States was born. There Washington held his levees. There Mrs. Adams and other brilliant women of the Revolution displayed their charms. There Witherspoon and Jonathan Edwards and George Whitefield sometimes preached. There Dr. Mason chided Alexander Hamilton for writing the Constitution of the United States without any God in it.

There negroes were sold in the slave-mart. There criminals were harnessed to wheelbarrows, and, like beasts of burden, compelled to draw, or were lashed through the street behind carts to which they were fastened. There fortunes have come to coronation or burial, since the day when reckless speculators, in powered hair and silver shoe-buckles, dodged Dugan, the Governor-General of his Majesty, clear down to yesterday at three o'clock.

The history of Wall Street is to a certain extent the financial, commercial, agricultural, mining, literary, artistic, moral, and religious history of this country. Only a few blocks long, it has reached from the Canadas to the Gulf of Mexico, from San Francisco to Bangor. There are the best men in this country, and there are the worst. Every thing, from unswerving integrity to *tip-top scoundrelism*—every thing, from heaven-born charity to bloodless Shylockism.

I want to put the plough in at the curbstone of Trinity and drive it clear through to Wall Street Ferry ; and so it shall go, if the horses are strong enough to draw the plough.

Wall Street stands as a type *of tried integrity and the most outrageous villainy.* Farmers who have only a few hundred dollars' worth of produce to put on the market have but little to test their character ; but put a man into the seven-times-heated furnace of Wall Street excitement, and he either comes out a Shadrach, with hair unsinged, or he is burned into a black moral cinder. No half-way work about it.

It is as honest to deal in stocks as to deal in iron, or coal, or hardware, or dry-goods. He who condemns all stock-dealings as though they were iniquities simply shows his own ignorance. Stop all legitimate speculation in this country, and you stop all banks, you stop all factories, you stop all storehouses, you stop all the great financial prosperities of this country.

A stock-dealer is only a commission-merchant under another name. He gets his commission on one style of goods. You, the grocer, get your commission on another style of goods. The dollar that he makes is just as bright and fair and honest a dollar as the dollar earned by the day laborer.

If I wanted to find integrity bomb-proof, I would go among the bankers and merchants of Wall Street , yet, because there have been such villainies enacted there at different times, some men have supposed that it is a great financial debauchery, and they hardly dare go near the street, or walk up and down it, unless they have buttoned up their pockets, and had their lives insured, or religiously crossed themselves.

Yet, if you start at either end of the street, and read the business signs, you will find the names of more men of integrity and Christian benevolence than you can find in the same space in any street of any of our cities.

When the Christian Commission and the Sanitary Commision wanted money to send medicines and bandages to the wounded, when bread-stuffs were wanted for famishing Ireland, when colleges were to be endowed and churches were to be supported, and missionary societies were to be equipped for their work of sending the Gospel all around the world, the first street to respond has been Wall Street, and *the largest responses* in all the land have come from Wall Street.

I have not so much admiration for the French Empress who stood in her balcony in Paris, and addressed an excited mob and quelled it, as I have admiration for that venerable banker on Wall Street who, in 1864, stood on the steps of his moneyed institution and quieted the fears of depositors, and bade peace to the angry wave of commercial excitement. " God did not allow the lions to hurt Daniel, and He will not allow the ' *bears* ' to hurt you."

But while that street is a type of tried integrity on the

one hand, it is also a type of *unbounded swindle* on the other. There are the spiders that wait for innocent flies. There are the crocodiles that crawl up through the slime to cranch the calf. There are the anacondas, with lifted loop, ready to crush the unwary. There are financial wreckers, who stand on the beach praying for a Caribbean whirlwind to sweep over our commercial interests.

And here *we must draw the line* between legitimate speculation and ruinous gambling. You, a stock operator without any property behind you, financially irresponsible, sell one hundred dollars of nothing and get paid for it. You sell one hundred shares at ten thousand dollars at thirty days. If at the end of thirty days you can get the scrip for nine thousand dollars, you have made a thousand. If at the end of thirty days you have to pay eleven thousand, then you have lost a thousand Now that is trafficking in fiction, that is bettering chances, that involves *the spirit of gambling* as much as anything that ever goes on in the lowest gambling hell of New York or Brooklyn.

DOINGS IN WALL STREET.

" Riches certainly make themselves wings; they fly away as an eagle toward heaven "—PROVERBS 23 5
[The Editor adds . " He that getteth riches, and not by right, shall leave them in the midst of his days, and at his end shall be a fool." JERE. 17 : 11.]

Money is a golden-breasted bird with silver beak. It alights on the office-desk, or in the counting-room, or on the parlor centre-table. Men and women stand and admire it. They do not notice that it has wings larger than a raven's larger than a flamingo's, larger than an eagle's. One wave of the hand of misfortune and it spreads its beautiful plumage and is gone—" as an eagle toward heaven," though sometimes I think it goes *in the other direction !*

INFLATION AND COLLAPSE.

What verification we have had of the flying capacity of riches in Wall Street! Encouraged by the revival of trade, and by the fact that Wall Street disasters of other years were so far back as to be forgotten, speculators ran up the stocks from point to point until innocent people on the outside supposed that the stocks would always continue to ascend.

They gathered in from all parts of the country. Large sums of money were taken into Wall Street, and small sums of money. The crash came, thank God, in time to warn off a great many who were on their way thither; for *the sadness of the thing* was that a great many of the young men of our cities who had saved a little money for the purpose of starting themselves in business, and who had $500, or $1,000, or $2,000, or $10,000, went into Wall Street and lost all. Stocks rose and fell and ruined! And my counsel is to invest in first mortgages and in Government bonds, and to stand clear of the Wall Street vortex, where so many have been swamped and swallowed. What a compliment it is to the healthy condition of our country that these disasters in no wise depress trade! I thank God that Wall Street's capacity to blast this country is gone forever.

And let me say it is no place for a man to go into business unless his moral principle is thoroughly settled. That is no place for a man to go into business who does not know when he is overpaid five dollars by mistake, whether he had better take it back again or not. That is no place for a man to go who has large funds in trust, and who is all the time tempted to speculate with them. That is no place for a man to go who does not quite know whether the laws of State forbid usury or patronize it.

O how many men have risked themselves in the vortex and gone down, for the simple reason that their integrity had not been thoroughly established. Remember poor Ketcham, how soon the flying hoofs of his iron grays clattered with him to destruction. Remember poor Gay, at thirty years of age astonishing the world with his fortunes and his forgeries. Remember that famous man whose steamboats and whose opera-houses could not atone for his adulterous rides through Central Park in the face of decent New York, and whose behavior on Wall Street, by its example, has blasted tens of thousands of young men of this generation.

I hold up the polluted memory to warn young men, whose moral principles are not thoroughly settled, to keep out of Wall Street. It is no place for a man who shivers under the blast of temptation. Let me say also to those who are doing legitimate business on that or similar streets of which that is a type, to stand firm in Christian principle. You are in a great commercial battle-field. Be courageous. There is such a thing as a hero of the Bank and a hero of the Stock Exchange. Be you that hero.

FASCINATIONS OF STOCK-GAMBLING.

At certain times, almost every prosperous merchant wakes up, and says: "Now, I have been successful in my line of trade, and I have a tolerable income; I think I shall go down to Wall Street and treble it in three weeks. There's my neighbor. He was in the same line of business; he has his three or four hundred thousand dollars from the simple fact that he went into Wall Street. I think I shall go too."

Here they come, retired merchants, who want to get a little excitement in their lethargic veins. Here they come, the trustees of great property, to fool everything away. Here they come, men celebrated for prudence, to trifle with the livelihoods of widows and orphans. Do you wonder that sometimes they become insane? It is insanity. Do you know, there are hundreds of young men in Brooklyn and New York who are perishing under the passion for stock-gambling? Do you know that in all Christian lands this is one of the greatest curses?

You know that for years men have been made heroes of and pictorialized and in various styles presented to the public, as though sometimes they were worthy of admiration if they have scattered the funds of banks, or swallowed great estates that did not belong to them. A different measure has been applied to the crime of Wall Street from that which has been applied to the spoils which the man carries up Rat Alley.

And our young men have been dazed with this quick accumulation. They have said: "That's the way to do it. What's the use of our plodding on with small wages or insignificant salary, when we may go into business life, and with some stratagem achieve such a fortune as that man has achieved?"

But nearly all the outsiders who go there on a little financial excursion lose all. The old spiders eat up the unsuspecting flies. I had a friend who put his hand on his hip pocket and said to me in substance: " I have there the value of a hundred and fifty thousand dollars." His home is to-day penniless. What was the matter? Wall Street. Of the vast majority who are victimized, you hear not one word. One great stock firm goes down, and whole columns of newspapers discuss their fraud or their disaster, and we are presented with their features and their biography. But where one such famous firm sinks, five hundred unknown men sink with them. The great steamer goes down, and all the little boats are swallowed in the same engulfment. Gambling is gambling, whether in stocks or bread-stuffs, or dice or race track betting. Exhilaration at the start, and a raving brain and a shattered nervous system and a sacrificed property and a destroyed soul at the last.

FAST IN THE STOCKS.

It must be very exhilarating to go into Wall Street, New York, or State Street, Boston, or Third Street, Philadelphia, and, depositing a small sum of money, run the risk of taking out a fortune.

One of the main pipes to this sewer of iniquity is business excitement. It is a most significant fact that nearly all the day gambling establishments in New York were found in proximity to Wall Street. Men went into the excitement of stock gambling. Getting through that at the close of business they went into other places of gambling that they might *keep up the excitement.* The howling, stamping, Bedlamitish crew of the old-fashioned Gold Room used to drop into the gambling saloons around about. The agitation in the Stock Exchange that you sometimes saw at the announcement of the word "North-western" or Rock Island" or "Erie" or "New York Central;" the rat-tat-tat of the auctioneer's mallet, the excitement of making "corners," and establishing "pools," and "carrying" stock, and a "break" from eighty to seventy, and the excited cry of "buyer three!" "buyer ten!" "taken!" "how many?" and the loss or the gain of hundreds and thousands of dollars in the flash of a moment disqualifies a man to go home, and he goes into gaming establishments near by. That has been the past history of a great many men. They went up the stairs amid the closed business offices until they came to the room darkly curtained and wooden shuttered, but richly furnished inside, and took their places at the roulette or the faro table. That is the way some of the best men of our great cities have been destroyed.

RELIGION IN BUSINESS.

O men of Wall Street, and of all streets, stand back from nefarious enterprises, join that great company of Christian men in New York and Brooklyn who are maintaining their integrity, notwithstanding all the pressure of temptation. In the morning, when you open business in the broker's office or in the banking-house, ask God's blessing, and when you close it pronounce a benediction upon it. A kind of business that a man cannot engage in with prayer is no business to do.

Remember, my friend, that all these scenes of business will soon have passed away, and by the law of God's eternal right all the affairs of your business life will be adjudicated. *Honesty pays best for both worlds.*

Remember that the man who gets his gain by iniquity will soon lose it all. One moment after his departure from life he will not own an opera house, he will not own a certificate of stock.

Stand close by Christ, and Christ will stand close by you. The greater the temptation, the more magnificent the reward. But, alas! for the stock-gambler—what will he do in the judgment? That day will settle everything. That to the stock-gambler will be a "break" at the "first call." No smuggling into heaven. *No "collaterals"* on which to trade your way in. Go in through Christ, the Lord, or you will forever stay out.

After you have done your last day's work on earth, and the hushed assembly stands around with bowed heads at your obsequies, God forbid that the most appropriate text for your funeral oration should be "As a partridge sitteth on eggs and hatcheth them not, so he that getteth riches, and not by right, shall leave them in the midst of his days, and at the end he shall be a fool."

> " Price of many a crime untold,
>   Gold, gold, gold, gold."

STOCK-GAMBLING A LAUGHING-STOCK.

" He that sitteth in the heavens shall laugh."

With such demonstration will God greet every kind of great sin and wickedness. Bad men build up villainies higher and higher. Good men almost pity God because He is so schemed against by men. Suddenly a pin drops out of the machinery of wickedness, or a secret is revealed, the foundation begins to rock; finally, the whole thing is demolished. What is the matter? I will tell you what is the matter. That crash of ruin is only the reverberation of God's laughter

On Wall Street a fraudulent man says: " I mean to have my million." He goes to work reckless of honesty, and he gets his first $100,000. He gets after a while his $200,000. After a while he gets his $500,000. "Now," he says, "I have only one more move to make, and I shall have my million." He gathers up all his resources; he makes that last grand move, he fails and loses all, and he has not enough money of his own left to pay the cost of the car to his home. People cannot understand this spasmodic revulsion. Some say it was a turn in Erie Railroad stock, or in Western Union, or in Illinois Central; some say it is Jay Gould; some say it is one speculator, some another. They all guess wrong. I will tell you what it is. "He that sitteth in the heavens laughs!"

A man in New York said he would be the richest man in the city. He left his honest work of chair-making, and got into the city councils some way, and in ten years stole fifteen million dollars from the city government. *Fifteen million dollars!* He held the Legislature of the State of New York in the grip of his right hand. Suspicions were aroused. The Grand Jury presented indictments. The whole land stood aghast. The man who expected to put half the city in his vest-pocket goes to Blackwell's Island; goes to Ludlow Street Jail; breaks prison, and goes across the sea; is re-arrested and brought back, and again remanded to jail. Why? "He that sitteth in the heavens laughs."

Rome was a great empire; she had Horace and Virgil among her poets; she had Augustus and Constantine among her emperors But what mean the defaced Pantheon, and the Forum turned into a cattle-market, and the broken-walled Collisoum, and the architectural skeleton of her great aqueducts? What was that thunder? "Oh!" you say, "that was the roar of the battering-rams against her walls" No. What was that quiver? "Oh," you say, "that was the tramp of hostile legions." No. The quiver and the roar were the outburst of omnipotent laughter from the defied and insulted heavens. Rome defied God and He laughed her down. Thebes defied God and He laughed her down. Nineveh defied God and He laughed her down. Babylon defied God and He laughed her down.

CHAPTER IX.

Amusements.

IT is the anniversary of *Herod's birthday.* The palace is lighted. The highways leading thereto are all ablaze with the pomp of invited guests. Lords, captains, merchant princes, the mighty men of the land, are coming to mingle in the festivities. The table is spread with all the luxuries that royal purveyors can gather. The guests, white-robed and anointed and perfumed, come in and sit at the table. Music! The jests evoke roars of laughter. Riddles are propounded. Repartee is indulged. Toasts are drank. The brain is befogged. The wit rolls on into uproar and blasphemy. They are not satisfied yet. Turn on more light. Pour out more wine. Music! Sound all the trumpets. Clear the floor for a dance. Bring in Salome, the beautiful and accomplished princess. The door opens, and in bounds the dancer. The lords are enchanted. Stand back and make room for the brilliant gyrations. These men never saw such "poetry of motion." Their souls whirl in the reel and bound with the bounding feet. Herod forgets crown and throne and everything but the fascinations of Salome. All the magnificence of his realm is as nothing now compared with the splendor that whirls on tiptoe before him. His body sways from side to side, corresponding with the motions of the enchantress. His soul is thrilled with the pulsations of the feet and bewitched with the taking postures and attitudes more and more amazing. After a while he sits in enchanted silence looking at the flashing, leaping, bounding beauty, and as the dance closes and the tinkling cymbals cease to clap and the thunders of applause that shook the palace begin to abate, the enchanted monarch swears to

239

the princely performer: "Whatsoever thou shalt ask of me I will give it thee, to the half of my kingdom." Now, there was in prison at that time a minister of the Gospel by the name of John the Baptist, and he had been making a great deal of trouble by preaching some very plain and honest sermons. He had denounced the sins of the king and brought down upon him the wrath of the females of the royal household. At the instigation of her mother, Salome takes advantage of the extravagant promise of the king and says, "Bring me the head of John the Baptist on a dinner plate." Hark to the sound of feet outside the door and the clatter of swords. The executioners are returning from their awful errand. Open the door. They enter, and they present the platter to Salome. What is on this platter? A new glass of wine to continue the uproarious merriment? No. Something redder and costlier—the ghastly, bleeding head of John the Baptist, the death glare still in the eye, the locks dabbled with the gore, the features still distressed with the last agony.

This woman, who had whirled so gracefully in the dance, bends over the awful burden without a shudder. She gloats over the blood, and with as much indifference as a waiting-maid might take a tray of empty glassware out of the room after an entertainment, Salome carries the dissevered head of John the Baptist, while all the banqueters shout with laughter, and think it a good joke that in so easy and quick a way they have got rid of an earnest and outspoken minister of the Gospel.

Well, there is no harm in a birthday festival. All the kings from Pharaoh's time had celebrated such occasions, and why not Herod? No harm in kindling the lights. No harm in spreading the banquet. No harm in arousing music. But from the riot and wassail that closed the scene of that day every pure nature revolts.

DANCING UNIVERSALLY POPULAR.

Dancing is the graceful motion of the body adjusted by art to the sound and measures of musical instrument or of the human voice. All nations have danced. The ancients thought that Castor and Pollux taught the art to the Lacedæmonians. But whoever started it, all climes have adopted it. In ancient times they had the festal dance, the military dance, the mediatorial dance, the bacchanalian dance, and queens and lords swayed to and fro in the gardens, and the rough backwoodsman with this exercise awakened the echo of the forest. There is something in the sound of lively music to evoke the movement of the hand and foot, whether cultured or uncultured. Passing down the street we unconsciously keep step to the sound of the brass band, while the Christian in church with his foot beats time while his soul rises upon some great harmony. While this is so in civilized lands, the red men of the forest have their scalp dances, their green-corn dances, their war dances.

DANCING IN ANCIENT TIMES.

The exercise was so utterly and completely depraved in ancient times that the church anathematized it. The old Christian fathers expressed themselves most vehemently against it. St. Chrysostom says: "The feet were not given for dancing but to walk modestly, not to leap impudently like camels." One of the dogmas of the ancient church reads: "A dance is the devil's possession, and he that entereth into a dance entereth into his possession. As many paces as a man makes in dancing, so many paces does he make to hell." Elsewhere the old dogmas declared this: "The woman that singeth in the dance is the princess of the devil, and those that answer are her clerks, and the beholders are his friends, and the music are his bellows, and the fiddlers are the ministers of the devil. For as when hogs are strayed, if the hogsherd call one all assemble together, so when the devil calleth one

woman to sing in the dance, or to play on some musical instrument, presently all the dancers gather together." This
indiscriminate and universal denunciation of the exercise
came from the fact that it was utterly and completely depraved

But we are not to discuss the customs of the olden times,
but customs now. We are not to take the evidence of the
ancient fathers, but our own conscience, enlightened by the
Word of God, is to be the standard.

Sybaris was a great city, and it once sent out three hundred horsemen in battle They had a minstrel who had
taught the horses of the army a great trick, and when the
old minstrel played a certain tune the horses would rear and
with their front feet seem to beat time to the music. Well,
the old minstrel was offended with his country, and he went
over to the enemy, and he said to the enemy : "You give
me the mastership of the army and I will destroy their troops
when those horsemen come from Sybaris. So they gave the
old minstrel the management, and he taught all the other
minstrels a certain tune.   Then when the cavalry troop came
up the old minstrel and all the other minstrels played a certain tune, and at the most critical moment in the battle when
the horsemen wanted to rush to the conflict, the horses reared
and beat time to the music with their forefeet, and in disgrace and rout the enemy fled." Ah ! my friends, I have
seen it again and again—the minstrels of pleasure, the minstrels of dissipation, the minstrels of godless association have
defeated people in the hardest fight of life. Frivolity has
lost the battle for ten thousand folk

How many people in America have stepped *from the
ball-room into the graveyard !* Consumptions and swift neu-
ralgias are close on their track Amid many of the glittering scenes of social life in America diseases stand right and
left and balance and chain. The breath of the sepulchre
floats up through the perfume, and the froth of Death's lip
bubbles up in the champagne.

A BRILLIANT VICTIM.

In my parish of Philadelphia there was a young woman brilliant as a spring morning. She gave her life to the world. She would come to religious meetings and under conviction would for a little while begin to pray, and then would rush off again into the discipleship of the world. She had all the world could offer of brilliant social position. One day a flushed and excited messenger asked me to hasten to her house, for she was dying. I entered the room. There were the physicians, there was the mother, there lay this disciple of the world. I asked her some questions in regard to the soul. She made no answer I knelt down to pray. I rose again, and desiring to get some expression in regard to her eternal interests, I said. " Have you any hope?" and then for the first her lips moved in a whisper as she said: " No hope!" Then she died. The world, she served it, and the world helped her not in the last.

With many life is a masquerade ball, and as at such entertainments gentlemen and ladies put on the garb of kings and queens or mountebanks or clowns and at the close put off the disguise, so a great many pass their whole life in a mask, taking off the mask at death. While the masquerade ball of life goes on, they trip merrily over the floor, gemmed hand is stretched to gemmed hand, gleaming brow bends to gleaming brow On with the dance! Flush and rustle and laughter of immeasurable merry-making. But after a while the languor of death comes on the limbs and blurs the eyesight Lights lower. Floor hollow with sepulchral echo. Music saddened into a wail. Lights lower. Now the maskers are only seen in the dim light. Now the fragrance of the flowers is like the sickening odor that comes from garlands that have lain long in the vaults of cemeteries Lights lower. Mists gather in the room Glasses shake as though quaked by sullen thunder. Sigh caught in the curtain. Scarf drops from the shoulder of beauty a shroud. Lights lower Over the slippery boards in dance of death glide jealousies, envies, revenges, lust, despair, and death. Stench of lamp-wicks almost extinguished. Torn garlands will not half cover the ulcerated feet. Choking damps. Chilliness. Feet still. Hands closed. Voices hushed. Eyes shut. Lights out.

THE THEATRE AND STAGE COSTUMES.

I do not go to theatres, so I must take the evidence of the actors and managers of theatres, such as Mr. John Gilbert, Mr. A. M. Palmer, and Mr. Daniel E. Bandmann. They have told us that the crime of undress is blasting the theatre, which by many is considered a school of morals, and indeed superior to the Church, and a forerunner of the millennium. *Mr. Palmer* says: " The bulk of the performances on the stage are degrading and pernicious. The managers strive to come just as near the line as possible without flagrantly breaking the law. There never have been costumes worn on a stage of this city, either in a theatre, hall, or ' dive,' so improper as those that clothe some of the chorus in recent comic opera productions." He says in regard to the female performers: " It is not a question whether they can sing, but just how little they will consent to wear." *Mr. Bandmann,* who has been twenty-nine years on the stage, and before almost all nationalities, says: " I unhesitatingly state that the taste of the present theatre-going people of America, as a body, is of a coarse and vulgar nature. The Hindoo would turn with disgust at such exhibitions, which are sought after and applauded on the stage of this country. Our shop-windows are full of and the walls covered with show-cards and posters which should be a disgrace to an enlightened country and an insult to the eye of a cultured community." *Mr. Gilbert* says: " Such exhibition is a disastrous one to the morals of the community. Are these proper pictures to put out for the public to look at, to say nothing of the propriety of females appearing in public dressed like that? It is shameful !"

I must take the testimony of the friends of the theatre

and the confirmation which I see on the board fences and in the show-windows containing the pictures of the way actresses dress. I suppose that those representations of play-house costume are true, for if they are not true, then those highly moral and religious theatres are swindling the public by inducing the people to the theatre by promises of spectacular nudity which they do not fulfil. Now, all this familiarizes the public with such improprieties of costume and depresses the public conscience as to what is allowable and right.

BEWARE OF CONTAMINATION.

I counsel you to beware lest you allow the dramatic element in human nature to lead you into contamination. To gratify that one taste you cannot afford to sacrifice your purity, your influence, your usefulness, your soul, as many have done. The amusements of life are merely the interstices, the parentheses, the interregnums of hard work, in preparation for other hard work. He who hunts for amusement and makes that his business, is like a man who hunts for *a lost diamond* among rocks, not regarding a precipice near by, and in the joy of finding the diamond stumbles five hundred feet off and down, the cormorants and the sea-gulls only knowing where he perished.

The amusements of life cannot pay you for the loss of your soul. I could not tell your character, I could not tell your prospects for this world or the next by the particular church you attend, but if you will tell me where you were last night, and where you were the night before, and where you have been the nights of the last month, I think I could guess where you will spend eternity.

O young men, I cannot but think of the immense parental anxieties which hover over you. "Oh!" says a young man, "my father and mother are dead." That is no reason why you should think they are not watching you. Do you think that when your mother with white and dying lips kissed you good-by and went up to God, that she left all interest for her boy behind? Oh, no! I suppose she has as much in-

terest in you now as she ever had. I do not believe you have
offered a prayer since that sad day that she has not stood
somewhere near, saying, " That is right," or that you have
been disposed to go to some place where you ought not to
go, that she has not stood by and said, " Don't go there, my
dear boy; that is wrong." You thought it was the sighing
of the wind No. *It was your mother.*

But many of you have parents living, and they are thinking about you this morning Perhaps they are away off in
the country; but I warrant you they are thinking of you,
planning for you, wanting to hear from you, expecting great
things of you. They may not say much, but every good or
bad thing they hear about you thrills them from the white
hair on the wrinkled brow to the foot that will soon stop in
the journey. As perhaps no one else will tell you how much
your parents think of you, I will tell you.

You need not go clear back to see how much David
thought of Absalom, or how much Hannah did for Samuel,
or how Rizpah stood driving the jackals of the wilderness
away from the rock on which her dead sons lay. I am talking about what your parents think of you. Oh, disappoint
not their expectations! Do not forget the advice they gave
you that last morning; do not go anywhere that would dis-
please them if they heard it. And if they are good, perhaps
you had better try their religion.

THE DRAMA OF LIFE.

As to the drama of your life and mine, it will soon end.
There will be *no encore* to bring us back after the curtain has
dropped. At the beginning of that drama of life stood a
cradle; at the end of it will stand a grave. The first act,
welcome. The last act, farewell. The intermediate acts,
banquet and battle, processions bridal and funeral, songs and
tears, laughter and groans.

It was not original with Shakespeare when he said, " All
the world's a stage, and all the men and women merely players." He got it from St. Paul, who, fifteen centuries before

that, had written, " We are made a spectacle unto the world, and to angels, and to men." A spectacle in a Coliseum fighting with wild beasts in an amphitheatre, the galleries full, looking down. Here we destroy a lion. Here we grapple with a gladiator. When we fall, devils shout. When we rise, angels sing A spectacle before gallery, above gallery, gallery above gallery. Gallery of our *departed kindred* looking down to see if we are faithful, and worthy of our Christian ancestry, hoping for our victory, wanting to throw us a garland, glorified children and parents, with cheer on cheer urging us on. *Gallery of the martyrs* looking down—the Polycarps, and the Ridleys, and the M'Kails, and the Theban Legion, and the Scotch Covenanters, and they of the Brussels market-place, and of Piedmont—crying down from the galleries, " God gave us the victory, and He will give it you."

Gallery of angels looking down—cherubic, seraphic, archangelic—clapping their wings at every advantage we gain. Gallery of the king from which there waves a scarred hand, and from which there comes a sympathetic voice, saying, " Be thou faithful unto death, and I will give thee a crown of life." Oh, the spectacle in which you and I are the actors! Oh, the piled-up galleries looking down!

Talk about the exciting scenes in a theatre. There was never anything enacted in Haymarket or Drury Lane theatre equal to the last spectacular Scene, the last day. Stage, a rocking earth. Enter dukes, lords, kings, clowns, beggars. No sword, no tinsel, no crown For footlights, the kindling flames of a world. For galleries, the clouds filled with angels. For orchestra, the trumpets that wake the dead. For applause, the clapping floods of the sea. For curtains, the heavens rolled together as a scroll. For last scene in the fifth act, the tramp of nations across the stage—these to the right, those to the left. " Behold, He cometh with clouds, and every eye shall see Him !"

TESTS OF AMUSEMENTS.

" Every tree is known by his own fruit."—LUKE 6 : 44.

I propose to lay down certain rules by which every person in this house may decide for himself *what is right and what is wrong* in the way of amusements and recreations.

The first test I want you to apply to every amusement is, Has it a healthful influence, or a baleful reaction? Exhilarant and rebounding spirits are in most peril of going into dangerous amusements. The gayer the horse, the more important to have a stout driver, the swifter the ship, the more important to have a strong helmsman; and all these people who have rebounding and exuberant spirits ought to be very cautious, and discipline themselves into *the right style of recreation* and amusement.

If you come from a place of amusement or recreation so nervous you cannot sleep, and you arise in the morning, not because you are slept out, but because your duty drags you from your pillow, you have been where you ought not. There are amusements that send one to the practical work of life bloodshot and yawning and stupid and nauseated. They are all bad—all that style of amusement. There are amusements that disgust one with the drudgery of every-day life—with tools of trade because they are not swords; with work-aprons because they are not robes; with the cattle because they are not infuriated bulls of the arena.

If any style of amusement gives you a longing for a life of romance and hair-breadth escapes, and love that takes poison and shoots itself, and makes you unpractical in the great duties of life—those amusements ought to be obnoxious to you as they are obnoxious to God. Our recreations were intended to build us up, and if they pull us down in our moral or physical health, they are bad amusements; and I charge you, O young men! steer clear of them.

Again: I want you not to go into any style of amusement which will lead you into expenditures beyond your means. Money spent for recreation is well spent. Do not be so silly as to come from a place of innocent recreation and say, " Now time is wasted and money wasted." It may yield you more profit for this world and the world to come than money that has brought you five thousand dollars from an investment.

But, oh, how many properties have been riddled with costly amusements! *The table has been robbed* to pay the club; the champagne has drowned the boy's primer; the table-cloth of the corner saloon is in debt to the wife's faded dress; excursions that in a day make a tour clear around a month's wages; ladies whose lifetime business it is to go shopping—all these have their echo in bankruptcies that appall the Church and shake the money-market, and send drunkenness staggering across the richly-figured carpet of the mansion, dashing into the mirror and drowning the carol of music in the whooping of bloated sons come home to break their old mother's heart.

They that go into amusements that they cannot afford, first borrow what they cannot earn, and then they steal what they cannot borrow. First into embarrassment, then into lying, then into theft; and when a man gets as far as that he does not stop short of the penitentiary. There are thousands of men who have enough salary to support them and support their families, but have not enough salary to support their expensive amusements; and in that direction they perish. How often it is that we ministers of the Gospel are requested to go over to New York and beg off some young man who has made a false entry or taken money from the drawer that did not belong to him, or made some financial shipwreck. We have sometimes been successful in begging him off, and getting the firm to try him over again, to give him one more chance before he is sent home to break his mother's heart, but sometimes we have not succeeded so well.

O merchants of New York and Brooklyn! if there be a leakage in the money-drawer, if the cash account did not come out last night aright, if there be something in the financial management of your store, would it not be well to look to see if you have not in your employ some one who is a victim of bad amusements? You pay enough salary to support that young man—honorably support him; but the amusements which he has entered into cannot be supported by any such salary, and you had better give the note of warning while warning may be of some good.

Sinful amusements open very brightly. The young man says, " Now I'm going to have a good time. I don't know where the money's coming from, but I'll get it somehow. Ah! what a beautiful day for a ride. Crack the whip. Away go the horses' hoofs racketing over the turnpike. Come, my boys, fill high the glasses Drink! Drink to health! Drink to long life! Drink to a good many rides like this!" Young men engaged in stores or shops or factories look out of the window and say, " I wonder where that young man gets his money? He gets no more salary than I get. I can't afford that: how can he afford it?"

Again: I charge you *not to make amusement your lifetime business.* Life is an earnest thing. I do not care whether you have been born in palace or hovel, affluent or pinched, you have got to work. If you do not sweat with toil you will sweat with disease. Besides that, you have a soul which is to be transfigured amid the pomps of a judgment day; and after the sea has chanted its last anthem, and the mountains have come down in avalanche of rock, you will be living in a realm where seraphs sing, or in a dungeon where demons howl.

Alas! that in a world where men have so much to do for themselves and so much to do for others, they can find nothing to do. Our amusements are only helps to hard work. Amusement is the bower in which business and philanthropy rest a little while on their way to stirring achievement. Amusements are the vines that grow up around the anvil and the blossoming of the hammers.

Alas for the man who spends his life in laboriously doing nothing—the days in hunting for sport, the nights in seeking out some *gas-lighted foolery !* No time to pray, no time to work, no time to read. Always with the sporting-jacket on, hunting game in the mountain or fish in the brook—not half so well off the man as the greyhound that runs at his side, or the fly-bait with which he whips the stream.

Our amusements are only the playing of the orchestra while the tragedy of life plunges through its five acts—infancy, childhood, manhood, old age, and death. Then exit the last chance for mercy. Enter the overwhelming realities of the eternal world.

Again: I charge you, stand clear of all amusements which lead you into bad company. If you belong to an organization where you have to meet with the intemperate, or the unclean, or the dishonest, or the abandoned, in God's name I beg you, quit it—quit it. I never knew a man yet who could stand evil association and be unhurt—never one. Out of the fourteen hundred millions of the race there never was one.

If your duty leads you among bad men, God will take care of you. If your style of work day by day carries you among those who are bad, God knows that, and He will take you through the furnace, and you will be unscorched. But I mean, when a man *deliberately chooses* bad association because he likes it, that man has started on *the road down.* Oh, I do not care what you call it, that association will despoil your soul. After you are destroyed, body, mind, and soul, what will they do for you? what will they do for your family? They will not give one cent to support your children after you are dead. They will not weep one tear at your burial. They will chuckle over your damnation.

AMUSEMENT VERSUS HOME.

Once more : I want you to stand clear from all amusements which interfere with your home happiness—all amusements that destroy domestic happiness. How many shattered homes in Brooklyn! Tens of thousands in the United States destroyed by sinful amusements—homes destroyed. The father went off, the mother went off, the child went off. Is there such a wanderer here? I should like to charm you

home by that imperial word—home ! home ! Do you know
that very soon you will be done with your home, and you
cannot bless it ?   Do you realize that soon, oh father, your
children will be out in the world, and all the influence for
good you have to bring upon them you must bring very
soon?   Do you know that death will crash in and break up
that conjugal relation ?   And alas for you if you stand by
the grave of one who perished through your neglect !

I saw a recreant husband stand at the death-bed of his
Christian wife.   She said to him, "*Do you see that ring ?*"
He said, "Yes, I see it."   She said, "Do you know who put
that ring there ?"   He said, "Yes, I put it there ; that is the
wedding-ring."   They both seemed overwhelmed with
memories.   And I do not know but that the chain of influences is going to draw you home and draw you to God and
Heaven: I do not know but that long chain of influences
has for its last link the wedding-ring.   So I lay hold of the
rope, I lay hold of the chain, and I pull for your eternal life.
By the hour when you stood in the church, or in the house at
the *wedding altar*, and promised to be faithful until death did
you part, in sorrow and in joy, in sickness and in health ;   by
the hour when you sat in *your new home* planning out a
bright future ;   *by the cradle* and the glad hour when one life
was spared and another given ;   *by the sick bed* from which the
little one lifted the hands, and you knew he must die, and
he put one arm around father's neck, and the other arm
around mother's neck and bound them with a dying
kiss ;   *by the grave* you can never think of without a rush
of tears ;   by the family Bible, where amid the story of
heavenly love is the short but expressive record of births
and deaths ;   by the judgment-day, where husbands and
wives, fathers and mothers, in immortal groups shall rise up
in shining array or shrink down into darkness—by all that,
I beg you, give your best love to your home.

I address you as Gehazi addressed the Shunammite,
when I look into your faces this day, and say, "Is it well
with thee ? is it well with thy husband ? is it well with the
child ?"   Go forth, then, and test all your amusements by

these four tests. Be happy in your work. Be happy in your recreations. When there are so many innocent amusements, do not plunge into the pernicious. Do not stop your ears to a Heaven full of songsters, and then listen to the hiss of a dragon. Do not turn your back upon the mountain-side, a-purple with wild flowers and dashing with nimble streams, to go with blistered feet climbing up the hot sides of fire-belching Cotopaxi. And if there be a man who is leading others astray, my last remark is to you : Let me say, if you are not only going astray yourself, but leading others astray, the judgment of God will meet you.

CHAPTER X.

Social Impurity.

"As an ox to the slaughter."—Prov. 7 : 22.

THERE is nothing in the voice or manner of the butcher to indicate to the ox that there is death ahead. The ox thinks he is going on to a rich pasture-field of clover, where all day long he will revel in the herbaceous luxuriance; but after a while the men and the boys close in upon him with sticks and stones and shouting, and drive him through bars and into a doorway, where he is fastened, and with a well-aimed stroke the axe fells him; and so the anticipation of the redolent pasture-field is completely disappointed. So many a young man has been driven on by temptation to what he thought would be paradisiacal enjoyment; but after a while influences with darker hue and swarthier arm close in upon him, and he finds that instead of making an excursion into a garden, he has gone "as an ox to the slaughter."

It seems to me that it is high time that pulpit and platform and printing-press speak out against the impurities of modern society. Fastidiousness and Prudery say: "Better not speak—you will rouse up adverse criticism; you will make worse what you want to make better; better deal in glittering generalities; the subject is too delicate for polite ears." But there comes a voice from heaven overpowering the mincing sentimentalities of the day, saying: "Cry aloud, spare not, lift up thy voice like a trumpet, and show my people their transgressions and the house of Jacob their sins."

The trouble is that when people write or speak upon this theme they are apt to cover it up with the graces of belles-lettres, so that the crime is made attractive instead of re-

254

pulsive. Lord Byron in " Don Juan" adorns this crime until
it smiles like a May queen. Michelet, the great French
writer, covers it up with bewitching rhetoric until it glows
like the rising sun, when it ought to be made loathsome as
a small-pox hospital. There are to-day influences abroad,
which if unresisted by the pulpit and the printing-press will
turn New York and Brooklyn into Sodom and Gomorrah,
fit only for the storm of fire and brimstone that whelmed
the cities of the plain.

A CRUSADE NEEDED.

You who are seated in your Christian homes, compassed
by moral and religious restraints, do not realize the gulf of
iniquity that bounds you on the north and the south and
the east and the west. While I speak there are tens of
thousands of men and women going over the awful plunge
of an impure life; and while I cry to God for mercy upon
their souls, I call upon you to marshal in the defence of your
homes, your Church, and your nation.

There is a banqueting-hall that you have never heard
described. You know all about the feast of Ahasuerus,
where a thousand lords sat. You know all about Belshazzar's carousal, where the blood of the murdered king spurted
into the faces of the banqueters. You may know of the scene
of riot and wassail when there was set before Esopus one
dish of food that cost $400,000. But I speak now of a dif-
ferent banqueting-hall. Its roof is fretted with fire. Its floor
is tessellated with fire. Its chalices are chased with fire. Its
song is a song of fire. Its walls are buttresses of fire. Solomon refers to it when he says: " Her guests are in the
depths of hell."

LIBERTINISM.

There has been a great deal of fascination thrown around
libertinism. Society is very severe upon the impurity that
lurks around the alleys and low haunts of the town. The

law pursues it, smites it, incarcerates it, tries to destroy
it. You know as well as I that society becomes lenient in
proportion as impurity becomes affluent or is in elevated
circles, and finally society is silent, or disposed to palliate.
Where is the judge, the jury, the police officer that dare
arraign the wealthy libertine ? He walks the streets, he rides
the parks, he flaunts his iniquity in the eyes of the pure.
The hag of uncleanness looks out of the tapestried window.
Where is the law that dares take the brazen wretches and
put their faces in an iron frame of a State's prison window ?

Sometimes it seems to me as if society were going back
to the state of morals of Herculaneum, when it sculptured
its vileness on pillars and temple wall, and nothing but the
lava of a burning mountain could hide the immensity of
crime. At what time God will rise up and extirpate these
evils upon society I know not, nor whether He will do it by
fire, or hurricane, or earthquake ; but a Holy God I do not
think will stand it much longer. I believe the thunderbolts
are hissing hot, and that when God comes to chastise the
community for these sins, against which He has uttered
Himself more bitterly than against any other, the fate of
Sodom and Gomorrah will be tolerable as compared with
the fate of our modern society, which knew better, but did
worse.

We want about ten thousand pulpits in America to thunder:
" All adulterers and whoremongers shall have their place in
the lake which burneth with fire and brimstone ; which is the
second death." It is hell on earth and hell forever. We
have got to understand in Brooklyn, and New York, and all
parts of this land that iniquity on Madison Square, of
Brooklyn Heights, or Beacon Hill is as damnable in the
sight of God as it is in the slums. Whether it has canopied
couch of eider-down, or dwells amid the putridity of a low
tenement house, God is after it in His vengeance. Yet the
pulpit of the Christian Church has been so cowed down on
this subject that it hardly dares speak, and men are almost
apologetic when they read the Ten Commandments.

FREE-LOVEISM.

Our American communities are suffering from the gospel of Free Loveism, which, fifteen or twenty years ago, was preached on some of the platforms of this country. I charge upon Free Loveism that it has blighted innumerable homes, and that it has sent innumerable souls to ruin. Free Loveism is bestial; it is worse—it is infernal. It has furnished this land with about one thousand divorces annually. In one county in the State of Indiana it furnished eleven divorces in one day before dinner. It has roused up elopements, North, South, East, and West. You can hardly take up a paper but you read of an elopement. As far as I can understand the doctrine of Free Loveism it is this : that every man ought to have somebody else's wife, and every wife somebody else's husband. They do not like our Christian organization of society, and I wish they would all elope, the wretches of one sex taking the wretches of the other, and start to-morrow morning for the great Sahara Desert, until the simoon shall sweep seven feet of sand all over them, and not one passing caravan for the next five hundred years bring back one miserable bone of their carcasses. Free Loveism ! It it *the double distilled extract of nux vomica,* ratsbane and adder's tongue. Never until society goes back to the old Bible and hears its eulogy of purity and its anathema of uncleanness—never until then will this evil be extirpated.

EXPLOSIONS OF SOCIAL LIFE.

Then look at the impurities of these great cities. Ever and anon there are reports in the newspapers that make the story of Sodom quite respectable ; for such things, Christ says, it were more tolerable for Sodom and Gomorrah than for the Chorazins and Bethsaidas of greater light. It is no unusual thing in our cities to see men in high position with two or

three families, or refined ladies willing solemnly to marry the
very swine of society, if they be wealthy. Brooklyn, whose
streets fifteen years ago were almost free from all sign of the
social evil, now night by night rivals upper Broadway in its
flamboyant wickedness. The Bible is all a-flame with denunci-
ations against an impure life, but many of the American minis
try utter not one point-blank word against this iniquity *lest
some old libertine throw up his church pew.* Machinery is
organized in all the cities of the United States and Canada by
which to put yearly in the grinding-mill of this iniquity thousands of the unsuspecting of the country farmhouses, one pro-
curess confessing last week in the courts that she had supplied the infernal market with *one hundred and fifty souls in
six months.* Oh! for five hundred *Pall Mall Gazettes* in
America to swing open the door of this lazar-house of social
corruption! Exposure must come before extirpation.

ALLEY SCENE.

Pass on through the alley. Open the door. Look at those
two eyes rising up out of the darkness and out from the
straw in the corner, coming toward you, and as they come
near you your light goes out. Strike another match Ah!
this is a babe, not like those beautiful children presented
in baptism. This little one never smiled; it never will smile.
A flower flung on an awfully barren beach. O Heavenly
Shepherd, fold that little one in Thy arms! Wrap around
you your shawl or your coat tighter, for the cold wind sweeps
through.

Strike another match. Ah! is it possible that the scarred
and bruised face of that young woman ever was looked into
by maternal tenderness? Utter no scorn. Utter no harsh
word. No ray of hope has dawned on that brow for many
a year. No ray of hope ever will dawn on that brow But
the light has gone out. Do not strike another light. It
would be a mockery to kindle another light in such a place
as that. Pass out and pass down the street. Our cities of

Brooklyn and New York and all our great cities are full of
such homes, and the worst time is the third watch of the
night. But while the city van carries the scum of this sin
from the prison to the police court morning by morning, it
is full time, if we do not want high American life to become
like that of the court of Louis XV., to put millionaire
Lotharios and the Pompadours of your brown-stone palaces
into a van of popular indignation, and drive them out of
respectable associations. What prospect of social purification can there be, as long as at summer watering-places it
is usual to see a young woman of excellent rearing, stand
and simper and giggle, and roll up her eyes sideways before
one of those first-class satyrs of fashionable life, and on the
ball-room floor join him in the dance, the maternal chaperone
meanwhile beaming from the wall on the scene? Matches
are made in heaven, they say. Not such matches ; for the
brimstone indicates the opposite region.

The evil is overshadowing all our cities. By some these
immoralities are called peccadilloes, gallantries, eccentrici-
ties, and are relegated to the realms of jocularity, and few
efforts are being made against it.

GOD BLESS THE "WHITE-CROSS"

movement, as it is called—the excellent and talented Miss
Frances Willard, its ablest advocate on this side the sea—an
organization making a mighty assault on this evil ! God forward the tracts on this subject distributed by the religious tract
societies of the land ! God help parents in the great work
they are doing, in trying to start their children with pure
principles ! God help all legislators in their attempt to in-
hibit this crime !

But, is this all ? Then it is only a question of time when
the last vestige of purity and home will vanish out of sight.
Human arms, human pens, human voices, human talents
are not sufficient. I begin to look up. I listen for artillery
rumbling down the sapphire boulevards of heaven. I watch

to see if in the morning light there be not the flash of descending scimetars. O for God! Does it not seem time for His appearance? Is it not time for all lands to cry out: "Let God arise, and let His enemies be scattered!"

[As a caution to young men, the Editor adds almost the last words of John B. Gough: "Young men, keep your record clean."]

CHAPTER XI.

Intemperance.

"And Noah planted a vineyard and drank of the wine and was drunken."

NOAH did the best and the worst thing for the world. He built an ark against the deluge of water, but introduced a deluge against which the human race has ever since been trying to build an ark—the deluge of drunkenness. In the opening chapters of the Bible we hear his staggering steps. Shem and Japhet tried to cover up the disgrace, but there he is, drunk on wine at a time in the history of the world when, to say the least, there was no lack of water.

Inebriation having entered the world, has not retreated. Abigail, the fair and heroic wife who saved the flocks of Nabal, her husband, from confiscation by invaders, goes home at night and finds him so intoxicated she cannot tell him the story of his narrow escape. Uriah came to see David, and David got him drunk, and paved the way for the despoliation of a household. Even the church bishops needed to be charged to be sober and not given to too much wine; and so familiar were the people of Bible times with the staggering and falling motion of the inebriate, that Isaiah, when he comes to describe the final dislocation of worlds, says: "The earth shall reel to and fro like a drunkard."

Ever since apples and grapes and wheat grew, the world has been tempted to unhealthful stimulants. But the intoxicants of the olden time were an innocent beverage, a harmless orangeade, a quiet syrup, a peaceful soda-water, as compared with the liquids of modern inebriation, into which a madness, and a fury, and a gloom, and a fire, and a suicide, and a retribution have mixed and mingled. Fermentation was always known, but it was not until a thousand years after Christ that distillation was invented.

THE ARCH FIEND OF THE NATIONS.

While we must confess that some of the ancient arts have been lost, the Christian era is superior to all others in the bad eminence of whiskey and rum and gin. The modern drunk is a hundred-fold worse than the ancient drunk. Noah in his intoxication became imbecile, but the victims of modern alcoholism have to struggle with whole menageries of wild beasts and jungles of hissing serpents and perditions of blaspheming demons. An arch fiend arrived in our world, and he built an invisible cauldron of temptation. He built that cauldron strong and stout for all ages and all nations. First, he squeezed into the cauldron the juices of the forbidden fruit of Paradise. Then he gathered for it a distillation from the harvest fields and the orchards of the hemispheres. Then he poured into this cauldron capsicum, and copperas, and logwood, and deadly nightshade, and assault and battery, and vitriol, and opium, and rum, and murder, and sulphuric acid, and theft, and potash, and cochineal, and red carrots, and poverty, and death, and hops.

But it was a dry compound, and it must be moistened, and it must be liquefied, and so the arch fiend poured into that cauldron the tears of centuries of orphanage and widowhood, and he poured in the blood of twenty thousand assassinations. And then the arch fiend took a shovel that he had brought up from the furnaces beneath, and he put that shovel into this great cauldron and began to stir, and the cauldron began to heave, and rock, and boil, and sputter, and hiss, and smoke, and the nations gathered around it with cups, and tankards, and demijohns, and kegs, and there was enough for all, and the arch fiend cried. "Aha! champion fiend am I. Who has done more than I have for coffins, and graveyards, and prisons, and insane asylums, and the populating of the lost world? And when this cauldron is emptied I'll fill it again, and I'll stir it again, and it will smoke again, and that smoke will join another smoke—the smoke of a torment that ascendeth forever and ever."

" I drove fifty ships on the rocks of Newfoundland and the Skerries and the Goodwins. I defeated the Northern army at Fredericksburg. I have ruined more senators than will gather next winter in the national councils. I have ruined more lords than will be gathered in the House of Peers. The cup out of which I ordinarily drink is a bleached human skull, and the upholstery of my palace is so rich a crimson because it is dyed in human gore, and the mosaic of my floors is made up of the bones of children dashed to death by drunken parents, and my favorite music, sweeter than Te Deum or triumphal march—my favorite music is the cry of daughters turned out at midnight on the street because father has come home from the carousal, and the seven-hundred-voiced shriek of the sinking steamer, because the captain was not himself when he put the ship on the wrong course. Champion fiend am I! I have kindled more fires, I have wrung out more agonies, I have stretched out more midnight shadows, I have opened more Golgothas, I have rolled more juggernauts, I have damned more souls than any other emissary of diabolism. Champion fiend am I!"

.

THE CAROUSAL.

"In that night was Belshazzar the King of the Chaldeans slain."
—DANIEL 5 : 30.

Bible pictures, like the works of the old masters, improve by age. Like Raphael's Transfiguration or Da Vinci's Last Supper, they are worth more now than ever before.

Night was about to come down upon Babylon. The shadows of her two hundred and fifty towers began to lengthen. The Euphrates rolled on, touched by the fiery splendors of the setting sun and gates of brass, burnished and glittering, opened and shut like doors of flame. The hanging gardens of Babylon, wet with the heavy dew, began to pour from starlit flowers and dripping leaf, a fragrance

for many miles around. The streets and squares were lighted
for dance and frolic and promenade. The theatres and galleries of art invited the wealth and pomp and grandeur of
the city to rare entertainments. Scenes of riot and wassail
were mingled in every street, and godless mirth and outrageous excess and splendid wickedness came to the king's
palace to do their mightiest deeds of darkness.

A royal feast to-night at the king's palace. Rushing up
to the gates are chariots upholstered with precious cloth
from Dedan and drawn by fire-eyed horses from Togarmah,
that rear and neigh in the grass by the charioteers, while a
thousand lords and women dismount dressed in all the splendor of Syrian emerald and the color blending of agate and
chasteness of coral, and the sombre glory of Tyrian purple,
and princely embroideries brought from afar by camels
across the desert and by ships of Tarshish across the sea.
Open wide the gates and let the guests come in. The cham-
berlains and cup-bearers are all ready. Hark to the rustle
of the silks and to the carol of the music. See the blaze of
the jewels. Lift the banners. Fill the cups. Clap the
cymbals. Blow the trumpets. Let the night go by with
song and dance and ovation, and let that Babylonish tongue
be palsied that will not say, "O King Belshazzar, live forever."

Ah, my friends, it was not any common banquet to which
these great people came. All parts of the earth had sent
their richest viands to that table. Brackets and chandeliers
flashed their light upon tankards of burnished gold. Fruits,
ripe and luscious, in baskets of silver entwined with leaves,
plucked from the royal conservatory. Vases, inlaid with
emerald and ridged with exquisite traceries, filled with nuts
that were thrashed from forests of different lands. Wine
brought from the royal vats foaming in the decanters and
bubbling in the chalices. Tufts of cassia and frankincense
wafting their sweetness from wall and table. Gorgeous banners unfolding in the breeze that came through the opening
window bewitched with the perfume of hanging gardens.

Fountains rising up from inclosures of ivory in jets of

crystal to fall in flattering rain of diamonds and pearls. Statues of mighty men looking down from niches in the wall upon crowns and shields brought from subdued empires. Idols of wonderful work standing on pedestals of precious stones. Embroidery stooping about the windows and wrapping pillars of cedar and drifting on floor inlaid with ivory and agate. Music mingling the thrum of harps and clash of cymbals and the blast of trumpets in one wave of transport that went rippling along the wall and breathing among the garlands and pouring down the corridors and thrilling the souls of a thousand banqueters.

The signal is given, and the lords and ladies, the mighty men and women of the land, come around the table. Pour out the wine. Let foam and bubble kiss the rim. Hoist every one his cup and drink to the sentiment: "O King Belshazzar, live forever!" Be-starred head-band and coronet of royal beauty gleam to the uplifted chalices as again and again and again they are emptied. Away with care from the palace! Tear royal dignity to tatters! Pour out more wine! Give us more light, wilder music, sweeter perfume! Lord shouts to lord, captain ogles to captain. Goblets clash, decanters rattle. There come in the obscene song and the drunken hiccough and the slavering lip and the guffaw of idiotic laughter, bursting from the lips of princes, flushed, reeling, bloodshot, and while mingling with it all I hear, " huzza, huzza, for great Belshazzar!"

What is that on the plastering of the wall? Is it a spirit? Is it a phantom? Is it God? The music stops. The goblets fall from the nerveless grasp. There is a thrill. There is a start. There is a thousand-voiced shriek of horror. Let Daniel be brought in to read that writing. He comes in. He reads it. "Weighed in the balances and found wanting."

Meanwhile the Assyrians who for two years had been laying a seige to that city took advantage of that carousal and came in. I hear the feet of the conquerors on the palace stairs. Massacre rushes in with a thousand gleaming knives. Death bursts upon the scene; and I shut the door of that banqueting-hall, for I do not want to look. There is nothing there but torn banners and broken wreaths and the slush of upset tankards and the blood of murdered women and the kicked and tumbled carcase of a dead king. " For in that night was Belshazzar the King of the Chaldeans slain."

There is a great difference between the opening of the banquet and of sin at its close. Young man, if you had looked in upon the banquet in the first few hours you would have wished you had been invited there and could sit at the feast. " Oh, the grandeur of Belshazzar's feast!" you would have said. But you look in at the close of the banquet, and your blood curdles with horror. The king of terrors has there a ghastlier banquet. Human blood is the wine, and dying groans are the music.

Sin has made itself a king in the earth. It has crowned itself. It has spread a banquet. It invites all the world to come to it. It has hung in its banqueting-hall the spoils of all kingdoms and the banners of all nations. It has gathered from all music. It has strewn from its wealth the tables and the floors and the arches. And yet how often is that banquet broken up, and how terrible is its end ; ever and anon there is a handwriting on the wall. A king falls. A great culprit is arrested. The knees of wickedness knock together. God's judgment like an armed host breaks in upon the banquet ; and that night is Belshazzar the King of the Chaldeans slain.

A WARNING VOICE FROM THE ASHES OF BABYLON.

Drunkenness is the greatest evil of this nation, and it takes no logical process to prove that a drunken nation cannot long be a free nation. So I go on showing you the perils that threaten the destruction of American institutions. I call your attention to the fact that drunkenness is not subsiding, certainly that it is not at a standstill, but that it is on an onward march, and it is a double quick. Beginning near by, I have seen more drunken people in Brooklyn and in

New York in the last six weeks than in any two years of my life, and so have you, if you have been passing up and down these streets much. There is more rum swallowed in this country, and of a worse kind, than was ever swallowed since the first distillery began its work of death. Where there was one drunken home there are ten drunken homes. Where there was one drunkard's grave there are twenty drunkards' graves.

According to United States Government figures, in 1840 there were 23,000,000 gallons of beer sold. Last year there were 551,000,000 gallons. According to the governmental figures, in the year 1840 there were 5,000,000 gallons of wine sold. Last year there were 25,000,000 gallons of wine. It is on the increase. Talk about crooked whiskey—by which men mean the whiskey that does not pay the tax to government—I tell you all strong drink is crooked   Crooked otard, crooked cognac, crooked schnapps, crooked beer, crooked wine, crooked whiskey, because it makes a man's path crooked, and his life crooked, and his death crooked, and his eternity crooked.

If I could gather all the armies of the dead drunkards and have them come to resurrection, and then add to that host all the armies of living drunkards, five and ten abreast, and then if I could have you mount a horse and ride along that line for review, you would ride that horse until he dropped from exhaustion, and you would mount another horse and ride until he fell from exhaustion, and you would take another and another, and you would ride along hour after hour, and day after day. Great hosts, in regiments, in brigades. Great armies of them. And then if you had voice enough stentorian to make them all hear, and you could give the command, "Forward, march!" their first tramp would make the earth tremble. I do not care which way you look in the community to-day, the evil is increasing.

I call your attention to the fact that there are thousands of people born with a thirst for strong drink—a fact too often ignored. Along some ancestral lines there runs the river of temptation There are children whose swaddling clothes are torn off the shroud of death.

THE DRUNKARD'S WILL.

Many a father has made a will of this sort: "In the name of God, amen. I bequeath to my children my houses and lands and estates, share and share shall they alike. Hereto I affix my hand and seal in the presence of witnesses." And yet, perhaps that very man has made another will that the people have never read, and that has not been proved in the courts. That will put in writing would read something like this: "In the name of disease and appetite and death, amen. I bequeath to my children my evil habits, my tankards shall be theirs, my wine-cup shall be theirs, my destroyed reputation shall be theirs. Share and share alike shall they in the infamy. Hereto I affix my hand and seal in the presence of all the applauding harpies of hell."

DRUG STORES.

From the multitude of those who have the evil habit born with them, this army is being augmented. And I am sorry to say that a great many of the drug stores are abetting this evil, and alcohol is sold under the name of bitters. It is bitters for this, and bitters for that, and bitters for some other thing, and good men deceived, not knowing there is any thraldom of alcoholism coming from that source, are going down, and some day a man sits with the bottle of black bitters on his table, and the cork flies out, and after it flies a fiend and clutches the man by his throat, and says: "Aha! I have been after you for ten years. I have got you now. Down with you, down with you!" Bitters! Ah! yes. They make a man's family bitter, and his home bitter, and his disposition bitter, and his death bitter, and his hell bitter. Bitters! A vast army all the time increasing. And let me also say that it is as thoroughly organized as any army, with commander-in-chief, staff officers, infantry, cavalry, batteries, sutlerships and flaming ensigns, and that every candidate for office in America will yet have to pronounce himself the friend or foe of the liquor traffic.

I have in my possession a circular of a brewers' association —a circular sent to all candidates for office ; it has been sent or will be sent—a form to be filled up saying whether the candidate is a friend of the liquor traffic or its enemy; and if he is an enemy of the business then the man is doomed ; or if he declines to fill up the circular and send it back, his silence is taken as a negative answer.

TAKE SIDES.

It seems to me it is about time for the 17,000,000 professors of religion in America to take sides. It is going to be an out-and-out battle between drunkenness and sobriety, between heaven and hell, between God and the devil. Take sides before there is any further national decadence ; take sides before your sons are sacrificed and the new home of your daughter goes down under the alcoholism of an embruted husband. Take sides while your voice, your pen, your prayer, your vote may have any influence in arresting the despoliation of this nation. If the 17,000,000 professors of religion should take sides on this subject, it would not be very long before the destiny of this nation would be decided in the right direction. Certainly, sermons setting forth the perils that threaten the destruction of our American institutions would be a very poorly planned course of sermons if they did not speak of drunkenness.

Is it a State evil? or is it a national evil? Does it belong to the North? or does it belong to the South? Does it belong to the East? or does it belong to the West? Ah! there is not an American river into which its tears have not fallen and into which its suicides have not plunged. What ruined that Southern plantation? Every field a fortune, the proprietor and his family once the most affluent supporters of summer watering-places. What threw that New England farm into decay and turned the roseate cheeks that bloomed

at the foot of the Green Mountains into the pallor of despair? What has smitten every street of every village, town,
and city of this continent with a moral pestilence? What
sends thousands of men on the first Tuesday in November
to the ballot-box, maudlin, incompetent, filthy, and blasphemous? Strong drink. To prove that this is a national
evil, I call up three States in opposite directions—Maine,
Iowa, and Georgia. Let them testify in regard to this.
State of Maine says: "It is so great an evil up here we have
anathematized it as a State." State of Iowa says : "It is so
great an evil out here we have prohibited it by constitutional
amendment." State of Georgia says : "It is so great an
evil down here that ninety counties of this State have made
the sale of intoxicating drink a criminality." So the word
comes up from all sources, and it is going to be a Waterloo,
and I want you to know on what side I am going to be when
that Waterloo is fully come, and I want you to be on the
right side. Either drunkenness will be destroyed in this
country, or the American Government will be destroyed.
Drunkenness and free institutions are coming into a death
grapple.

O how many are waiting to see if something cannot be
done! Thousands of drunkards waiting who cannot go ten
minutes in any direction without having the temptation
glaring before their eyes or appealing to their nostrils, they
fighting against it with enfeebled will and diseased appetite,
conquering, then surrendering, conquering again and surrendering again, and crying: "How long, O Lord, how long
before these infamous solicitations shall be gone?" And how
many mothers there are waiting to see if this national curse cannot lift! Is that the boy that had the honest breath who comes
home with breath vitiated or disguised? What a change!
How quickly those habits of early coming home have been
exchanged for the rattling of the night-key in the door long
after the last watchman has gone by and tried to see that
everything was closed up for the night! Oh, what a change
for that young man who we had hoped would do something
in merchandise, or in artisanship, or in a profession that

would do honor to the family name long after mother's wrinkled hands are folded from the last toil! All that exchanged for startled look when the door-bell rings, lest something has happened. And the wish that the scarlet-fever twenty years ago had been fatal, for then he would have gone directly to the bosom of his Saviour. But alas, poor old soul, she has lived to experience what Solomon said : "A foolish son is a heaviness to his mother."

O what a funeral it will be when that boy is brought home dead! And how mother will sit there and say : " Is this my boy that I used to fondle and that I walked the floor with in the night when he was sick? Is this the boy that I held to the baptismal font for baptism ? Is this the boy for whom I toiled until the blood burst from the tips of my fingers that he might have a good start and a good home? Lord, why hast Thou let me live to see this ? Can it be that these swollen hands are the ones that used to wander over my face when rocking him to sleep ? Can it be that this is the swollen brow that I once so rapturously kissed ? Poor boy! how tired he does look. I wonder who struck him that blow across the temples ! I wonder if he uttered a dying prayer! Wake up, my son ! Don't you hear me? Wake up ! O he can't hear me ! Dead, dead, dead ! 'O Absalom, my son, my son, would God that I had died for thee O Absalom, my son, my son !'"

I am not much of a mathematician, and I cannot estimate it ; but is there any one here quick enough at figures to estimate how many mothers there are waiting for something to be done ? Ay, there are many wives waiting for domestic rescue. He promised something different from that when, after the long acquaintance and the careful scrutiny of character, the hand and the heart were offered and accepted. What a hell on earth a woman lives in who has a drunken husband ! O Death, how lovely thou art to her, and how soft and warm thy skeleton hand ' The sepulchre at midnight in winter is a king's drawing-room compared with that woman's home. It is not so much the blow on the head that hurts as the blow on the heart. The rum fiend

came to the door of that beautiful home and opened the
door and stood there, and said : " I curse this dwelling with
an unrelenting curse. I curse that father into a maniac, I
curse that mother into a pauper. I curse those sons into
vagabonds. I curse those daughters into profligacy. Cursed
be bread-tray and cradle. Cursed be couch and chair and
family Bible with record of marriages and births and deaths.
Curse upon curse." O how many wives are there waiting
to see if something cannot be done to shake these frosts of
the second death off the orange-blossoms! Yea, God is
waiting, the God who works through human instrumentali-
ties, waiting to see whether this nation is going to overthrow
this evil; and if it refuse to do so God will wipe out the
nation as He did Phœnicia, as He did Rome, as He did
Thebes, as He did Babylon. Ay, He is waiting to see what
the Church of God will do. If the Church does not do its work,
then He will wipe it out as He did the Church of Ephesus,
Church of Thyatira, Church of Sardis. The Protestant and
Roman Catholic Churches to-day stand side by side with an
impotent look, gazing on this evil, which costs this country
more than a billion dollars a year, to take care of the 800,000
paupers, and the 315,000 criminals, and the 30,000 idiots, and
to bury the 75,000 drunkards.

TO THE RESCUE!

There is the Bengal tiger of drunkenness that prowls
around, and instead of attacking it, how many of us hide
under the church pew or the communion table ? There is
so much invested in it, we are afraid to assault it ; millions
of dollars in barrels, in vats, in spigots, in corkscrews, in gin
palaces with marble floors and Italian top-tables, and chased
ice-coolers, and in the strychnine, and the logwood, and the
tartaric acid, and the nux vomica, that go to make up our
" pure" American drinks.

I looked with wondering eyes on *the " Heidelberg tun."*
It is the great liquor vat of Germany, which is said to hold
eight hundred hogheads of wine, and only three times in a
hundred years has it been filled. But, as I stood and looked

at it, I said to myself: "That is nothing—eight hundred hogsheads. Why our American vat holds four million five hundred thousand barrels of strong drinks, and we keep three hundred thousand men with nothing to do but to see that it is filled." O, to attack this great monster of intemperance requires you to rally all your Christian courage. Through the press, through the pulpit, through the platform, you must assault it. Would to God that all our American Christians would band together, not for crack-brained fanaticism, but for holy Christian reform.

A GRAND CRUSADE.

To-day—not in the millennium, but to-day—the Church holds the balance of power in America; and if Christian people—the men and the women who profess to love the Lord Jesus Christ and to love purity and to be the sworn enemies of all uncleanness and debauchery and sin—if all such would march side by side and shoulder to shoulder, this evil would soon be overthrown. Think of 300,000 churches and Sunday-schools in Christendom marching shoulder to shoulder! How very short a time it would take them to put down this evil, if all the churches of God— trans-Atlantic and cis-Atlantic—were armed on this subject!

Protagoras boasted that out of the sixty years of his life forty years he had spent in ruining youth ; but the arch fiend of the nations may make the more infamous boast that all its life it has been ruining the bodies, minds, and souls of the human race.

I indict this evil as the regicide, the fratricide, the patricide, the matricide, the uxoricide of the century. Yet under what innocent and delusive and mirthful names alcoholism deceives the people! It is a "cordial." It is "bitters." It is an "eye-opener." It is an "appetizer." It is a "digester." It is an "invigorator." It is a "settler." It is a "night-cap." Why don't they put on *the right labels*—" Essence of Perdition," "Conscience Stupefier," "Five Drachms of Heart-ache," "Tears of Orphanage," "Blood of Souls," "Scabs of an

Eternal Leprosy," "Venom of the Worm That Never
Dies"? Only once in a while is there anything in the title
of liquors to even hint their atrocity, as in the case of *sour
mash.* That I see advertised all over It is an honest
name, and any one can understand it. Sour mash! That
is, it makes a man's disposition sour, and his associations
sour, and his prospects sour, and then it is good to mash his
body, and mash his soul, and mash his business, and mash
his family. Sour mash! One honest name at last for an
intoxicant! But through lying labels of many of the
apothecaries' shops, good people, who are only a little under-
tone in health, and wanting of some invigoration, have unwittingly got on their tongue the fangs of this cobra, that
stings to death so large a ratio of the human race.

THE EVIL OF DRUNKENNESS.

Whether you live in Brooklyn or New York, or Chicago or
Cincinnati, or Savannah or Boston, or in any of the cities of
this land, count up the saloons on that street, and see they are
far out of proportion to the increase of the population. You
people who are so precise and particular lest there should be
some imprudence or rashness in attacking the rum traffic,
will have your son some night pitched into your front door
dead drunk, or your daughter will come home with her children because her husband has, by strong drink, been turned
into a demoniac. The rum fiend has despoiled whole streets of
good homes in all our cities. Fathers, brothers, sons on the
funeral pyre of strong drink! Fasten tighter the victims!
Stir up the flames! Pile on the corpses! More men, women,
and children for the sacrifice! Let us have whole generations on fire of evil habit; and at the sound of the cornet,
flute, harp, sackbut, psaltery, and dulcimer let all the people
fall down and worship King Alcohol, or you shall be cast
into the fiery furnace of the rum power.

THE DRAM-SHOP.

is a great caldron of iniquity in our time. Anacharsis said
that the vine bore three grapes: the first was Pleasure, the
next was Drunkenness, and the next Misery. Every saloon
above ground or under ground is a fountain of iniquity. It
may have a license and it may go along quite respectably for
a while, but after a while the cover will fall off and the color
of the iniquity will be displayed.

"Oh," says some one, "you ought to be easier on such
a traffic as that when it pays such a large revenue to the
government, and helps support your schools and your great
institutions of mercy." And then I think of what William
E. Gladstone said—I think it was the first time he was Chan-
cellor of the Exchequer—when men engaged in the ruinous
traffic came to him and said their business ought to have
more consideration from the fact that it paid such a large
revenue to the English Government. Mr. Gladstone said:
"Gentlemen, *don't worry yourselves about the revenue;* give
me thirty millions of sober people, and we'll have revenue
enough and a surplus."

We might in this country—this traffic perished—have
less revenue, but we would have more happy homes, and we
would have more peace, and we would have fewer people in
the penitentiary, and there would be tens of thousands of
men who are now on the road to hell who would start on the
road for heaven.

But the financial ruin is a very small part of it. This
iniquity of which I speak takes everything that is sacred out
of the family, everything that is holy in religion, everything
that is infinite in the soul, and tramples it under foot. The
marriage-day has come. The twain are at the altar. Lights
flash. Music sounds. Gay feet go up and down the drawing-room. Did ever a vessel launch on such a bright and
beautiful sea? The scene changes. Dingy garret. No fire.
On a broken chair a sorrowful wife. Last hope gone. Poor,
forsaken, trodden under foot, she knows all the sorrows of
being a drunkard's wife. "Oh," she says, "he was the kind-

est man that ever lived, he was so noble, he was so good! God never made a grander man than he was, but the drink did it, the drink did it!" Some day she will press her hands against her temples and cry: "Oh, my brain, my brain!" or she will go out on the abutment of the bridge some moonlight night, and look down on the glassy surface and wonder if under that glassy surface there is not some rest for a broken heart.

Lorenzo de Medici was very sick, and some of his superstitious friends thought if they could dissolve a certain number of pearls in a cup and then he would drink them, it would cure him of the disease. So they went around and they gathered up all the beautiful pearls they could find, and they dissolved them in a cup, and the sick man drank them. Oh, it was an expensive draught. But I tell you of a more expensive draught than that. Drunkenness puts into its cup the pearl of physical health, the pearl of domestic happiness, the pearl of respectability, the pearl of Christian hope, the pearl of an everlasting heaven, and presses it to the hot lips.

I tell you *the dram-shop is the gate of hell.* The trouble is they do not put up the right kind of a sign. They have a great many different kinds of signs now on places where strong drink is sold. One is called the "restaurant," and another is called the "saloon," and another is called the "hotel," and another is called the "wine-cellar," and another is called the "sample-room." What a name to give one of those places! A "sample-room." I saw a man on the steps of one of those "sample-rooms" the other day, dead drunk. I said to myself: "I suppose *that is a sample!*" I tell you it is the gate of hell.

A CONEY ISLAND TRAGEDY.

In front of the Brooklyn Tabernacle this scene occurred: Sabbath morning a young man was entering for divine worship. A friend passing along the street said: "Joe, come along with me; I am going down to Coney Island, and we'll have a gay Sunday." "No," replied Joe; "I have started to go to Church, and I am going to attend service here." "O Joe," his friend said, "you can go to Church any time! The day is bright, and we'll go to Coney Island, and we'll have a splendid time." The temptation was too great, and the twain went to the beach, spent the day in drunkenness and riot. The evening train started up from Brighton. The young men were on it. Joe, in his intoxication, when the train was in full speed, tried to pass around from one car to another, and fell and was crushed. Under the lantern, as Joe lay bleeding his life away on the grass, he said to his comrade: "John, that was a bad business, your taking me away from church; it was a very bad business. You ought not to have done that, John. I want you to tell the boys to-morrow when you see them that rum and Sabbath-breaking did this for me. And, John, while you are telling them, I will be in hell, and it will be your fault."

BEATS THE BARD OF AVON.

The greatest of dramatists, in the tragedy of the Tempest, sends staggering across the stage Stephano, the drunken butler; but across the stage of human life strong drink sends kingly and queenly and princely natures staggering forward against the footlights of conspicuity, and then staggering back into failure, till the world is impatient for their disap-. pearance, and human and diabolic voices join in hissing them off the stage.

A TRAGEDY IN FIVE ACTS.

Act the first: A young man starting off from home; parents and sisters weeping to have him go. Wagon rising over the hill. Farewell kiss flung back. Ring the bell and let the curtain fall.

Act the second: The marriage altar. Full organ. Bright lights. Long white veil trailing through the aisle. Prayer and congratulation, and exclamation of, How well she looks!"

Act the third. A woman waiting for staggering steps. Old garments stuck into the broken window-pane. Marks of hardship on the face The biting of the nails of bloodless fingers. Neglect and cruelty and despair. Ring the bell and let the curtain drop.

Act the fourth · Three graves in a dark place—grave of the child that died for lack of medicine, grave of the wife that died of a broken heart, grave of the man that died of dissipation. Oh, what a blasted heath with three graves! Plenty of weeds, but no flowers. Ring the bell and let the curtain drop.

Act the fifth : A destroyed soul's eternity. No light. No music. No hope. Anguish coiling its serpents around the heart. Blackness of darkness forever. But I cannot look any longer. Woe! woe! I close my eyes to this last act of the tragedy. Quick! Quick! Ring the bell and let the curtain drop. " Rejoice, O young man, in thy youth; and let thy heart cheer thee in the days of thy youth; but know thou, that for all these things God will bring thee into judgment." " There is a way which seemeth right unto a man, but the end thereof are the ways of death."

A WRECK.

A man was found at the foot of Canal Street. As they picked him up from the water, and brought him to the Morgue, they saw by the contour of his forehead that he had great mental capacity. He had entered the newspaper profession. He had gone down in health. He took to artificial stimulus. He went down further and further, until one summer day, hot and hungry, and sick and in despair, he flung himself off the dock. They found in his pocket a reporter's pad, a lead-pencil, a photograph of some one who had loved him long ago.

NO STOPPING.

So far back as 959 King Edgar of England made a law that the drink-cup should have pins fastened at a certain point in the side, so that the indulger might be reminded to stop before he got to the bottom. But there are no pins projecting from the sides of the modern wine-cup or beer-mug, and the first point at which millions stop is at the gravelly bottom of their own grave.

"You must stop drinking," says the doctor, "and quit the fast life you are leading, or it will destroy you." The patient suffers paroxysm after paroxysm, but under skilful medical treatment he begins to sit up, begins to walk about the room, begins to go to business. And, lo! he goes back to the same grog-shops for his morning dram, and his evening dram, and the drams between. Flat down again. Same doctor. Same physical anguish Same medical warning.

Now the illness is more protracted, the liver is more stubborn, the stomach more irritable, and the digestive organs are more rebellious. But after a while he is out again, goes back to the same dram shops, and goes the same round of sacrilege against his physical health.

He sees that his downward course is ruining his household, that his life is a perpetual perjury against his marriage vow, that that broken-hearted woman is so unlike the roseate young wife that he married, that her old schoolmates do not recognize her, that his sons are to be taunted for a lifetime by the father's drunkenness, that the daughters are to pass into life under the scarification of a disreputable ancestor. He is drinking up their happiness, their prospects for this life, and perhaps, for the life to come. Sometimes an appreciation of what he is doing comes upon him. His nervous system is all a jangle. From crown of head to sole of foot he is one aching, rasping, crucifying, damning torture. Where is he? In hell on earth Does it reform him?

After a while he has delirium tremens, with a whole jungle of hissing reptiles let out on his pillow, and his screams horrify the neighbors as he dashes out of his bed, crying: "Take these things off me!" As he sits, pale and convales- cent, the doctor says: "Now I want to have a plain talk with you, my dear fellow. The next attack of this kind you will have you will be beyond all medical skill, and you will die. He gets better and goes forth into the same round again. This time medicine takes no effect. Consultation of physicians agree in saying there is no hope. Death ends the scene.

AN IMPORTANT DISCOVERY.

Dr. Sax, of France, has recently discovered something which all drinkers ought to know. He has found out that alcohol in every shape, whether of wine or brandy or beer, contains parasitic life called bacillus potumaniæ. By a power- ful microscope these living things are discovered, and when you take strong drink you take them into the stomach, and then into your blood, and getting into the crimson canals of life they go into every tissue of your body, and your entire organism is taken possession of by these noxious infinitesi- mals. When in delirium tremens a man sees every form of reptilian life, it is only these parasites of the brain in exag- gerated size. It is not a hallucination that the victim is suf- fering from. He only sees in the room what is actually crawling and rioting in his own brain. Every time you take strong drink you swallow these maggots, and every time the imbiber of alcohol in any shape feels vertigo or rheumatism or nausea, it is only the jubilee of these maggots Efforts are being made for the discovery of some germicide that can kill the parasites of alcoholism, but the only thing that will ever extirpate them is abstinence from alcohol and teetotal abstinence, to which I would before God swear all these young men and old.

A DREADFUL CROP.

America is a fruitful country, and we raise large crops of wheat and corn and oats, but the largest crop we raise in

this country is *the crop of drunkards.* With sickle made out
of the sharp edges of the broken glass of bottle and demi-
john they are cut down, and there are whole swathes of them,
whole winrows of them, and it takes all the hospitals and
penitentiaries and grave-yards and cemeteries to hold this
harvest of hell. Some of you are going down under this
evil, and the never-dying worm of alcoholism has wound
around you one of its coils, and by next New Year's Day it
will have another coil around you, and it will after a while
put a coil around your tongue and a coil around your brain
and a coil around your lung and a coil around your foot and
a coil around your heart; and some day this never-dying
worm will with one spring tighten all the coils at once, and
in the last twist of that awful convolution you will cry out,
" Oh, my God !" and be gone.

THE HISTORY OF A FRIEND.

I could give you the history of one of the best friends I
ever had. Outside of my own family I never had a better
friend. He welcomed me to my home at the West. He
was of splendid personal appearance, but he had an ardor of
soul and a warmth of affection that made me love him like
a brother. I saw men coming out of the saloons and gamb-
ling-hells, and they surrounded my friend, and they took him
at the weak point—his social nature—and I saw him going
down, and I had a fair talk with him—for I never yet saw a
man you could not talk with on the subject of his habits, if
you talked with him in the right way. I said to him, "Why
don't you give up your bad habits and become a Christian?"
I remember now just how he looked, leaning over his counter, as he replied, " I wish I could. Oh, sir, I should like to
be a Christian, but I have gone so far astray I can't get
back!"

So the time went on. After a while the day of sickness
came. I was summoned to his sick-bed. I hastened. It
took me but a very few moments to get there. I was surprised as I went in. I saw him in his ordinary dress, fully

dressed, lying on top of the bed. I gave him my hand, and he seized it convulsively and said, "Oh, how glad I am to see you! Sit down there." I sat down, and he said, "Mr. Talmage, just where you sit now my mother sat last night. She has been dead twenty years. Now, I don't want you to think I am out of my mind, or that I am superstitious; but, sir, she sat there last night, and she said, 'Roswell, I wish you would do better—I wish you would do better.' I said, 'Mother, I wish I could do better; I try to do better, but I can't. Mother, you used to help me; why can't you help me now?' And, sir, I got out of bed, for it was a reality, and I went to her, and threw my arms around her neck, and I said, 'Mother, I will do better, but you must help; I can't do this alone.'" I knelt and prayed. That night his soul went to the Lord that made it. Arrangements were made for the obsequies. The question was raised whether they should bring him to the church. Somebody said, "You cannot bring such a dissolute man as that into the church." I said, "You will bring him in church; he stood by me when he was alive, and I will stand by him when he is dead. Bring him." As I stood in the pulpit and saw them carrying the body up the aisle, I felt as if I could weep tears of blood.

On one side the pulpit sat his little child of eight years, a sweet, beautiful little girl, that I have seen him hug convulsively in his better moments. He put on her all jewels, all diamonds, and gave her all pictures and toys, and then he would go away, as if hounded by an evil spirit, to his cups and the house of shame—a fool to the correction of the stocks. She looked up wonderingly. She knew not what it all meant. She was not old enough to understand the sorrow of an orphan. On the other side sat the men who ruined him; they were the men who had poured the worm wood into the orphan's cup, they were the men who had bound him hand and foot. I knew them How did they seem to feel? Did they weep? No. Did they say, "What a pity that so generous a man should be destroyed?" No. Did they sigh repentingly over what they had done? No; they sat there, looking as vultures look at the carcass of a lamb whose heart they have ripped out. So they sat and looked at the coffin-lid, and I told them the judgment of God upon those who had destroyed their fellows. Did they reform? I was told they were in the places of iniquity that night after my friend was laid in Oakwood Cemetery, and they blasphemed and they drank. Oh, how merciless men are, especially after they have destroyed you! Do not look to men for comfort or help.

That friend, whom I cannot think of without emotion, was a Samson in strength, but Delilah sheared him, and the Philistines put his eyes out, and they threw him into prison, and he made sport for them; but in the hour of his death he rose up and took hold of the two-pillared curse of God against intemperance and threw himself forward, and down upon him and upon his comrades came the crashing thunders of eternal catastrophe.

OTHER VICTIMS.

Others are ruined by the common and all-destructive habit of treating customers. And it is a treat on their coming to town, a treat while the bargaining progresses, a treat when the purchase is made, and a treat as he leaves town. Others, to drown their troubles, submerge themselves with this worse trouble. Oh, the world is battered and bruised and blasted with this growing evil. It is more and more entranced and fortified. They have millions of dollars subscribed to marshal and advance the alcoholic forces. They nominate and elect, and govern the vast majority of the office-holders of this country. On their side they have enlisted the mightiest political power of the centuries. And behind them stand all the myrmidons of the nether world, Satanic and Apollyonic and diabolic. It is beyond all human effort to overthrow this Bastile of decanters or capture this Gibraltar of rum jugs. And while I approve of all human agencies of reform, I would utterly despair if we had nothing else. But what cheers me is that our best troops are yet to come. Our chief artillery is in reserve. Our greatest commander has not yet fully taken the field. If a hell is on their side, all heaven is on our side. Now "Let God arise, and let His enemies be scattered."

AN EMBLEM FROM EGYPT.

"And there shall be a great cry throughout all the land of Egypt."
—Exodus 11 : 6.

This was the worst of the ten plagues. The destroying angel at midnight flapped his wing over the land, and there was one dead in each house. Lamentation and mourning and woe through all Egypt. That destroying angel has fled the earth, but *a far worse* has come. He sweeps through these cities. It is the destroying angel of strong drink. Far worse devastation wrought by this second than by the first. The calamity in America worse than the calamity in Egypt. Thousands of the slain, millions of the slain. No arithmetic can calculate their number.

Who could think that the ripe clusters of the vineyard and the golden sheaves of the harvest field could be used for the world's damage and the world's death?

Once upon a time four fiends met in the lost world. They resolved that the people of our earth were too happy, and these four infernals came forth to our earth on embassy of mischief. The one fiend said : " I'll take charge of the vine-yards." Another said, "I'll take charge of the grain fields." Another said, " I'll take charge of the dairy." Another said, " I'll take charge of the music." The four fiends met in the great Sahara Desert, with skeleton fingers clutched each other in handshake of fidelity, kissed each other good-by with lip of blue flame, and parted on their mission.

The fiend of the vineyard came in one bright morning amid the grapes, and sat down on a root of twisted grapevine in sheer discouragement. The fiend knew not how to damage the vineyard, or, through it, how to damage the world. The grapes were so ripe and beautiful and luscious. They be-witched the air with their sweetness. There seemed to be so much health in every bunch ; and while the fiend sat

here in utter indignation and disappointment, he clutched at
cluster and squeezed it in perfect spite, and lo ! his hand was
red with the blood of the vineyard, and the fiend said:
" That reminds me of *the blood of broken hearts ;* I'll strip
the vineyard and I'll squeeze out all the juice of the grapes,
and I'll allow the juices of the grapes to stand until they rot,
and I'll call the process fermentation." And there was a
great vat prepared, and people came with their cups and
their pitchers, and they dipped up the blood of the grapes,
and they drank and drank and went away drinking, and they
drank until they fell in long lines of death, so that when the
fiend of the vineyard wanted to return to his home in the
pit, he stepped from carcass to carcass and walked down
amid a great causeway of the dead.

Then the second fiend came into *the grain field.* He
waded chin-deep amid the barley and the rye. He heard all
the grain talking about bread, and prosperous husbandry,
and thrifty homes. He thrust his long arms into the grain
field and pulled up the grain and threw it into the water
and made beneath it great fires—fires lighted with a spark
from his own heart—and there was a grinding, and a
mashing, and a stench, and the people came with their
bottles and they dipped up the fiery liquid, and they drank,
and they blasphemed, and they staggered, and they fought,
and they rioted, and they murdered, and the fiend of the
pit, the fiend of the grain field, was so pleased with their
behavior that he changed his residence from the pit to a
whiskey barrel, and there he sat by the door of the bung-
hole laughing in high merriment at the thought that out of
anything so harmless as the grain of the field he might turn
this world into a seeming pandemonium.

The fiend of the dairy saw the cows coming home from
the pasture-field, full-uddered, and as the maid milked he
said : " I'll soon spoil all that mess ; I'll add to it brandy,
sugar, and nutmeg, and I'll stir it into a *milk punch,* and
children will drink it, and some of the temperance people will
drink it, and if I can do them no more harm, I'll give them a
headache, and then I'll hand them over to the more vigor-

ous fiends of the Satanic delegation." And then the fiend of the dairy leaped upon the shelf and danced until the long row of shining milkpans almost quaked

The fiend of the music entered a grogshop, and there were but few customers. Finding few customers he swept the circuit of the city, and he gathered up the musical instruments, and after nightfall he marshalled a band, and the trombones blew, and the cymbals clapped, and the drums beat, and the bugles called, and the people crowded in, and they swung around in merry dance, each one with a wineglass in his hand ; and the dance became wilder and stronger and rougher until the room shook, and the glasses cracked and the floor broke, and the crowd dropped into hell.

Then the four fiends—the fiend of the vineyard, and of the grain field, and of the dairy, and of the music hall—went back to their home, and they held high carnival because their work had been so well done ; and Satan rose from his throne and announced that there was no danger of the earth's redemption so long as these four fiends could pay such tax to the diabolic And then all the demons, and all the sprites, and all the fiends filled their glasses and clicked them, and cried "Let us drink—drink to the everlasting prosperity of the liquor traffic. Here's to woe, and darkness, and murder, and death. Drink ! Drink !"

But whether by allegory or by appalling statistics this subject is presented, you know as well as I that it is impossible to exaggerate the evils of strong drink. A plague ! A plague ! I shall show you that it is a plague of suffering to the inebriate.

LOSS OF GOOD NAME.

God has so arranged it that no man loses his reputation except by his own act. The world may assault a man, and all the powers of darkness may assault him—they cannot capture him so long as his heart is pure and his life is pure All the powers of earth and hell cannot take that Gibraltar. If a man is right, all the bombardment of the world for five, ten,

twenty, forty years will only strengthen him in his position.
So that all you have to do is to keep yourself right. Never
mind the world. Let it say what it will. It can do you no
damage. But as soon as it is whispered " he drinks," and it
can be proved, he begins to go down.

What clerk can get a position with such a reputation?
What store wants him? What Church of God wants him for
a member? What dying man wants him for an executor?
" He drinks!" Young man, your reputation is your capital.
Your father gave you a good education, or as good an education as he could afford to give you. He started you in
city life. He could furnish you no means, but he has surrounded you with Christian influences and a good memory
of the past. Now, young man, under God you are with
your own right arm to achieve your fortune, and as your
reputation is your capital, do not bring upon it suspicion by
going in and out of liquor establishments, or by an odor of
your breath, or by any glare of your eye, or by any unnatural flush on your cheeks. You lose your reputation and
you lose your capital.

The subject comes over me like the waves of the Atlantic for power. O! when I see the influences abroad in Brooklyn and New York to destroy young men, I hardly know
what to say. For the young men themselves all sympathy
have I, and all compassion. For those who deal out the
deadly stuff, all pity that they should bring upon themselves
the condemnation of good society and the retributions of
God. But for the liquor establishments themselves, for the
rum-selling restaurants, may God Almighty consume them
with the brightness of His coming.

LOSS OF SELF-RESPECT.

The inebriate suffers also the plague in the fact that he
loses his self-respect, and when you destroy a man's self-
respect there is not much left of him. Just as soon as a
man finds he is a slave, he loses his self-respect. Then a
man will do things he would not do otherwise, he will say

things he would not say otherwise. He has lost his self-respect.

The fact is that man cannot stop, or he would stop now. He is bound hand and foot by the Philistines, and they have shorn his locks and put his eyes out, and made him grind in *the mill of a great horror.* After he is three-fourths gone in this slavery, the first thing he will be anxious to impress you with is that he can stop at any time he wants to. His family become alarmed in regard to him, and they say : " Now do stop this ; after a while, it will get the mastery of you." " O ! no," he says, " I can stop at any time ; I can stop now, I can stop to-morrow ; I can stop at any time." His most confidential friends say : " Why, I'm afraid you are losing your balance with that habit ; you are going a little further than you can afford to go ; you had better stop." " O ! no," he says, " I can stop at any time ; I can stop now." He goes on further and further.

He cannot stop. I will prove it. He loves himself, and he knows nevertheless that strong drink is depleting him in body, mind, and soul. He knows he is going down, that he has less self-control, less equipoise of temper than he used to. Why does he not stop? Because he cannot stop. I will prove it by going still further. He loves his wife and children. He sees that his habits are bringing disgrace upon his home. The probabilities are they will ruin his wife and disgrace his children. He sees all this, and he loves them. Why does he not stop ? He cannot stop.

I had *a very dear friend*, generous to a fault. He had given thousands and tens of thousands of dollars to Bible societies, tract societies, missionary societies, asylums for the poor, the halt, the lame, the blind, the imbecile. I do not believe for twenty years anybody asked him for a dollar or fifty dollars, or a hundred dollars for charity but he gave it. I never heard of anybody asking him for help, but he gave it. But he was under the power of strong drink, and he went on down, down, down. His family implored him, saying : " You are going too far in that habit ; you had better stop." He replied . " I can stop any time ; I am my own

master; I can stop." He went on down, down. His friends
advised and cautioned him. He said : "Don't be afraid of
me ; I am my own master; I can stop now ; I know what I
am doing." He went on down until he had the *delirium
tremens.* On down until he had the *delirium tremens* twice.
After the second time the doctor said : " If you ever have
an attack like this again you will die ; you'd better stop."
He said : "I can stop any time ; I can stop now." He went
on down. He is dead. What slew him? Rum! Rum!
Among the last things he said was that he could stop any
time. He could not stop. He could not stop.

O my young friends, I want to tell you that there is a
point in inebriation beyond which if a man go he cannot stop.
But sometimes a man will be more frank than that. A victim of strong drink said to a reformer : " It is impossible for
me to stop ; I realize it. But if you should tell me I couldn't
have a drink until to-morrow night unless I had all my fingers cut off, I would say, ' Bring the hatchet and cut them
off.'" I had a very dear friend in Philadelphia whose nephew
came to him and was talking about his trouble and confessed it. He confessed he could not stop. My friend said,
" You must stop." He said, "I can't stop. If there stood
a cannon, and it was loaded, and there was a glass of wine on
the mouth of the cannon, and I knew you would fire it off if
I approached, I would start to get that glass of wine. I
must have it. I can't get rid of this habit. I can't get away
from it." O! it is awful for a man to wake up and feel that
he is a captive. I hear him soliloquizing, saying : " I might
have stopped three months ago, but I can't stop now. Dead
but not buried. I am *a walking corpse.* I am an apparition
of what I once was. I am a caged immortal and my soul
beats against the wires of my cage on this side and beats
against the wires of my cage on the other side, until there is
blood on the wires, and blood on the soul, but I can't get
out. Destroyed without remedy !"

LOSS OF USEFULNESS.

Do you know, some of the men who have fallen into the ditch were once in the front rank in churches and in the front rank in reformatory institutions? Do you know they once knelt at the family altar, and once carried the chalice of the holy communion on sacramental days? Do you know they once stood in the pulpit and preached the Gospel of the Son of God.

We will not forget the scene witnessed four or five years ago in church when a man rose in the midst of the audience, stepped into the aisle, and walked up and down. Everybody saw that he was intoxicated. The ushers led him out, and his poor wife took his hat and overcoat and followed him to the door. Who was he? He had once been a mighty minister of the Gospel of Jesus Christ, had often preached in this very city. *What slew him?* Strong drink.

O! what must be the feeling of a man who has destroyed his capacity for usefulness? Do not be angry with that man. Do not lose your patience with him. Do not wonder if he says strange things and gets irritated easily in the family. He has the Pyrenees, and the Andes, and the Alps, and the Himalayas on him. Do not try to persuade him that there is no future punishment. Do not go into any argument to prove to him that there is no hell. He knows there is. He is there now!

LOSS OF PHYSICAL HEALTH.

The older people in this audience can remember Doctor Sewell going through this country electrifying great audiences by demonstrating to them the effect of strong drink upon the human stomach. I am told he had eight or ten diagrams which he presented to the people, showing the different stages in the progress of the disease, and I am told tens of thousands of people turned back from that ulcerous sketch and swore eternal abstinence from all intoxicants. God only knows what the drunkard suffers. Pain files on every nerve, and travels every muscle, and gnaws on every bone, and stings with every poison, and pulls with every torture. What reptiles crawl over his shivering limbs! What spectres stand by his midnight pillows! What groans tear the air! Talk of the rack, talk of the funeral pyre, talk of the Juggernaut—he suffers them all at once.

See the attendants stand back from *that ward in the hospital* where the inebriates are dying. They cannot stand it. The keepers come through it and say: "Hush up, now, stop making this noise. Be still! You are disturbing all the other patients. Keep still now!" Then the keepers pass on, and after they get past then the poor creatures wring their hands and say: "O! God. Help, help! Give me rum, give me rum! O! God. Help! Take the devils off of me. O! God. O! God." And they shriek, and they blaspheme, and they cry for help, and then they ask the keepers to slay them, saying: "Stab me, strangle me, smother me. O! God. Help, help! Rum! Give me rum. O! God. Help!" They tear out their hair by the handful, and they bite their nails into the quick "O! God," they say, "help! O! God, help, help, help!" This is no fancy picture. It is transpiring in a hospital at this moment. It went on last night while you slept ; and more than that, that is *the death some of you will die* unless you stop! I see it coming. God help you to stop before you go so far that you cannot stop.

LOSS OF HOME.

I do not care how much a man loves his wife and children, if this habit gets the mastery over him—this habit of strong drink—he will do the most outrageous things. If need be, in order to get strong drink he would sell them all into everlasting captivity. There are hundreds and thousands of homes in New York and Brooklyn that have been utterly blasted of it. I am speaking of *no abstraction.* Is there anything so disastrous to a man for this life and for the life to come? Do you tell me that a man can be happy

when he knows he is breaking his wife's heart and clothing
his children with rags? There are little children in the
streets to-day, barefooted, unkempt, uncombed, want written on every patch of their faded dress, and on every wrinkle
of their prematurely old countenance, who would have been
in the house of God this morning as well clad as you had it
not been that strong drink drove their parents down into
penury and then down into the grave. O! rum, rum, thou
despoiler of homes, thou foe of God, thou recruiting officer
of the pit, I hate thee, I hate thee!

LOSS OF THE SOUL.

But my subject takes a deeper tone when it tells you that
the inebriate suffers the loss of the soul. The Bible intimates that if we go into the future world unforgiven the appetites and passions which were regnant here will torment
us there. I suppose when the inebriate wakes up in the lost
world, there will be *an infinite thirst* clawing upon him. In
this world he could get strong drink. However poor he was
in this world, he could beg or he could steal five cents to get
a drink that would for a little while slake his thirst; but in
eternity where will the rum come from? Dives wanted one
drop of water, but could not get it. Where will the inebriate get the draught he so much requires, so much demands.
No one to brew it. No one to mix it. No one to pour it.
No one to fetch it. Millions of worlds now for the dregs
that were thrown on the sawdusted floor of the restaurant.
Millions of worlds now for the rind flung out from the punch-
bowl of an earthly banquet. Dives called for water. The
inebriate calls for rum.

If a fiend from the lost world should come up on a mission to a grog-shop, and having finished the mission in the
grog-shop, should come back, taking on the tip of his wing
one drop of alcoholic beverage, what excitement it would
make all through the world of the lost; and if that one drop
of alcoholic beverage should drop from the wing of the fiend
upon the tongue of the inebriate, how he would spring up

and cry: "That's it; that's it! Rum! Rum! That's it!" And all the caverns of the lost would echo with the cry, "Give it to me. Rum! Rum!" Ah! my friends, the inebriate's sorrow in the next world will not be the absence of God, or holiness, or light; it will be the absence of rum. "Look not thou upon the wine when it is red, when it giveth his color in the cup, when it moveth itself aright; at the last it biteth like a serpent, and stingeth like an adder."

When I see this plague in the land, and when I see this destroying angel sweeping across our great cities, I am sometimes indignant, and sometimes humiliated. When a man asks me: " What are you in favor of for the subjugation of this evil?" I answer, " I am ready for anything that is reasonable." You ask me "Are you in favor of Sons of Temperance?" Yes. " Are you in favor of Good Samaritans?" Yes. "Are you in favor of Good Templars?" Yes. "Are you in favor of a prohibitory law?" Yes. "Are you in favor of the pledge?" Yes. Combine all the influences, O Christian reformers and philanthropists. Combine them all for the extirpation of this evil.

Thirty women in one of the Western States banded together, and with an especial ordination from God they went forth to the work and shut up all the grog-shops of a large village. Thirty women, with their song and with their prayer; and if one thousand or two thousand Christian men and women with an especial ordination from God should go forth feeling the responsibility of their work and discharging their mission, they could in this city shut up all the grog-shops, put an end to this mighty vice of strong drink, and redeem our beloved city.

But I must not dwell on generalities; I must come to specifics. If there is any sermon I dislike it is a sermon on generalities. I want personalities.

ARE YOU ASTRAY? BEWARE!

I must say that unless you quit this evil habit, within ten years, as to your body, you will lie down in a drunkard's

grave, and as to your immortal soul, you will lie down in a
drunkard's hell! It is *a hard thing to say*, but it is true, and
I utter the warning lest I have your blood upon my soul.
Beware! As to-day you open the door of your wine closet,
let the decanter flash that word upon your soul, " Beware!"
As you pour out the beverage let the foam at the top spell
out the word, " Beware!" In the great day of God's judgment, when a hundred million drunkards shall come up to
get their doom, I want you to testify that in love of your
soul and in fear of God, I gave you warning in regard to that
influence which has already been felt in your home, blowing
out some of its lights—premonition of the blackness of darkness forever.

O! if you could only hear Intemperance with *drunkards'
bones drumming on the top of the wine cask* the dead march of
the immortal souls, you would kneel down and pray God
that rather than your children should ever become the victims of this evil habit, you might carry them out to Greenwood and put them down in the last slumber, waiting for
the flowers of spring to come over the grave—sweet prophecies of the resurrection. God hath a balm for such a wound,
but what flower of comfort ever grew on the blasted heath
of a drunkard's sepulchre?

Is it not time for me to pull out from the great organ of
God's Word, with many banks of keys, the *tremulo* stop?
" Look not upon the wine when it is red, when it moveth
itself aright in the cup, for at the last it biteth like a serpent
and stingeth like an adder." Ay, is it not time for me to
pull out the trumpet stop? " Awake, ye drunkards, and
weep, and howl, all ye drinkers of wine."

WINE-DRINKING CONVIVIALITIES.

Away with these wine-drinking convivialities! How dare
you, the father of a household, trifle with the appetites of
our young people? Perhaps out of regard for the minister,
or some other weak temperance man, you have the decanter
in a side-room, where, after refreshments, only a select few

are invited ; and you come back with a glare in your eye and
a stench in your breath that show that you have been out
serving the devil. The excuse which Christian men often
give for this is, that it is necessary, after such late eating, by
some sort of stimulant to help digestion. My plain opinion
is that, if a man have no more control over his appetite than
to stuff himself until his digestive organs refuse to do their
office, he ought not to call himself a man, but rather to class
himself among the beasts that perish. I take the words of
the Lord Almighty, and cry: "Woe unto him that giveth
his neighbor drink, that puttest thy bottle to him!"

HOLIDAY TEMPTATIONS.

Young man, take it as the counsel of a friend when I bid
you be cautious where you spend your winter evenings.
Thank God that you have lived to see the glad winter days
in which your childhood was made cheerful by the faces of
fathers and mothers, brothers and sisters, some of whom,
alas! will never again wish you a " Happy New Year " or " A
Merry Christmas." Let no one tempt you out of your sobriety. I have seen respectable young men of the best families drunk on New Year's Day. The excuse they gave for
the inebriation was that the ladies insisted on their taking it.
There have been instances where the delicate hand of woman
hath kindled a young man's taste for strong drink, who after
many years, when the attractions of that holiday scene were
all forgotten, crouched, in her rags and her desolation and
her woe, under the uplifted hand of the drunken monster
who, on that New Year's morning so long ago, took the glass
from her hand. And so the woman stands on the abutment
of the bridge on the moonlit night, wondering if down under the water there is not some quiet place for a broken
heart. She takes one wild leap—and all is over!

THE PAWNBROKER'S SPOILS.

Oh, mingle not with the harmless beverage of your fes-
tive scene this poison of adders! Mix not with the white

sugar of the cup the snow of this awful leprosy! Mar not the clatter of cutlery at the holiday feast with the clink of a madman's chain! Stop and look into the window of that pawnbroker's shop. Elegant furs. Elegant watches. Elegant scarfs. Elegant flutes. People stand with a pleased look gazing at these things; but I look with a shudder, as though I had seen into a window of hell. Whose elegant watch was that? It was a drunkard's. Whose furs? They belonged to a drunkard's wife. Whose flute? Whose shoes? Whose scarf? They belonged to a drunkard's child. If I could I would take the three brazen balls hanging at the doorway and clang them together until they tolled the awful knell of the drunkard's soul. The pawnbroker's shop is only one eddy of the great stream of municipal drunkenness.

NOBLE ALTRUISM.

Stand back, young man! Take not the first step in the path that leads there. Let not the flame of strong drink ever scorch your tongue. You may tamper with these things and escape, but your influence will be wrong. Can you not make a sacrifice for the good of others? When the good ship London went down the captain was told that there was a way of escape in one of the life-boats. He said: " No, I will go down with the passengers." All the world acknowledged that heroism.

THE BRAND ON THE BARREL.

Can you not deny yourself insignificant indulgences for the good of others? Be not allured by the fact that you drink only the moderate beverages. You take only ale, and a man has to drink a large amount of it to become intoxicated. Yes; but there's not in all the city to-day an inebriate that did not begin with ale. " XXX "—what does that mark mean? " XXX " on the beer barrels; " XXX " on the brewer's dray; " XXX " on the door of the gin shop; " XXX " on the side of the bottle. Not being able to find

any one who could tell me what this mark means, I have had
to guess that the whole thing was an allegory: "XXX"—
that is, thirty heart-breaks, thirty agonies, thirty desolated
homes, thirty chances for a drunkard's grave, thirty ways to
perdition. "XXX!" If I were to write a story, the first
chapter would be "XXX," the last the pawnbroker's shop.
Be watchful! At this season all the allurements to dissipation will be especially busy. Let not your flight to hell be
in the winter.

TEMPTATIONS OF YOUNG WRITERS FOR THE PRESS.

To bear up under the tremendous nervous strain, they
are tempted to artificial stimulus, and how many thousands
have gone down under that pressure God only knows. They
must have something to counteract the wet, they must have
something to keep out the chill, and after a scant night's
sleep they must have something to revive them for the morning's work. This is what made *Horace Greeley* such a stout
temperance man. He told me that he had seen so many of
his comrades go down under that temptation.

O my brother of the newspaper profession, what you cannot do without artificial stimulus, God does not want you to
do! There is no halfway ground for our literary people between teetotalism and dissipation. Your professional success, your domestic peace, your eternal salvation, will depend upon your theories in regard to artificial stimulus. I
have had so many friends go down under the temptation,
their brilliancy quenched, their homes blasted, that I cry out
in the words of another: "Look not thou upon the wine
when it is red, when it giveth its color in the cup; at the last
it biteth like a serpent, and stingeth like an adder."

LOVES A "SHINING MARK."

"Oh," says some man, "I am kind, I am indulgent to
my family, I am right in many respects, I am very generous,
and I have too grand and generous a moral nature to be

oveithrown in that way." Let me say that the persons who
are in the most peril have the largest hearts, the best education, the brightest prospects. This sin chooses the fattest
lambs for its sacrifice. The brightest garlands are by this
carbuncled hand of drunkenness torn off the brow of the
poet and the orator. Charles Lamb, answer! Thomas Hood,
answer! Sheridan, the English orator, answer! Edgar A.
Poe, answer! Thomas Marshall, answer!

Oh, come and look over into it while I draw off the cover
—hang over it and look down into it. and see the seething,
boiling, loathsome, smoking, agonizing, blaspheming hell of
the drunkard. Young man, be master of your appetites
and passions. Oh, there are hundreds—might I not say
thousands?--of young men in this house this morning—
young men of fair prospects. Put your trust in the Lord
God, and all is well. But *you will be tempted.* Perhaps you
may this moment be addressed on the first Sabbath of your
coming to the great city, and I give you this brotherly counsel.
I speak not in a perfunctory way. I speak as an older
brother talks to a younger brother. I put my hand on your
shoulder this day and commend you to Jesus Christ, who
Himself was a young man and died while yet a young man,
and has sympathy for all young men. O! be master, by the
grace of God, of your appetites and passions!

STUDENT VICTIM.

When I was at school in New Brunswick, I heard of an
incident that occurred one evening, of a young man brought
home by his comrades from a place of evil entertainment,
the young man intoxicated and helpless. I had the house
pointed out to me the next day, where he was carried up
the steps; then his comrades rang the door-bell, and father
and mother came down, and the comrades pitched the
young man into the door-way, and said, " There he is, drunk
as a fool IIa! ha!"

THE CONTRAST.

Oh, it is beautiful to see a young man standing upright where thousands of other young men fall! You will move in honorable circles all your days, and some old friend of your father will meet you, and say: " My son, how glad I am to see you look so well. Just like your father, for all the world I thought you would turn out well when I used to hold you on my knee."

But here is a young man who takes the other route. The voices of sin charm him away. He reads bad books, lives in vicious circles, loses the glow from his cheek, the sparkle from his eye, and the purity from his soul. The good shun him. Down he goes, little by little. They who knew him when he came to town, while yet lingering on his head was a pure mother's blessing, and on his lip the dew of a pure sister's kiss, now pass him and say: " What an awful wreck!" His eyes bleared with frequent carousals, his cheek bruised in the grog-shop fight, his lip swollen with evil indulgences. Look out what you say to him : for a trifle he will take your life. Lower down and lower down ; until, outcast of God and man, he lies in the almshouse a blotch of loathsomeness.

Sometimes he calls out for God, and then for more drink. Now he prays, now curses, now laughs as fiends laugh, then bites his nails to the quick, then runs both hands through the shock of hair that hangs about his head like the mane of a wild beast, then shivers until the cot shakes with unutterable terror ; then, with uplifted fist, fights back the devils or clutches the serpents that seem winding him in their coil ; then asks for water, which is instantly consumed by his cracked lips. Going his round some morning, the surgeon finds him dead. Straighten the limbs. You need not try to comb out or shove back the matted locks. Wrap him in a sheet. Put him in a box. Two men will carry it down to the wagon at the door. With chalk write on the top of the box the name of the destroyed. Do you know who it is? That is you, O man, if, yielding to the temptations to a disipated life, you go out and perish. There is a way that seemeth bright and fair, but the end thereof is death.

RECKLESS INFATUATION.

Alas! how many take no warning. They make me think of Cæsar on his way to assassination, fearing nothing; though his statue in the hall crashed into fragments at his feet, and a scroll containing the names of the conspirators was thrust into his hands, yet walking right on to meet the dagger that was to take his life. This infatuation of strong drink is so mighty in many a man that though his fortunes are crashing, and his health is crashing, and his domestic interests are crashing, and we hand him a long scroll containing the names of perils that await him, he goes straight on to physical and mental and moral assassination. In proportion as any style of alcoholism is pleasant to your taste, and stimulating to your nerves, and for a time delightful to all your physical and mental constitution, is the peril awful. Remember Jonathan and the forbidden honey in the woods of Beth-aven.

THE PLUNGE.

Life is full of excitement and full of mirth. Cheeks flush. Eyes flash. Watch-chain jingles. Cup foams. They swagger, they jostle decent men off the sidewalk, they blaspheme God, they parody the hymn they learned at their mother's knee; and when you point out the perils of their course, they say, "Who cares?" And when you counsel them to do right, they say, "Who are you?" Some night, going down the street, you hear a shriek in a grog-shop, and the rattle of the watchman's club, and the rush of the police. What is the matter! A young man killed in a grog-shop fight. Carry him home to his father's house. Father and and mother will come, and they will wash the blood off the wounds and close the eyes in death; and they will forgive him, though he cannot ask now to be forgiven.

The mother will go out in the garden and gather the most

beautiful flowers she can find, and she will twist them into a chaplet and lay them on his silent heart, and brush back from his bloated brow the long locks which were once her pride, and the air will resound with the father's cry, "O my son, my poor son!"

BROKEN HEARTS.

There is many a young man proud of his mother, who would strike into the dust any man who would insult her, who is at this moment himself, by his evil-doing and his bad habits, sharpening a dagger to plunge through that mother's heart. *A telegram* brought in from afar. He went bloated and scarred into the room and he stood by the lifeless form of his mother.

Her hair gray; it had turned gray in sorrow. Those eyes had wept floods of tears over his wandering. That still white hand had done him many a kindness and had written many a loving invitation and good counsel. He had broken her old heart. He came into the room and threw himself on the casket and he sobbed outright: "Mother, mother!" But those lips that had kissed him in infancy and uttered so many kind words spake not: they were sealed. Rather than have such a memory come on my soul, I would prefer to have roll over on me the Alps and the Himalayas.

A young man, through the intercession of metropolitan friends, gets a place in a bank or store. He is going to leave his country home. That morning, they are up early in the old homestead. The trunk is on the wagon. Mother says: "My son, *I put a Bible in the trunk*, I hope you will read it often." She wipes the tears away with her apron. "Oh," he says, "come, don't you be worried, I know how to take care of myself. Don't be worried about me." The father says: "My son, be a good boy and write home often, your mother will be anxious to hear from you." Crack! goes the whip, and over the hills goes the wagon. Five years have passed on, and *a dissipated life* has done its work for that young man. There is a hearse coming up in front of the old home-

stead. The young men of the neighborhood who have stayed
on the farm come in and say : " Is it possible? Why, he
doesn't look natural, does he ? Is that the fair brow we used
to know ? is that the healthy cheek we used to know? It
can't be possible that is he." The parents stand looking at
the gash in the forehead from which the life oozed out, and
they lift their hands and say : " O my son Absalom, my son,
my son Absalom ; would God I had died for thee, O Absalom, my son, my son."

STOP IN TIME.

Here is a young man who says : " I cannot see why they
make such a fuss about the intoxicating cup. Why, it is ex-
hiliarating. It makes me feel well. I can talk better,
think better, feel better. I cannot see why people have
such a prejudice against it." A few years pass on and
he wakes up and finds himself in the clutches of an evil
habit which he tries to break but cannot ; and he cries out :
" O Lord God, help me !" It seems as though God would
not hear his prayer, and in an agony of body and soul he
cries out : " It biteth like a serpent and it stingeth like an
adder."

YOUNG MEN OF AMERICA,

pass over into the army of teetotalism. Whiskey, good to
preserve corpses, ought never to turn you into a corpse.
Tens of thousands of young men have been dragged out of
respectability, and out of purity, and out of good character,
and into darkness by this infernal stuff called strong drink.
Do not touch it ! Do not touch it !

A PERORATION.

Ministers and speakers are very apt to close with a peroration, and they generally roll up some grand imagery to express what they have to say. I close with a peroration

mightier than was ever uttered by mere human lips. Two quotations. The first is this: " Who hath woe? who hath bab-bling? who hath wounds without cause? They that tarry long at the wine, they that go to seek mixed wine. Look not upon the wine when it is red, when it giveth its color in the cup, for at the last it biteth like a serpent and stingeth like an adder." This is the other quotation. Make up your mind as to which is the more impressive. I think the last is the mightier: " Rejoice, O young man, in thy youth, and let thy heart cheer thee in the days of thy youth, and walk thou in the sight of thine own eyes; but know thou that for all these things God will bring thee into judgment."

YOUR ONLY HOPE.

Have you gone so far you think you cannot get back? Did I say that a man might go to a point in inebriation where he could not stop? Yes, I said it, and I reiterate it; but I want you also to understand that while the man him-self, of his own strength, cannot stop, God can stop any man. You have only to lay hold of the strong arm of the Lord God Almighty. He can stop you. _You_ cannot.

A few summers ago I went over to New York one Sab-bath evening, and, in a room in the Fourth Ward, New York, where a religious service was being held for reformed drunkards, I heard a revelation that I had never heard before —fifteen or twenty men standing up and testifying not only that their hearts had been changed by the grace of God, but that the grace of God had extinguished their thirst. They went on to say that they had reformed at different times before, but immediately fallen, because they were doing the whole work in their own strength: " But as soon as we gave our hearts to God," they said, " and the love of the Lord Jesus Christ has come into our soul, the thirst has all gone. We have no more disposition for strong drink."

It was a new revelation to me, and I have proclaimed it again and again in the hearing of those who have far gone astray; and I stand here to-day to tell you that the grace of the Lord Jesus Christ can not only save your soul, but save your body. I look off to-day upon the desolation. Some of you are far on in this habit, although there may be no outward indications of it—you never have staggered along the street—the vast majority of people do not know that you stimulate; but God knows, and you know; and by human calculations there is not one chance out of five thousand that you will ever be stopped.

ANOTHER CASE TO THE POINT.

There is a man who was for ten years a hard drinker. The dreadful appetite had sent down its roots around the palate and the tongue, and on down until they were interlinked with the vitals of body, mind, and soul; but he has not taken any stimulants for two years. What did that? Not temperance societies. Not prohibition laws. Not moral suasion. Conversion did it.

I could tell you of a tragic scene, when once at the close of the service I found a man in one of the front seats, wrought upon most mightily. I said to him, "What is the matter?" He replied, "I am a captive of strong drink; I came from the West; I thought, perhaps, you could do me some good; I find you can't do me any good; I find there is no hope for me." I said, "Come into this side room and we will talk together."

"Oh, no," he said, "there's no need of my going in; I am a lost man; I have a beautiful wife; I have four beautiful children; I had a fine profession; I have had a thorough education; I had every opportunity a man ever had, but I am a captive of strong drink; God only knows what I suffer."

I said, "Be encouraged; come in here, and we'll talk together about it." "No," he said, "I can't come; you can't do me any good. I was on the Hudson River Railroad yesterday, and coming down, I resolved never again to touch a drop of strong drink. While I sat there a man came in—a low creature—and sat by me; he had a whiskey flask, and he said to me: 'Will you take a drink?' I said 'no;' but oh, how I wanted it! and as I said no, it seemed that the liquor curled up around the mouth of the flask and begged, 'Take me! take me! take me!' I felt I couldn't resist it, and yet I was determined not to drink, and I rushed out on the platform of the car, and I thought I would jump off; we were going at the rate of forty miles an hour, and I didn't dare to jump; the paroxysm went off, and I am here to-night."

I said, "Come in, I'll pray for you, and commend you to God." He came in trembling. Some of you remember. After the service, we walked up the street. I said, "You have an awful struggle. I'll take you into a drug-store; perhaps the doctor can give you some medicine that will help you in your struggle, though, after all, you will have to depend upon the grace of God." I said to the doctor, "Can you give this man something to help him in his battle against strong drink?" "I can," replied the doctor, and he prepared a bottle of medicine. I said, "There is no alcohol in this—no strong drink?" "None at all," said the doctor. "How long will this last?" I inquired. "It will last him a week." "O!" I said, "give us another bottle."

We passed out into the street and stood under the gas-light. It was getting late, and I said to the man, "I must part with you. Put your trust in the Lord, and He will see you through. You will make use of this medicine when the paroxysm of thirst comes on." A few weeks passed away, and I got a letter from Boston saying, "Dear friend, I enclose the money you paid for that medicine. I have never used any of it. The thirst has entirely gone away from me. I send you two or three newspapers to show you what I have been doing since I came to Boston." I opened the newspapers and saw accounts of meetings of two or three thousand people to whom this man had been preaching righteousness, temperance, and judgment to come. I have heard from him again and again since. He is faithful now, and will be, I know, faithful to the last. O this work of soul-saving!

CHAPTER XII.

Corrupt Literature.

THE printing-press is the mightiest agency on earth for good or evil. The position of a minister of religion standing in his pulpit is a responsible position, but it does not seem to me so responsible a position as that of the editor and the publisher. At what distant point of time, at what distant cycle of eternity, will cease the influence of the four great departed editors of New York—Henry J. Raymond, Horace Greeley, James Gordon Bennett, and William Cullen Bryant? Men die, but the literary influences they project go on forever.

Taking into consideration the fact that there are now New York and Brooklyn dailies with a circulation of over five hundred thousand copies, and taking into consideration that there are three weekly periodicals with about one million of circulation, I want you to sit down and cipher out, if you can, how far up, and how far down, and how far out reaches the influence of the American printing-press. I believe that God has made the printing-press to be the chief agent in the world's correction and evangelization, and that the great final battle of the world will be fought, not with guns and swords, but with types and presses, a gospelized and purified literature triumphing over and trampling under foot and crushing out a corrupt literature. God speed the cylinders of an honest, intelligent, aggressive, Christian printing-press!

MULTIPLICATION OF BOOKS.

"Of making many books there is no end."—ECCLESIASTES 12 : 12.

This was written centuries before the art of printing was invented, and in ages of the world when books were chiselled in stone, and baked in clay and impressed in wax, and scratched on the bark of trees, and written on parchment. It was no unusual thing for a man to walk a hundred miles to read a book. We are told of volumes that were chained to pillars and to walls in order that men might make long pilgrimages and read them, and not be tempted to carry them away.

A Sicilian scholar parted with his entire estate to get one copy of Livy; Jerome ruined himself financially in buying the works of Origen, and if in those ages of the world Solomon was amazed at the vast literature abroad, and said in his time, "of making many books there is no end," what would he say if he could now descend and make the tour of our American and English publishing houses? Books on all subjects. Books of all styles. Books in all places. Books. Books.

The greatest blessing that has come to this world since Jesus Christ came is good journalism, and the worst scourge unclean journalism. You must apply the same law to the book and the newspaper. The newspaper is a book swifter and in more portable shape. Under unclean literature, under pernicious books and newspapers, tens of thousands have gone down ; the bodies of the victims in the penitentiaries, in the dens of shame, and some of the souls in the asylums for the imbecile and the insane, more of the souls already having gone down in an avalanche of horror and despair.

The London plague was nothing to it. That counted its victims by the thousands ; this modern pest shovels its millions into the charnel-house of the morally dead. The longest train of cars that ever rolled over the Erie track, or the Hudson, is not long enough, or large enough, to hold the beastliness and the putrefaction which has been gathered up in the bad books and newspapers of America for the last twenty years.

A WORSE THAN FROG PLAGUE.

There is almost a universal aversion to frogs, and yet with the Egyptians they were honored, they were sacred,

and they were objects of worship while alive, and after death
they were embalmed, and to-day their remains may be found
among the sepulchres of Thebes. These creatures, so attractive once to the Egyptians, at divine behest became obnoxious and loathsome, and they went croaking and hop-
ping and leaping into the palace of the king, and into the
bread-trays and the couches of the people; and even the
ovens, which now are uplifted above the earth and on the
side of chimneys, then being small holes in the earth with
sunken pottery, were filled with frogs when the housekeepers
came to look at them. If a man sat down to eat, a frog
alighted on his plate. If he attempted to put on a shoe, it
was preoccupied by a frog. If he attempted to put his head
upon a pillow, it had been taken possession of by a frog.
Frogs high and low and everywhere ; loathsome frogs, slimy
frogs, besieging frogs, innumerable frogs, great plague of
frogs.

What made the matter worse, the magicians said there
was no miracle in this, and they could by sleight-of-hand
produce the same thing, and they seemed to succeed, for by
sleight-of-hand wonders may be wrought. After Moses had
thrown down his staff and by miracle it became a serpent,
and then he took hold of it and by miracle it again became
a staff, the serpent-charmers imitated the same thing, and
knowing that there were serpents in Egypt which by a peculiar pressure on the neck would become as rigid as a stick
of wood, they seemed to change the serpent into the staff,
and then, throwing it down, the staff became a serpent. So
likewise these magicians tried to imitate the plague of frogs,
and perhaps by smell of food attracting a great number of
them to a certain point, or by shaking them out from a hidden place, the magicians sometimes seemed to accomplish the
same miracle. While these magicians made the plague worse
none of them tried to make it better.

Now that plague of frogs has come back upon the earth.
It is abroad to-day   It is smiting this nation. It comes in
the shape of corrupt literature. These frogs hop into the
store, the shop, the office, the banking-house, the factory—

into the home, into the cellar, into the garret, on the drawing-room table, on the shelf of the library. While the lad is reading the bad book and the teacher's face is turned the other way one of these frogs hops upon the page. While the young woman is reading the forbidden novelette after retiring at night, reading by gaslight, one of these frogs leaps upon the page. Indeed, they have hopped on the news-stands of the country, and the mails at the post-office shake out in the letter-trough hundreds of them.

The plague has taken, at different times, possession of this country. It is one of the most loathsome, one of the most frightful, one of the most ghastly of the ten plagues of our modern cities. There is a vast number of books and newspapers printed and published which ought never to see the light. They are filled with a pestilence that makes the land swelter with a moral epidemic. The literature of a nation decides the fate of a nation. Good books, good morals. Bad books, bad morals.

SALACIOUS LITERATURE.

I begin with the lowest of all the literature, that which does not even pretend to be respectable—from cover to cover a blotch of leprosy. There are many whose entire business it is to dispose of that kind of literature. They display it before the schoolboy on his way home. They get the catalogues of colleges and young ladies' seminaries, take the names and the post-office addresses, and send their advertisements and their circulars and their pamphlets and their books to every one of them.

The president of one of the finest young ladies' seminaries on the Atlantic coast being absent one day, one of these miscreants came in and secured a catalogue. The president returning and hearing of it, had his fears excited, and he reported the case to official authority. For two weeks that man was hunted, and he was hunted down, and in his possession were found not only the catalogue of that institution, but the catalogues of fourteen colleges, and in

eight of them already he had done the damning work   In
the possession of these dealers in impure literature were
found nine hundred thousand names and post-office addresses, to whom it was thought it might be profitable to
send these corrupt things.

In the year 1873 there were one hundred and sixty-five
establishments engaged in publishing salacious literature.
From one publishing house there went out twenty different
styles of corrupt books.   Although twenty-four tons of salacious literature have been destroyed by the Society for the
Suppression of Vice, still there is enough of it left in this
country to bring down upon us the thunderbolts of an incensed God   What has been very remarkable is the fact
that more of those publishers of impure literature lived in
the City of Brooklyn than any other city—lived here, did
business in New York, had their factories, some on this side
the river, some on the other side the river, but they dared
to have their residences in this City of Churches.   All of
them now driven out, or for the most part driven out, these
vultures will alight in other fields, and they must be pursued
and exterminated from Christendom.

In the year 1868 the field had become so great in this
country that the Congress of the United States passed a law
forbidding the transmission of impure literature through
the United States mails; but there were large loops in that
law through which criminals might crawl out, and the law
was a dead failure—that law of 1868   But in 1873 another
law was passed by the Congress of the United States against
the transmission of corrupt literature through the mails—a
grand law, a potent law, a Christian law—and under that
law multitudes of these scoundrels have been arrested, their
property confiscated, and they themselves thrown into the
penitentiaries where they belonged.

Against that good and wholesome and Christian law no
good man could make any objection ; but it stirred up the
animosity and the indignation of a great many people, and
they sent up a petition to Congress to compel that body to
repeal that good, Christian law.   The petition rolled up to

the door of the House of Representatives asking for the repeal of the law, and the head name on the petition was Robert G. Ingersoll, *the champion blasphemer of America.* He appealed to the House of Representatives with others. That body refused to grant the petition. Then Mr. Ingersoll made application to the Senate of the United States, and that body also refused, so that both Houses of Congress rejected the petition.

That application for the repeal of that good law against the transmission of corrupt and obscene literature through the mails of the United States, only demonstrates what you and I know, that the same infidelity which wipes its feet on the Bible and spits in the face of God is the worst foe of American society. I do not wonder that when Robert G. Ingersoll applied to the Mayor of Toronto for permission to lecture in that city, the Mayor of Toronto replied: " No, sir; you may have no God in the United States, but we have one up here in Canada, and you shall not stand here and blaspheme Him."

One of the filthiest creatures who had been sending corrupt literature through the mails of the United States was arrested, tried, condemned and put in the Penitentiary. A petition went to President Hayes asking him to pardon the culprit. President Hayes looked over the whole case, saw there was no excuse for the infamy, that there were no mitigating circumstances, and he declined to pardon the miscreant. Then a company of what are called " Liberalists" got together in a meeting and passed a resolution of *" deepest sympathy"*—these were the two words—" deepest sympathy" for that culprit, and the resolution of " deepest sympathy" for that culprit was offered by Robert G. Ingersoll, and the resolution was passed amid great acclamation of the people present.

Ah! my friends, the day will come when it will be demonstrated—and if no one else will undertake the work, I will —that while Christianity is the mother of all the virtues, Infidelity is the foster-mother of all the vices of this century, not one excepted. Any man who could ask for the repeal

of that good law against the sending of corrupt literature
through the mails of the United States, any man that could
do that is the enemy of every decent home in America, and
has offered an insult to every clean-minded man and every
pure-hearted woman in Christendom.

HOW ARE THE FROGS TO BE SLAIN?

Now, my friends, how are we to war against this corrupt
literature? and how are the frogs of this Egyptian plague
to be slain? First of all, by the prompt and inexorable execution of the law. Let all good postmasters and United
States district attorneys, and detectives and reformers con-
cert in their action to stop this plague. When Sir Rowland
Hill spent his life in trying to secure cheap postage not only
for England, but for all the world, and to open the blessing of
the post-office to all honest business and to all messages of
charity, and kindness, and affection, for all healthful inter-
communication, he did not mean to make vice easy or to fill
the mail-bags of the United States with *the scabs of such a
leprosy.*

It ought not to be in the power of every bad man who
can raise a one-cent stamp for a circular, or a two-cent
stamp for a letter, to blast a man or destroy a home. I was
glad when I saw how Jay Gould pounced upon the culprit
who was desecrating our magnificent post-office system.
That the culprit lived on Fifth Avenue instead of Elm
Street only made the matter more outrageous. The New
York Post-Office never did better work than when they detailed fifty postmen to watch the letter-boxes, and the Police Department of New York City never did better work
than when they detailed fifty detectives to make summary
arrests. The postal service of this country must be clean,
must be kept clean, and we must all understand that the
swift retributions of the United States Government hover
over every violation of the letter-box.

There are thousands of men and women in this country,
some for personal gain, some through innate depravity,

some through a spirit of revenge, who wish to use this great avenue of convenience and intelligence for purposes revengeful, salacious, and diabolic. Wake up the law. Wake up all its penalties. Let every court-room on this subject be a Sinai thunderous and aflame. Let the convicted offenders be sent for the full term to Sing Sing or Harrisburg, and hurl that Governor from his chair who shall dare to pardon before the expiration of the sentence.

I am not talking about what cannot be done. . I am talking now about what is being done. A great many of the printing-presses that gave themselves entirely to the publication of salacious literature have been stopped, or have gone into business less obnoxious. What has thrown off, what has kept off the rail-trains of this country for some time back nearly all the leprous periodicals? Those of us who have been on the rail-trains have noticed a great change. Why have nearly all those indecent periodicals been kept off the rail-trains? Who effected it? These societies for the purification of railroad literature gave warning to the publishers and warning to railroad companies, and warning to conductors, and warning to newsboys, to keep the infernal stuff off the trains.

Cleveland and Rock Island and Ann Arbor and other cities have successfully prohibited the most of that literature even from going on the news-stands. Terror has seized upon the publishers and the dealers in impure literature from the fact that over six hundred arrests have been made, and the aggregate time for which the convicted have been sentenced to the prison is over one hundred and fifty years, and from the fact that over one million three hundred thousand of their circulars have been destroyed, and the business is not as profitable as it used to be.

How have so many of the news-stands of our great cities been purified? How has so much of this iniquity been balked? By moral suasion? Oh no. You might as well go into a jungle of the East Indies and pat a cobra on the neck, and with profound argument try to persuade it that it is morally wrong to bite and to sting and to poison anything.

The only answer to your argument would be an uplifted head and a hiss, and a sharp, reeking tooth struck into your arteries. The only argument for a cobra is a shot-gun, and the only argument for these dealers in impure literature is the clutch of the police and bean-soup in a penitentiary. The law! The law! I invoke the law to consummate the work so grandly begun!

HEALTHFUL LITERATURE.

Another way in which we are to drive back this plague of Egyptian frogs is by filling the minds of our boys and girls with a healthful literature.

A good book—who can exaggerate its power? Benjamin Franklin said that his reading of Cotton Mather's "Essays To Do Good," in childhood gave him holy aspirations for all the rest of his life.

A clergyman, many years ago, passing to the Far West, stopped at a hotel. He saw a woman copying something from Doddridge's "Rise and Progress." It seemed that she had borrowed the book, and there were some things she wanted especially to remember. The clergyman had in his satchel a copy of Doddridge's "Rise and Progress," and so he made her a present of it. Thirty years passed on The clergyman came that way and he asked where the woman was, whom he had seen long ago They said : "She lives yonder in that beautiful house." He went there and said to her. "Do you remember me?" She said . "No, I do not." He said : "Do you remember a man gave you Dodd-ridge's 'Rise and Progress' thirty years ago?" "O yes; I remember. *That book saved my soul.* I loaned the book to all my neighbors, and they read it and they were converted to God, and we had a revival of religion which swept through the whole community. We built a church and called a pastor. You see that spire yonder, don't you? That church was built as the result of that book you gave me thirty years ago."

O the power of a good book! But, alas! for the influ-

ence of a bad book. *John Angell James*, than whom England
never had a holier minister, stood in his pulpit at Birming-
ham and said : " Twenty-five years ago a lad loaned to me
an infamous book. He would loan it only fifteen minutes,
and then I had to give it back; but that book has haunted
me like a spectre ever since. I have in agony of soul, on my
knees before God, prayed that He would obliterate from my
soul the memory of it; but I shall carry the damage of it
until the day of my death." The assassin of Sir William
Russell declared that he got the inspiration for his crime by
reading what was then a new and popular novel, "Jack
Sheppard." "Homer's Iliad " made Alexander the Warrior. Alexander said so. The story of Alexander made
Julius Cæsar and Charles XII. both men of blood.

Have you in your pocket or in your trunk or in your
desk at business a bad book, a bad picture, a bad pamphlet ?
In God's name, I warn you to destroy it. There are good
books, good histories, good biographies, good works of fiction, good books of all styles with which we are to fill the
minds of the young, so that there will be no more room for
the useless and the vicious than there is room for chaff in a
bushel measure which is already filled with Michigan wheat.

Against every bad pamphlet send a good pamphlet ;
against every unclean picture send an innocent picture;
against every scurrilous song send a Christian song; against
every bad book send a good book ; and then it will be as it
was in ancient Toledo, where the Toletum missals were kept
by the saints in six churches, and the sacrilegious Romans
demanded that those missals be destroyed, and that the
Roman missals be substituted ; and the war came on, and I
am glad to say that, the whole matter having been referred
to champions, the champion of the Toletum missals with
one blow brought down the champion of the Roman missals.

So it will be in our day. The good literature, the Christian literature, in its championship for God and the truth,
will bring down the evil literature in its championship for
the devil. I feel tingling to the tips of my fingers and
through all the nerves of my body, and all the depths of my

soul, the certainty of our triumph. Cheer up, O men and women who are toiling for the purification of society! Toil with your faces in the sunlight. "If God be for us, who, *who* can be against us?"

Thus one way in which we shall fight back this corrupt literature and kill the frogs of Egypt is by rolling over them the Christian printing-press, which shall give plenty of healthful reading to all adults.

We see so many books that we do not understand what a book is. Stand it on end. Measure it, the height of it, the depth of it, the length of it, the breadth of it. You cannot do it. Examine the paper and estimate the progress made from the time of the impressions on clay, and then on to the bark of trees, and from the bark of trees to papyrus, and from papyrus to the hide of wild beasts, and from the hide of wild beasts on down until the miracles of our modern paper manufactories, and then see the paper, white and pure as an infant's soul waiting for God's inscription. A book! Examine the type of it. Examine the printing of it and see the progress from the time when Solon's laws were written on oak planks and Hesiod's poems were written on tables of lead, and the Sinaitic commands were written on tables of stone, on down to Hoe's perfecting printing-press. It took all the universities of the past, all the martyr fires, all the civilizations, all the battles, all the victories, all the defeats, all the glooms, all the brightnesses, all the centuries, to make it possible. A book! It is the chorus of the ages—it is the drawing-room in which kings and queens and orators and poets and historians and philosophers come out to greet you. If I worshipped anything on earth I would worship that. If I burned incense to any idol, I would build an altar to that. Thank God for good books, healthful books, inspiring books, Christian books, books of men, books of women, Book of God. It is with these good books that we are to overcome corrupt literature. Upon the frogs swoop with these eagles.

I depend much for the overthrow of iniquitous literature upon the mortality of books. Even good books have a hard struggle to live. Polybius wrote forty books; only five of them left. Thirty books of Tacitus have perished. Twenty books of Pliny have perished. Livy wrote one hundred and forty books: only thirty-five of them remain. Eschylus wrote one hundred dramas; only seven remain. Euripides wrote over a hundred; only nineteen remain. Varro wrote the biographies of over seven hundred great Romans. All that wealth of biography has perished. If good and valuable books have such a struggle to live, what must be the fate of those that are diseased and corrupt and blasted at the very start? They will die as the frogs when the Lord turned back the plague. The work of Christianization will go on until there will be nothing left but good books, and they will take the supremacy of the world. May you and I live to see the illustrious day!

GOOD AND BAD RESULTS.

If I have placed before you, fathers and mothers, young men and young women, tests by which you may know what a good newspaper is and what a bad newspaper, what good books, and what bad books, I have done a work that I shall not be ashamed of on that day when God shall try every man's work of what sort it is. Encourage good literature. Do not begrudge the three or five pennies you pay for your morning newspaper. In every possible way, encourage the literature of the world so far as it is pure; so far as it is bad, denounce it. Do not purchase bad books even out of curiosity. You remember that one column of a good newspaper may save your soul, and that one paragraph of a bad newspaper may damn it.

Crowd your minds with good books, and there will be no room for the bad. When Thomas Chalmers was riding beside a stage-driver and the horses were going beautifully, the stage-driver drew his long lash and struck the ear of the leader. It seemed to Thomas Chalmers a great cruelty, and he said, "Why did you strike that horse; he is going splendidly." "Ah!" said the stage-driver, "do you see that frightful object along the road? I never in the world would

have got that horse along there if I hadn't given him something else to think of!" Thomas Chalmers went home and
wrote his immortal sermon, " The Expulsive Power of a
New Affection."

WHAT BOOKS AND NEWSPAPERS SHALL WE READ?

Shall we make our minds the receptacle of everything
that bad authors have a mind to write? Shall we make no
distinction between the tree of life and the tree of death?
Shall we stoop down and drink out of the trough which
the wickedness of men has filled with pollution and shame?
Shall we chase the fantastic will-o'-the-wisps across the
swamp, and mire in impurity when we may walk in the
blooming gardens of God? You and I must decide for our
present welfare and our everlasting happiness what we shall
read, and we cannot afford to make a mistake. God help
me this morning, and help you, that I may present the right
theory, and that we may all be enabled to adopt it.

Standing as we do chin deep in the fictitious literature
of the day, the question is asked us, What novels shall we
read, if we read any? Shall we read any? What advice
shall we give to young people in regard to this matter?

FICTITIOUS LITERATURE.

There are good, pure, honest, Christian novels—those
that elevate the heart and purify the life. A novel is history and poetry combined—the history of things around
us, with the licenses and the assumed names of poetry.
The world will never be able to pay the debt of obligation it
owes to such fictitious writers as Hawthorne, and M'Kenzie,
and Landor, and Hunt, and Arthur, and Marion Harland,
and others whose names easily occur to you. No one has
ever better set forth the follies of high life than did Miss
Edgeworth. No one has ever more faithfully embalmed the
memories of the past than has Walter Scott. Cooper's novels are healthy with the breath of seaweed and the air of the

American forest. Charles Kingsley has done wonders in curing the morbidity of the world, and showing the poetry of strong muscle and good health and fresh air. Thackeray has brought the world under obligation by his caricature of the pretenders to gentility and high blood. Charles Dickens has built his monument in his own books, which are an ever-lasting plea for the poor and an anathema against injustice.

Now, it is certain that this style of books rightly read and read in right proportion with other books, will have an elevating and purifying and ennobling and enlarging influence; but I have to deplore, as you will deplore, the fact that there is a pernicious tide of novels setting in in this country. It is coming in like a freshet overflowing all the banks of decency and common-sense. Some of the most reputable publishing houses of the country are printing them. Some of the religious papers are commending them. You find them in the school-girl's desk, in the young man's trunk, in the steamboat cabin, on the table of the reception-room.

You see a light in your child's room late at night. You go in and say, " What are you doing?" The boy says, " I am reading." You say, " What are you reading ?" " Reading a book." " Well, what is the book?" You take hold of the book, and you see it is a bad book, and you say "Where did you get this book?" " Oh," he says, " I borrowed it !" There is always some one glad to loan a bad book to your boy. Pernicious literature everywhere! I charge upon it the destruction of tens of thousands of immortal souls, and I bid you wake up to this *tremendous evil*

I am going to gather all the books together, novels good and bad, travels true and false, histories faithful and inaccurate, legends beautiful and monstrous—all catalogues, all chronicles, all family, city, state, and national libraries, and I will pile them up in one great pyramid of literature, and bring to bear upon it certain grand, glorious, unmistakable, and infallible Christian texts, so that instead of going away saying, I recommend this, or denounce that, every man and every woman with an awakened conscience will be able to decide for himself and for herself.

I. In the first place, I counsel you to avoid all those books which give *false portraiture of human life*. Life is neither a tragedy nor a farce, men are not all knaves or heroes, women are neither angels nor furies, and yet much of the literature of the day would seem to give you the idea that instead of life being an earnest, practical thing, it is a fantastic and extravagant thing.

How are that young man and that young woman prepared for the duties of the day who by reading romances last night waded through stories of magnificent knavery and wickedness? An indiscriminate reader of novels is inane, useless, and a nuisance, unfit for store, bank, office, factory, street, home—anywhere. A woman who is an indiscriminate reader of novels is unfitted for her duty as wife, mother, sister, daughter. There she is at midnight, bending over the romance. Hair dishevelled, countenance vacant, hand tremulous, cheek pale, bursting into tears at the story of an unfortunate lover!

There she is, by day, when she ought to be busy, gazing for one long hour at—nothing! Biting her finger-nails into the quick! The carpets that were plain before on the floor of the home, will be plainer, now that in the romance she has been walking through tessellated halls of castles, beside plumed princesses, or lounging in the arbor with polished desperado. Oh, these indiscriminate readers of fiction, they are unfitted for this life, which .is a tremendous discipline. They are unfitted for the furnaces of trial through which they have to pass. They are unfitted for this life, where all we gain is achieved by hard, long-continued, exhaustive and tremendous work!

Again: I counsel you to avoid all those books which, while they have good in them, have also a large admixture of evil. What has been your history in the reading of books which were partly good and partly bad? Which stuck the longest, the good or the bad? The bad. Most human intellects are so fashioned that they allow the small particles of good like a sieve to fall through, and hold the great cinders. There is here and there an intellect, which, like a loadstone plunged amid steel and brass filings, gathers up the steel and repels the brass filings; but it is the exception.

The best man that ever lived cannot afford to read a bad book, unless he read it for professional purposes, for the purpose of making the world better, just as a doctor may go through a small-pox hospital, or through a lazaretto studying disease that he may go forth and benefit the world with his theories in regard to health and in regard to sickness. But you go into a bad book to get the good out of it and you will make a terrible mistake. You will plunge through a hedge of burrs to get one blackberry, and you will get *more burrs than blackberries.*

You say the evil in the book is so insignificant it will not amount to anything. I tell you that the scratch of a pin has sometimes produced lock-jaw. You go out of curiosity prying into a bad book, and you are making as dangerous an experiment as the man who should take a lighted torch into a gunpowder mill to find out whether really there is any danger of its blowing up. He will find out, but the experiment will never be of any advantage to anybody.

Years ago there was on exhibition in New York *a black leopard,* a very dangerous animal, but very beautiful. A gentleman stood looking through the bars of the cage at the black leopard. It seemed so mild, so quiet, so beautiful, he felt as if he would like to stroke the sleek hide. He stood a little while considering whether it would be safe. Everything seemed safe and he put his hand through the bars of the cage and stroked the sleek and beautiful hide of the black leopard; but no sooner had he touched it than it sprang upon him, and he pulled forth his arm and his hand mauled and bleeding, and *ready for amputation.* Look out how you toy with iniquity. It may be very beautiful, very attractive, and seem very placid; but you attempt to stroke it, and you may pull forth your soul torn and bleeding under the clutch of the black leopard.

You say, "*How are we to find out* what books are good or

bad without reading them?" Every bad book has something suspicious about it. There is something suspicious in
the index or in the engraving. You take any book to any
intelligent man, and in five minutes by shuffling the leaves
and looking at the index he can tell you whether it is a good
book or a bad one, and out of a thousand attempts he will
not make one mistake. This reptile of bad literature carries
a *warning rattle.*

BOOKS THAT CORRUPT THE IMAGINATION.

I command you to avoid all books that arouse the base
passions. I do not refer now to the bad book the villain has
under his arm, standing at the street corner waiting for the
school to come out, then looking up and down the street,
and finding no police near by, offers the book to your boy
on his way home. I do not refer to that, but I refer to literature which evades the law, and is written in polished
style, and with acute plot sounds the tocsin that arouses all
the baser passions of the soul.

Many years ago, there was a lady who came forth as an
authoress under the assumed name of *George Sand.* She
smoked cigars. She dressed like a gentleman. She wrote
in style ardent and eloquent, mighty in its gloom, terrible in
its unchastity, vivid in its portraiture, damnable in its influence, putting forth an evil which has never relaxed, but has
hundreds of copyists. So much worse now are many of
these French books coming to America than anything
George Sand ever wrote that if she were alive now she
might be thought almost a reformer.

Right under the nostrils of your great cities there is a
reeking, unwashed literature enough to poison all the fountains of public virtue and smite your sons and daughters as
with the wing of a destroying angel, and it is high time that
ministers of religion should blow the trumpet and rally the
troops of righteousness, all armed to the teeth in this battle
against a corrupt literature.

Here is a man who begins to read French novels. "They

are so charming," he says, " I will go out and see for myself whether all these things are so." He opens the gate of a sinful life. He goes in. A sinful sprite meets him with her wand. She waves her wand and it is all enchantment. Why, it seems as if the angels of God had poured out vials of perfume in the atmosphere. As he walks on he finds the hills becoming more radiant with foliage, and the ravines more resonant with the falling water. Oh what a charming landscape he sees !

But that sinful sprite with her wand meets him again ; but now she reverses the wand and all the enchantment is gone. The cup is full of poison. The fruit turns to ashes. All the leaves of the bower are forked tongues of hissing serpents. The flowing fountains fall back in a dead pool, stenchful with corruption. The luring songs become curses and screams of demoniac laughter. Lost spirits gather about him, and feel for his heart, and beckon him on with " Hail brother ! Hail, blasted spirit, hail !" He tries to get out. He comes to the front door where he entered and tries to push it back, but the door turns against him ; and in the jar of that shutting door he hears these words: " This night is Belshazzar the King of the Chaldeans slain." Sin may open bright as the morning ; it closes dark as the night.

BOOKS WHICH ARE APOLOGETIC FOR CRIME.

It is a deplorable fact that some of the richest bookbindery and the finest rhetoric are brought into the service of sin. Now, sin is loathsome anyhow. It is born in shame and it dies howling in the darkness. In this world it is scourged with a whip of scorpions, and afterward it is pursued by God's thunders of wrath across a boundless desert of ruin and woe.

All those books that represent sin as happy and congratulated, and sin as finally successful are an insult to God and a blasting influence to the human race. *Sin is never happy.* " There is no peace, saith my God, to the wicked." Sin is never finally successful. " The way of the wicked He

turneth upside down." Those books that represent the
opposite of this, that sin is happy, that sin is finally successful, are slanders on the human race and an outrage on God,
who made the human race. If you present carnality, do not
present it as looking from behind embroidered curtains, or
through the lattice of a royal seraglio, but as writhing in the
agonies of a city hospital.

Cursed of God and man be all those books which would
try to make impurity decent and iniquity right and hypocrisy
honorable! Cursed be all those books swarming with libertines and desperadoes, filling the minds of young people
with sin and whirling them into iniquity! Ye authors who
write them, ye publishers who print them, ye booksellers
who sell them, you will be cut to pieces after a while, if not
with the indignation of the community, then with the wrath
of that God who will by no means clear the guilty. A
mighty responsibility that man undertakes who has anything
to do with iniquitous literature.

·

INSANITY INDUCED.

The hour strikes midnight. She is bending over the
depraved romance. The cheeks are flushed with the color
that soon dies out. Hot tears fall. Breath is quick and
irregular. The hand trembles as though a guardian angel
were trying to shake the book out of her grasp. The sweat
on the brow is the spray dashed up from the river of death.
She laughs; the sound drops dead. Four o'clock in the
morning! The day will soon look upon her as though she
were a detained spectre of the night. Soon in the mad-
house, she will mistake the ringlets for coiling serpents, and
she will thrust her white hand through the bars, and smite
her head, and push it as though to shove the scalp from the
skull, crying, "*my brain! my brain!*" *Mad! Mad!*

Oh, stand off from such an accursed literature! Why go
sounding among the reefs and the warning buoys of such a
dangerous coast when there is a vast ocean where you may
voyage all sail set?

Why are fifty per cent of the criminals in the jails and penitentiaries of the United States to-day under twenty-one years of age? Many of them under seventeen, under sixteen, under fifteen, under fourteen, under thirteen. Walk along one of *the corridors of the Tombs* prison in New York and look for yourselves. Bad books, bad newspapers, bewitched them as soon as they got out of the cradle. Beware of all those stories which end wrong. Beware of all those books which make the road that ends in perdition seem to end in Paradise. Do not glorify the dirk and the pistol. Do not call the desperado brave or the libertine gallant. Teach our young people that if they go down into the swamps and marshes to watch the jack-o'-lanterns dance on the decay and rottenness, they will catch the malaria and death.

APOLOGIES.

"O!" says some one, "I am a business man, and I have no time to examine what my children read. I have no time to inspect the books that come into my household." If your children were threatened with typhoid fever, would you have time to go for the doctor? Would you have time to watch the progress of the disease? Would you have time for the funeral? In the presence of my God I warn you of the fact that your children are threatened with moral and spiritual typhoid, and that unless the thing be stopped, it will be to them funeral of body, funeral of mind, funeral of soul. Three funerals in one day.

My word is to this vast multitude of young people: Do not touch, do not borrow, do not buy a corrupt book or a corrupt picture. A book will decide a man's destiny for good or for evil.

INFIDEL BOOKS.

Who can calculate the soul-havoc of a Rousseau, going on with a very enthusiasm of iniquity, with fiery imagination seizing upon all the impulsive natures of his day, or David Hume, who employed his life as a spider employs its summer, in spinning out silken webs to trap the unwary, or Voltaire, the most learned man of his day, marshalling a great host of sceptics, and leading them out in the dark land of infidelity, or Gibbon, who showed an uncontrollable grudge against religion in his history of one of the most fascinating periods of the world's existence—the decline and fall of the Roman Empire—a book in which, with all the splendors of his genius, he magnified the errors of Christian disciples, while with a sparseness of notice that never can be forgiven he treated of the Christian heroes of whom the world was not worthy?

I had one book in my library of which I have never thought with any comfort. It was an infidel book, which I bought for the purpose of finding out the arguments against Christianity. A gentleman in my library one day said, "Can I borrow that book?" I said, "Certainly." That book came back with some passages marked as having especially impressed him, and when I heard that he had gone down in a shipwreck off Cape Hatteras I asked myself the question, "I wonder if anything he saw in that book which he borrowed from me could have affected his eternal destiny?"

I remember one infidel book in the possession of my student companion. He said, "De Witt, would you like to read that book?" "Well," said I, "I would like to look at it." I read it a little while. I said to him, "I dare not read that book; you had better destroy it, I give you my advice, you had better destroy it. I dare not read that book. I have read enough of it." "Oh," he said, "haven't you a stronger mind than that? Can't you read a book you don't exactly believe, and not be affected by it?" I said, "You had better destroy it." He kept it.

He read it. He poured over it. He read it and re-read it. He read it until he gave up his Bible. He read it until he gave up his belief in the existence of a God. He read it until he gave up his good morals. He read it until body, mind, and soul were ruined—the body smitten with disease, the mind deranged—and he went into the insane asylum, and the story of that book, that one infidel book, will never be told in this world.

I read too much of it. I read about fifteen or twenty pages of it. I wish I had never read it. It never did me any good; it did me harm. I have often struggled with what I read in that book. I rejected it, I denounced it, I cast it out with infinite scorn, I hated it, yet sometimes it has troubled me. You cannot afford to read a bad book, young man, you cannot afford it.

PERNICIOUS PICTORIALS

Are also doing a tremendous work of death. You find these death-warrants on all the streets. For a good, healthful picture we have great admiration. What a good author may take four hundred pages to present, a good engraver could present on the half side of a pictorial. Costly paintings are the aristocracy of art; engraving is the democracy of art. The best part of a picture that cost $10,000 you may buy for ten cents. I say the best part. So we ought to rejoice in the multiplication of pictures. It is the intense, it is the quick way of presenting a truth.

A man never gets over his love for pictures. The little child is entranced with them; we all are entranced with them. If a book be presented to us, we first look at the pictures. Multiply them. After the children are gathered after the evening repast, put before them the pictures. Nail them to the wall of the nursery—the pictures. Put them on the couch of the invalid. Strew them all through the railroad cars and steamboat cabins to refresh the travellers. Gather pictures in your albums and portfolios. Bless God for pictures and may they multiply all over the earth these messengers of knowledge and of mercy.

But the unclean pictorials are doing a work vast for death and perdition. Many a young man for ten cents buys his everlasting undoing. It poisons his soul, his soul may poison ten other souls, they may poison hundreds, the hundreds thousands, the thousands millions. It will take the measuring line of eternity to tell how far out has gone the influence of that one unclean pictorial. He may unroll it amid the roaring mirth of his comrades; but if they could see the result on the young man's heart and life, instead of laughing they would weep.

The queen of death holds a banquet every night, and these unclean pictorials are the printed invitations to the guests. Alas! that the fair brow of American art should be blotched with this plague-spot, and that philanthropists, worried about lesser evils, should give so little time to this calamity. Young men, have nothing to do with these pictures. Do not take the *moral strychnine* into your soul. Do not take up this nest of coiling adders and put it in your pocket. Do not patronize the news-stand that sells them.

A man is *no better than the picture he loves to look at.* I will give you $1000 reward for any young man who remains pure, and yet has the regular habit of buying unclean pictorials—$1000 reward for one specimen. Ah, my friends, Satan sometimes failing to get a soul by inducing him to read a bad book captures him by getting him to look at an impure periodical! When Satan goes fishing he does not care whether it is a long line or a short line, if he only hauls his victim in.

EXAMINE YOUR LIBRARIES.

And after you have got through your libraries, examine the stand where the pictorials and newspapers are, and if you find anything there that cannot stand the test of the judgment day, do not give it to others—that would despoil them; do not sell it—that would be getting the price of blood; but kindle a fire on your kitchen hearth or in your back yard, and put the poison in and keep stirring the blaze until everything has gone to ashes from preface to appendix.

EPHESIAN MAGIC BOOKS.

"Many of them also which used curious arts brought their books together, and burned them before all men : and they counted the price of them, and found it fifty thousand pieces of silver.—Acts 19 : 19.

Paul had been stirring up Ephesus with some lively sermons about the sins of that place. Among the more important results was the fact that the citizens brought out their bad books, and in a public place made a bonfire of them. I see the people coming out with their arms full of Ephesian literature, and tossing it into the flames. I hear an economist standing by, and saying, "Stop this waste. Here are seven thousand five hundred dollars' worth of books—do you propose to burn them all up? If you don't want to read them yourselves, sell them, and let somebody else read them. "No," said the people, "if these books are not good for us, they are not good for anybody else, and we shall stand and watch until the last leaf has turned to ashes. They have done us a world of harm, and they shall never do others harm." Hear the flames crackle and roar!

Well, my friends, one of the wants of the cities of this country is a great bonfire of bad books and newspapers. We have enough fuel to make a blaze two hundred feet high. Many of the publishing-houses would do well to throw into the blaze the entire stock of goods. Bring forth the insufferable trash and put it into the fire, and let it be known, in the presence of God, and angels, and men that you are going to rid your homes of the overtopping and underlying curse of profligate literature.

A DAY OF RECKONING.

We must not forget that there is an eternity behind us, and there is an eternity before us, and anything that will unfit us for the coming eternity is a very bad investment ; and alas' for that man or that woman who, resolved to adhere to iniquitous literature, goes right on in that way. The Lord will stop you after a while. The day is coming.

A TERRIBLE FATE.

You shall be cut to pieces, if not by an aroused community, then at last by the hail of divine vengeance, and you shall be swept to the lowest pit of perdition as the murderers of souls. I tell you, though you may escape in this world, you will be ground at last under the hoof of eternal calamities, and you will be chained to the rock, and you will have the vultures of despair clawing at your soul, and those whom you have destroyed will come around to torment you, and to pour hotter coals of fury upon your head, and rejoice eternally in the outcry of your pain, and the howl of your damnation.

CHAPTER XIII.

Traps for Young Men.

IT may be almost impossible to take a castle by siege—
straightforward siege—but suppose in the night there is a
traitor within, and he goes down and draws the bolt and
swings open the great door, and then the castle falls immediately. That is the trouble with the hearts of the young;
they have foes without and foes within. There are a great
many who try to make our young people believe that it is a
sign of weakness to be pure. The man will toss his head and
take dramatic attitudes and tell of his own indiscretions, and
ask the young man if he would not like to do the same.
And they call him verdant, and they say he is green and un-
sophisticated, and wonder how he can bear the Puritanical
strait-jacket. They tell him he ought to break from his
mother's apron-strings, and they say, " I will show you all
about town. Come with me. You ought to see the world.
It won't hurt you. Do as you please, it will be the making
of you." After a while the young man says, " I don't want
to be odd, nor can I afford to sacrifice these friends, and I'll
go and see for myself." From the gates of hell there goes
a shout of victory. Farewell to all innocence—farewell to
all early restraints favorable to that innocence which, once
gone, never comes back.

How many traps there are set for our young people!
That is what makes parents so anxious. Here are tempta-
tions for every form of dissipation and every stage of it.
The young man, when he first goes into dissipation, is very
particular where he goes. It must be a fashionable hotel.
He could not be tempted into these corner nuisances, with
red-stained glass and a mug of beer painted on the sign-board.
You ask the young man to go into that place and he would

331

say: "Do you mean to insult me?" No; it must be a marble-floored bar-room. There must be no lustful pictures behind the counter; there must be no drunkard hiccoughing while he takes his glass. It must be a place where elegant gentlemen come in and click their cut glass and drink to the announcement of flattering sentiment. But the young man cannot always find that kind of a place; yet he has a thirst and it must be gratified. The down-grade is steeper now, and he is almost at the bottom. Here they sit in an oyster cellar around a card-table, wheezing, bloated, and bloodshot, with cards so greasy you can hardly tell who has the best hand. But never mind; they are only playing for drink. Shuffle away! shuffle away! The landlord stands in his shirt-sleeves with hands on his hips, watching the game and waiting for another call to fill up the glasses.

It is the hot breath of eternal woe that flushes that young man's cheek. In the jets of gaslight I see the shooting out of the fiery tongue of the worm that never dies. The clock strikes twelve; it is the tolling of the bell of eternity at the burial of a soul. Two hours pass on, and they are all sound asleep in their chairs. Landlord says, "Come, now, wake up; it's time to shut up." They look up and say, "What?" "It's time to shut up." Push them out into the air. They are going home. Let the wife crouch in the corner, and the children hide under the bed. They are going home! What is the history of that young man? He began his dissipation at the Fifth Avenue Hotel, and completed his damnation in the worst grog-shop in Navy Street.

CITY SNARES.

I have made up my mind that our city life is destroying too many young men. There comes, in every September and October, a large influx of those between sixteen and twenty-four years of age, and *New York and Brooklyn damn at least a thousand of them every year.* They are shovelled off and down with no more compunction than that with which a coal-heaver scoops the anthracite into a dark cellar. What with the wine-cup and the gambler's dice, and the scarlet enchantress, no young man without the grace of God is safe ten minutes.

There is much discussion about which is the worst city of the continent. Some say New York, some say New Orleans, some say Chicago, some say St. Louis. What I have to say is, you cannot make much comparison between the infinities, and in all our cities the temptation seems infinite. We keep a great many mills running day and night. No rice-mills or cotton-mills. Not mills of corn or wheat, but mills for grinding up men. Such are all the grog-shops, licensed and unlicensed. Such are all the gambling saloons. Such are all the houses of infamy. And we do the work according to law, and we turn out a new grist every hour, and grind up warm hearts and clear heads; and the earth about a cider-mill is not more saturated with the beverage than the ground about all these mind-destroying institutions is saturated with the blood of victims.

We say to Long Island neighborhoods and villages, "Send us more supply;" and to Westchester and Ulster and all the other counties of New York, "Send us more men and women to put under the wheels." Give us full chance, and we could grind up in the municipal mill five hundred a day. We have enough machinery; we have enough men who can run them. Give us more homes to crush! Give us more parental hearts to pulverize! Put into the hopper the wardrobes and the family Bibles, and the livelihoods of wives and children. Give us more material for these mighty mills, which are wet with tears and sulphurous with woe, and trembling with the earthquakes of an incensed God, who will, unless our cities repent, cover us up as quick and as deep as in August, of the year 79, Vesuvius avalanched Herculaneum.

But sin does not stop here. It comes to the door of the drawing-room. There are men of leprous hearts that go into the very best classes of society. They are so fascinating— they have such a bewitching way of offering their arm. Yet

the poison of asps is under the tongue, and their heart is
hell. At first their sinful devices are hidden, but after a
while they begin to put forth their talons of death. Now
they begin to show really what they are. Suddenly—
although you could not have expected it, they were so
charming in their manner, so fascinating in their address—
suddenly a cloud, blacker than was ever woven of midnight
or hurricane, drops upon some domestic circle. There is
agony in the parental bosom that none but the Lord God
Almighty can measure—an agony that wishes that the children of the household had been swallowed by the grave, when
it would be only a loss of body instead of a loss of soul.

What is the matter with that household? They have
not had the front windows open in six months or a year.
The mother's hair suddenly turned white; father, hollow-
cheeked and bent over prematurely, goes down the street.
There has been no death in that family—no loss of property.
Has madness seized upon them? No! no! A villain, kid-
gloved, patent-leathered, with gold chain and graceful manner, took that cup of domestic bliss, elevated it high in the
air until the sunlight struck it, and all the rainbows danced
about the brim, and then dashed it down in desolation and
woe, until all the harpies of darkness clapped their hands
with glee, and all the voices of hell uttered a loud ha! ha!
Oh, there are scores and hundreds of homes that have been
blasted, and if the awful statistics could be fully set before
you, your blood would freeze into a solid cake of ice at the
heart.

YOUNG MEN FROM THE COUNTRY.

I do not feel so sorry for young men who were born in
the city and who have had all these temptations described
before them until they know what they are—I am not so
sorry for them as I am for those who come from country
homes and are easily betrayed and easily overthrown. Oh,
young man from the farmhouse among the hills, what did
your parents do to you that you should do this to them?

Why will you, by going into a life of dissipation, break the
heart of her who gave you birth? Look at her hand, so
distort are the knuckles. Why? Working for you. Look
at the back, so bent. Why? Carrying your burdens. Oh,
dissipated young man, write home by the first mail to-morrow, cursing your mother's gray hair, cursing the chair in
which she sits, cursing the cradle in which she rocked you.
"Oh," you say, "I cannot, I cannot." You are doing worse
than that. There is something on your forehead now.
What is it? Run your finger over your forehead. What is
it? It is red. It is the blood of a broken heart.

I am more in sympathy with such persons who have
come from the country life to the city life because *I was a
country lad* myself, and saw not until fifteen years of age, a
great city. O! how stupendous New York seemed to me
that morning I arrived at Courtland Street Ferry. I came
to the city my soul all awake for the amusements and the
hilarities of the world. No soul ever more awake, or more
sympathetic with all the sports and amusements of life than
my soul was, and I have sometimes thought it was quite
strange I was not captured of evil and dragged down. I
was talking with a man of the world about it some time ago,
and though he pretended to be only a man of the world, he
said: "I guess, sir, there must have been some prayers hovering over your head—prayers that have been answered!"

BEHAVIOR MAKES THE ABODE.

I have noticed that a man never likes a city where he has
not behaved well! Swartout did not like New York, nor
did Parkman like Boston, and people who have *a free ride
in the prison van* never like the city that furnishes the vehicle.
When I find Argos, and Rhodes, and Smyrna trying to
prove themselves the birthplace of Homer, I conclude right
away that Homer behaved well.

NO HALF WAY.

[The Editor here remarks, that, to be safe, one must shun all sin as he would a serpent, and treat it as he would poison.]

"Death in the pot."—2 KINGS 4 : 40.

Elisha had gone down to lecture to the students in the theological seminary at Gilgal. He found the students very *hungry, as students are apt to be.* It is very seldom the world makes large provision for those who give themselves to intellectual toil. In order that these students may be prepared to hear what Elisha says, he first feeds their hunger. He knew very well it is useless to talk, to preach, to lecture, to argue with hungry men.

So Elisha recognizing this common-sense principle, which every Christian ought to recognize, sends servants out to get food for these hungry students. They pick up some good, healthful herbs, but they happen to pick up also some coloquintida, a bitter, poisonous, deathful herb. They bring all these herbs, they put them into the boiling-pot, they stir them up, and then a portion of this food is brought to the students and their professors. Seated at the table, one of the hungry students begins immediately to eat, and he happens to get hold of some of the coloquintida. He knew it by the taste. He cries out: "Poison, poison! O thou man of God, there is death in the pot!" Consternation is thrown over the whole group. What a fortunate thing it was that this student so early found the coloquintida in the mixture at the table! You will by reference find the story is precisely as I have mentioned it.

Well, in our day there are great caldrons of sin and death. Coloquintida of mighty temptation is pressed into it. Some dip it out, and taste, and reject it, and live. Others dip it out, taste it, keep on, and die. And it is the business of every minister of religion and every man who wishes well to the human race, and who wants to keep the world back from its follies and its sufferings, to cry out : " Beware ! poison,

poison! Look out for this caldron! Stand back! Beware!"

In Florence there is a fresco by Giotto that for many ages was covered up by two thicknesses of whitewash. It is only within a very few years that the artist's hand has come and removed that covering, and the fresco comes out as fair and beautiful as it was before. You say it was *a great sacrilege* thus to cover up a fine fresco. Yes, but it is a sadder thing that the image of God in the human soul should have been covered up and obliterated. The work is beyond any human hand to restore the divine lineaments. Sin has done an awful work in our world. It has gone out through all the ages, it has mixed up a great caldron of trouble and suffering and pain, and the whole race is poisoned—poisoned in body, poisoned in mind, poisoned in soul. But blessed be God that the Gospel of Jesus Christ is the antidote, and where there was sin there shall be pardon, and where there was suffering there shall be comfort, and where there was death there shall be life.

AN INDOLENT LIFE.

One of the most awful caldrons of iniquity is an indolent life. All the rail-trains down the Hudson River, all the rail-trains on the Pennsylvania route, all the trains on the Long Island road bring to these cities young men to begin commercial life. Do you know what one of their great temptations is? It is the example of indolent people in our cities. They are in all our cities. They dress better than some who are industrious. They have access to all places of amusement—plenty of money, and yet idle. They hang around our great hotels—the Pierrepont House, the Fifth Avenue, the Windsor, the Brunswick, the Stuyvesant, the Gilsey House—all our beautiful hotels, you find them around there any day—men who do nothing, never earn anything, yet well-dressed, having plenty. Why should I work? Why should you work? Why drudge and toil in bank and shop and office, or on the scaffolding, or by the anvil, when these men get along so well and do not work?

Some of them hang around the City Halls of our great cities, toothpick in their mouth, waiting for some crumb to fall from the office-holder's table. Some of them hang around the City Hall for the city van bringing criminals from the station-houses. They stand there and gloat over it— really enjoy the disgrace and suffering of those poor creatures as they get out of the city van and go into the courts.

Where do they get their money? That is what you ask. That is what I ask. Only four ways of getting money, only four: by inheritance, by earning it, by begging it, by stealing it; and there are a vast multitude among us who get their living not by inheritance, nor by earning it, nor by begging it. I do not like to take the responsibility of saying how they get it!

Now, these men are *a constant temptation.* Why should I toil and wear myself out in the bank, or the office, or the store, or the shop, or the factory? These men have nothing to do. They get along a great deal better. And that is the temptation under which a great many young men fall. They begin to consort with these men, these idlers, and they go down the same awful steeps. The number of men in our cities who are trying to get their living by their wits and by sleight-of-hand is all the time increasing.

A New York merchant saw a young man, one of his clerks, in half disguise, going into a very low place of amusement. The merchant said to himself: "I must look out for that clerk; he is going in bad company and going in bad places; I must look out for him." A few months passed on, and one morning the merchant entered his store, and this clerk of whom I have been speaking came up in assumed consternation and said: "Oh, sir, the store has been on fire; I have put out the fire, but there are a great many goods lost; we have had a great crowd of people coming and going." Then the merchant took the clerk by the collar and said: "I have had enough of this; you cannot deceive me; where are those goods that you stole ?" The young man instantly confessed his villainy.

O the numbers of people in these great cities who are trying to get their living not honestly ! And they are a mighty temptation to the industrious young man who cannot understand it. While these others have it so easy they have it so hard. Horatius of olden time was told that he could have just *as much ground as he could plough* around with a yoke of oxen in one day. He hooked up the oxen to the plough, and he cut a very large circle and ploughed until he came to the same point where he started, and all that property was his. But I have to tell you to-day that just so much financial, just so much moral, just so much spiritual possession you will have as you compass with your own industries, and just so much as from the morning of your life to the evening of your life you can plough around with your own hard work. " Go to the ant, thou sluggard, consider her ways and be wise."

HOW SWIFT THE RIVER !

I was on the St. Lawrence River and the current was very swift, and I said : "Captain, how swift the river is." "Oh," he replied, " not much here, but seventy-five miles on further it is ten times swifter, and we employ an Indian pilot, and we give him a thousand dollars a summer to take us through between the Thousand Islands and between the rocks." Every man who comes from the country to the city life comes from smooth water into the rapids. There are thousands of islands of enchantment and many rocks of peril. Oh, I wonder if you are going to have good pilotage.

Do you know, my brother, that the report of your dissipation has already got back to the old homestead ? " Oh, no," you say, " that isn't possible." It is possible. There are always people ready to carry bad news, and of these people that desire to carry bad news there is an accursed old gossip wending her infernal step toward the old homestead.

She has been there. She sat down in a chair and she wriggled about for a while and said she could not stay a great while. But she said to your parents. "Do you know *your son gambles?* do you know your son drinks?" And the old people got very white about the lips, and your mother said : "Just open the door a little, so we may have fresh air." And after this bad messenger went away your mother came out and sat down on the steps where you used to play, and she cried and cried and cried, and took off her spectacles, and with her apron wiped off the mist of tears.

After a while she will be very sick and the old gig of the country doctor will come up the country lane, and the horse will be tied at the swinging gate, and the prescriptions will fail, and she will get worse and worse, and in her last delirium she will talk about nothing but you. And then the farmers will come to the funeral. They will tie their horses to the rail of the fence, and they will talk over what ailed the departed, and one will say it was intermittent, and another will say it was congestion, and another will say it was premature old age. Oh, no. It will be neither intermittent, nor congestion, nor premature old age ; but it will be recorded in the book of God Almighty that *you killed her !*

Our language is very fertile in describing crime. Slaying a man, that is homicide; slaying a brother, that is fratricide; slaying a father, that is patricide; slaying a mother, that is matricide. But you go on in that way, oh, wandering and dissipated soul, and it will take two words to describe your crime—patricide and matricide. Oh, come home to thy God, come home to thy father's God, thy mother's God. Just fold your hands to-day and say with another:

> "For sinners, Lord, Thou camest to bleed,
> And I'm a sinner vile indeed ,
> Lord, I believe Thy grace is free,
> O ! magnify that grace in me."

Do not let the world destroy you. Do not get swindled out of Heaven !

DIVERSITY OF TEMPTATIONS.

I have heard men in mid-life say they had never been led into temptation. If you have not felt temptation it is because you have not tried to do right. A man hoppled and handcuffed, as long as he lies quietly, does not test the power of the chain; but when he rises up, and with determination resolves to snap the handcuff or break the hopple, then he finds the power of the iron. And there are men who have been for ten and twenty and thirty years bound hand and foot by evil habits who have never felt the power of the chain, because they have never tried to break it. It is very easy to go on down with the stream and with the wind, lying on your oars; but just turn around and try to go against the wind and the tide, and you will find it is a different matter. As long as we go down the current of our evil habit we seem to get along quite smoothly; but if after a while we turn around and head the other way, toward Christ and pardon and heaven, oh, then how we have to lay to the oars! You will have your temptation. You one kind, you another, you another, not one person escaping.

It is all folly for you to say to some one, " I could not be tempted as you are." The lion thinks it is so strange that the fish should be caught with a hook. The fish thinks it is so strange that the lion should be caught with a trap. You see some man with a cold, phlegmatic temperament, and you say, " I suppose that man has not any temptation." Yes, as much as you have. In his phlegmatic nature he has a temptation to indolence and censoriousness and over-eating and drinking; a temptation to ignore the great work of life; a temptation to lay down an obstacle in the way of all good enterprises. The temperament decides the styles of temptation; but sanguine or lymphatic, you will have temptation; Satan has a grappling-hook just fitted for your soul. A man never lives beyond the reach of temptation. You say when a man gets to be seventy or eighty years of age he is safe from all Satanic assault. You are very much mistaken. A man at eighty-five years of age has as many temptations as a man at twenty-five. They are only different styles of temptation. Ask the aged Christian whether he is never assaulted of the powers of darkness. If you think you have conquered the power of temptation, you are very much mistaken.

A man who wanted the Papal throne pretended he was very weak and sickly, and if he was elected he would soon be gone. He crawled upon his crutches to the throne, and having attained it he was strong again. He said, "It was well for me while I was looking for the sceptre of another that I should stoop, but now that I have found it, why should I stoop any longer?" and he threw away his crutches and was well again. How illustrative of the power of temptation! You think it is a weak and crippled influence; but give it a chance, and it will be a tyrant in your soul, it will grind you to atoms.

COMMERCIAL PHARISEES.

This title photographs all those who are abhorrent of small sins, while they are reckless in regard to magnificent thefts. You will find many a merchant who, while he is so careful that he would not take a yard of cloth or a spool of cotton from the counter, without paying for it, and who, if a bank cashier should make a mistake and send in a roll of bills five dollars too much, would despatch a messenger in hot haste to return the surplus, yet who will go into a stock company in which, after awhile, he gets control of the stock, and then waters the stock and makes one hundred thousand dollars appear like two hundred thousand dollars. He only stole one hundred thousand dollars by the operation. Many of the men of fortune made their wealth in that way.

One of those men engaged in such unrighteous acts, that evening—the evening of the very day when he watered the stock—will find a wharf-rat stealing a newspaper from the basement doorway, and will go out and catch the urchin by the collar, and twist the collar so tightly that the poor fellow

cannot say it was thirst for knowledge that led him to the
dishonest act; tighter and tighter will he grip, saying, "I
have been looking for you a long while, you stole my paper
four or five times, haven't you? you miserable wretch." And
then the old stock-gambler, with a voice they can hear three
blocks, will cry out, "Police! police!" That same man, the
evening of the day in which he watered the stock, will kneel
with his family in prayers, and thank God for the prosperity
of the day, then kiss his children good-night with an air
which seems to say, "I hope you will all grow up to be as
good as your father." Prisons for sins insectile in size, but
palaces for crimes dromedarian. No mercy for sins animalcule in proportion, but great leniency for mastodon iniquity.
A poor boy slyly takes from the basket of a market woman
a choke-pear—saving some one else from the cholera—and
you smother him in the horrible atmosphere of Raymond
Street Jail, or New York Tombs, while his cousin, who has
been skilful enough to steal fifty thousand dollars from the
city, you will make a candidate for the New York Legislature!

There is a great deal of uneasiness and nervousness now
among some people in our time who have gotten unright
eous fortunes; a great deal of nervousness about dynamite.
I tell them that God will put under their unrighteous fortunes something more explosive than dynamite—the earthquake of His omnipotent indignation. It is time that we
learn in America that sin is not excusable in proportion as
it declares large dividends and has outriders in equipage.
Many a man is riding to perdition, postilion ahead and
lackey behind. To steal one copy of a newspaper is a gnat;
to steal many thousands of dollars is a camel. There is
many a fruit-dealer who would not consent to steal a basket
of peaches from a neighbor's stall, but who would not scruple
to depress the fruit market; and as long as I can remember,
we have heard every summer the peach crop of Maryland is
a failure, and by the time the crop comes in, the misrepresentation makes a difference of millions of dollars. A man

who would not steal one peach basket, steals fifty thousand peach baskets.

Go down in the summer-time into the Mercantile Library, in the reading-rooms, and see the newspaper reports of the crops from all parts of the country, and their phraseology is very much the same, and the same men wrote them, methodically and infamously carrying out the huge lying about the grain crop from year to year, and for a score of years. After a while there will be a "corner" in the wheat market, and men who have a contempt for a petty theft, will burglarize the wheat-bin of a nation, and commit larceny upon the American corn-crib. And some of the men will sit in churches, and in reformatory institutions, trying to strain out the small gnats of scoundrelism, while in their grain elevators and their store-houses they are fattening huge camels, which they expect, after a while, to swallow. Society has to be entirely reconstructed on this subject. We are to find that a sin is inexcusable in proportion as it is great. I know in our time the tendency is to charge religious frauds upon good men. They say, "O what a class of frauds you have in the Church of God in this day!" And when an elder of a church, or a deacon, or a minister of the Gospel, or a superintendent of a Sabbath-school, turns out a defaulter, what display heads there are in many of the newspapers. Great-primer type. Five-line pica. "Another Saint Absconded!" "Clerical Scoundrelism;" "Religion at a discount!" "Shame on the Churches!" Yet there are a thousand scoundrels outside the Church to where there is one inside the Church, and the misbehavior of those who never see the inside of a church is so great it is enough to tempt a man to become a Christian to get out of their company. But in all circles, religious and irreligious, the tendency is to excuse sin in proportion as it is mammoth. Even John Milton, in his "Paradise Lost," while he condemns Satan, gives such a grand description of him you have hard work to suppress your admiration O this straining out of small sins like gnats, and this gulping down great iniquities like camels!

SIN WILL OUT.

The smallest iniquity has a thousand tongues, and they will blab out an exposure. Saul was sent to destroy the Canaanites, their sheep and their oxen. But when he got down there among the pastures he saw some fine sheep and oxen too fat to kill, and so he thought he would steal them. He drove them towards home, but stopped to report to the prophet how well he had executed his commission, when in the distance the sheep began to bleat and the oxen to bellow. The secret was out, and Samuel said to the blushing and confounded Saul: "What means this bleating of the sheep that I hear and the lowing of the cattle?" Aye, my hearers, you cannot keep an iniquity quiet. At just the wrong time the sheep will bleat and the oxen will bellow. Achan cannot steal the Babylonish garment without getting stoned to death, nor Benedict Arnold betray his country without having his neck stretched. Look over the police arrests, these thieves, these burglars, these adulterers, these counterfeiters, these highwaymen, these assassins. They all thought they could bury their iniquity so deep down that it would never come to resurrection. But there was some shoe that answered to the print in the sand, some false keys found in possession, some bloody knife that whispered of the deed, and the public indignation, and the anathema of outraged law hurled him into the Tombs or hoisted him on the gallows. At the close of the battle between the Dauphin of France and the Helvetians, Burchard Monk was so elated with the victory that he lifted his helmet to look off upon the field, when a wounded soldier hurled a stone that struck his uncovered forehead and he fell. Sin always leaves some point exposed, there is no safety in iniquity. Francis the First, King of France, was discussing how it was best to get his army into Italy. Amaril, the court fool, sprang out from the corner and said to the king and his staff-officers: "You had better be thinking how you will get your army back out of Italy after once you have entered." In other words, it is easier for us to get into sin than to get out of it. Do not think that you can hide any great and protracted sin in your hearts. In an unguarded moment it will slip off of the lip, or some slight occasion may for a moment set ajar this door of hell that you wanted to keep closed. But suppose that in this life you hide it, and you get along with that transgression burning in your heart, as a ship on fire within for days may hinder the flame from bursting out by keeping down the hatchways, yet at last, in the Judgment, that iniquity will blaze out before God and the universe.

HISSED OFF THE STAGE.

" Men shall clap their hands at him, and shall hiss him out of his place."—JOB 27: 23

This allusion seems to be dramatic. The Bible more than once makes such allusion. Paul says : " We are made a theatre (or spectacle) to angels and to men." The theatre is so old that no one can fix the date of its birth. Archilochus, Simonides, and Solon, who wrote for it dithyrambics, lived about six or seven hundred years before Christ. It is evident from the text that some of the habits of the theatre-goers were known in Job's time, because in the text he describes an actor hissed off the stage. The impersonator comes on the boards, and either through lack of study of the part he is to take, or inaptness, or other incapacity, the spectators are offended, and express their disapprobation and disgust first by over-applause, attempting by great clapping of hands to drown out what he says, and, that failing to stop the performer, they put their tongue against their teeth, and make terrific sibilation until he disappears behind the curtain. " Men shall clap their hands at him, and shall hiss him out of his place."

EVERY MAN HAS A PART.

My text suggests that each one of us is put on the stage of this world to take some part. Each one is assigned a place, no supernumeraries hanging around the drama of life to take this or that or the other part, as he may be called upon.

No one can take our place. We can take no other place. Ay, it is not the impersonation of another; we ourselves are the real Merchant of Venice or the real Shylock; the real filial Cordelia or the real cruel Regan; the real Portia or the real Lady Macbeth. The tragedian of the playhouse, at the close of the third scene of the fifth act, takes off the attire of Gonzalo or Edward Mortimer or Henry V., and resigns the character in which for three hours he appeared. But we never put off our character, and no change of apparel can make us any one else than that which we eternally are. McCullough, the actor, was no more certainly appointed on any occasion to appear as Spartacus, or Edwin Forrest as King Lear, or Charlotte Cushman as Meg Merrilies, or John Kemble as Macbeth, or Cooke as Richard III., or Kean as Othello, than you and I are expected to take some especial and particular part in the great drama of human and immortal life. Through what hardship and suffering and discipline these artists went year after year that they might be perfected in their parts, you have often read. But we, put on the stage of this life to represent charity and faith and humility and helpfulness—what little preparation we have made, although we have three galleries of spectators—earth and heaven and hell! Have we not been more attentive to the part taken by others than to the part taken by ourselves, and while we needed to be looking at home and concentring on our own duty, we have been criticising the other performers, and saying: "That was too high," or "too low," or "too feeble," or "too extravagant," or "too tame," or "too demonstrative," while we were making ourselves a dead failure and preparing to be ignominiously hissed off the stage?

Now, compare some of these goings out of life with the departure of men and women who in the drama of life took the part that God assigned them, and then went away honored of men, and applauded of the Lord Almighty.

A CONSECRATED HOME.

It is about fifty years ago that in a comparatively small

apartment of the city a newly-married pair set up a home. The first guest that was invited in that residence was the Lord Jesus Christ, and the Bible given the bride on the day of her espousals was the guide of that household. Days of sunshine were followed by days of shadow. Did you ever know a home that for fifty years had no vicissitude?

Years passed on, and there were in that home hilarities, but they were good and healthful; and sorrows, but they were comforted. Marriages as bright as orange-blossoms could make them, and burials in which all hearts were riven. They have a family lot in the cemetery, but all the place is illuminated with stories of resurrection and reunion. The children of the household that lived have grown up, and they are all Christians, the father and mother leading the way, and the children following. What care the mother took of wardrobe and education and character and manners! How hard she sometimes worked! When the head of the household was unfortunate in business she sewed until her fingers were numb and bleeding at the tips. And what close calculation of economies, and what ingenuity in refitting the garments of the elder children for the younger! And only God kept account of that mother's sideaches and headaches and heartaches and the tremulous prayers by the side of the sick child's cradle, and by the couch of this one fully grown. The neighbors often noticed how tired she looked, and old acquaintances hardly knew her in the street; but without complaint she waited and toiled and endured and accomplished all these years.

AN EXIT.

The children are out in the world, an honor to themselves and their parents. After a while the mother's last sickness comes. Children and grandchildren, summoned from afar, come softly into the room one by one, for she is too weak to see more than one at a time. She runs her dying fingers lovingly through their hair, and tells them not to cry, and that she is going now, but they will all meet again in a little while, in a better world, and then kisses them good-by and "God bless and keep you, my dear child!" The day of the obsequies comes, and the officiating clergyman tells the story of wifely and motherly endurance, and many hearts on earth and in heaven echo the sentiment ; and as she is carried off the stage of this mortal life there are cries of " Faithful unto death, she hath done what she could," while overpowering all the voices of earth and heaven is the plaudit of the God who watched her from first to last, saying: " Well done, good and faithful servant; thou hast been faithful over a few things, I will make thee ruler over many things. Enter thou into the joy of thy Lord."

But what became of the father of that household? He started out as a young man in business and had small income, and having got a little ahead, sickness in the family swept it all away. He went through all the business panics of forty years, met many losses, and suffered many betrayals, but kept right on trusting in God, whether business was good or poor, setting his children a good example, giving them the best of counsel ; and never a prayer did he offer for all those years but they were mentioned in it. He is old now, and realizes it cannot be long before he must quit all these scenes ; but he is going to leave his children an inheritance of prayer and Christian principles which all the defalcations of earth can never touch ; and as he goes out of the world the Church of God blesses him, and the poor ring his door-bell to see if he is any better, and his grave is surrounded by a multitude who went on foot and stood there before the procession of carriages came up, and some say, " There will be no one to take his place," and others say, " Who will pity me now?" and others remark, " He shall be held in everlasting remembrance." And as the drama of his life closes, all the vociferations and bravos and encores that ever shook the amphitheatres and the Drury Lanes and the Covent Gardens and the Haymarkets and the Coliseums of earthly spectacle were tame and feeble compared with the long, loud thunders of approval that shall break from the cloud of witnesses in the piled-up gallery of the heavens. Choose ye between the life that shall close by being hissed off the stage and the life that shall close amid the acclamations supernal and archangelic.

SHAKESPEARE'S WILL.

O men and women on the stage of life, many of you in the first act of the drama, and others in the second, and some of you in the third, and a few in the fourth, and here and there one in the fifth, but all of you between entrance and exit, I quote to you as the peroration of this sermon the most suggestive passage that Shakespeare ever wrote, although you never heard it recited. The author has often been claimed as infidel and atheistic, so the quotation shall be not only religiously helpful to ourselves, but grandly vindicatory of the great dramatist. I quote from his last will and testament: " In the name of God, Amen. I, William Shakespeare, of Stratford-upon-Avon, in the County of Warwick, gentleman, in perfect health and memory (God be praised), do make this my last will and testament in manner and form following. First, I commend my soul into the hands of God, my Creator, hoping and assuredly believing through the only merits of Jesus Christ, my Saviour, to be made partaker of life everlasting." Then follow the bequests and the signature: " By me, William Shakespeare." " Witnesses to the publishing hereof, F. Collyns, Jesse Shaw, John Robinson, Hamnet Sadler, Robert Whattcott."

WINTER TEMPTATIONS.

There is something in the winter season that not only tests our physical endurance, but, especially in the city, tries our moral character. It is the winter months that ruin morally and forever many of our young men. We sit in the house on a winter's night, and hear the storm raging on the outside, and imagine the helpless crafts driven on the coast ; but, if our ears were only good enough, we could on any

winter night hear the crash of *a hundred moral shipwrecks.*
Many who come in September to town by the first of
March will have been blasted   It only takes one winter to
ruin a young man.   When the long winter evenings have
come many of our young men will improve them in forming
a more intimate acquaintance with books, contracting higher
social friendships, and strengthening and ennobling characters.   But not so with all.   I will show you before I get
through that at this season of the year temptations are
especially rampant, and my counsel is, Look out how you
spend your winter nights!

THE DEVIL'S HARVEST TIME.

I remark, first, that there is no season of the year in
which vicious allurements are so active.   In warm weather
places of dissipation win their tamest triumphs.   People do
not feel like going, in the hot nights of summer, among the
blazing gas-lights, or breathing the fetid air of assemblages.
The receipts of most grog-shops in a December night are
three times what they are in any night in July or August.
I doubt not there are larger audiences in the casinos in win-
ten than in the summer weather.   Iniquity plies a more
profitable trade.   December, January, and February are
harvest months for the devil.   The play-bills of the low entertainments then are more charming, the acting is more exquisite, the enthusiasm of the spectators more bewitching.
Many a young man who makes out to keep right the rest of
the year capsizes now.   When he came to town in the
autumn his eye was bright, his cheek rosy, his step elastic;
but before spring, as you pass him you will say to your
friend, "What is the matter with that young man?"   The
fact is, that one winter of dissipation has done the work of
ruin.

FATAL PARTIES.

This is the season for parties, and if they are of the right
kind our social nature is improved and our spirits are cheered

up. But many of them are not of the right kind, and our young people, night after night, are kept in the whirl of unhealthy excitement, until their strength fails, and their spirits are broken down, and their taste for ordinary life corrupted; and by the time the spring weather comes they are in the doctor's hands or sleeping in the cemetery. The certificate of their death is made out, and the physician, out of regard for the family, calls the disease by some Latin name, when the truth is that they died of too many parties.

SLAIN BY EVIL HABITS.

There are tens of thousands of young men every year coming from the country to our great cities. They come with brave hearts and grand expectations. They think they will be Rufus Choates in the law, or Drapers in chemistry, or A. T. Stewarts in merchandise. The country lads sit down in the village grocery, with their feet on the iron rod around the red-hot stove, in the evening, talking over the prospects of the young man who has gone off to the city. Two or three of them think that perhaps he may get along very well and succeed, but the most of them prophesy failure, for it is very hard to think that those whom we knew in boyhood will ever make any stir in the world.

But our young man has a fine position in a dry-goods store. The month is over. He gets his wages. He is not accustomed to have so much money belonging to himself. He is a little excited, and does not exactly know what to do with it, and he spends it in some places where he ought not. Soon there come up new companions and acquaintances from the bar-rooms and the saloons of the city. Soon that young man begins to waver in the battle of temptation, and soon his soul goes down. In a few months, or few years, he has fallen. He is morally dead. He is a mere corpse of what he once was. The harpies of sin snuff up the taint and come on the field. His garments gradually give out. He has pawned his watch. His health is failing him. His credit perishes. He is too poor to stay in the

city, and he is too poor to pay his way home to the country.
Down! down! Why do the low fellows of the city now
stick to him so closely? Is it to help him back to a moral
and spiritual life? Oh, no! I will tell you why they stay;
they are the Philistines stripping the slain.

TRY, TRY AGAIN!

With an insight into human nature such as no other man
ever reached, Solomon sketches the mental operations of
one who, having stepped aside from the path of rectitude,
desires to return. With a wish for something better he
said, "When shall I awake? When shall I come out of
this horrid nightmare of iniquity?" But, seized upon by
uneradicated habit, and forced down hill by his passions, he
cries out, "I will seek it yet again. I will try it once more."

Our libraries are adorned with an elegant literature addressed to young men, pointing out to them all the dangers
and perils of life—complete maps of the voyage, showing
all the rocks, the quicksands, the shoals. But suppose a
man has already made shipwreck; suppose he is already off
the track; suppose he has already gone astray, how is he to
get back? That is a field comparatively untouched. I
propose to address myself to such. There are those in this
audience who, with every passion of their agonized soul, are
ready to hear such a discussion. They compare themselves
with what they were ten years ago, and cry out from the
bondage in which they are incarcerated. Now, if there be
any in this house, here with an earnest purpose, yet feeling they are beyond the pale of Christian sympathy, and
that the sermon can hardly be expected to address them,
then, at this moment, I give them my right hand, and call
them brother. Look up. There is glorious and triumphant hope for you yet. I sound the trumpet of Gospel deliverance. The Church is ready to spread a banquet at
your return, and the hierarchs of heaven will fall into line of
bannered procession at the news of your emancipation. So
far as God may help me, I propose to show what are the

obstacles of your return, and then how you are to sur-
mount those obstacles.

MORAL GRAVITATION.

The first difficulty in the way of your return is the force
of *moral gravitation.* Just as there is a natural law which
brings down to the earth anything you throw into the air,
so there is a corresponding moral gravitation. In other
words, it is easier to go down than it is to go up; it is
easier to do wrong than it is to do right. Call to mind the
comrades of your boyhood days—some of them good, some
of them bad—which most affected you? Call to mind the
anecdotes that you have heard in the last five or ten years—
some of them are pure and some of them impure. Which
the more easily sticks to your memory? During the years
of your life you have formed certain courses of conduct—
some of them good, some of them bad. To which style of
habit did you the more easily yield? Ah, my friends, we
have to take but a moment of self-inspection to find out that
there is in all our souls a force of moral gravitation! But
that gravitation may be resisted. Just as you may pick up
from the earth something and hold it in your hand toward
heaven, just so, by the power of God's grace, a soul fallen
may be lifted toward peace, toward pardon, toward heaven.
Force of moral gravitation in every one of us, but power in
God's grace to overcome that force of moral gravitation.

EVIL HABITS HARD TO GIVE UP.

I know there are those who say it is very easy for them
to give up evil habits. I do not believe them. Here is a
man given to intoxication. He knows it is disgracing his
family, destroying his property, ruining him, body, mind, and
soul. If that man, being an intelligent man, and loving his
family, could easily give up that habit, would he not do so?
The fact that he does not give it up proves it is hard to
give it up.

Yet the trouble is that many make a *disgraceful surren-der.* As we all know, there is honorable and dignified surren-der, as when a small host yields to superior numbers. It is no humiliation for a thousand men to yield to ten thousand. It is better than to keep on when there can be no result ex-cept that of massacre. But those who surrender to sin make a surrender when on their side they have enough re-serve forces to rout all the armies of Perdition, whether led on by what a demonographer calls Belial, or Beelzebub, or Apollyon, or Abaddon, or Ariel. At the time of it there was much talk about the abdication of Alexander of Bulgaria, but what a paltry throne was that from which the unhappy king descended, compared with the abdication of that young man, or middle-aged man, or old man, who quits the throne of his opportunity and turns his back upon a heavenly throne, and tramps off into ignominy and everlasting exile! That is an abdication enough to shake a universe. In Persia they will not have a blind man on the throne, and when a reigning monarch is jealous of some ambitious rela-tive, he has his eyes extinguished so that he cannot possibly ever come to crowning. And that suggests the difference between the way sin and divine grace takes hold of a man. The former blinds him so he may never reach a throne, while the latter illumines the blind that he may take coronation.

EASY TO GO DOWN STREAM.

It is a very easy thing to sail down stream, the tide carrying you with great force; but suppose you turn the boat up stream, is it so easy then to row it? As long as we yield to the evil inclinations in our hearts, and our bad habits, we are sailing down stream; but the moment we try to turn, we put our boat in the rapids just above Niagara, and try to row upstream. Take a man given to the habit of *using to-bacco*, as most of you do, and let him resolve to stop, and he finds it very difficult. Twenty one years ago I quitted that habit, and I would as soon dare to put my right hand in the fire as once to indulge in it Why? Because it was such a

terrific struggle to get over it.   Now, let a man be advised
by his physician to give up the use of tobacco.   He goes
around not knowing what to do with himself.   He cannot
add up a line of figures.   He cannot sleep nights.   It seems
as if the world had turned upside down.   He feels his business
is going to ruin.   Where he was kind and obliging he is
scolding and fretful.   The composure that characterized him
has given way to a fretful restlessness, and he has become a
complete fidget.   What power is it that has rolled a wave of
woe over the earth and shaken a portent in the heavens?
He has tried to stop smoking or chewing!   After a while he
says, "I am going to do as I please   The doctor doesn't
understand my case.   I'm going back to my old habit."
And he returns.   Everything assumes its usual composure.
His business seems to brighten.   The world becomes an
attractive place to live in.   His children, seeing the difference,
hail the return of their father's genial disposition.   What
wave of color has dashed blue into the sky, and greenness
into the mountain foliage, and the glow of sapphire into the
sunset?   What enchantment has lifted a world of beauty
and joy on his soul?   He has gone back to tobacco!

O! the fact is, as we all know in our own experience,
that habit is a taskmaster; as long as we obey it, it does not
chastise us, but let us resist and we find we are to be lashed
with scorpion-whips and bound with ship-cable, and thrown
into the track of bone-breaking Juggernauts!   During the
war of 1812 there was a ship set on fire just above Niagara
Falls, and then, cut loose from its moorings, it came on
down through the night and tossed over the Falls.   It was
said to have been a scene brilliant beyond all description.
Well, there are thousands of men on fire of evil habit, coming
down through the rapids and through the awful night of
temptation toward the eternal plunge.   Oh! how hard it is
to arrest them.   God only can arrest them.

Suppose a man after five, or ten, or twenty years of evil-
doing, resolves to do right?   Why, all the forces of darkness
are allied against him.   He cannot sleep nights.   He gets
down on his knees in the midnight and cries, "God help me!"

He bites his lip. He grinds his teeth. He clenches his fist in a determination to keep his purpose. He dare not look at the bottles in the window of a wine-store. It was one long, bitter, exhaustive, hand-to-hand fight with inflamed, tantalizing, and merciless habit.

When he thinks he is entirely free, the old inclinations pounce upon him like a pack of hounds with their muzzles tearing away at the flanks of one poor reindeer. In Paris there is a sculptured representation of Bacchus, the god of revelry. He is riding on a panther at full leap. Oh, how suggestive! Let every one who is speeding on bad ways understand he is not riding a docile and well-broken steed, but he is riding a monster, wild and bloodthirsty, going at a death-leap.

How many there are who resolve on a better life and say, "When shall I awake?" but, seized on by their old habits, cry, "I will try it once more; I will seek it yet again!" Years ago there were some Princeton students who were skating, and the ice was very thin, and some one warned the company back from the air-hole, and finally warned them entirely to leave the place. But one young man with bravado, after all the rest had stopped, cried out, "One round more!" He swept around and went down, and was brought out a corpse. My friends, there are thousands and tens of thousands of men losing their souls in that way. It is the "one round more."

FOUR PLAIN QUESTIONS.

Are your habits as good as when you left your father's house? Have you a pool ticket in your pocket? Have you a fraudulent document? Have you been experimenting to see how accurate an imitation you could make of your employer's signature? O! you have good blood. Remember your father's prayers. Remember your mother's example Turn not in an evil way Have you been going astray? Come back. Have you ventured out too far?

Why, my brother, there have been too many prayers

offered for you to have you go overboard. And there are those venturing down into sin, and my heart aches to call them back.

At Brighton Beach or Long Branch you have seen men go down into the surf to bathe, and they waded out farther and farther, and you got anxious about them. You said, " I wonder if they can swim?" And then you stood and shouted, "Come back! come back! You will be lost! you will be lost!" They waved their hands back, saying, " No danger." They kept on wading deeper down and farther out from shore, until after a while a great wave with a strong under-tow took them out, and their corpses the next day were dashed on the beach. So I see men wading into sin farther and farther—farther from God—and I call to them, "Come back! come back! You will be lost! you will be lost!" They wave their hands back, saying, "No danger, no danger." Deeper down and deeper down, until after a while a wave sweeps them out and sweeps them off forever. O, come back! The one farthest away may come.

I have shown you obstacles because I want you to under-stand I know all the difficulties in the way; but I am now to tell you how Hannibal may scale the Alps, and how the shackles may be unriveted, and how the paths of virtue for-saken may be regained. First of all, my brother, throw yourself on God. Go to Him frankly and earnestly, and tell Him these habits you have, and ask Him if there is any help in all the resources of omnipotent love, to give it to you. Do not go with a long rigmarole people call prayer, made up of "ohs" and "ahs" and "forever and forever amens!" Go to God and cry for help! help! help! and if you cannot cry for help just look and live. I remember in the war I was at Antietam, and I went into the hospitals after the battle, and I said to a man, "Where are you hurt?" He made no answer, but held up his arm, swollen and splintered. I saw where he was hurt. The simple fact is, when a man has a wounded soul, all he has to do is to hold it up before a sympathetic Lord and get it healed. It does not take any long prayer. Just hold up the wound. Oh, it is no small thing when a

man is nervous and weak and exhausted, coming from his
evil ways, to feel that God puts two omnipotent arms around
about him and says, " Young man, I will stand by you! The
mountains may depart and the hills be removed, but I will
never fail you." And then, as the soul thinks the news is
too good to be true, and cannot believe it, and looks up in
God's face, God lifts His right hand and takes an oath, an
affidavit, saying, " As I live, saith the Lord God, I have no
pleasure in the death of him that dieth."

IRRELIGION A SLAUGHTERER !!!

I think many young men are slaughtered through irreli-
gion. Take away a young man's religion, and you make
him the prey of evil. We all know that the Bible is the only
perfect system of morals. Now, if you want to destroy the
young man's morals, take his Bible away? How will you do
that? Well, you will caricature his reverence for the Scriptures; you will take all those incidents of the Bible which
can be made mirth of—Jonah's whale, Samson's foxes,
Adam's rib—then you will caricature eccentric Christians or
inconsistent Christians; then you will pass off as your own
all those hackneyed arguments against Christianity, which
are as old as Tom Paine, as old as Voltaire, as old as sin.
Now you have captured his Bible, and you have taken his
strongest fortress. the way is comparatively clear, and all
the gates of his soul are set open in invitation to the sins of
earth and the sorrows of death, that they may come in and ,
drive the stake for their encampment.

A steamer fifteen hundred miles from shore with broken
rudder and lost compass, and hull leaking fifty gallons the
hour, is better off than a young man when you have robbed
him of his Bible. Have you ever noticed how despicably
mean it is to take away the world's Bible without proposing
a substitute? It is meaner than to come to a sick man, and
steal his medicine; meaner than to come to a cripple and
steal his crutch; meaner than to come to a pauper and steal
his crust; meaner than to come to a poor man and burn his

house. It is the worst of all larcenies to steal the Bible, which has been the crutch and medicine and food and eternal home to so many. Slaughter a young man's faith in God, and there is not much left to slaughter.

Now, *what has become of the slaughtered?* Well, some of them are in their father's or mother's house, broken down in health, waiting to die ; others are in the hospital ; others are in Greenwood, or, rather, their bodies are, for their souls have gone on to retribution. Not much prospect for a young man who started in life with good health, and good education, and a Christian example set him, and opportunity of useful-ness, who gathered all his treasures and put them in one box, and dropped it into the sea.

Now, how is this wholesale slaughter to be stopped? There is no one but is interested in that question. Young man, arm yourself ! The object of my sermon is to put a weapon in each of your hands for your own defence. Wait not for Young Men's Christian Associations to protect you, or churches to protect you. Appeal to God for help.

There is no class of persons that so stir my sympathies as young men in great cities. Not quite enough salary to live on, and all the temptations that come from that deficit. Invited on all hands to drink, and their exhausted nervous system seeming to demand stimulants. Their religion cari-catured by most of the clerks in the store and most of the operatives in the factory. The rapids of temptation and death rushing against that young man forty miles the hour, and he in a frail boat headed up stream, with nothing but a broken oar to work with. Unless Almighty God help him he will go under. Ah ! do not depend upon human resolu-tion, which may be dissolved in the foam of the wine-cup, or may be blown out with the first gust of temptation. Here is the helmet, the sword of the Lord God Almighty. Clothe yourself in that panoply, and you shall not be put to con-fusion. Sin pays well neither in this world nor the next, but right-thinking and right-believing and acting will take you in safety through this life, and in transport through the next.

Have a room somewhere that you can call your own.

Whether it be the back parlor of a fashionable boarding-house or a room in the fourth story of a cheap lodging, I care not. Only have that one room your fortress. Let not the dissipator or unclean step over the threshold. If they come up the long flight of stairs and knock at the door, meet them face to face, and kindly yet firmly refuse them admittance. Have a few family portraits on the wall, if you brought them with you from your country home. Have a Bible on the stand. If you can afford it, and you can play on one, have an instrument of music—harp or flute or cornet or melodeon or violin or piano. Every morning, before you leave that room, pray. Every night, after you come home in that room, pray. Make that room your Gibraltar, your Sebastopol, your Mount Zion. Let no bad book or newspaper come into that room any more than you would allow a cobra to coil on your table.

Then look to God. Nobody else will take care of you. Your help will not come up two or three or four flights of stairs; your help will come through the roof, down from heaven, from that God who in the six thousand years of the world's history never betrayed a young man who tried to be good and Christian.

"O!" you say, "you don't know where I came from; you don't know what my history has been; you don't know what iniquity I have plotted; I have gone through the whole catalogue of sin." My brother, I do not know the story, but I tell you this: the door of mercy is wide open. "Though your sins be as scarlet they shall be as snow; though they be red like crimson, they shall be as wool." Though you have been polluted with the worst of crimes, though you have been smitten with the worst of leprosies, though you have been fired with all evil passions, this moment on your brow, hot with iniquitous indulgences, may be set the flashing coronet of a Saviour's forgiveness.

MERCY FOR ALL.

"I am a gambler," says one man. There is mercy for you. "I am a libertine," says another. There is mercy for you.

"I have plunged into every abomination." Mercy for you. The door of grace does not stand ajar to-night, nor half swung around on the hinges. It is wide, wide open; and there is nothing in the Bible, or in Christ, or God, or earth, or heaven, or hell, to keep you out of the door of safety, if you want to go in. Christ has borne your burdens, fought your battles, suffered for your sins. The debt is paid, and the receipt is handed to you, written in the blood of the Son of God—will you have it? Oh, decide the matter now! Decide it here! Fling your exhausted soul down at the feet of an all-compassionate, all-sympathizing, all-pitying, all-pardoning Jesus. The laceration on His brow, the gash in His side, the torn muscles and nerves of His feet beg you to come.

But remember, one inch outside the door of pardon and you are in as much peril as though you were a thousand miles away.

THE WORST MAY HOPE.

Blessed be God for such a Gospel as this! "Cut the slices thin," said the wife to the husband, "or there will not be enough to go all around for the children; cut the slices thin." Blessed be God, there is a full loaf for every one that wants it, bread enough and to spare. No thin slices at the Lord's table. I remember when a certain hospital in Philadelphia was opened during the war, a telegram came saying, "There will be three hundred wounded men to-night, be ready to take care of them;" and from my church there went some twenty or thirty men and women to look after these poor wounded fellows. As they came, some from one part of the land, some from another, no one asked whether this man was from Oregon, or from Massachusetts, or from Minnesota, or from New York. There was a wounded soldier, and the only question was how to take off the rags most gently, and put on the bandage, and administer the cordial. And when a soul comes to God, He does not ask where you came from or what your ancestry was.

Healing for all your wounds. Pardon for all your guilt. Comfort for all your troubles.

If you do not know how to come, it may be helpful to seek Christian advice. Every Christian man is bound to help you. First of all, seek God; then seek Christian counsel. And, if you want to get back, quit all your bad associations. What chance is there for that young man I saw along the street, four or five young men with him, halting in front of a grog shop, urging him to go in, he resisting, violently resisting, until after a while they forced him to go in? Give up your bad companions, or give up heaven. It is not ten bad companions that destroy a man, nor five bad companions, nor three bad companions, but one; one unholy intimacy will fill your soul with moral distemper. In all the ages of the Church there has not been an instance where a man kept one evil associate and was reformed. Among the fourteen hundred million of the race not one instance. Go home to-day, open your desk, take out letter paper, stamp, and envelope, and then write a letter something like this:

" My old companions : I start this day for heaven. Until I am persuaded you will join me in this, farewell "

Then sign your name, and send the letter by the first post. Then gather up the energies of body, mind, and soul, and, appealing to God for success, declare this day everlasting war against all drinking habits, all gaming practices, all houses of sin. Half-and-half work will amount to nothing, it must be a Waterloo. Shrink back now, and you are lost. Push on and you are saved. A Spartan general fell at the very moment of victory, but he dipped his finger in his own blood and wrote on a rock near which he was dying, " Sparta has conquered !" Though your struggle to get rid of sin may seem to be almost a death struggle, you can dip your finger in your own blood and write on the Rock of Ages, " Victory through our Lord Jesus Christ."

GLORIOUS NEWS.

O what glorious news it would be for some of these young men to send home to their parents in the country'

They go to the post-office every day or two to see whether there are any letters from you. How anxious they are to hear. You might send them for a holiday present a book from one of our best publishing houses, or a complete wardrobe from the importer's palace, it would not please them half so much as the news you might send home to-morrow that you had given your heart to God. I know how it is in the country. The night comes on. The cattle stand under the rack through which burst the trusses of hay. The horses just having frisked up from the meadow at the nightfall stand knee-deep in the bright straw that invites them to lie down and rest. The perch of the hovel is full of fowl, their feet warm under the feathers. In the old farm-house at night no candle is lighted, for the flames clap their hands about the great back log, and shake the shadow of the group up and down the wall.

Father and mother sit there for half an hour, saying nothing. I wonder what they are thinking of. After awhile the father breaks the silence and says, " Well, I wonder where our boy is in town to-night?" and the mother answers, " In no bad place, I warrant you, we always could trust him when he was home, and since he has been away there have been so many prayers offered for him, we can trust him still." Then, at eight o'clock—for they retire early in the country—they kneel down and commend you to that God who watches in country and in town, on the land and on the sea.

Some one said to a Grecian general, " What was the proudest moment in your life?" He thought a moment and said, " The proudest moment in my life was when I sent word home to my parents that I had gained the victory." And the proudest and most brilliant moment in your life will be the moment when you can send word to your parents that you have conquered your evil habits by the grace of God, and become eternal victor. Oh, despise not parental anxiety!

The time will come when you will have neither father nor mother, and you will go around the place where they used to watch you, and find them gone from the house, and gone from the field, and gone from the neighborhood. Cry as loud for forgiveness as you may over the mound in the churchyard, they will not answer.

And then you will take out the white lock of hair that was cut from your mother's brow just before they buried her, and you will take the cane with which your father used to walk, and you will think and think and wish that you had done just as they wanted you to, and would give the world if you had never thrust a pang through their dear old hearts God pity the young man who has brought disgrace on his father's name! *God pity the young man who has broken his mother's heart!* Better if he had never been born—better if in the first hour of his life, instead of being laid against the warm bosom of maternal tenderness, he had been coffined and sepulchred. There is no balm powerful enough to heal the heart of one who has brought parents to a sorrowful grave, and who wanders about through the dismal cemetery, rending the hair, and wringing the hands, and crying, "Mother! Mother!" O that by all the memories of the past, and by all the hopes of the future, you would yield your heart to God! May your father's God and your mother's God be your God forever!

CHAPTER XIV.

Defences of Young Men.

"And the Lord opened the eyes of the young man."—II. KINGS 6 : 17.

ONE morning in Dothan, a young theological student was scared by finding himself and Elisha the prophet, upon whom he waited, surrounded by a whole army of enemies. But venerable Elisha was not scared at all, because he saw the mountains full of defence for him, in chariots made out of fire, wheels of fire, dash-board of fire, and cushion of fire, drawn by horses with nostrils of fire, and mane of fire, and haunches of fire, and hoofs of fire—a supernatural appearance that could not be seen with the natural eye. So the old minister prayed that the young minister might see them also, and the prayer was answered, and the Lord opened the eyes of the young man, and he also saw the fiery procession, looking somewhat, I suppose, like the Adirondacks or the Alleghanies in their autumnal resplendence.

Many young men, standing among the most tremendous realities, have their eyes half shut or entirely closed May God grant that the truth may open wide your eyes to your safety, your opportunity and your destiny.

A GOOD HOME.

A mighty defence for a young man is *a good home.* Some of you may look back with tender satisfaction to your early home. It may have been rude and rustic, hidden among the hills, and architect or upholsterer may never have planned or adorned it. But all the fresco on princely walls never looked so enticing to you as those rough-hewn rafters. You can think of no park or arbor of trees planted on fashionable country-seat so attractive as the plain brook that ran in front of the old farm-house and sung under the weeping

366

willows. No barred gateway, adorned with statue of bronze, and swung open by obsequious porter in full dress, has half the glory of the swing gate. Many of you have a second dwelling-place, your adopted home, that also is sacred forever. There you built the first family altar. There your children were born. All those trees you planted. That room is solemn, because once in it, over the hot pillow, flapped the wing of death. Under that roof you expect when your work is done, to lie down and die. You try with many words to tell the excellency of the place, but you fail. There is only one word in the language that can describe your meaning. It is home. That young man is comparatively safe who goes out into the world with a charm like this upon him. The memory of parental solicitude, watching, planning and praying, will be to him a shield and a shelter. I never knew a man faithful both to his early and adopted home, who at the same time was given over to any gross form of dissipation or wickedness. He who seeks his enjoyment chiefly from outside association, rather than from the more quiet and unpresuming pleasures of which I have spoken, may be suspected to be on the broad road to ruin. Absalom despised his father's house, and you know his history of sin and his death of shame. If you seem unnecessarily isolated from your kindred and former associates, is there not some room that you can call your own? Into it gather books and pictures, and a harp. Have a portrait over the mantel. Make ungodly mirth stand back from the threshold. Consecrate some spot with the habit of prayer. By the memory of other days, a father's counsel, and a mother's love, and a sister's confidence, call it home.

INDUSTRIOUS HABITS.

Many young men, in starting upon life in this age, expect to make their way through the world by the use of their wits rather than the toil of their hands. A boy now goes to the city and fails twice before he is as old as his father was when he first saw the spires of the great town.

Sitting in some office, rented at a thousand dollars a year, he is waiting for the bank to declare its dividend, or goes into the market expecting before night to be made rich by the rushing up of the stocks. But luck seemed so dull he resolved on some other tack. Perhaps he borrowed from his employer's money-drawer and forgets to put it back, or for merely the purpose of improving his penmanship makes a copy-plate of a merchant's signature. Never mind, all is right in trade. In some dark night there may come in his dreams a vision of Blackwell's Island, or of Sing Sing, but it soon vanishes. In a short time he will be ready to retire from the busy world, and amid his flocks and herds culture the domestic virtues. Then those young men who once were his schoolmates, and knew no better than to engage in honest work, will come with their ox-teams to draw him logs, and with their hard hands help heave up his castle. This is no fancy picture. It is every-day life. I should not wonder if there were some rotten beams in that beautiful palace. I should not wonder if dire sicknesses should smite through the young man, or if God should pour into his cup of life a draught that would thrill him with unbearable agony. I should not wonder if his children should become to him a living curse, making his home a pest and a disgrace. I should not wonder if he goes to a miserable grave, and beyond it into the gnashing of teeth. The way of the ungodly shall perish.

My young friends, there is no way to genuine success, except through toil either of the head or hand. At the battle of Crecy, in 1346, the Prince of Wales, finding himself heavily pressed by the enemy, sent word to his father for help. The father, watching the battle from a wind-mill, and seeing that his son was not wounded and could gain the day if he would, sent word: "No, I will not come. Let the boy win his spurs, for, if God will, I desire that this day be his with all its honors." Young man, fight your own battle, all through, and you shall have the victory. Oh, it is a battle worth fighting. Two monarchs of old fought a duel, Charles V. and Francis, and the stakes were kingdoms,

Milan and Burgundy. You fight with sin, and the stake is heaven or hell.

Do not get the fatal idea that you are a genius, and that, therefore, there is no need of close application. It is here where multitudes fail. I had rather be an ox than an eagle, plain, and plodding and useful, rather than high flying and good for nothing but to pick out the eyes of carcases. *Extraordinary capacity without work is extraordinary failure.* There is no hope for that person who begins life resolved to live by his wits, for the probability is that he has not any. It was not safe for Adam, even in his unfallen state, to have nothing to do, and, therefore, God commanded him to be a farmer and horticulturist. He was to dress the garden and keep it, and had he and his wife obeyed the divine injunction and been at work, they would not have been sauntering under the trees and hankering after that fruit which destroyed them and their posterity ; proof positive for all ages to come that those who do not attend to their business are sure to get into mischief.

I do not know that the prodigal in Scripture would ever have been reclaimed had he not given up his idle habits, and gone to feeding swine for a living. " Go to the ant, thou sluggard, consider her ways and be wise ; which having no guide, overseer, or ruler, provideth her meat in the summer and gathereth her food in the harvest." The devil does not so often attack the man who is busy with the pen, and the book, and the trowel, and the saw, and the hammer. He is afraid of those weapons. But woe to the man whom this roaring lion meets with his hands in his pockets.

DRUDGERY NECESSARY.

Do not demand that your toil always be elegant, and cleanly and refined. There is a certain amount of drudgery through which we must all pass, whatever be our occupation. You know how men are sentenced a certain number of years to prison, and after they have suffered and worked out the time, then they are allowed to go free. And so it is

with all of us. God passed on us the sentence : " By the
sweat of thy brow shalt thou eat bread." We must endure our time of drudgery, and then after a while, we will
be allowed to go into comparative liberty. We must be
willing to endure the sentence. We all know what drudgery
is connected with the beginning of any trade or profession,
but this does not continue all our lives, if it be the student's,
or the merchant's, or the mechanic's life. I know you have,
at the beginning, many a hard time, but after a while these
things will become easy. You will be your own master.
God's sentence will be satisfied. You will be discharged
from prison.

Bless God that you have a brain to think, and hands to
work, and feet to walk with, for in your constant activity,
O young man, is one of your strongest defences. Put your
trust in God and do your level best. That child had it right
when the horses ran away with the load of wood and he sat
on it. When asked if he was frightened, he said : "*No, I
prayed to God and hung on like a beaver.*"

RESPECT FOR THE SABBATH

will be to the young man another preservative against evil.
God has thrust into the toil and fatigue of life a recreative
day, when the soul is especially to be fed. It is no new-
fangled notion of a wild-brained reformer, but an institution
established at the beginning. God has made natural and
moral laws so harmonious that the body as well as the soul
demands this institution. Our bodies are seven-day clocks,
that must be wound up as often as that, or they will run
down. Failure must come sooner or later to the man who
breaks the Sabbath. Inspiration has called it the Lord's
Day, and he who devotes it to the world is guilty of robbery.
God will not let the sin go unpunished either in this world
or the world to come

This is the statement of a man who had broken this divine
enactment : " I was engaged in manufacturing on the Lehigh
River. On the Sabbath I used to rest, but never regarded

God in it. One beautiful Sabbath when the noise was all
hushed, and the day was all that loveliness could make it, I
sat down on my piazza, and went to work inventing a new
shuttle. I neither stopped to eat nor drink till the sun went
down. By that time I had the invention completed. The
next morning I exhibited it, and boasted of my day's work,
and was applauded. The shuttle was tried and worked well,
but that Sabbath Day's work cost me thirty thousand dollars. We branched out and enlarged, and the curse of heaven
was upon me from that day onward."

While the Divine frown must rest upon him who tramples
upon this statute, God's special favor will be upon that young
man who scrupulously observes it. This day properly observed, will throw a hallowed influence over all the week.
The song and sermon and sanctuary will hold back from pre-
sumptuous sins. That young man who begins the duties of
life with either secret or open disrespect of the holy day, I
venture to prophesy, will meet with no permanent successes.
God's curse will fall upon his ship, his store, his office, his
studio, his body and his soul. "The way of the wicked He
turneth upside down." In *one of the old fables* it was said that
a wonderful child was born in Bagdad, and a magician could
hear his footsteps six thousand miles away. But I can hear
in the footstep of that young man on his way to the house
of worship this morning the step not only of a life-time of
usefulness, but the on-coming step of eternal ages of happiness yet millions of years away.

A NOBLE IDEAL,

and confident expectation of approximating to it, is an infallible defence. The artist completes in his mind the great
thought that he wishes to transfer to the canvas or the marble before he takes up the crayon or the chisel. The architect plans out the entire structure before he orders the
workmen to begin ; and though there may for a long while
seem to be nothing but blundering and rudeness, he has in
his mind every Corinthian wreath and Gothic arch and Byzan-

tine capital. The poet arranges the entire plot before he begins to chime the first canto of tingling rhythms. And yet, strange to say, there are men who attempt to build their character without knowing whether in the end it shall be a rude Tartar's tent or a St. Mark's of Venice—men who begin to write the intricate poem of their lives without knowing whether it shall be a Homer's Odyssey or a rhymester's botch. Nine hundred and ninety-nine men out of a thousand are living without any great life-plot. Booted and spurred and plumed, they urge their swift coursers in the hottest haste. I ask: "Halloo, man, whither away?" His response is, "Nowhere." Rush into the busy shop or store of many a one, and taking the plane out of the man's hand and laying down the yard stick, say: "What, man, is all this about—so much stir, and sweat?" The reply will stumble and break down between teeth and lips. Every day's duty ought only to be the filling up of the main plan of existence. Let men be consistent. If they prefer misdeeds to correct courses of action, then let them draw out the design of knavery and cruelty and plunder. Let every day's falschood and wrong-doing be added as coloring to the picture. Let bloody deeds red-stripe the picture, and the clouds of a wrathful God hang down heavily over the canvas, ready to break out in clamorous tempest. Let the waters be chafed, and froth-tangled, and green with immeasurable depths. Then take a torch of burning pitch and scorch into the frame the right name for it. If one entering upon sinful directions would only in his mind or on paper draw out in awful reality this dreadful future, he would recoil from it and say: "Am I a Dante, that by my own life I should write another Inferno?" But if you are resolved to live a life such as God and good men will approve, do not let it be a vague dream, an indefinite determination, but in your mind or upon paper, sketch it in all its minutiæ. You cannot know the changes to which you may be subject, but you may know what always will be right and what always will be wrong. Let gentleness and charity and veracity and faith stand in the heart of the sketch. On some still brook's bank make a

lamb and a lion lie down together. Draw two or three of
the trees of life, not frost-stricken nor ice-glazed, nor wind-
stripped, but with thick verdure waving like the palms of
heaven. On the darkest cloud place the rainbow, that pillow of the dying storm. You need not burn the title on
the frame. The dullest will catch the design at a glace, and
say : " That is the road to heaven."

Ah, me! On this sea of life, what innumerable ships,
heavily laden and well-rigged, yet seem bound for no port.
Swept every whither of wind and wave, they go up by the
mountains, they go down by the valleys, and are at their
wits' end. They sail by no chart, they watch no star, they
long for no harbor. I beg every young man to-day to draw
out a sketch of what, by the grace of God, he means to be.
Think no excellence so high that you cannot reach it. He
who starts out in life with a high ideal of character, and
faith in its attainment, will find himself encased from a thousand temptations. There are magnificent possibilities before
each of you young men of the stout heart, and the buoyant
step, and the bounding spirit I would marshal you for
grand achievement. God now provides for you the field,
and the armor, and the fortifications ; who is on the Lord's
side ? The captain of the Zouaves in ancient times, to encourage them against the immense odds on the side of their
enemies, said : " Come, my men, look these fellows in the
face. They are six thousand, you are three hundred.
Surely the match is even." That speech gave them the
victory. Be not, my hearers, dismayed at any time by what
seems immense odds against you. Is fortune, is want of
education, are men, are devils against you, though the
multitudes of earth and hell confront you, stand up to the
charge. With a million against you, the match is just even.
Nay, you have a decided advantage " If God be for us, who
can be against us ?" Thus protected, you need not spend
much time in answering your assailants.

Many years ago word came to me that two impostors, as
temperance lecturers, had been speaking in Ohio, in various
places, and giving their experience, and they told their au

dience that they had long been intimate with me, and had become drunkards by dining at my table, where I had always liquors of all sorts. Indignant to the last degree, I went down to Patrick Campbell, Chief of the Brooklyn Police, saying that I was going to start that night for Ohio to have those villains arrested, and I wanted him to tell me how to make the arrest. He smiled and said: "Do not waste your time by chasing these men. Go home and do your work, and they can do you no harm." I took his counsel, and all was well. Long ago I made up my mind that if one will put his trust in God and be faithful to duty, he need not fear any evil. Have God on your side, young man, and all the combined forces of earth and hell can do you no damage.

RELIGIOUS PRINCIPLE.

And this leads me to say that the mightiest defence for a young man is the possession of religious principle. Nothing can take the place of it. He may have manners that would put to shame the gracefulness and courtesy of a Lord Chesterfield. Foreign languages may drop from his tongue. He may be able to discuss literature and laws and foreign customs. He may wield a pen of unequalled polish and power. His quickness and tact may qualify him for the highest salary of the counting-house. He may be as sharp as Herod and as strong as Samson, with as fine locks as those which hung Absalom, still he is not safe from contamination. The more elegant his manner, and the more fascinating his dress, the more peril. Satan does not care for the allegiance of a cowardly and illiterate being. He cannot bring him into efficient service. But he loves to storm that castle of character which has in it the most spoils and treasures. It was not some crazy craft creeping along the coast with a valueless cargo that the pirate attacked, but the ship, full-winged and flagged, plying between great ports, carrying its millions of specie. The more your natural and acquired accomplishments, the more need of the religion of

Jesus. That does not cut in upon or hack up any smooth-
ness of disposition or behavior. It gives symmetry. It arrests that in the soul which ought to be arrested, and pro-
pels that which ought to be propelled. It fills up the
gullies. It elevates and transforms. To beauty it gives
more beauty, to tact more tact, to enthusiasm of nature
more enthusiasm. When the Holy Spirit impresses the
image of God on the heart, He does not spoil the canvas.
If in all the multitudes of young men upon whom religion
has acted you could find one nature that had been the least
damaged, I would yield this proposition.

You may now have enough strength of character to repel
the various temptations to gross wickedness which assail
you, but I do not know in what strait you may be thrust at
some future time. Nothing short of the grace of the Cross
may then be able to deliver you from the lions. You are
not meeker than Moses, nor holier than David, nor more
patient than Job, and you ought not to consider yourself
invulnerable. You may have some weak point of character
that you have never discovered, and in some hour when you
are assaulted the Philistines will be upon thee, Samson.
Trust not in your good habits, or your early training, or
your pride of character; nothing short of the arm of Almighty God will be sufficient to uphold you. You look forward to the world sometimes with a chilling despondency.
Cheer up, I will tell you how you may make a fortune.
"Seek first the kingdom of God and his righteousness and
all other things will be added unto you." I know you do
not want to be mean in this matter. Give God the fresh-
ness of your life. You will not have the heart to drink down
the brimming cup of life, and then pour the dregs on God's
altar. To a Saviour so infinitely generous you have not the
heart to act like that That is not brave, that is not honorable, that is not manly. Your greatest want in all the world
is a new heart. In God's name I tell you that. And the
Blessed Spirit presses through the solemnities and privileges
of this holy hour. Put the cup of life eternal to your thirsty
lips. Thrust it not back. Mercy offers it, bleeding mercy,

long-suffering mercy. Reject all other friendships, be ungrateful for all other kindness, prove recreant to all other bargains, but despise God's love for your immortal soul—don't you do that.

I would like to see some of you this hour press out of the ranks of the world and lay your conquered spirit at the feet of Jesus. This hour is no wandering vagabond, staggering over the earth, it is a winged messenger of the skies whispering mercy to thy soul. Admiral Farragut, one of the most admired men of the American Navy, early became a Christian, and, seated not long before his death, at Long Branch, he was giving some friends an account of his early life. He said: "My father went down in behalf of the United States Government to put an end to Aaron Burr's rebellion. I was a cabin-boy, and went along with him. I could swear like an old salt. I could gamble in every style of gambling. I knew all the wickedness there was at that time abroad. One day my father cleared everybody out of the cabin except myself, and locked the door. He said: 'David, what are you going to do? What are you going to be?' 'Well,' I said, 'father, I am going to follow the sea.' 'Follow the sea! and be a poor miserable, drunken sailor, kicked and cuffed about the world, and die of a fever in a foreign hospital?'

" 'Oh, no!' I said, 'father, I will not do that; I will tread the quarter-deck and command as you do.' 'No, David,' my father said, ' no, David, a person that has your principles and your bad habits will never tread the quarter-deck or command.'

"My father went out and shut the door after him, and I said then, 'I will change; I will never swear again, I will never drink again, I will never gamble again;' and, gentlemen, by the help of God, I have kept those three vows to this time. I soon after that became a Christian, and that decided my fate for time and for eternity."

CHAPTER XV.

The Termini of Two City Roads.

" Ponder the path of thy feet."—PROV. 4 : 26.

THE COUNTRY HOME.

IT was Monday, September 20, at a country depot. Two young men were to take the cars for the city. Father brought them in a wagon with two trunks. The evening before, at the old home, was rather a sad time. The neighbors had gathered in to say good-by. Indeed, all the Sunday afternoon there had been a strolling that way from adjoining farms, for it was generally known that the two boys the next morning were going to the city to live; and the whole neighborhood was interested, some hoping they would do well, and others, without saying anything, hoping for them a city failure. Sitting on the fence talking over the matter, the neighbors would interlard their conversation about the wheat crop of last summer, and the apple crop yet to be gathered, with remarks about the city prospects of Edward and Nicholas, for those were the names of the two young men. Edward seventeen, and Nicholas nineteen; but Edward, although two years younger, being a little quicker to learn, knew as much as Nicholas.

Father and mother on Monday morning had both resolved to go to the depot with the boys, but the mother at the last moment backed out, and she said that somehow she felt quite weak that morning, and had no appetite for a day or two, and so concluded to say good-by at the front door of the old place. Where she went and what she did after the wagon left, I leave other mothers to guess. The breakfast things stood almost till noon before they were cleared away. But little was said on the way to the railroad sta-

tion. As the locomotive whistle was heard coming around
the curve, the father put out his hand—somewhat knotted
at the knuckles, and one of the joints stiffened years ago by
a wound from a scythe—and said ; " Good-by, Edward,
good-by, Nicholas! Take good care of yourselves and write
as soon as you get there, and let us know how they treat
you. Your mother will be anxious to hear."

LANDED IN THE CITY

they sought out, with considerable inquiry of policemen on
street corners and questioning of car-drivers, the two commercial establishments to which they were destined—so far
apart that thereafter they seldom saw each other ; for it is
astonishing how far apart two persons can be in a large city,
especially if their habits are different, practically a hundred
miles from Bowling Green to Canal Street, or even from
Atlantic Avenue to Fulton.

Edward being the youngest, we must look after him
first. He never was in so large a store in all his life. Such
interminable shelves, such skilful imitation of real men and
women to display goods on, such agility of cash boys, such
immense stock of goods, and a whole community of employees. His head is confused, as he seems dropped like a
pebble in the great ocean of business life. " Have you seen
that green-horn from the country?" whispers young man to
young man. " He is in such and such a department. We
will have to break him in some night."

Edward stuck at his new place all day, so homesick that
any moment he could have cried aloud, if his pride had not
suppressed everything. Here and there a tear he carelessly
dashed off as though it were from influenza or a cold in the
head. But some of you know how a young man feels when
set down in a city of strangers, thereafter to fight his own
battles, and no one near by seeming to care whether he lives
or dies.

But that evening, as the hour for closing has come, there
are two or three young men who sidle up to Edward and

ask him how he likes the city, and where he expects to go
that night, and if he would like them to show him the sights.
He thanks them, and says he shall have to take some even
ings for unpacking and making arrangements, as he had just
arrived, but that after a while he will be glad to accept their
company. After spending two or three evenings in his
boarding-house room, walking up and down, looking at the
bare wall, or an old chromo hung there at the time that religious newspapers by such prizes advanced their subscrip-
tion lists, and after an hour toying with the match-box, and
ever and anon examining his watch to see if it is time to retire, and it seems that ten o'clock at night, or even nine
o'clock, will never come, he resolves to accept the chaperon-
ing of his new friends at the store. The following night
they are all out together. Although his salary is not large,
he is quite flush with pocket money, which the old folks
gave him after saving by for some time. He cannot be
mean, and these friends are doing all this for his pleasure,
and so he pays the bills. At the door of places of enchantment, his companions cannot find the change, and they accidentally fall behind just as the ticket office is approached, or
they say they will make it all right, and will themselves pay
the next time. Edward, accustomed to farm life or village
life, is dazed and enchanted with the glitter of spectacular
sin. Plain and blunt iniquity Edward would have immediately repulsed, but sin accompanied by bewitching orchestra,
sin amid gilded pillars and gorgeous upholstery, sin arrayed
in all the attractions that the powers of darkness in combina-
tion can arrange to magnetize a young man, is very different
from sin in its loathsome and disgusting shape.

But after being a few nights late out, he says: " I must
stop. My purse won't stand this. My health won't stand
this. My reputation won't stand this." Indeed, one of the
business firm, one night from his private box, in which he
applauded a play wherein attitudes and phraseology occurred which if taken or uttered in his own parlor would
have caused him to shoot or stab the actor on the spot—
from this high-priced box sees in a cheaper place the new

clerk of his store, and is led to ask questions about his habits, and wonders how, on the salary the house pays him, he can do as he does. Edward, to recover his physical vigor and his finances, stopped awhile, and spent a few more evenings examining the chromo on the wall, and counting the matches in the match-box.

"Confound it!" cried the young man, "I cannot stand this life any longer, and I must go out and see the world." The same young men, and others of a now larger acquaintance, are ready to escort him. There is never any lack of such guidance. If a man wants to go the whole round of sin, he can find plenty to take him, a whole regiment who knows the way. But after a while Edward's.

MONEY IS ALL GONE.

He has received his salary again and again, but it was spent before he got it, borrowing a little here and a little there. What shall he do now? Why, he has seen in his rounds of the gambling table men who put down a dollar and took up ten, put down a hundred and took up a thousand Why not he! To reconstruct his finances he takes a hand, and wins: is so pleased he takes another hand, and wins; is in a frenzy of delight, and takes another hand and loses all.

When he first came to the city Edward was disposed to keep Sunday in quietness, reading a little, and going occasionally to hear a sermon. Now, Sunday is a day of carousal. He is full of intoxicants by 11 o'clock in the day, and staggers into one of the licensed rumholes of the city.

Some morning, Edward, his breath stenchful with rum, takes his place in the store. He is not fit to be there. He is listless or silly or impertinent, or in some way incompetent, and a messenger comes to him and says: "The firm desire to see you in the private office."

The gentleman in the private office says: "Edward, we will not need you any more. We owe you a little money for services since we paid you last, and here it is."

"What is the matter?" says the young man. "I cannot understand this. Have I done anything?"

The reply is: "We do not wish any words with you. Our engagement with each other is ended."

"Out of employment!" What does that mean to a good young man? It means opportunity to get another and perhaps a better place. It means opportunity for mental improvement and preparation for higher work. "Out of employment!" What does that mean to a dissipated young man? It means a lightning express train on a down grade on the Grand Trunk to Perdition.

It is now only five years since Edward came to town. He used to write home once a week at the longest. He has not written home for three months. "What can be the matter?" say the old people at home. One Saturday morning the father puts on the best apparel, of his wardrobe, and goes to the city to find out.

"Oh, he has not been here for a long while," say the gentlemen of the firm. "Your son, I am sorry to say, is on the wrong track."

The old father goes hunting him from place to place, and comes suddenly upon him, that night, in a place of abandonment.

The father says: "My son, come with me. Your mother has sent me to bring you home. I hear you are out of money and good clothes, and you know as long as we live you can have a home. Come right away," he says, putting his hand on the young man's shoulder.

In angry tone, Edward replies: "Take your hands off me! You mind your own business! I will do as I please! Take your hands off me, or I will strike you down! You go your way, and I will go mine!"

THE CONTRAST.

That Saturday night, or rather Sunday morning—for it was by this time two o'clock in the morning—the father goes to the city home of Nicholas, and rings the bell, and rings again and again, and it seems as if no answer would be given, but after a while a window is hoisted and a voice cries, " Who's there?"

" It is I," says the old man

" Why, father, is that you?"

In a minute the door is opened and the son says, " What in the world has brought you to the city at this hour of the night?"

"Oh! Edward has brought me here   I feared your mother would go stark crazy, not hearing from him, and I find out that it is worse with him than I suspected."

" Yes," said Nicholas, " I had not the heart to write you any thing about it.   I have tried my best with him, and all in vain.   But it is after two o'clock," says Nicholas to his father, "and I will take you to bed."

On a comfortable couch in that house the old father lies down, coaxing sleep for a few hours, but no sleep comes. Whose house is it?   That of his son Nicholas.   The fact is, that Nicholas, soon after coming to the city, became indispensable in the commercial establishment where he was placed.   He knew, what few persons know, that while in all departments of business and mechanism and art, there is a surplus of people of ordinary application and ordinary diligence, there is a great scarcity, and always has been a great scarcity, of people who excel.   Plenty of people to do things poorly or tolerably well, but very few clerks, or business men, or mechanics who can do splendidly well.   Appreciating this, Nicholas had resolved to do so grandly that the business firm could not do without him.   Always at his place a little after everybody had gone, as extremely polite to those who declined purchasing, as to those who made large purchases.   He drank no wine, for he saw it was the empoisonment of multitudes ; and when any one asked him to take something, he said " No" with the peculiar intonation that meant no.   His conversation was always as pure as if his sisters had been listening.

He went to no place of amusement where he would be ashamed to die.   He never betted or gambled, even at a

church fair! When he was at the boarding-house, after he
had got all the artistic development he could possibly receive
from the chromo on the wall, he began to study that which
would help him to promotion—penmanship, biographies
of successful men; or he went forth to places of innocent
amusement and to Young Men's Christian Associations, and
was not ashamed to be found at a church prayer-meeting.
He rose from position to position and from one salary to
another salary.

Only five years in town and yet he has rented his own
house, or a suite of rooms, not very large, but a home large
enough in its happiness to be a type of Heaven. In the
morning, as the old father, with handkerchief in hand, comes
crying downstairs to the table, there are four persons, one
for each side : the young man, and opposite to him the best
blessing that a God of infinite goodness can bestow, namely,
a good wife ; and on another side, the high chair filled with
dimpled and rollicking glee, that makes the grandfather
opposite smile outside, while he has a broken heart within.

Well, as I said, it was Sabbath, and Nicholas and his
father, knowing that there is no place so appropriate for a
troubled soul as the house of God, find their way to church.
It is communion day, and what is the old man's surprise to
see his son pass down the aisle with one of the silver chalices,
showing him to be a church official. The fact was, that
Nicholas from the start in city life honored God, and God
had honored him. When the first wave of city temptation
struck him, he had felt the need of divine guidance and
divine protection, and in prayer had sought a regenerated
heart, and had obtained that mightiest of all armor, that
mightiest of all protection, that mightiest of all reinforce-
ments, the multipotent and omnipotent grace of God, and
you might as well throw a thistle down against Gibraltar,
expecting to destroy it, as with all the combined temptations
of earth and hell, try to overthrow a young man who can
truthfully say, " God is my refuge and strength."

But that Sabbath afternoon, while in the back room
Nicholas and his father are talking over any attempt at the

reclamation of Edward, there is a ringing of the door-bell and a man with the uniform of a policeman stands there, and a man with some embarrassment, and some halting, and in a round-about way says, that in a fight in some low haunt of the city Edward had been hurt. He says to Nicholas: "I heard that he was some relation of yours."

"Hurt? Is he badly hurt?"

"Yes, very badly hurt."

"Is the wound mortal?"

"Yes; it is mortal. To tell you the whole truth, sir," says the policeman, "although I can hardly bear to tell you, he is dead."

".Dead!" cries Nicholas. And by this time the whole family are in the hallway. The father says: "Just as I feared. It will kill his mother when she hears of it. Oh, my son, my son! Would God I had died for thee! Oh, my son, my son!"

"Wash off the wounds," says Nicholas, "and bring him right here to my house, and let there be all respect and gentleness shown him. It is the last we can do for him."

Oh, what obsequies! The next-door neighbors hardly knew what was going on; but Nicholas and the father and mother knew. Out of the Christian and beautiful home of the one brother is carried the dissolute brother. No word of blame uttered. No harsh thing said. On a bank of camellias is spelled out the word "Brother." Had the prodigal been true and pure and noble in life, and honorable in death, he could not have been carried forth with more tenderness, or slept in a more beautiful casket, or been deposited in a more beautiful garden of the dead. Amid the loosened turf the brothers who left the country for city life five years before now part forever. The last scene of *the fifth act of an awful tragedy* of human life is ended.

What made the difference between these two young men? Religion. The one depended on himself, the other depended on God. They started from the same home, had the same opportunities of education, arrived in the city on the same day, and if there is any difference, Edward had the advantage, for he was brighter and quicker, and all the neighbors prophesied greater success for him than for Nicholas.

THE TREMENDOUS SECRET.

Voices come up out of this audience and say, " Did you know these brothers?"   "Yes; knew them well."   "Did you know their parents?"   "Yes; intimately."   What was the city, what the street, what the last names of these young men?   You have excited our curiosity; now tell us all.

I will.   Nothing in these characters is fictitious except the names   They are in every city, and in every street of every city, and in every country.   Not two of them, but ten thousand.   Aye, aye!   Right before me to-day, and on either side of me, and above me, they sit and stand, the invulnerable through religious defence and the blasted of city allurements.   Those who shall have longevity in beautiful homes, and others who shall have early graves of infamy. And I am here to-day in the name of Almighty God to give you the choice of the two characters, the two histories, the two experiences, the two destinies, the two worlds, the two eternities.

Standing with you at the forks of the road something makes me think that if to-day I set before the people the termini of the two roads, they will all of them take the right one.   There are before me in this house and in the invisible audience back of this—for journalism has generously given me every week full opportunity to address the people in all the towns and cities of Christendom—I say, in the visible and invisible audience, there are many who have not fully made up their minds which road to take.   "Come with us!" cry all the voices of righteousness.   "Come with us!" cry all the voices of sin.

Oh, man and woman, ponder the path of thy feet!   See which way you are going   Will you have the destiny of Edward or Nicholas?   There comes a crisis in the history of every man.   We seldom understand that turning-point until it is far past.   The road of life is forked, and I read on two sign-boards: "This is the way to happiness." "This is the way to ruin." How apt we are to pass the forks of the road without thinking whether it comes out at the door of bliss or the gates of darkness.

A PARTING AT A THEATRE.

Many years ago I stood on the anniversary platform with a minister of Christ who made this remarkable statement: "Thirty years ago two young men started out in the evening to attend the Park Theatre, New York, where a play was to be acted in which the cause of religion was to be placed in a ridiculous and hypocritical light. They came to the steps. The consciences of both smote them. One started to go home, but returned again to the door, and yet had not courage to enter, and finally departed. But the other young man entered the pit of the theatre. It was the turning-point in the history of those two young men. The man who entered was caught in the whirl of temptation. He sank deeper and deeper in infamy; he was lost. That other young man was saved, and he now stands before you to bless God that for more than twenty years he has been permitted to preach the Gospel."

"Rejoice, O young man, in thy youth, and let thy heart cheer thee in the days of thy youth; but know thou that for all these things God will bring thee into judgment."

CHAPTER XVI.

Gospel Trumpet Peals.

"Blow ye the trumpet in Zion and sound an alarm in my Holy Mountain."—JOEL 2. 1.

WARNING AND INVITATION.

AT some time you have been hit by the Gospel arrow. You felt the wound of that conviction, and you plunged into the world deeper; just as the stag, when the hounds are after it, plunges into Scroon Lake, expecting in that way to escape. Jesus Christ is on your track to-day, impenitent man! not in wrath, but in mercy. Oh, ye chased and panting souls! here is the stream of God's mercy and salvation, where you may cool your thirst. Stop that chase of sin to-day. By the red fountain that leaped from the heart of my Lord, I bid you stop. There is mercy for you—mercy that pardons; mercy that heals; everlasting mercy. Is there in all this house anyone who can refuse the offer that comes from the heart of the dying Son of God?

There is in a forest in Germany, a place called the "Deer Leap," two crags about eighteen yards apart, between a fearful chasm. This is called the "Deer Leap," because once a hunter was on the track of a deer, it came to one of these crags; there was no escape for it from the pursuit of the hunter, and in utter despair it gathered itself up and in the death agony attempted to jump across. Of course it fell, and was dashed on the rocks far beneath. Here is a path to heaven. It is plain, it is safe. Jesus marks it out for every man to walk in. But here is a man who says: "I won't walk in that path; I will take my own way." He comes on up until he confronts the chasm that divides his soul from heaven. Now, his last hour has come, and he re-

solves that he will leap that chasm from the heights of earth
to the heights of heaven. Stand back, now, and give him
full swing, for no soul ever did that successfully. Let him
try. Jump! Jump! He misses the mark, and he goes down,
depth below depth, "destroyed without remedy."   Men!
angels! devils! what shall we call that place of awful catastrophe? Let it be known forever as "*The Sinner's Death
Leap.*"

TIME AND ETERNITY.

We all come under the divine satire when we make the
questions of time more prominent than the questions of
eternity. Come, let us all go into the confessional. Are
not all tempted to make the question, Where shall I live
now, greater than the question, Where shall I live forever?
How shall I get more dollars here, greater than the question,
How shall I lay up treasures in heaven? How shall I pay
my debts to man, greater than the question, How shall I
meet my obligations to God? How shall I gain the world,
greater than the question, What if I lose my soul? Why did
God let sin come into the world, greater than the question,
How shall I get it extirpated from my nature? What shall I
do with the twenty or forty or seventy years of my sublunar
existence, greater than the question, What shall I do with
the millions of cycles of my post-terrestrial existence? Time,
how small it is! Eternity, how vast it is! The former more
insignificant in comparison with the latter than a gnat is insignificant when compared with a camel. We dodged. We
said, "That doesn't mean me, and that doesn't mean me,"
and with a ruinous benevolence we are giving the whole
away.

But let us all surrender to the charge. What an ado about
things here! What poor preparation for a great eternity!
As though a minnow were larger than a behemoth, as though
a swallow took wider circuit than an albatros, as though a
nettle were taller than a Lebanon cedar, as though a gnat

were greater than a camel, as though a minute were longer than a century, as though time were higher, deeper, broader, than eternity. So the truth which flashed with lightning of wit as Christ uttered it, is followed by the crashing thunders of awful catastrophe to those who make the questions of time greater than the questions of the future, the oncoming, overshadowing future. O eternity! eternity! eternity!

TIME OUR ONLY OPPORTUNITY.

King Alfred, before modern time-pieces were invented, used to divide the day into three parts, eight hours each, and then had three wax candles. By the time the first candle had burned to the socket, eight hours had gone, and when the second candle had burned to the socket, another eight hours had gone, and when all the three candles were gone out, then the day had passed. Oh, that some of us, instead of calculating our days and nights and years by any earthly time-piece, might calculate them by the numbers of opportunities and mercies which are burning down and burning out, never to be relighted, lest at last we be amid the foolish virgins who shall cry, "Our lamps have gone out!"

SOLEMN THOUGHT.

Xerxes looked off on his army. There were two million men—perhaps the Finest Army ever marshalled. Xerxes rode along the lines, reviewed them, came back, stood on some high point, looked off upon the two million men, and burst into tears. At that moment, when every one supposed he would be in the greatest exultation, he broke down in grief. They asked him why he wept. "Ah!" he said, "I weep at the thought that so soon all this host will be dead." So I stand looking off upon the host of immortal men and women, and realize the fact, that soon the places which know them now will know them no more, and they will be gone—whither? whither? There is a stirring idea which the poet put in very peculiar verse when he said:

> " 'Tis not for man to trifle ; life is brief,
>   And sin is here ;
> Our age is but the falling of a leaf—
>   A dropping tear.
> Not many lives, but only one have we—
>   One, only one ,
> How sacred should that one life ever be—
>   That narrow span !"

Not one surplus second have you to spare. Quick, quick, quick !

Great God, is life such an uncertain thing? If I bear a little too hard with my right foot on the earth, does it break through into the grave? Is this world which swings at the speed of thousands of miles an hour around the sun going with tenfold more speed toward the judgment day? Oh, I am overborne with the thought, and in the conclusion I cry to one and I cry to the other : "Oh, time! Oh, eternity !"

ETERNITY FOR TIME.

How little care do we bestow upon the railroad depot where we stop twenty minutes to dine ! We dash in and we dash out again. We do not examine the architecture of the building, nor the face of the caterer. We supply our hunger, we pay our money, and we put on our hat and take our place in the train What is that depot as compared with the place for which we are bound? Now, my friends, this world is only a stopping-place on the way to a momentous destination, and yet how many of us sit down as though we had consummated our journey, as though we had come to the final depot, when our stopping here is as compared with our stopping there as is twenty minutes to twelve hours—yea, as the one hundredth part of a second compared with ten thousand million years !

Would Spain sell us Cuba for a bushel of wheat? Would England sell us India for a ton of coal? Would Venice sell us all her pictures for an American school-boy's sketch? Ah! that would be a better bargain for England, Spain,

and Venice than that man makes who gives his eternity for
time. Yet how many there are who are saying to-day,
"Give me the world's dollars, and you may have the eternal
rewards! Give me the world's applause, and you may have
the garlands of God. Give me twenty, or forty, or sixty
years of worldly successes, and I don't care what becomes
of the future. Go away from me, God and angels, and all
thoughts of the future!"

SOON TO LEAVE ALL.

Where are Crœsus and Cleopatra, and Æsopus, who had
one dish of food that cost one million four hundred thousand
dollars; and Lentulus, who had a pond of fish worth a hundred and seventy-five thousand dollars; and Scaurus, who
bought a country seat for twenty-nine million dollars; and
Tiberius, who left at death a fortune of one hundred and
eighteen millions one hundred and twenty thousand dollars?
Where are they?

What is the use of your struggling for that which you
cannot keep? As long as you have clothes, and food, and
shelter and education for yourselves and your children, and
the means for Christian generosity, be satisfied. You worry,
and tug, and sweat, and wear your self out for that which
cannot satisfy. Whole flocks of crows' feet on your temples and cheeks before they ought to have come there. You
are ten years older than you ought to be, and yet you cannot take along with you into the future world even the two
pennies on your eyelids to keep them shut after you are
dead. And yet you hold on to this world with the avidity
of the miser who persisted in having his bonds and mortgages and notes of hand in the bosom of his dressing-gown
while he was dying, and in the last moment held his parchment in such a tight grip that the undertaker after death
must almost break the man's fingers in order to get the
bonds away.

Men are actually making that choice, while there are
others who have done far differently. When they tried to

bribe with money Martin Luther, some one said, "There's no use trying to do that—that Dutch beast cares nothing for gold." When they tried, by giving him a cardinal's hat, to bribe Savonarola, he stood up in his pulpit and cried out, " I will have no red hat save that of martyrdom, colored with my own blood." These men chose Christ amid great persecutions; but how many there are in this day, when Christianity seems to be popular, who are ashamed of Christ and not willing to take the hardships—the seeming hardships—of His religion! And, alas! for them, for long after the crash of the world's demolition they shall find that in all these years they were turning their backs upon the palaces of heaven, scrabbling on the door of this world's treasure house, the saliva of a terrific lunacy on their lips—horribly and overwhelmingly playing the fool.

A FICKLE WORLD.

Xerxes garlanded and knighted the steerman of his boat in the morning, and hanged him the evening of the same day. Fifty thousand people stood around the columns of the national capitol, shouting themselves hoarse at the Presidential inaugural, and in four months so great were the antipathies, that a ruffian's pistol in Washington depot expressed the sentiment of a great multitude. The world sits in its chariot and drives tandem and the horse ahead is Huzza, and the horse behind is Anathema. Lord Cobham, in King James' time, was applauded, and had $35,000 a year, but was afterward execrated, and lived on scraps stolen from the royal kitchen. Alexander the Great after death remained unburied for thirty days, because no one would do the honor of shovelling him under. The Duke of Wellington refused to have his iron fence mended because it had been broken by an infuriated populace in some hour of political excitement, and he left it in ruins that men might learn what a fickle thing is human favor.

MAKING A GOD OF THE WORLD.

Sad mistake! for this world as a god is like something I saw the other day in the museum of Strasburg, Germany —the figure of a virgin in wood and iron. The victim in olden time was brought there, and this figure would open its arms to receive him, and once enfolded, the figure closed with a hundred knives and lances upon him, and then afterward let him drop one hundred and eighty feet sheer down. So the world first embraces its idolaters, then closes upon them with many tortures, and then lets them drop forever down. The highest honor the world could confer was to make a man Roman emperor; but out of sixty-three emperors, it allowed only six to die peacefully in their beds.

The dominion of this world over multitudes is illustrated by the names of coins of many countries. They have their pieces of money, which they call sovereigns and half sovereigns, crowns and half crowns, Napoleons and half Napoleons, Fredericks, and double Fredericks, and ducats, and Isabellinos, all of which names mean not so much usefulness, as dominion.

A GREAT CHEAT.

The world is a great cheat, so many thousand miles in diameter, and so many thousand miles in circumference. If I should put this audience under oath, one half of them would swear that this world is a liar. It is a bank which makes large advertisement of what it has in the vaults and of the dividends that it declares, and tells us that if we want happiness, all we have got to do is to come to that bank and apply for it. In the hour of need, we go to that bank to get happiness, and we find that the vaults are empty; all reliabilities have absconded and we are swindled out of everything.

Many of you have tried the garden of this world's delight You have found it has been a chagrin. So it was with Theodore Hook. He made all the world laugh. He makes us laugh now when we read his poems, but he could not make his own heart laugh. While in the midst of his festivities he confronted a looking-glass, and he saw himself and said : "There, that is true. I look just as I am, done up in body, mind, and purse." So it was of Shenstone in his garden. He sat down amid those bowers and said· "I have lost my road to happiness. I am angry and envious and frantic and despise everything around me, just as it becomes a madman to do."

WORLD HUNTING.

"In the morning he shall devour the prey, and at night he shall divide the spoil."—GEN. 49 : 27.

There is in this chapter such an affluence of simile and allegory, such a mingling of metaphors, that there are a thousand thoughts in it not on the surface. Old Jacob, dying, is telling the fortunes of his children. He prophesies the devouring propensities of Benjamin and his descendants. With his dim old eyes he looks off and sees the hunters going out to the fields, ranging them all day, and at night-fall coming home, the game slung over the shoulder; and reaching the door of the tent the hunters begin to distribute the game, and one takes a coney and another a rabbit and another a roe. "In the morning he shall devour the prey, and at night he shall divide the spoil." Or, it may be a reference to the habits of wild beasts that slay their prey, and then drag it back to the cave or lair, and divide it among the young

FASCINATION OF KILLING.

There is nothing more fascinating than the life of a hunter. On a certain day in all England you can hear the crack of the sportsman's gun, because grouse-hunting has begun; and every man who takes pleasure in destroying life, and can afford the time and ammunition, and can draw a trigger, starts for the fields. On the 20th of October our woods and forests will resound with the shock of firearms, and will be tracked by pointers and setters, because the quail will then be a lawful prize for the sportsman. Xenophon grew eloquent in regard to the art of hunting In the far East, people, elephant-mounted, chase the tiger. The American Indian darts his arrow at the buffalo, until the frightened herd tumble over the rocks. European nobles are often found in the fox-chase and at the stag-hunt. Francis I. was called the father of hunting. Moses declares of Nimrod, "He was a mighty hunter before the Lord." Therefore, in all ages of the world, the imagery of my text ought to be suggestive, whether it means a wolf after a fox or a man after a lion. "In the morning he shall devour the prey, and at night he shall divide the spoil."

A MORNING HUNT.

I take my text, in the first place, as descriptive of those people who in the morning of their life give themselves up to hunting the world, but afterward, by the grace of God, in the evening of their, life divide among themselves the spoils of Christian character. There are aged Christian men and women in this house who, if they gave testimony, would tell you that in the morning of their life they were after the world as intensely as a hound after a hare, or as a falcon swoops upon a gazelle. They wanted the world's plaudits and the world's gains. They felt that if they could get this world they would have everything.

Some of them started out for *the pleasures of the world.* They thought that the man who laughed loudest was happiest. They tried repartee and conundrum and burlesque and madrigal. They thought they would like to be Tom Hoods or Charles Lambs or Edgar A. Poes. They mingled wine and music and the spectacular. They were worshippers of the harlequin and the Merry Andrew and the buffoon and the jester. Life was to them foam and bubble and cachinnation and roystering and grimace. They were so full of glee

they could hardly repress their mirth even on solemn occasions, and they came near bursting out hilariously even at
the burial, because there was something so dolorous in the
tone or countenance of the undertaker.

After a while misfortune struck them hard on the back.
They found there was *something they could not laugh at*.
Under their late hours their health gave way, or there was a
death in the house. Of every green thing their soul was
exfoliated. They found out that life was more than a joke.
From the heart of God there blazed into their soul an earnestness they had never felt before. They awoke to their sin-
fulness and their immortality, and here they sit to-day at
sixty or seventy years of age, as appreciative of all innocent
mirth as they ever were, but they are bent on a style of
satisfaction which in early life they never hunted—the evening of their days brighter than the morning. In the morning
they devoured the prey, but at night they are dividing the
spoil.

HUNTING THE DOLLAR—THE MONEY-GOD.

Then there are others who started out for financial success. They see how limber a man's back is when he bows
down before some one transpicuous. They felt they would
like to see how the world looked from the window of a
three-thousand-dollar turnout. They thought they would
like to have the morning sunlight tangled in the headgear of
a dashing span. They wanted the bridges in the park to
resound under the rataplan of their swift hoofs. They
wanted a gilded baldrick, and so they started on the dollar
hunt. They chased it up one street and chased it down
another. They followed it when it burrowed in the cellar.
They treed it in the roof. Wherever a dollar was expected
to be they were. They chased it across the ocean. They
chased it across the land. They stopped not for the night.
Hearing that dollar even in the darkness thrilled them as
an Adirondack sportsman is thrilled by a loon's laugh.
They chased that dollar to the money vault. They chased

it to the Government treasury. They routed it from under
the counter. All the hounds were out—all the pointers and
setters. They leaped the hedges for that dollar and they
cried: " Hark, away! a dollar! a dollar!" and when at last
they came upon it and had actually captured it, their excitement was like that of a falconer who has successfully flung
his first hawk. In the morning of their life, oh, how they
devoured the prey!

RETURN FROM THE CHASE.

There came a better time to their souls. They found out
that an immortal nature cannot live on Government bonds.
They took up a Northern Pacific bond, and there was a hole
in it through which they could look into the uncertainty of
all earthly treasures. They saw some Ralston, living at the
rate of twenty-five thousand dollars a month, leaping from
San Francisco wharf because he could not continue to live
at the same ratio. They saw the wizen and paralytic bankers
who had changed their souls into molten gold stamped with
the image of the earth, earthy. They saw some great souls
by avarice turned into homunculi; and they said to themselves, " I will seek after higher treasure."

From that time they did not care whether they walked
or rode if Christ walked with them; nor whether they lived
in a mansion or a hut if they dwelt under the shadow of the
Almighty; nor whether they were robed in French broad-
cloth or in homespun if they had the robe of the Saviour's
righteousness; nor whether they were sandalled with mo-
rocco or calf-skin if they were shod with the preparation of
the Gospel. Now, you see peace on their countenance.
Now, that man says " What a fool I was to be enchanted
with this world! Why, I have more satisfaction in five
minutes in the service of God than I had in all the first
years of my life, while I was gain-getting. I like this evening of my day a great deal better than I did the morning.
In the morning I greedily devoured the prey, but now it is
evening, and I am gloriously dividing the spoil."

My friends, this world is a poor thing to hunt. It is healthful to go out in the woods and hunt. It rekindles the lustre of the eye. It strikes the brown of the autumnal leaf into the cheek. It gives to the rheumatic limbs a strength to leap like the roe. Christopher North's pet gun, the muckle-mounted Meg, going off in the summer in the forests, had its echo in the winter time in the eloquence that rang through the University halls of Edinburgh. It is healthy to go hunting in the fields; but I tell you that it is belittling and bedwarfing and belaming for a man to hunt this world. The hammer comes down on the gun-cap, and the barrel explodes and kills you instead of that which you are pursuing.

When you turn out to hunt the world, the world turns out to hunt you; and as many a sportsman aiming his gun at a panther's heart has gone down under the striped claws, so while you have been attempting to devour this world, the world has been devouring you. So it was with Lord Byron. So it was with Coleridge. So it was with Catherine of Russia. Henry II. went out hunting for this world, and its lances stuck through his heart. Francis I. aimed at the world, but the assassin's dagger put an end to his ambition and his life with one stroke. Mary Queen of Scots, wrote on the window of her castle:

> " From the top of all my trust
> Mishap hath laid me in the dust."

The Queen Dowager of Navarre was offered for her wedding-day a costly and beautiful pair of gloves, and she put them on, but they were poisoned gloves and they took her life. Better a bare hand of cold privation than a warm and poisoned glove of ruinous success.

IS IT WELL WITH THY SOUL?

A man may be sound in body, and he may have luxuriant investments, and have high social position, and yet instead of it being well with him there may be everlasting diseases wasting his soul, and awfully and overwhelmingly it may be ill with him. All those estates will go out of your hands, all these friends will vanish from your earthly association : but God has planted in you a light which will burn on after the last ember of a consuming world is trampled out and extinguished.

> " There is a life that always lives,
> There is a death that never dies."

Considering the fact that you are so invested, and that eternity presses on toward you, and that soon your naked soul will step out and up into the presence of the eternal God in judgment, ought not the question of my text resound through the deepest depths of your immortal nature while I cry out : " Is it well with thy soul?" You have an undefined longing in your soul. You tried money-making; that did not satisfy you. You tried office under Government ; that did not satisfy you. You tried pictures and sculptures ; but works of art did not satisfy you. You are as much discontented with this life as *the celebrated French author*, who felt that he could not any longer endure the misfortunes of the world, and who said : "At four o'clock this afternoon I shall put an end to my own existence. Meanwhile, I must toil on up to that time for the sustenance of my family." And he wrote on until the clock struck four, when he folded up his manuscript, and, by his own hand, concluded his earthly life. Grace alone satisfies the soul with a high, deep, all-absorbing, and eternal satisfaction. It comes, and it offers the most unfortunate man so much of this world as is best for him, and throws all heaven into the bargain.

THE TWO SCALES.

The wealth of Crœsus, and of all the Stewarts, and of all the Barings, and all the Rothschilds is only a poor, miserable shilling compared with the eternal fortunes that Christ offers you to-day. In the far East, there was a king who used once a year to get on one scale, while on the other scale were placed gold and silver and gems ; indeed, enough were placed there to balance the king; then, at the close of the weighing, all those treasures were thrown among the populace. But Christ to-day steps on one scale, and on the other are all the treasures of the universe, and He says: "All are yours—all height, all depth, all length, all breadth, all eternity; all are yours."

THE PROPERTY SOLD.

When a man passes himself over to the world he parts with his whole nature in four instalments. He pays down the first instalment, and one fourth of his nature is gone. He pays down the second instalment, and one half of his nature is gone. He pays down the third instalment, and three quarters of his nature are gone; and after many years have gone by he pays down the fourth instalment, and, lo! his entire nature is gone. Then he comes up to the world and says. " Good morning. I have delivered to you the goods. I have passed over to you my body, my mind, and my soul; and I have come now to collect the two hundred and fifty thousand dollars." "Two hundred and fifty thousand dollars?" says the world. "What do you mean?" "Well," you say, " I come to collect the money you owe me, and I expect you now to fulfil your part of the contract." "But," says the world, " *I have failed. I am bankrupt.* I cannot possibly pay that debt. I have not for a long while expected to pay it." "Well," you then say, "give me back the goods." "Oh, no," says the world; "they are all gone. I cannot give them back to you." And there you stand on the confines of eternity, your spiritual character gone, staggering under the consideration that you have sold yourself for nought.

I tell you the world is a liar; it does not keep its promises. It is a cheat, and it fleeces everything it can put its hands on. It is a bogus world. It is a six-thousand-year-old swindle. Even if it pays the two hundred and fifty thousand dollars for which you contracted, it pays them in bonds that will not be worth anything in a little while. Just as a man may pay down ten thousand dollars in hard cash and get for it worthless scrip—so the world passes over to you the two hundred and fifty thousand dollars in that shape which will not be worth a farthing to you a thousandth part of a second after you are dead. " Oh," you say, " it will help to bury me, anyhow " Yes, my brother, that is all.

Post mortem emoluments are of no use to you The treasures of this world will not pass current in the future world; and if all the wealth of the Bank of England were put in the pocket of your shroud, and you in the midst of the Jordan of death were asked to pay three cents for your ferriage, you could not do it. There comes a moment in your existence beyond which all earthly values fail ; and many a man has wakened up in such a time to find that he has sold out for eternity, and has nothing to show for it. I should as soon think of going to Chatham Street to buy silk pocket-handkerchiefs with no cotton in them, as to go to this world ' expecting to find any permanent happiness It has deceived and deluded every man that has ever put his trust in it.

BUSINESS CLOSED.

I went to see a worldling die. As I went into the hall I saw its floor was tessellated, and its wall was a picture-gallery. I found his death-chamber adorned with tapestry until it seemed as if the clouds of the setting sun had settled in the room. The man had given forty years to the world— his wit, his time, his genius, his talent, his soul. Did the world come in to stand by his death-bed, and, clearing off the phials of bitter medicine, put down any compensation ? Oh, no! The world does not like sick and dying people, and leaves them in the lurch. It ruined this man, and then left him. He had a magnificent funeral. All the ministers wore scarfs, and there were forty-three carriages in line ; but the departed man appreciated not the obsequies.

Cyrus, the Conqueror, thought for a little while that he was making a fine thing out of this world, and yet before he came to his grave he wrote out this pitiful epitaph for his

monument · "I am Cyrus. I occupied the Persian Empire.
I was king over Asia. Begrudge me not this monument."
But the world in after years ploughed up his sepulchre
What difference now does it make to Napoleon III. whether
he triumphed or surrendered at Sedan? whether he lived at
the Tuilleries or at Chiselhust, whether he was Emperor or
exile? They laid him out in his coffin in the dress of a field-
marshal. Did that give him any better chance for the next
world than if he had been laid out in a plain shroud?

Oh, ye who have tried this world, is it a satisfactory portion? Would you advise your friends to make the investment? No. "Ye have sold yourselves for nought." Your
conscience went. Your hope went. Your Bible went. Your
heaven went. Your God went. When a sheriff under a writ
from the courts sells a man out, the officer generally leaves a
few chairs and a bed, and a few cups and knives; but in
this awful vendue in which you have been engaged the auctioneer's mallet has come down upon body, mind, and soul :
Going! Gone!

A BAD BARGAIN.

History tells us of one who resolved that he would have
all his senses gratified at one and the same time, and he ex-
pended thousands of dollars on each sense. He entered a
room, and there were the first musicians of the land pleasing
his ear, and there were fine pictures fascinating his eye, and
there were costly aromatics regaling his nostril, and there
were the richest meats, and wines, and fruits, and confections
pleasing the appetite, and there was a soft couch of sinful
indulgence on which he reclined ; and the man declared afterward that he would give ten times what he had given if
he could have one week of such enjoyment, even though he
lost his soul by it. Ah! that was the rub. He did lose his
soul by it !

FAMOUS VENDORS.

The world clapped its hands and stamped its feet in honor of *Charles Lamb*; but what does he say? "I walk up and down, thinking I am happy, but feeling I am not." Call the roll, and be quick about it. *Samuel Johnson*, the learned! Happy? "No. I am afraid I shall some day get crazy." *William Hazlitt*, the great essayist! Happy? "No I have been for two hours and a half going up and down Paternoster Row, with a volcano in my breast." *Smollet*, the witty author! "No. I am sick of praise and blame, and I wish to God that I had such circumstances around me that I could throw my pen into oblivion." *Buchanan*, the world-renowned writer, exiled from his own country, appealing to Henry VIII. for protection! Happy? "No. Over mountains covered with snow, and through valleys flooded with rain, I come a fugitive." *Molière*, the popular dramatic author! Happy? "No. That wretch of an actor just now recited four of my lines without the proper accent and gesture. To have the children of my brain so hung, drawn, and quartered, tortures me like a condemned spirit."

Ah! my brother, the soul that you have bartered for less than a mess of pottage, what is it worth? How could you do so? Did you think that your soul was a mere trinket, which for a few pennies you could buy in a toy shop? Did you think that your soul, if once lost, might be found again, if you went out with torches and lanterns? Did you think that your soul was short-lived, and that, panting, it would soon lie down for extinction? Or had you no idea what your soul was worth? Did you ever put your forefinger on its eternal pulses? Have you never felt the quiver of its peerless wing? Have you not known that, after leaving the body, the first step of your soul reaches to the stars, and the next step to the furthest outposts of God's universe, and that it will not die until the day when the everlasting Jehovah expires? Oh. my brother, what possessed you that you should part with your soul so cheap? "Ye have sold yourselves for nought."

A SUIT FOR REPLEVIN.

I want to engage in a litigation for the recovery of that soul of yours. I want to show that you have been cheated out of it. I want to prove, as I will, that you were crazy on that subject, and that the world, under such circumstances, has no right to take the title-deed from you; and if you will join me I shall get a decree from the High Chancery Court of Heaven reinstating you into the possession of your soul. "Oh," you say, "I am afraid of law-suits; they are so expensive, and I cannot pay the cost." Then have you forgotten the last half of my text? "Ye have sold yourselves for nought; and ye shall be redeemed *without money.*"

Money is a good for a great many things, but it cannot do anything in this matter of the soul. You cannot buy your way through. Dollars and pounds sterling mean nothing at the gate of mercy. If you could buy your salvation, heaven would be a great speculation, an extension of Wall Street. Bad men would go up and buy out the place, and leave us to shift for ourselves. But as money is not a lawful tender, what is? I will answer, Blood! Whose? Are we to go through the slaughter? Oh, no; it wants richer blood than ours. It wants a king's blood. It must be poured from royal arteries. It must be a sinless torrent. But where is the king? I see a great many thrones and a great many occupants, yet none seem to be coming down to the rescue. But after awhile the clock of night in Bethlehem strikes twelve, and the silver pendulum of a star swings across the sky, and I see the King of Heaven rising up, and He descends, and steps down from star to star, and from cloud to cloud, lower and lower, until He touches the sheep-covered hills, and then on to another hill, this last skull-covered: and there, at the sharp stroke of persecution, a rill incarnadine trickles down, and we who could not be redeemed by money are redeemed by precious and imperial blood.

We have in this day professed Christians who are so rarefied and etherealized that they do not want a religion of blood. What do you want?' You seem to want a religion of brains. The Bible says, "In the blood is the life." No atonement without blood. Ought not the apostle to know? What did he say? "Ye are redeemed not with corruptible things, such as silver and gold; but by the precious blood of Christ." You put your lancet into the arm of our holy religion and withdraw the blood, and you leave it a mere corpse, fit only for the grave. Why did God command the priests of old to strike the knife into the kid, and the goat, and the pigeon, and the bullock, and the lamb? It was so that when the blood rushed out from these animals on the floor of the ancient tabernacle the people should be compelled to think of the coming carnage of the Son of God. No blood, no atonement.

THE ACCUSING BLOOD.

I think that God intended to impress us with the vividness of that color. The green of the grass, the blue of the sky, would not have startled and aroused us like this deep crimson. It is as if God had said: "Now, sinner, wake up and see what the Saviour endured for you. This is not water. This is not wine. It is blood. It is the blood of my own Son. It is the blood of the Immaculate. It is the blood of a God." Without the shedding of blood is no remission. There has been many a man who in courts of law has pleaded " not guilty," who nevertheless has been condemned because there was blood found on his hands, or blood found in his room; and what shall we do in the last day if it be found that we have recrucified the Lord of Glory, and have never repented of it? You must believe in the blood or die. No escape. Unless you let the sacrifice of Jesus Christ go in your stead you yourself must suffer. It is either Christ's blood or your blood.

THE COST OF RECOVERY.

"Oh," says some one, "the thought of blood sickens me." Good. God intended it to sicken you with your sin.

Do not act as though you had nothing to do with that Cal
varean massacre. You had. Your sins were the implements of torture. Those implements were not made of
steel, and iron, and wood, so much as out of your sins.
Guilty of this homicide, and this regicide, and this deicide,
confess your guilt to-day. Ten thousand voices of heaven
bring in the verdict against you of guilty, guilty. Prepare
to die, or believe in that blood. Stretch yourself out for the
sacrifice, or accept the Saviour's sacrifice. Do not fling
away your one chance.

It seems to me as if all heaven were trying to bid in your
soul. The first bid it makes is the tears of Christ at the
tomb of Lazarus ; but that is not a high enough price. The
next bid heaven makes is the sweat of Gethsemane ; but it
is too cheap a price. The next bid heaven makes seems to
be the whipped back of Pilate's hall ; but it is not a high
enough price. Can it be possible that heaven cannot buy
you in? Heaven tries once more. It says, " I bid this time
for that man's soul the tortures of Christ's martyrdom, the
blood on His temple, the blood on His cheek, the blood on
His chin, the blood on His hand, the blood on His side, the
blood on His knee, the blood on His foot—the blood in
drops, the blood in rills, the blood in pools coagulated beneath the cross ; the blood that wet the tips of the soldiers'
spears, the blood that plashed warm in the faces of His enemies." Glory to God, that bid wins it ! The highest price
that was ever paid for anything was paid for your soul
Nothing could buy it but blood! The estranged property
is bought back Take it. " Ye have sold yourselves for
nought, and ye shall be redeemed without money," Christ,
the surety, paying your debts; Christ, the divine Cyrus,
loosening your Babylonish captivity.

SAVING POWER.

The grace of God is *able to convert a soul.* People
laughed at the missionaries in Madagascar because they
preached ten years without one convert; but there are

thirty-three thousand converts in Madagascar to-day. People laughed at Dr. Judson, the Baptist missionary, because he kept on preaching in Burmah five years without a single convert ; but there are twenty thousand Baptists in Burmah to-day. People laughed at Dr. Morrison, in China, for preaching there seven years without a single conversion ; but there are fifteen thousand Christians in China to-day. People laughed at the missionaries for preaching at Tahiti for fifteen years without a single conversion, and at the missionaries for preaching in Bengal seventeen years without a single conversion ; yet in all those lands there are multitudes of Christians to-day. But why go so far to find evidences of the Gospel's power to save a soul ? "We are witnesses." We have been as really changed as Gourgis, the heathen, who went into a prayer-meeting with a dagger and a gun, to disturb the meeting and destroy it, but the next day was found crying : " Oh ! my great sins ! Oh ! my great Saviour !" and for eleven years preached the Gospel of Christ to his fellow mountaineers, the last words on his dying lips being " Free grace !" Oh, it was free grace !

" Why," said one upon whom the great change had come, " sir, I feel just as though I were somebody else." There was a sea-captain who swore all the way from New York to Havana, and from Havana to San Francisco, and when he was in port he was worse than when he was on sea. What power was it that washed his tongue clean of profanities, and made him a psalm-singer ? Conversion by the Holy Spirit. There are thousands of people to-day who are no more what they once were than a water-lily is nightshade, or a morning lark is a vulture, or day is night.

ALL OF GRACE.

One of John Bunyan's great books is entitled, " Abounding Grace.' " It is all of grace that I am saved" has been on the lips of hundreds of dying Christians *The boy Sammy* was right when, being examined for admission into church membership, he was asked, "Whose work was your salva-

tion?" and he answered, " Part mine and part God's."
Then the examiner asked, " What part did you do,
Sammy?" and the answer was, " I opposed God all I could,
and He did the rest!"   O, the height of it, the depth of it,
the length of it, the breadth of it,—the grace of God!   Grace,
that saved the publican, that saved Lydia, that saved the
dying thief, that saved the jailer, that saved me.   But the
riches of that grace will not be fully understood until Heaven
breaks in upon the soul.

Among the thousands of words in the language, there is
no more queenly word.   It means free and unmerited kindness.   My text has no monopoly of the word.   One hundred and twenty-nine times does the Bible eulogize grace.
It is a door swung wide open to let into the pardon of God
all the millions who choose to enter it.   John Newton sang
of it:

> " Amazing grace, how sweet the sound
> That saved a wretch like me!"

Philip Doddridge put it into hymnology when he wrote:

> " Grace, 'tis a charming sound,
>   Harmonious to the ear ;
> Heaven with the echo shall resound,
>   And all the world shall hear."

Yes, grace, free grace, sovereign grace, omnipotent grace!

I present you, not an abstraction or a chimera, or anything like guess-work, but *affidavits of the best men and
women*, living and dead.   Two witnesses in court will estab-
lish a fact.   Here are not two witnesses, but thousands of
witnesses—millions of witnesses, and in heaven a great multitude of witnesses that no man can number, testifying that
there is power in this religion to convert the soul, to give
comfort in trouble, and to afford composure in the last
hour.

If ten men should come to you when you are sick with
appaling sickness, and say they had the same sickness, and
took a certain medicine, and it cured them, you would probably take it.   Now, suppose ten other men should come up

and say, "We don't believe that there is anything in that medicine." "Well," I say, "have you tried it?"

"No. I never tried it, but I don't believe there is anything in it." Of course you discredit their testimony. The sceptic may come and say, "There is no power in your religion." "Have you ever tried it?" "No, no." "Then avaunt!" Let me take the testimony of the millions of souls that have been converted to God, and comforted in trial, and solaced in the last hour. We will take their testimony as they cry, "We are witnesses!"

Some time ago Professor Henry, of Washington, discovered a new star, and the tidings sped by submarine telegraph, and all the observatories of Europe were watching for that new star. Oh, hearer, looking out through the darkness of thy soul, canst thou see a bright light beaming on thee? "Where?" you say, "where? How can I find it?" Look along by the line of the Cross of the Son of God. Do you not see it trembling with all tenderness and beaming with all hope? It is the star of Bethlehem.

> "Deep horror then my vitals froze,
>   Death-struck I ceased the tide to stem,
> When suddenly a star arose—
>   It was the Star of Bethlehem."

SOUL-HUNTING.

In our day, hunting is a sport, but in the lands and the times infested with wild beasts, it was a matter of life or death with the people. It was very different from going out on a sunshiny afternoon with a patent breech-loader, to shoot reed-birds on the flats, when Pollux and Achilles and Diomedes went out to clear the land of lions and tigers and bears. My text sets forth Nimrod as a hero when it presents him with broad shoulders and shaggy apparel and sun-browned face, and arm bunched with muscle—"a mighty hunter before the Lord." I think he used the bow and the arrow with great success, practicing archery.

I have thought that if it is such a grand thing and such a

brave thing to clear wild beasts out of a country, is it not a better and braver thing to hunt down and destroy those great evils of society that are stalking the land with fierce eye and bloody paw and sharp tusk and quick spring? I have wondered if there is not such a thing as soul-hunting, by which those who have been flying from the truth, may be captured for God and heaven. The Lord Jesus, in His sermon used the art of angling for an illustration when He said, " I will make you fishers of men." And so I think I have authority for using hunting as an illustration of Gospel truth; and I pray God that there may be many a man in this congregation who shall begin to study Gospel archery, of whom it may, after a while, be said, " He was a mighty hunter before the Lord.' If you want to succeed in hunting, be sure of your weapon. There was something very fascinating about the archery of olden times. Perhaps you do not know what they could do with the bow and arrow. Why, the chief battles fought by the English Plantagenets were with the long bow. They would take the arrow of polished wood, and feather it with the plume of a bird, and then it would fly from the bow-string of plaited silk. The broad fields of Agincourt, and Solway Moss, and Neville's Cross, heard the loud thrum of the archer's bow-string Now, my Christian friends, we have a mightier weapon than that It is the arrow of the Gospel; it is a sharp arrow; it is a straight arrow; it is feathered from the wing of the dove of God's Spirit; it flies from a bow made out of the wood of the cross. As far as I can estimate or calculate, it has brought down four hundred million souls. Paul knew how to bring the notch of that arrow on to that bow-string, and its whirr was heard through the Corinthian theatres, and through the court-room, until the knees of Felix knocked together. It was that arrow that stuck in Luther's heart when he cried out, "Oh, my sins! Oh, my sins!" If it strike a man in the head, it kills his skepticism; if it strike him in the heel, it will turn his step, if it strike him in the heart, he throws up his hands, as did one of old when wounded in the battle, crying, " Oh, Galilean, Thou hast conquered."

In the armory of the Earl of Pembroke, there are old corselets which show that the arrow of the English used to go through the breast-plate, through the body of the warrior, and out through the back-plate. What a symbol of that Gospel which is sharper than a two-edged sword, piercing to the dividing asunder of soul and body, and of the joints and marrow! Would to God we had more faith in that Gospel! The humblest man in this house, if he had enough faith in him, could bring a hundred souls to Jesus—perhaps five hundred Just in proportion as this age seems to believe less and less in it, I believe more and more in it. What are men about that they will not accept their own deliverance? There is nothing proposed by men that can do anything like this Gospel.

GOSPEL WEAPON.

The full power of the Gospel has not yet been touched. As a sportsman throws up his hand and catches the ball flying through the air, just so easily will this Gospel, after a while, catch this round world flying from its orbit, and bring it back to the heart of Christ. Give it full swing, and it will pardon every sin, heal every wound, cure every trouble, emancipate every slave, and ransom every nation Ye Christian men and women who go out this afternoon to do Christian work, as you go into the Sunday-schools, and the lay preaching stations, and the penitentiaries, and the asylums, I want you to feel that you bear in your hand a weapon, compared with which the lightning has no speed, and avalanches have no heft, and the thunderbolts of heaven have no power; it is the arrow of the omnipotent Gospel. Take careful aim. Pull the arrow clear back until the head strikes the bow. Then let it fly. And may the slain be many!

WHERE TO HUNT.

If you want to be skilful in spiritual hunting you must hunt in unfrequented and secluded places. Why does the hunter go three or four days in the Pennsylvania forests or over Raquette Lake into the wilds of the Adirondacks? It is the only way to do. The deer are shy, and one "bang" of the gun clears the forest. From the California stage you see, as you go over the plains, here and there a coyote trotting along, almost within range of the gun—sometimes quite within range of it. No one cares for that; it is worthless. *The good game is hidden* and secluded. Every hunter knows that. So, many of the souls that will be of most worth for Christ, and of most value for the Church, are secluded. They do not come in your way. You will have to go where they are. Yonder they are, down in that cellar, yonder they are, up in that garret. Far away from the door of any church, the Gospel arrow has not been pointed at them. The tract distributor and the city missionary sometimes just catch a glimpse of them, as a hunter through the trees gets a momentary sight of a partridge or roebuck.

The trouble is we are waiting for the game to come to us. We are not good hunters. We are standing in Schermerhorn Street, expecting that the timid antelope will come up and eat out of our hand. We are expecting that the prairie fowl will light on our church-steeple. It is not their habit. If the church should wait ten millions of years for the world to come in and be saved, it will wait in vain. The world will not come. What the church wants now is to lift their feet from damask ottomans, and put them in the stirrups. We want a pulpit on wheels. The church wants not so much cushions as it wants saddle-bags and arrows. We have got to put aside the gown and the kid-gloves, and put on the hunting-shirt. We have been fishing so long in the brooks that run under the shadow of the church that the fish know us, and they avoid the hook, and escape as soon as we come to the bank, while yonder is Upper Saranac and Big Tupper's Lake, where the first swing of the Gospel net would break it for the multitude of the fishes. There is outside work to be done. What is that I see in the backwoods? It is a tent. The hunters have made a clearing and camped out. What do they care if they have wet feet, or if they have nothing but a pine branch for a pillow, or for the northeast storm? If a moose in the darkness steps into the lake to drink, they hear it right away. If a loon cry in the midnight, they hear it. So in the service of God we have exposed work. *We have got to camp out and rough it.*

SKILL IN HUNTING.

The archers of old times studied their art. They were very precise in the matter. The old books gave special directions as to how the archer should go, and as to what an archer should do. He must stand erect and firm, his left foot a little in advance of his right foot. With his left hand he must take hold of the bow in the middle, and then, with the three fingers and the thumb of his right hand, he should lay hold of the arrow and affix it to the string—so precise was the direction given. But how clumsy we are about religious work! How little skill and care we exercise! How often our arrows miss the mark! Oh, that we might learn the art of doing good, and become "mighty hunters before the Lord!"

If Mithridates liked hunting so well that for seven years he never went in-doors, what enthusiasm ought we to have who are hunting for immortal souls! If Domitian practiced archery until he could stand a boy down in the Roman amphitheatre, with a hand out, the fingers outstretched, and then the king could shoot an arrow between the fingers without wounding them, to what drill and practice ought not we to subject ourselves in order to become spiritual archers and "mighty hunters before the Lord!" The old archers took the bow, put one end of it down beside the foot, elevated the other end, and it was the rule that the bow should be just the size of the archer, if it were just his size, then he would go into the battle with confidence. Let me say that your power to project good in the world will correspond exactly to your own spiritual stature. In other words, the first thing, in preparation for Christian work, is personal consecration.

How much awkward Christian work there is done in the world! How many good people there are who drive souls away from Christ instead of bringing them to Him! Religious blunderers, who upset more than they right. Their gun has a crooked barrel, and kicks as it goes off. They are like a clumsy comrade who goes along with skilful hunters—at the very moment he ought to be most quiet, he is cracking an elder or falling over a log and frightening away the game.

Truman Osborne, one of the evangelists who went through this country some years ago, had a wonderful art in the right direction. He came to my father's house one day, and while we were all seated in the room, he said, "Mr. Talmage, are all your children Christians?" Father said, "*Yes, all but De Witt.*" Then Truman Osborne looked down into the fireplace, and began to tell a story of a storm that came on the mountains, and all the sheep were in the fold; but there was one lamb outside that perished in the storm. Had he looked me in the eye, I should have been angered when he told me that story; but he looked into the fireplace, and it was so pathetically and beautifully done that I never found any peace until I was inside the fold, where the other sheep are.

If you want to be successful in spiritual hunting, you need not only to bring down the game, but bring the game in. I think one of the most beautiful pictures of Thorwaldsen is his "Autumn." It represents a sportsman coming home and standing under a grape-vine. He has a staff over his shoulder, and on the other end of that staff are hung a rabbit and a brace of birds. Every hunter brings home the game. No one would think of bringing down a reindeer or whipping up a stream for trout, and letting them lie in the woods. At eventide the camp is adorned with the treasures—beak and fin and antler.

If you go out to hunt for immortal souls, not only bring them down under the arrow of the Gospel, but bring them into the Church of God, the grand home and encampment we have pitched this side the skies. Fetch them in, do not

let them lie out in the open field. They need our prayers
and sympathies and help. That is the meaning of the
Church of God—help. O ye hunters for the Lord! not only
bring down the game, but bring it in.

SOUL-SAVING.

Near my summer residence there is a life-saving station
on the beach. There are all the ropes and rockets, the boats,
the machinery, for getting people off shipwrecks Summer before last I saw there fifteen or twenty men who were
breakfasting, after having just escaped with their lives and
nothing more. Up and down our coasts are built these useful structures, and the mariners know it, and they feel that
if they are driven into the breakers there will be apt from
shore to come a rescue. The churches of God ought to be
so many soul-saving stations, not so much to help those who
are in smooth waters, as those who have been shipwrecked.
Come, let us run out the life-boats! And who will man
them?

I would rather, in a mud-scow, try to weather the worst
cyclone that ever swept up from the Caribbean than risk
my immortal soul in useless and perilous discussions. They
remind me of a company of sailors standing on Ramsgate
pier-head, from which the life-boats are usually launched,
and coolly discussing the different style of oar-locks, and
how deep a boat ought to set in the water, while a hurricane
is in full blast, and there are three steamers crowded with
passengers going to pieces in the offing.

An old tar, the muscles of his face working with nervous
excitement, cries out, "This is no time to discuss such
things. Man the lifeboat! Who will volunteer? Out with
her into the surf! Pull, my lads, pull for the wreck? Ha!
ha! Now we have them. Let them in, and lay them down
on the bottom of the boat. Jack, you try to bring them to.
Put these flannels around their hands and feet, and I will
pull for the shore. God help me! There! Landed!
Huzza!" When there are so many struggling in the waves

of sin and sorrow and wretchedness, let all else go but salvation for time and salvation forever.

One Monday morning, at about two o'clock, while her nine hundred passengers were sound asleep in her berths, dreaming of home, the steamer *Atlantic* crashed into Mars Head. But see this brave quartermaster pushing out with the life-line until he gets to the rock, and see these fishermen gathering up the shipwrecked, and taking them into the cabins, and wrapping them in the flannels snug and warm, and see that minister of the Gospel with three other men getting into a life-boat and pushing out for the wreck, pulling away across the surf, and pulling away until they saved one more man, and then getting back with him to the shore.

Well, our world has gone into a worse shipwreck. Sin drove it on the rocks. The old ship has lurched and tossed on the tempests of six thousand years. Out with the life-line!

RESCUE THE PERISHING.

Why did not that heroic minister of the Gospel of whom I have spoken sit down and take care of those men on the beach, wrapping them in flannels, kindling fire for them, seeing that they got plenty of food? Ah, he knew that there were others who would do that! He says; "Yonder are men and women freezing in the rigging of that wreck. Boys, launch the boat!" And now I see the oar-blades bend under the strong pull, but before they reached the rigging a woman was frozen and dead. She was washed off, poor thing! But he says: "There is a man to save;" and he cries out: "Hold on five minutes longer and I will save you. Steady! Steady! Give me your hand. Leap into the life-boat. Thank God, he is saved!" So there are those who are safe on the shore of God's mercy, but there are some who are freezing in the rigging of sin, and surrounded by perilous storms. Pull away, my lads! Let us reach them. Alas, one is washed off and gone! There is one more to be saved. Let us push out for that one. " Clutch the rope, oh dying man! Clutch it as with a death-grip. Steady now on the slippery places. Steady! There! Saved! Saved!" Just as I thought. For Christ has declared that there are some still in the breakers who shall come ashore.

When the Schiller went down, out of three hundred and eighty people only forty were saved. When the Ville du Havre went down, out of three hundred and forty, about fifty were saved. And out of the soul-wrecked how many will get to the shore of heaven?

Some years ago there came down a fierce storm on the sea-coast, and a vessel got in the breakers and was going to pieces. They threw up some signals of distress, and the people on the shore saw them. They put out in a life-boat. They came on, and they saw the poor sailors, almost ex- hausted, clinging to a raft ; and so afraid were the boatmen that the men would give up before they got to them, they gave them three rounds of cheers, and cried: " Hold on, there! Hold on! We'll save you!" After a while the boat came up. One man was saved by having the boat- hook put in the collar of his coat ; and some in one way, and some in another ; but they all got into the boat. "Now," says the captain, " for the shore Pull away now, pull!" The people on the land were afraid the life-boat had gone down. They said : " How long the boat stays. Why, it must have been swamped, and they have all perished to- gether."

But as the boat swept through the boiling surf and came to the pier-head, the captain waved his hand over the ex- hausted sailors that lay flat on the bottom of the boat, and cried: " All saved! Thank God! All saved!"

Oh! shipwrecked souls, I have come for you. I cheer you with this Gospel hope. God grant that we may row with you into the harbor of God's mercy. And when the glorified gather on the pier-heads of heaven to watch and to listen, may we be able to report all saved! Young and old, good and bad! All saved! Saved from sin, and death, and hell. Saved for time. Saved for eternity. And so shall it come to pass that you all escape safe to land.

If a boat in any harbor should get in distress, from the men of war, and from the sloops, and from the steamers, the flying paddles would pull to the rescue. And if now you would lift one signal of distress, all these voyagers of eternity would bear down toward you and bring you relief. But no. You are like a ship on fire at sea. They keep the hatches down, and the captain is frenzied, and he gives orders that no one hail the passing ships. He says, " I shall either land this vessel in Hamburg or on the bottom of the ocean, and I don't care which." Yonder is a ship of the White Star Line passing. Yonder one of the National Line. Yonder one of the Cunard Line. Yonder one of the Inman Line. But they know not there is any calamity happening on that one vessel. Oh, if the captain would only put his trumpet to his lip and cry out, " Lower your boats! Bear down this way! We are burning up! Fire! Fire!" No, no No signal is given. If that vessel perishes, having hailed no one, whose fault will it be? Will it be the fault of the ship that hid its calamity, or will it be the fault of the vessels that, passing on the high seas, would have been glad to furnish relief if it had been only asked? In other words, my brother, if you miss heaven it will be your own fault.

My friends, religion is either a sham or a tremendous reality. If it be a sham, let us disband our churches and Christian associations. If it be a reality, then great populations are on the way to the bar of God unfitted for the ordeal, and what are we doing?

A great sermon dropped into an audience of hundreds of thousands will do its work; but if this world is ever to be brought to God, it will be through little sermons preached by private Christians *to an audience of one.* The sister's letter postmarked at the village ; the word uttered in your hearing : half of smiles and half of tears ; the religious postscript to a business letter , the card left at the door when you had some kind of trouble , the anxious look of some one across a

church aisle while an earnest sermon was being preached,
swung you into the kingdom of God.

GOSPEL SHIP.

The great Gospel ship is the finest vessel in the universe
and can carry more passengers than any craft ever constructed,
and you could no more wreck it than you could wreck the
throne of God Almighty. I wish all the people would come
aboard of her. I could not promise a smooth voyage, for
ofttimes it will be tempestuous, and a chopped sea, but I
could promise safe arrival for all who took passage on that
Great Eastern, so called by me because its commander came
out of the East, the star of the East a badge of His authority.

But a vast multitude do not take regular passage. They
are like those who at Paul's shipwreck came in on broken
pieces of the ship. There is something about them that excites in me an intense interest. I am not so much interested in those that could swim. They got ashore as I expected. A mile of water is not a very great undertaking for
a strong swimmer. But I cannot stop thinking about those
on broken pieces of the ship. Their theology broken in
pieces, and their life broken in pieces, and their habits broken
in pieces, and their worldly and spiritual prospects broken in
pieces, and yet I believe they are going to reach the shining
shore, and I am encouraged by the experience of those people who are spoken of in the words, "Some on broken pieces
of the ship."

The object I have in view is to encourage all those who
cannot take the whole system of religion as we believe it,
but who really believe something, to come ashore on that
one plank. If you can come in on the grand old ship, I
would rather have you get aboard, but if you can find only
a piece of wood as long as the human body, or a piece as
wide as the outspread human arms, and either of them is a
piece of the cross, come in on that piece. Come in on that
one narrow beam, the beam of the cross   Let all else go and
cling to that. Put that under you, and with the earnestness

of a swimmer struggling for his life put out for shore. There is a great warm fire of welcome already built, and already many, who were as far out as you are, are standing in its genial and heavenly glow. The angels of God's rescue are wading out into the surf to clutch your hand, and they know how exhausted you are, and all the redeemed prodigals of heaven are on the beach with new white robes to clothe all those who come in on broken pieces of the ship.

I CAME IN ON A PLANK.

I knew Christ was the Saviour of sinners, and that I was a sinner, and I got ashore, and so can you if you cling to that plank. I was in danger of being farther out to sea than any of the two hundred and seventy-six in the Mediterranean breakers. I floundered a long while in the sea of sin and doubt, and it was as rough as the Mediterranean on the fourteenth night when they threw the grain overboard, but I saw there was mercy for a sinner, and that plank I took, and I have been warming myself by the bright fire on the shore ever since. And so may you. If you have not a whole ship fashioned in the theological dry docks to bring you to wharfage, you have at least a plank: You say "I do not like Princeton theology, or New Haven theology, or Andover theology." I do not ask you on board either of these great men-of-war, their portholes filled with the great siege-guns of ecclesiastical battle. But I do ask you to take the one plank of the Gospel that you do believe in and strike out for the pearl-strung beach of heaven. You are like a man out there in that Mediterranean tempest and tossed in the Melita-breakers, refusing to come ashore until he can mend the pieces of the broken ship. I hear him say: "I won't go in on any of these planks until I know in what part of the ship they belong. When I can get the windlass in the right place, and the sails set, and that keel-piece where it belongs, and that floor timber right, and these ropes untangled, I will go ashore. I am an old sailor, and know all about ships for forty years, and as soon as I can get the vessel afloat in good shape I will come in." A man drifting by on a piece of wood overhears him and says: "You will drown before you get that ship reconstructed. Better do as I am doing. I know nothing about ships, and never saw one before I came on board this, and I cannot swim a stroke, but I am going ashore on this shivered timber." The man in the offing while trying to mend his ship goes down. The man who trusted to the plank is saved. Oh, my brother, let your smashed-up system of theology go to the bottom while you come in on a splintered spar!

I bethink myself that there are some here whose opportunity or whose life is a mere wreck, and they have only a small piece left. You started in youth with all sails set and everything promised a grand voyage, but you have sailed in the wrong direction or have foundered on a rock. You have only a fragment of time left. Then come in on that one plank.

The past you cannot recover. Get on board that old ship you never will. Have you only one more year left, one more month, one more week, one more day, one more hour—come in on that, and so "escape safe to land."

CHAPTER XVII.

Three Trumpet Peals.

IT is said that when Charlemagne's host was overpowered by three armies of the Saracens in the Pass of Roncesvalles, his warrior, Roland, in terrible earnestness, seized a trumpet, and blew it with such terrific strength that the opposing army reeled back with terror ; but at the third blast of the trumpet it broke in two. I see your soul fiercely assailed by all the powers of earth and hell, and I put the trumpet of the Gospel to my lips and blow it three times. Peal the first : " Seek ye the Lord while He may be found." Peal the second : "Call ye upon Him while He is near." Peal the third : " Now is the accepted time ; now is the day of salvation." Does not the host of sin fall back ? But the trumpet does not, like that of Roland, break in two. As it was handed down to us from the lips of our fathers, we hand it down to the lips of our children, and tell them to sound it when we are dead. Hear the three peals, one after another.

PEAL FIRST.

"Seek ye the Lord while He may be found."—ISA. 55 : 6.

What Paul was among the apostles, Isaiah was among the prophets. A circular letter. Standing on a mountain of inspiration, looking out into the future, beholding Christ advancing and anxious that all men might know Him ; his voice rings down the ages: "Seek ye the Lord while He may be found." "Oh," says some one, "that was for olden times." No, my friend. If you have travelled in other lands you have taken a circular letter of credit from some banking-house in New York, and in St. Petersburg, or Ven-

ice, or Rome, or Antwerp, or Brussels, or Paris, you presented that letter and got financial help immediately. And
I want you to understand that the text, instead of being
appropriate for one age, or for one land, is a circular letter
for all ages and for all lands, and wherever it is presented
for help, the help comes: "Seek ye the Lord while He may
be found."

I come with no hair-spun theories of religion, with no
nice distinctions, with no elaborate disquisition; but with a
plain talk on the matters of personal religion. I feel that
the message will be the savor of life unto life, or of death
unto death. In other words, the Gospel of Christ is a powerful medicine; it either kills or cures.

Now you know very well that to seek a thing is to
search for it with earnest endeavor. If you want to see a
certain man in New York, and there is a matter of $10,000
connected with your seeing him, and you cannot at first find
him, you do not give up the search. You look in the direc-
tory, but cannot find the name, you go in circles where you
think, perhaps, he may mingle, and, having found the part
of the city where he lives, but perhaps not knowing the
street, you go through street after street, and from block to
block, and you keep on searching for weeks and for months.

You say: "It is a matter of $10,000 whether I see him
or not." O that men were as persistent in seeking for
Christ! Had you one half that persistence you would long
ago have found Him who is the joy of the forgiven spirit.
We may pay our debts, we may attend church, we may relieve the poor, we may be public benefactors, and yet all our
life never seek God. O that the Spirit of God would help
while I try to show you, first, *how* to seek the Lord, and in
the next place, *when* to seek Him. "O seek ye the Lord
while He may be found."

I remark, in the first place, you are to seek the Lord
through earnest and believing prayer. God is not an auto-
crat or a despot seated on a throne with His arms resting on
brazen lions, and a sentinel pacing up and down at the foot
of the throne. God is a father seated in a bower, waiting

for His children to come and climb on His knee, and get His kiss and His benediction.

O impenitent soul, have you ever tried the power of prayer? God says He is loving, and faithful, and patient. Do you believe that? You are told that Christ came to save sinners. Do you believe that? You are told that all you have to do to get the pardon of the Gospel is to ask for it. Do you believe that? Then come to Him and say: "O Lord, I know Thou canst not lie. Thou hast told me to come for pardon, and I could get it. I come, Lord. Keep Thy promise, and liberate my captive soul."

O that you might have an altar in the parlor, in the kitchen, in the store, in the barn, for Christ will be willing to come again to the manger to hear prayer. He would come in your place of business, as He confronted Matthew, the Tax Commissioner. If a measure should come before Congress that you thought would ruin the nation, how you would send in petitions and remonstrances. And yet there has been enough sin in your heart to ruin it forever, and you have never remonstrated or petitioned against it. If your physical health failed, and you had the means, you would go and spend the summer in Germany, and the winter in Italy, and you would think it a very cheap outlay if you had to go all round the earth to get back your physical health. Have you made any effort, any expenditure, any exertion for your immortal and spiritual health? No, you have not taken one step

O that you might now begin to seek after God with earnest prayer. Some of you have been working for years and years for the support of your families. Have you given one half day to the working out of your salvation with fear and trembling? I tell you, first of all, if you want to find the Lord, you must pray, and pray, and pray.

I remark, again, you must seek the Lord through Bible study, the book for seekers. When people are anxious about their souls, there are those who recommend good books. That is all right. But I want to tell you that the Bible is the best book in such circumstances. Baxter wrote,

"A Call to the Unconverted," but the Bible is the best call to the unconverted. Philip Doddridge wrote, "The Rise and Progress of Religion in the Soul," but the Bible is the best rise and progress. John Angell James wrote "Advice to the Anxious Inquirer," but the Bible is the best advice to the anxious inquirer.

O the Bible is the very book you need, anxious and inquiring soul! A dying soldier said to his mate : "Comrade, give me a drop !" The comrade shook up the canteen, and said :

"There isn't a drop of water in the canteen."

"Oh," said *the dying soldier*, "that's not what I want ; feel in my knapsack for my Bible " and his comrade found the Bible, and read him a few of the gracious promises, and the dying soldier said · "Ah, that's what I want There isn't anything like the Bible for a dying soldier, is there, comrade ?" O blessed book while we live. Blessed book when we die !

But I come now to the last part of my text. It tells us *when* we are to seek the Lord. "While He may be found." When is that ? Old age ? You may not see old age. To-morrow ? You may not see to-morrow. To-night ? You may not see to-night.

O ye dying, yet immortal men, "Seek the Lord while He may be found."

A DESPAIRING OCTOGENARIAN.

I want you to take the hint that there is a time when He cannot be found. There was a man in New York, eighty years of age, who said to a clergyman that came in, " Do you think that a man at eighty years of age can get pardoned ?" " Oh, yes," said the clergyman. The old man said : "I can't ; when I was twenty years of age the Spirit of God came to my soul, and I felt the importance of attending to these things, but I put it off. I rejected God, and since then I have had no feeling " "Well," said the minister, "wouldn't you like to have me pray with you?" " Yes," replied the old man, " but it will do no good. You can pray with me if you like." The minister knelt down and prayed, and commended the man's soul to God. It seemed to have no effect upon him. After a while the last hour of the man's life came, and through his delirium a spark of intelligence seemed to flash, and with his last breath he said : "*I shall never be forgiven!*" "O seek the Lord while He may be found."

PEAL SECOND.

"Call ye upon Him while He is near." [Last clause of the same verse as above.]—ISA. 55 : 6.

Now He is a God nigh at hand, soon He may be a God afar off.

One Sabbath night years ago in my church in Brooklyn a young man appeared at the end of the platform and said to me, "I have just come off the sea." I said, "When did you arrive?" Said he, "I came into port this afternoon. I was in a great 'blow' off Cape Hatteras this last week, and I thought that I might as well go to heaven as to hell. I thought the ship would sink; but, sir, I never very seriously thought about my soul until to-night." I said to him, "Do you feel that Christ is able and willing to save you?" "Oh, yes," he replied, "I do." "Well," I said, "now are you willing to come and be saved by Him?" "I am," he said. "Well, will you now, in the prayer we are about to offer, give yourself to God for time and eternity?" "I will," he said. Then we knelt in prayer, and after we had got through praying he told me the great transformation had taken place. He did not wait till God was afar off, as in the following:

A young man, at the close of a religious service, was asked to decide the matter of his soul's salvation. He said, "I will not do it to-night." Well, the Christian man kept talking with him, and he said, "I insist that to-night you either take God or reject him." "Well," said the young man, "if you put it that way, I will reject Him. There now, the matter's settled." On his way home on horseback, he knew not that a tree had fallen aslant the road, and he was going at full speed, and he struck the obstacle and dropped lifeless. That night his Christian mother heard the riderless horse plunging about the barn, and suspecting that something terrible was the matter, she went out and came to the place where her son lay, and she cried out, " O Henry! dead, and not a Christian. Oh, my son! my son! dead and not a Christian. O Henry! Henry! dead and not a Christian." God keep us from such a catastrophe! O, do not thus put off calling upon God till you are finally left to reject Him and are lost! Right about face! for you are going in the wrong direction. While you are in a favorable mood for it, enter into life. Here, and just now, decide everything that makes for peace and heaven. Agassiz says that he has stood at one place in the Alps where he could throw a chip into the water in one direction, and it would roll on into the German Ocean, or he could throw a chip into the water in another direction, and it would reach the Black Sea by the Danube, or he could throw a chip in another direction, and it would enter the Mediterranean, by the Rhone. How far apart the Mediterranean and the Black Sea and the German Ocean! Standing to-day on this Alps of Gospel privilege, you can project your soul into the right currents, and it will roll on into the ocean of life, or project it in the wrong direction, and it will roll into the sea of death. But how far apart the two distances! May God help us to appreciate more and more the momentous meaning of the words, "Call ye upon Him while He is near." We are thus prepared to hear.

PEAL THIRD.

"Behold! NOW is the accepted time; behold! now is the day of salvation!" 2 Cor. 6: 2.

There are those who say: " I would like to become a Christian. I have been waiting a good while for the right kind of influences to come;" and still you are waiting.

A SPECTATOR AT GETTYSBURG.

A gentleman told me that at the battle of Gettysburg he stood upon a height looking off upon the conflicting armies. He said it was the most exciting moment of his life; now one army seeming to triumph, and now the other. After a while the host wheeled in such a way that he knew in five minutes the whole question would be decided. He said the emotion was almost unbearable. There is just such a time to-day with you, O impenitent soul—the forces of light on the one side, and the siege-guns of hell on the other side, and in a few moments the matter will be settled for eternity.

There is a time which mercy has set for leaving port. If you are on board before that you will get a passage for heaven. If you are not on board, you miss your passage for heaven. As in law courts a case is sometimes adjourned from time to time, and from year to year till the bill of costs eats up the entire estate, so there are men who are adjourning the matter of religion from time to time, and from year to year until heavenly bliss is the bill of costs the man will have to pay for it.

CRISIS IN DISEASE.

Sin is an awful disease. I hear people say with a toss of the head and with a trivial manner: "Oh, yes, I'm a sinner." Sin is an awful disease. It is leprosy. It is dropsy. It is consumption. It is all moral disorders in one. Now you know there is a crisis in disease. Perhaps you have had some illustration of it in your family. Sometimes the physician has called, and he has looked at the patient and said: "That case was simple enough, but the crisis has passed. If you had called me yesterday or this morning I could have cured the patient. It is too late now; the crisis has passed." Just so it is in the spiritual treatment of the soul —there is a crisis. Before that, life! After that, death! O my dear brother, as you love your soul do not let the crisis pass unattended to!

LOST CHANCE.

There are some who can remember instances in life when, if they had bought a certain property, they would have become very rich. A few acres that would have cost them almost nothing were offered them. They refused them. Afterward a large village or city sprang up on those acres of ground and they see what a mistake they made in not buying the property. There *was* an opportunity of getting it. It never came back again. And so it is in regard to a man's spiritual and eternal fortune. There is a chance; if you let that go, perhaps it never comes back. Certainly, that one never comes back.

"Oh," you say, "religion I am going to have; it is only a question of time." My brother, I am afraid that you may lose heaven the way Louis Philippe lost his Empire. The Parisian mob came around the Tuileries. The National Guard stood in defence of the palace, and the commander said to Louis Philippe: "Shall I fire now? Shall I order the troops to fire? With one volley we can clear the place." "No," said Louis Philippe, "not yet." A few minutes passed on, and then Louis Philippe, seeing the case was hopeless, said to the general: "Now is the time to fire." "No," said the general, "it is too late now; don't you see that the soldiers are exchanging arms with the citizens? It is too late." Down went the throne of Louis Philippe. Away from the earth went the House of Orleans, and all because the King said: "Not yet, not yet." May God forbid that any of you should adjourn this great subject of religion and postpone assailing your spiritual foes until it is too late—too late, you losing a throne in heaven the way that Louis Philippe lost a throne on earth.

> "When the Judge descends in might,
> Clothed in majesty and light.
> When the earth shall quake with fear,
> Where, O where, wilt thou appear?"

Procrastination is a notorious thief of time and murderer of the soul.

POSTPONEMENT USELESS.

Why defer this matter, oh my dear hearer? Have you any idea that sin will wear out? that it will evaporate? that it will relax its grasp, that you may find religion as a man accidentally finds a lost pocket-book? Ah, no! No man ever became a Christian by accident, or by the relaxing of sin. The embarrassments are all the time increasing. The hosts of darkness are recruiting, and the longer you postpone this matter the steeper the path will become. O fly for refuge! The avenger of blood is on the track! The throne of judgment will soon be set; and, if you have anything to do toward your eternal salvation, you had better do it now, for the redemption of the soul is precious, and it ceaseth forever!

Have you ever imagined what will be the soliloquy of the soul on that day unpardoned, as it looks back upon its past life? "Oh," says the soul, "I am lost! Notwithstanding all the opportunities I have had of being saved, I am lost! O Thou long-suffering Lord God Almighty, I am lost! O day of judgment, I am lost! O father, mother, brother, sister, child in glory, I am lost!" And then as the tide goes out, your soul goes out with it—farther from God, farther from happiness, and I hear your voice fainter, and fainter, and fainter: "Lost! Lost! Lost! Lost! Lost!" And, O my dear friend, perhaps it is with you

NOW OR NEVER!!

Those persons play the fool who, while they admit the righteousness of religion, set it down for future attendance. Do you know how many times the word "Now" occurs in the Bible? Over two hundred times. One of the shortest words in the Bible, and yet one of the grandest in meaning and ramifications. When does the Bible say is the best time to repent? Now. When does the Bible say that God will forgive? Now. When does God say is the only safe time to attend to the matters of the soul? Now. But that word

" Now" melts away as easily as a snowflake in the evening
rain. Where is the " now" of the dead of last year? the
" now" of the dead of last month? the " now" of the dead
of last week? the " now" of the dead of yesterday? Time
picked it up in its beak and flew away with it.

Swammerdam and other naturalists tell us there are insects which within the space of one minute are born, fulfil
their mission, celebrate their nuptials, and die ; but this wonderful " now " is more short lived than they. It is a flash, a
stroke, a glance. Its cradle is its grave. If men catch it at
all, it is with quick clutch. Millions of men have lost their
soul immortal because they did not understand the momentum and the ponderosity of that one word. All the strate-
gic powers of hell are exerted in trying to substract from the
energy and emphasis of that word. They say it is only a
word of three letters, while there is a better word of eight
letters—" to-morrow." They say, " Throw away that small
word and take this other grand one ;" and so men say, " Give
us ' to-morrow ' and take away from us ' now ', " and between
those two words is the Appian way of death, and a great
multitude throng that road, jostling and elbowing each other,
hastening on swifter and swifter to die. For how much
would you walk the edge of the roof of your house? For
how much would you come out on the most dangerous peak
of the Matterhorn and wave your cap? You say, " No
money could induce me to do it." And yet you stand to-
day with one foot on a crumbling moment and the other
foot lifted, not knowing where you will put it down, while
the distance between you and the bottom of the depth beneath you no plummet can measure, no arithmetic calculate,
no wing of lightning cleave. And yet the Bible tells us that
unless a man has a new heart he cannot get into heaven ;
and some of you are not seeking for that new heart. In
Mexico sometimes the ground suddenly opens, and a man
standing near the gap can see down an appalling distance.
But, oh, if to-day, at your feet, there should open the chasms
of the lost world, how you would fling yourself back and cry,
" God save me—now ! now ! now !"

I greet you to-day, my brother, in the very gate of eternity. Some of us may live a longer and some of us may live a shorter time; but at the longest, life is so short that we all stand on the door-sill of the great future. The next step— all the angels of God cannot undo the consequences. Will your exit from this life be a rising or a falling? The righteous go up. The Saviour helps them. Ministering spirits meet them. The doors of Paradise open to receive them. Up! up! up! O! what a grand thing it is to die with a strong faith in God, like that which Stonewall Jackson had when, in his expiring moments, he said : "Let us cross over the river, and lie down under the shade." But to leave this world unprepared is falling—falling from God, falling from hope, falling from peace, falling from heaven—swiftly, wildly, forever falling.

So it was with one who had been eminent for his intelligence, but who had omitted all preparation for the future world, and had come down to his last hour. He said to his wife, seated by the bedside, "O don't talk to me about pain ; *it is the mind, woman,* it is the mind! Of all the years of my life, I never lived one minute for heaven. It is awfully dark here," he whispered, "it is awfully dark. I seem to stand on the slippery edge of a great gulf. I shall fall! I am falling!" And with a shriek, as when a man tumbles over a precipice, he expired. Wise, for this world ; about the matters of his immortal soul, he was all his life-long playing the fool.

I will take the case of some one and ask you what you think about that case. He has been all his life amid Bibles and churches, so that he knows his duty. Christ has offered to do all for that man that a divine Saviour can offer to do for a dying soul. Heaven has been offered him, yea, been pushed upon him, and yet he has not accepted it, and to-day he sits deliberately allowing his chances for life to go away from him. What do you say of that one?" "Hallucinated," says one ; "Monomaniacal," says another ; "Playing the fool," says another. Oh, how many there are taking just that position! There is such a thing as pyromania, an insanity which disposes one to destroy buildings by fire : but who would have thought that there was a pyromania of the immortal nature, and that any one could be so struck through with that insanity as to have a desire and disposition to consume the soul?

I cannot consent to have you lose your souls. Come with me, and as in the summer time we go down to the beach and bathe in the waters, so to-day let us join hands and wade down into the summer sea of God's forgiveness. Roll over us, tides of everlasting love, roll over us! Dear Lord, we knock at the door of mercy—not as the demented knock, not knowing what they want, but knocking at the door of mercy, because we want to come in, while others run their meaningless hands up and down the panels, and scrabble at the gate, in the presence of God, and men, and angels, and devils, playing the fool.

THE ACCEPTED TIME.

Present opportunities will soon be gone forever. The conductor of a rail-train was telling me of the fact that he was one night standing by his train on a side track, his train having been switched so that an express train might dart past unhindered. He said while he stood there in the darkness, beside his train on the side-track, he heard the thunder of the express in the distance. Then he saw the flash of the headlight. The train came with fearful velocity, nearer and nearer, until after a while, when it came very near, by the flash of the headlight, he saw that the switchman had not attended to his duty—either through intoxication or indifference,—and that train, unless something were done immediately, would rush on the side-track, and dash the other train to atoms. He shouted to the switchman, " Set up that switch!" and with one stroke the switch went back, and the express thundered on. Oh men and women, going on toward the eternal world, swift as the years, swift as the months, swift as the days, swift as the hours, swift as the

minutes, swift as the seconds: On what track are you running? Toward light or darkness? Toward victory or defeat? Toward heaven or hell? Set up that switch! Cry
aloud to God!   " Behold!   Now is the accepted time ; behold now is the day of salvation!"   Now!   O if I could
only write on every heart in three capital letters that word
N-O-W—Now ! now ! now !

CHAPTER XVIII.

The Story of Naaman.

HERE we have a warrior sick, not with pleurisies, or rheumatisms, or consumptions, but with a disease worse than all these put together; a red mark has come out on the forehead, precursor of complete disfigurement and dissolution. I have something awful to tell you. General Naaman, the commander-in-chief of all the Syrian forces, has the leprosy! It is on his hands, on his face, on his entire person.

Get out of the way of the pestilence! If his breath strike you, you are a dead man. The commander-in-chief of all the forces of Syria! And yet he would be glad to exchange conditions with the boy at his stirrup, or the hostler that blankets his charger. The news goes like wildfire all through the realm, and the people are sympathetic, and they cry out, "Is it possible that our great hero who overthrew Ahab, and around whom we came with such vociferation when he returned from victorious battle—can it be possible that our grand and glorious Naaman has the leprosy?"

Yes. Everybody has something he wishes he had not. —David, an Absalom to disgrace him; Paul, a thorn to sting him; Job, carbuncles to plague him; Samson, a Delilah to shear him; Ahab, a Naboth to deny him; Haman, a Mordecai to irritate him; George Washington, childlessness to afflict him; John Wesley, a termagant wife to pester him; Leah, weak eyes; Pope, a crooked back; Byron, a club foot; John Milton, blind eyes; Charles Lamb, an insane sister; and you, and you, and you, and you, something which you never bargained for, and would like to get rid of. The reason of this is, that God does not want this world to

435

be too bright, otherwise we would always want to stay, and eat these fruits, and lie on these lounges, and shake hands in this pleasant society. We are only in the vestibule of a grand temple. God does not want us to stay on the doorstep, and therefore he sends aches, and annoyances, and sorrows, and bereavements of all sorts to push us on, and push us up toward riper fruits, and brighter society, and more radiant prosperities. *God is only whipping us ahead.*

The reason that Edward Payson and Robert Hall had more rapturous views of heaven than other people had was because, through their aches and pains, God pushed them nearer up to it. If God dashes out one of your pictures, it is only to show you a brighter one. If He sting your foot with gout, your brain with neuralgia, your tongue with an inextinguishable thirst, it is only because He is preparing to substitute a better body than you ever dreamed of, when the mortal shall put on immortality. It is to push you on, and push you up toward something grander and better, that God sends upon you, as He did upon General Naaman, something you do not want.

Seated in his Syrian mansion—all the walls glittering with the shields which he had captured in battle; the corridors crowded with admiring visitors who just wanted to see him once; music, and mirth, and banqueting filling all the mansion, from tesselated floor to pictured ceiling—Naaman would have forgotten that there was anything better, and would have been glad to stay there ten thousand years. But oh, how the shields dim, and how the visitors fly from the hall, and how the music drops dead from the string, and how the gates of the mansion slam shut with sepulchral bang, as you read the closing words of the eulogium : " He was a leper ! He was a leper !"

There was one person more sympathetic with General Naaman than any other person. Naaman's wife walks the floor, wringing her hands and trying to think what she can do to alleviate her husband's suffering. All remedies have failed. The surgeon-general and the doctors of the royal staff have met, and they have shaken their heads as much

as to say, "No cure; no cure." I think that the office-
seekers had all folded up their recommendations and gone
home. Probably most of the employees of the establishment had dropped their work and were thinking of looking
for some other situation. What shall now become of poor
Naaman's wife? She must have sympathy somewhere. In
her despair she goes to a little Hebrew captive, a servant-
girl in her house, to whom she tells the whole story; as
sometimes, when overborne with the sorrows of the world,
and finding no sympathy anywhere else, you have gone out
and found in the sympathy of some humble domestic—
Rose, or Dinah, or Bridget—a help which the world could
not give you. What a scene it was! One of the grandest
women in all Syria in cabinet council with a waiting-maid
over the declining health of the mighty general! "I know
something," says the little captive maid, "I know something," as she bounds to her bare feet. "In the land from
which I was stolen there is a certain prophet known by the
name of Elisha, who can cure almost everything, and I
shouldn't wonder if he could cure my master. Send for him
right away." "Oh, hush!" you say. "If the highest medical talent in all the land cannot cure that leper, there is no
need of your listening to any talk of a servant-girl." But do
not scoff, do not sneer. The finger of that little captive
maid is pointing in the right direction. Forgetting her own
personal sorrows, she sympathizes with the suffering of her
master, and recommends him to the famous Hebrew
prophet.

No wonder the advice of this little Hebrew captive threw
all Naaman's mansion and Benhadad's palace into excitement.

With face scarified and ridged and inflamed by the pestilence, and aided by those who supported him on either
side, he staggers out to the chariot. Hold fast the fiery
coursers of the royal stable, while the poor sick man lifts his
swollen feet and pain-struck limbs into the vehicle. Bolster
him up with the pillows, and let him take a lingering look
· at his bright apartment, for perhaps the Hebrew captive

may be mistaken, and the next time Naaman comes to that place he may be a dead weight on the shoulders of those who carry him—an expired chieftain seeking sepulture amid the lamentations of an admiring nation. Good-by, Naaman!

Let the charioteer drive gently over the hills of Hermon, lest he jolt the invalid. Here goes the bravest man of all his day, a captive of a horrible disease. As the ambulance winds through the streets of Damascus the tears and prayers of all the people go after the world-renowned invalid. Perhaps you have had an invalid go out from your house on a health excursion You know how the neighbors stood around and said, "Ah, he will never come back again alive!" Oh, it was a solemn moment, I tell you, when the invalid had departed, and you went into the room to make the bed, and to remove the medicine phials from the shelf, and to throw open the shutters so that the fresh air might rush into the long-closed room! Good-by, Naaman! There is only one cheerful face looking at him, and that is the face of the little Hebrew captive, who is sure he will get cured and who is so glad she helped him.

As the chariot winds out and the escort of mounted courtiers, and the mules laden with sacks of gold and silver and embroidered suits of apparel, went through the gates of Damascus and out on the long way, the hills of Naphtali and Ephraim look down on the procession, and the retinue goes right past the battle-fields where Naaman, in the days of his health, used to rally his troops for fearful onset; and then the procession stops and reclines awhile in the groves of olives and oleander, and General Naaman so sick—so very, very sick!

How the countrymen gaped as the procession passed! They had seen Naaman go past like a whirlwind in days gone by, and had stood aghast at the clank of his war-equipments, but now they commiserate him. They say, "Poor man, he will never get home alive! Poor man!" General Naaman wakes up from a restless sleep in the chariot, and he says to the charioteer, "How long before we shall reach this prophet Elisha's?" The charioteer says to a waysider, " How far is it to Elisha's house?" He says, " Two miles." " Two miles." Then they whip up the lathered and fagged-out horses. The whole procession brightens up at the prospect of speedy arrival.

By and by the charioteers shout, "Whoa!" to the horses, and the tramping hoofs and grinding wheels cease shaking the earth.

"Come out, Elisha, come out, you have company; the grandest company that ever came to your house has come to it now." No stir inside Elisha's house. The fact was, the Lord had informed Elisha that the sick captain was coming, and just how to treat him. Indeed, when you are sick and the Lord wants you to get well, He always tells the doctor how to treat you; and *the reason we have so many bungling doctors* is because they depend upon their own strength and instruction, and not on the Lord God; and that always makes malpractice Come out, Elisha, and attend to your business. General Naaman and his retinue waited and waited and waited. The fact was, Naaman had two diseases—pride and leprosy; the one was as hard to get rid of as the other. Elisha sits quietly in his house and does not go out. After a while, when he thinks he has humbled this proud man, he says to a servant, "Go out and tell General Naaman to bathe seven times in the River Jordan, out yonder five miles, and he will get entirely well."

The message comes out. "What!" says the commander-in-chief of the Syrian forces, his eye kindling with an animation which it had not shown for weeks, and his swollen foot stamping on the bottom of the chariot, regardless of pain. " What! Isn't he coming out to see me? Why, I thought certainly he would come and utter some cabalistic words over me, or make some enigmatical passes over my wounds. Why, I don't think he knows who I am. Isn't he coming out? I won't endure it any longer. Charioteer, drive on! Wash in the Jordan! Ha! ha! The slimy Jordan—the muddy Jordan—the monotonous Jordan. I wouldn't be seen by any one washing in such a river as that.

Why, we watered our horses in a better river than that on our way here. The beautiful river, the jaspar-paved river of Pharpar. Besides that, we have in our country another Damascene river, Abana, with foliaged bank and torrent ever swift and ever clear, under the flickering shadows of sycamore and oleander. Are not Abana and Pharpar, rivers of Damascus, better than all the waters of Israel?"

I suppose Naaman felt very much as we would feel if, by way of medical prescription, some one should tell us to go and wash in the Danube or the Rhine. We would answer, "Are not the Connecticut or the Hudson just as good?" Or, as an Englishman would feel if he were told, by way of medical prescription, he must go and wash in the Mississippi or St. Lawrence. He would cry out, "Are not the Thames and the Mersey just as well?" The fact was that haughty Naaman needed to learn what every Englishman and every American needs to learn—that when God tells you to do a thing, you must go and do it, whether you understand the reason or not.

Well, General Naaman could not stand the test. The charioteer gives a jerk to the right line until the bit snaps in the horse's mouth, and the whirr of the wheels and the flying of the dust show the indignation of the great commander. "He turned and went away in a rage." So people now often get mad at religion, and go away in a rage. So, after all, it seems that this health excursion of General Naaman is to be a dead failure. That little Hebrew captive might as well have not told him of the prophet, and this long journey might as well not have been taken. Poor, sick, dying Naaman! are you going away in high dudgeon and worse than when you came? As his chariot halts a moment, his servants clamber up in it and coax him to do as Elisha said. They say: "It's easy. If the prophet had told you to walk for a mile on sharp spikes in order to get rid of this awful disease you would have done it. It is easy. Come, my lord, just get down and wash in the Jordan. You take a bath every day, anyhow, and in this climate it is so hot that it will do you good. Do it on our account, and for the sake

of the army you command, and for the sake of the nation
that admires you. Come, my lord, just try this Jordanic
bath." "Well," he says, "to please you I will do as you
say." The retinue drive to the brink of the Jordan. The
horses paw and neigh to get into the stream themselves and
cool their hot flanks. General Naaman, assisted by his
attendants, gets down out of the chariot and painfully comes
to the brink of the river, and steps in until an inclination of
the head will thoroughly immerse him. He bows once into
the flood, and comes up and shakes the water out of nostrils
and eyes ; and his attendants look at him and say, "Why,
general, how much better you look." And he bows a
second time into the flood and comes up, and the wild stare
is gone out of his eye. He bows the third time in the flood
and comes up, and the shrivelled flesh has got smooth again.
He bows the fourth time into the flood and comes up, and
the hair that had fallen out is restored in thick locks again
all over the brow. He bows the fifth time into the flood
and comes up, and the hoarseness has gone out of his throat.
He bows the sixth time and comes up, and all the soreness
and anguish have gone out of the limbs. "Why," he says,
"I am almost well, but I will make a complete cure," and he
bows the seventh time into the flood ; and he comes up, and
not so much as a fester, or scale, or an eruption as big as the
head of a pin is to be seen on him. He steps out on the
bank and says, "Is it possible?" And the attendants look
and say, "Is it possible?" And as, with the health of an
athlete he bounds back into the chariot and drives on, there
goes up from all his attendants a wild "Huzza! huzza!"

WHAT TO DO.

You notice that this General Naaman did two things in
order to get well. The first was—he got out of his chariot.
He might have stayed there with his swollen feet on the
stuffed ottoman, seated on that embroidered cushion, until
his last gasp, he would never have got any relief. He had
to get down out of his chariot. And you have got to get

down out of the chariot of your pride if you ever become a
Christian. You cannot drive up to the cross with a coach-
and-four, and be *saved among all the spangles.*

But he had not only to get down out of his chariot. He
had to wash. O my hearer, there is a flood brighter than
any other. Zechariah called it the "fountain open for sin
and uncleanness." William Cowper called it the "fountain
filled with blood." Plunge once, twice, thrice, four times,
five times, six times, seven times. It will take as much as
that to cure your soul. Oh, wash, and be clean!

I suppose that was a great time at Damascus when General Naaman got back. The charioteers did not have to
drive slowly any longer, lest they jolt the invalid; but as the
horses dashed through the streets of Damascus, I think the
people rushed out to hail back their chieftain. Naaman's
wife hardly recognized her husband; he was so wonderfully
changed she had to look at him two or three times before
she made out that it was her restored husband. And the
little captive maid, she rushed out, clapping her hands, and
shouting, "Did he cure you? Did he cure you?" Then
music woke up the palace, and the tapestry of the windows
was drawn away, that the multitude outside might mingle
with the princely mirth inside, and the feet went up and
down in the dance, and all the streets of Damascus that
night echoed and re-echoed with the news, " Naaman
is cured! Naaman is cured!"

But a gladder tune than that it would be if the soul
should get cured of its leprosy. The swiftest white horse
hitched to the King's chariot would rush the news into the
Eternal City. Our loved ones before the throne would welcome the glad tidings. Your children on earth, with more
emotion than the little Hebrew captive, would notice the
change in your look, and the change in your manner, and
would put their arms around your neck and say, " Mother,
I guess you must have become a Christian. Father, I think
you have got rid of the leprosy." O Lord God of Elisha,
have mercy on us!

CHAPTER XIX.

The Well at the Gate.

"Oh that one would give me drink of the water of the well of Bethlehem, which is by the gate." II SAM 23 15.

WAR, always distressing, is especially ruinous in harvesttime. When the crops are all ready for the sickle, to have them trodden down by cavalry horses, and heavy supplytrains gullying the fields, is enough to make any man's heart sick. When the last great war broke out in Europe, and France and Germany were coming into horrid collision, I rode past their golden harvest-fields and saw tents pitched and the trenches dug in the very midst of the ripe fields, the long scythe of battle sharpening to mow down harvests of men in great winrows of the dead. It was at this season of harvest that the army of the Philistines came down upon Bethlehem. Hark to the clamor of their voices, the neighing of their chargers, the blare of their trumpets and the clash of their shields!

Let David and his men fall back! The Lord's host sometimes loses the day. But David knew where to hide. He had been brought up in that country. Boys are inquisitive, and they know all about the region where they were born and brought up If you should go back to the old homestead, you could, with your eyes shut, find your way to the meadow, or the orchard, or the hill back of the house, with which you were familiar thirty or forty years ago. So David knew the Cave of Adullam. Perhaps, in his boyhood days, he had played "hide-and-seek" with his comrades all about the old cave; and though others might not have known it, David did Travellers say there is only one way of getting into that cave, and that is by a very narrow path, but David was stout and steady-headed and steady-nerved;

and so, with his three brave staff-officers, he goes along that path, finds his way into the cave, sits down, looks around at the roof and the dark passages of the mountain, feels very weary with the forced march, and water he must have, or die.

I do not know but there may have been drops trickling down the side of the cavern, or that there may have been some water in the goat-skin slung to his girdle ; but that was not what he wanted. He wanted a deep, full, cold drink, such as a man gets only out of an old well with moss-covered bucket. David remembered that very near that cave of Adullam there was such a well as that, a well to which he used to go in boyhood—the well of Bethlehem ; and he almost imagines that he can hear the liquid plash of that well, and his parched tongue moves through his hot lips as he says, " Oh, that one would give me drink of the water of the well of Bethlehem, which is by the gate !"

It was no sooner said than done. The three brave staff-officers bound to their feet and start. Brave soldiers will take even a hint from the commander. But between them and the well lay the host of the Philistines ; and what could three men do with a great army ? Yet where there is a will there is a way, and, with their swords slashing this way and that, they make their path to the well. While the Philistines are amazed at the seeming fool-hardiness of these three men, and cannot make up their minds exactly what it means, the three men have come to the well. They drop the bucket. They bring up the water. They pour it in the pail, and then start for the cave. "Stop them !" cry the Philistines. " Clip them with your swords! Stab them with your spears! Stop those three men !" Too late ! They have got around the hill. The hot rocks are splashed with the overflowing water from the vessel as it is carried up the cliffs. The three men go along the dangerous path, and with cheeks flushed with the excitement, and all out of breath in their haste, they fling their swords red with the skirmish, to the side of the cave, and cry out to David : " There, captain of the host, is what you wanted, a drink of the well of Bethlehem, which is by the gate !"

David had known hundreds of wells of water, but he wanted to drink from that particular one, and he thought nothing could slake his thirst like that. And unless your soul and mine can get access to the Fountain open for sin and uncleanness, we must die. That fountain is the well of Bethlehem. It was dug in the night. It was dug by the light of a lantern—the star that hung down over the manger. It was dug not at the gate of Cæsar's palaces, not in the park of a Jerusalem bargain-maker. It was dug in a barn. The camels lifted their weary heads to listen as the work went on. The shepherds, unable to sleep, because the heavens were filled with bands of music, came down to see the opening of the well. The angels of God, at the first gush of the living water, dipped their chalices of joy into it, and drank to the health of earth and heaven, as they cried, "Glory to God in the highest, and on earth peace." Sometimes in our modern barns the water is brought through the pipes of the city to the very nostrils of the horses or cattle; but this well in the Bethlehem barn was not so much for the beasts that perish as for our thirst-smitten race, desert-travelled and simoon-struck. Oh, my soul, weary with sin, stoop down and drink to-day out of that Bethlehem well!

Bring me some of that water. Whosoever drinketh of that water shall never thirst. " Oh, that one would give me drink of the water of the well of Bethlehem, which is by the gate "

A few days ago I was in the country, thirsty after a long walk. And I came in, and my child was blowing soap bubbles, and they rolled out of the cup, blue, and gold, and green, and sparkling, and beautiful, and orbicular, and in so small a space I never saw more splendor concentrated. But she blew once too often and all the glory vanished into suds. Then I turned and took a glass of water, and was refreshed. And so far as soul thirst is concerned, I put against all the blowing of glittering soap bubbles a pure draught of water from salvation's well.

The Gospel well, like the one here spoken of, is a captured well. David remembered the time when that good water of Bethlehem was in the possession of his ancestors. His father drank there, his mother drank there. He remembered how the water tasted when he was a boy.

David thought of that well, that boyhood well, and he wanted a drink of it, but he remembered that the Philistines had captured it. When those three men tried to come up to the well in behalf of David, they saw swords gleaming around about it And this is true of this Gospel well The Philistines have at times captured it. When we come to take a full, old-fashioned drink of pardon and comfort, do not their swords of indignation and sarcasm flash? Why, the skeptics tell us that we cannot come to that fountain! They say the water is not fit to drink, anyhow. "If you are really thirsty now, there is the well of philosophy, there is the well of art, there is the well of science." They try to substitute, instead of our boyhood faith, a modern mixture. They say a great many beautiful things about the soul, and they try to feed our immortal hunger on rose-leaves, and mix a mint-julep of worldly stimulants, when nothing will satisfy us but a drink of the water of the well of "Bethlehem, which is at the gate."

I tell you the old Gospel well is a captured well. I pray God that there may be somewhere in the elect host three anointed men, with courage enough to go forth in the strength of the omnipotent God, with the glittering swords of truth, to hew the way back again to that old well.

Depend upon it, that well will come into our possession again, though it has been captured. If there be not three anointed men in the Lord's host, with enough consecration to do the work, then the swords will leap from Jehovah's buckler, and the Eternal Three will descend—God the Father, God the Son, God the Holy Ghost—conquering for our dying race the way back again to "the water of the well of Bethlehem, which is by the gate."

The Gospel well, like the one spoken of, is a well at the gate. The traveller stops the camel to-day, and gets down, and dips out of the valley of the East, some very beautiful, clear, bright water, and that is out of the very well that

David longed for. Do you know that that well was at the gate, so that nobody could go into Bethlehem without going right past it? And so it is with this Gospel well—it is at the gate. It is, in the first place, *at the gate of purification*.

Angel of the Covenant, dip thy wing into this living fountain to-day, and wave it over us, that our souls may be washed in "the water of the well of Bethlehem, which is by the gate!"

This well is at *the gate of comfort*. Do you know where David was when he uttered the words of the text. He was in the cave of Adullam. That is where some of you are now. And I break through the armed ranks of your sorrows to-day, and bring to your parched lips "a drink of the water of the well of Bethlehem which is by the gate."

Finally, the Gospel well is *at the gate of heaven*. After you have been on a long journey, and you come in, all be-dusted and tired to your home, the first thing you want is refreshing ablution, and I am glad to know that after we get through the pilgrimage of this world—the hard, dusty pilgrimage—we will find a well at the gate. In that one wash, away will go our sins and sorrows. I do not care whether cherub or seraph, or my own departed friends in that blessed land, place to my lips the cup, the touch of that cup will be life, will be heaven! I was reading of how the ancients sought for the fountain of perpetual youth. They thought if they could only find and drink out of that well, the old would become young again, the sick would be cured, and everybody would have eternal juvenescence. Of course they could not find it. Eureka! I have found it! "the water of the well of Bethlehem, which is by the gate."

I think we had better make a bargain with those who leave us, going out of this world from time to time, as to where we will meet them. Travellers parting appoint a place of meeting. They say: "We will meet at Rome, or we will meet at Stockholm, or Vienna, or Jerusalem, or Bethlehem." Now, when we come to stand by the death-pillow of those who are leaving us for the far land, do not let us weep as though we would never see them again, but let us, there standing, appoint a place where we will meet. Where shall it be? Shall it be on the banks of the river? No; the banks are too long. Shall it be in the temple? No, no ; there is such a host there—ten thousand times ten thousand. Where shall we meet our loved ones? Let us make an appointment to meet at the well by the gate. Oh, heaven ! Sweet heaven ! Dear heaven ! Heaven, where our good friends are ! Heaven, where Jesus is ! Heaven ! Heaven !

But there comes a revulsion of feeling when I know there are souls dying of thirst notwithstanding the well at the gate. Between you and the well of heaven there is a great army of sin ; but Christ is ready to clear a way to that well, and I am glad to know that you may come yet. The well is here—the well of heaven. Come , I do not care how feeble you are. Let me take hold of your arm, and steady you up to the well-curb. " Ho, every one that thirsteth, come."

CHAPTER XX.

Character-Building.

PLUMB-LINE RELIGION.

"And the Lord said unto me, Amos, what seest thou? And I said, a plumb-line."—Amos 7:8

I WANT you to notice this fact, that when a man gives up the straight up-and-down religion in the Bible for any new-fangled religion, it is *generally to suit his sins.* You first hear of his change of religion, and then you hear of some swindle he has practised in Colorado mining stock, telling some one if he will put in ten thousand dollars he can take out a hundred thousand, or he has sacrificed his chastity, or plunged into irremediable worldliness. His sins are so broad he has to broaden his religion, and he becomes as broad as temptation, as broad as the soul's darkness, as broad as hell. They want a religion that will allow them to keep their sins, and then at death say to them: "Well done, good and faithful servant," and that tells them: "All is well, for there is no hell." What a glorious heaven they hold before us! Come, let us go in and see it. There is Herod and all the babes he massacred. There is Charles Guiteau, and Jim Fiske, and Robespierre, the friend of the French guillotine, and all the liars, thieves, house-burners, garroters, pick-pockets and libertines of all the centuries. They have all got crowns, and thrones, and harps, and sceptres, and when they chant they sing: "Thanksgiving, and honor, and glory, and power to the Broad Religion that lets us all into heaven without repentance, and faith in those disgraceful dogmas of ecclesiastical old-fogy-ism." All sorts of religions are putting forth their pretensions. Some have a spiritualistic religion, and their chief work is with ghosts, and others a religion of political economy, proposing to put an end to human misery by a new style of taxation, and there is a humanitarian religion that looks after the body of men and lets the soul look after itself, and there is a legislative religion that proposes to rectify all wrongs by enactment of better laws, and there is an æsthetic religion that by rules of exquisite taste would lift the heart out of its deformities, and religions of all sorts, religions by the peck, religions by the square foot, and religions by the ton—all of them devices of the devil that would take the heart away from *the only religion that will ever effect anything* for the human race, and that is the straight up-and-down religion written in the book, which begins with Genesis and ends with Revelation, the religion of the skies, the old religion, the God-given religion, the everlasting religion, which says, "Love God above all and your neighbor as yourself." All religions but one begin at the wrong end, and in the wrong place. Bible religion demands that we first get right with God. It begins at the top and measures down, while the other religions begin at the bottom and try to measure up. They stand at the foot of the wall, up to their knees in the mud of human theory and speculation, and have a plummet and a string tied fast to it. And they throw the plummet this way, and break a head there, and throw the plummet another way and break a head there, and then they throw it up, and it comes down upon their own pate. Fools! Why will you stand at the foot of the wall measuring up when you ought to stand at the top measuring down?

PLUMB-LINE RECTITUDE.

The solid masonry of the world has to me a fascination. Walk about some of the triumphal arches and the cathedrals, four or six hundred years old, and see them stand as erect as when they were builded, walls of great height, for centuries not bending a quarter of an inch this way or that.

So greatly honored were the masons who builded these walls that they were free from taxation and called "free" masons. The trowel gets most of the credit for these buildings, and its clear ringing on stone and brick has sounded across the ages. But there is another implement of just as much importance as the trowel, and my text recognizes it. Bricklayers and stone-masons, and carpenters, in the building of walls, use an instrument made of a cord, at the end of which a lump of lead is fastened. They drop it over the side of the wall, and, as the plummet naturally seeks the centre of gravity in the earth, the workman discovers where the wall recedes, and where it bulges out, and just what is the perpendicular. Our text represents God as standing on the wall of character, which the Israelites had built, and, in that way, testing it. "And the Lord said unto me, Amos, what seest thou? And I said, A plumb-line." What the world wants is a straight up-and-down religion. Much of the so-called piety of the day bends this way and that, to suit the times. It is horizontal, with a low state of sentiment and morals. We have all been building a wall of character, and it is glaringly imperfect, and needs reconstruction. How shall it be brought into perpendicular? Only by the divine measurement. "And the Lord said unto me, Amos, what seest thou? And I said, A plumb-line."

The whole tendency of the times is to make us act by the standard of what others do. If they play cards, we play cards. If they dance, we dance. If they read certain styles of book, we read them. We throw over the wall of our character the tangled plumb line of other lives and reject the infallible test which Amos saw.

PLUMB-LINE TRAFFIC.

The divine plumb-line needs to be thrown *over all merchandise.* Nothing would make times so good, and the earning of a livelihood so easy, as the universal adoption of the law of right. Suspicion strikes through all bargain-making. Men who sell know not whether they will ever get

the money. Purchasers know not whether the goods ship-
ped will be according to the sample. And what with the
large number of clerks who are making false entries and then
absconding to Canada, and the explosion of firms that fail
for millions of dollars, honest men are at their wits' end to
make a living. He who stands up amid all the pressure and
does right is accomplishing something toward the establishment of a high commercial prosperity. I have deep sympathy for the laboring classes who toil with hand and foot.
But we must not forget the business men, who, without any
complaint or bannered processions through the street, are
enduring a stress of circumstances terrific.

To feel right and to do right under all this pressure requires martyr grace, requires divine support, requires celestial reinforcement. But you will be wise to preserve your
equilibrium and your honesty and your faith, and throw
over all the counters and shelves and casks, the measuring
line of divine light   "And the Lord said unto me, Amos,
what seest thou ? And I said, A plumb-line."

LEANING TOWER OF PISA.

The question for me should not be what I think is right,
but what God thinks is right. This perpetual reference to
the behavior of others, as though it decided anything but
human fallibility, is a mistake as wide as the world. There
are *ten thousand plumb-lines in use,* but only one is true and
exact, and that is the line of God's eternal right. There is a
mighty attempt being made to reconstruct and fix up the
Ten Commandments. To many they seem too rigid. *The
tower of Pisa* leans over about thirteen feet from the perpendicular, and people go thousands of miles to see its graceful
inclination, and, by extra braces and various architectural
contrivances, it is kept leaning from century to century.
Why not have the ten granite blocks of Sinai set a little
aslant ? Why not have the pillar of truth a leaning tower ?
Why is not an ellipse as good as a square ? Why is not an

oblique as good as straight up and down ? My friends, we must have a standard ; shall it be God's or man's ?

This subject gives me a grand opportunity of saying a useful word to all young men who are now forming habits for a lifetime. Of what use to a stone-mason or a bricklayer is a plumb-line ? Why not build the wall by the unaided eye and hand ? Because they are insufficient, because if there be a deflection in the wall it cannot further on be corrected. Because by the law of gravitation, a wall must be straight in order to be symmetrical and safe. A young man is in danger of getting a defect in his wall of character that may never be corrected. One of the best friends I ever had died of delirium tremens at sixty years of age, though he had not since twenty-one years of age—before which he had been dissipated—touched intoxicating liquor until that particular carousal that took him off. Not feeling well in the street on a hot summer day, he stepped into a drug store, just as you and I would have done, and asked for a dose of something to make him feel better. And there was alcohol in the dose, and that one drop aroused the old appetite, and he entered the first liquor store, and stayed there until thoroughly under the power of rum. He entered his home a raving maniac, his wife and daughters fleeing from his presence, until he was taken to the city hospital to die. The combustible material of early habit had lain quiet nearly forty years, and that one spark ignited it.

Remember that the wall may be one hundred feet ʻhigh, and yet a deflection one foot from the foundation affects the entire structure. And if you live a hundred years and do right the last eighty years, you may nevertheless do something at twenty years of age that will damage all your earthly existence. All you who have built houses for yourselves, or for others, am I not right in saying to these young men, you cannot build a wall so high as to be independent of the character of its foundation ? A man before thirty years of age may commit enough sin to last him a lifetime. Now, John, or George, or Henry, or whatever be your Christian name or surname, say here and now : " No wild oats for me, no cigars or cigarettes for me, no wine or beer for me, no nasty stories for me, no Sunday sprees for me , I am going to start right and keep on right.   God help me, for I am very weak.   From the throne of eternal righteousness let down to me the prinples by which I can be guided in building everything from foundation to cap-stone.   Lord God, by the wounded hand of Christ, throw me a plumb-line."

CHAPTER XXI.

Heaven.

THE WAY TO HEAVEN.

You have heard of the Appian way. It was three hundred and fifty miles long. It was twenty-four feet wide, and on either side the road was a path for foot passengers. It was made out of rocks cut in hexagonal shape and fitted together. What a road it must have been! Made of smooth, hard rock, three hundred and fifty miles long. No wonder that in the construction of it the treasures of a whole empire were exhausted. Because of invaders, and the elements, and Time—the old conqueror who tears up a road as he goes over it—there is nothing left of that structure excepting a ruin. But I have to tell you of a road built before the Appian Way, and yet it is as good as when first constructed. Millions of souls have gone over it. Millions more will come.

> "The prophets and apostles, too,
> Pursued this road while here below ;
> We therefore will, without dismay,
> Still walk in Christ, the good old way."

"An highway shall be there, and a way, and it shall be called The Way of Holiness ; the unclean shall not pass over it, but it shall be for those; the wayfaring men, though fools, shall not err therein. No lion shall be there, nor any ravenous beast shall go up thereon, it shall not be found there ; but the redeemed shall walk there ; and the ransomed of the Lord shall return, and come to Zion with songs and everlasting joy upon their heads : they shall obtain joy and gladness, and sorrow and sighing shall flee away."

455

THE KING'S HIGHWAY.

In the diligence you dash on over the St.-Bernard pass of the Alps, mile after mile, and there is not so much as a pebble to jar the wheels. You go over bridges which cross chasms that make you hold your breath; under projecting rock; along by dangerous precipices, through tunnels adrip with the meltings of the glaciers, and, perhaps, for the first time, learn the majesty of a road built and supported by governmental authority. Well, my Lord the King decided to build a highway from earth to heaven.

It should span all the chasms of human wretchedness, it should tunnel all the mountains of earthly difficulty; it should be wide enough and strong enough to hold fifty thousand millions of the human race, if so many of them should ever be born. It should be blasted out of the "Rock of Ages," and cemented with the blood of the Cross, and be lifted amid the shouting of angels and the execration of devils.

The King sent His Son to build that road. He put head, and hand, and heart to it, and after the road was completed waved His blistered hand over the way, crying: "It is finished!" Napoleon paid fifteen million francs for the building of the Simplon Road, that his cannon might go over for the devastation of Italy; but our King, at a greater expense, has built a road for a different purpose, that the banners of heavenly dominion might come down over it, and all the redeemed of earth travel up over it.

Being a King's highway, of course, it is well built. Bridges splendidly arched and buttressed have given way, and crushed the passengers who attempted to cross them. But Christ, the King, would build no such thing as that. The work done, He mounts the chariot of His love, and multitudes mount with Him, and He drives on and up the steep of heaven, amid the plaudits of gazing worlds! The work is done—well done—gloriously done—magnificently done.

A CLEAN ROAD.

Many a fine road has become miry and foul because it has not been properly cared for; but my text says the unclean shall not walk on this one. Room on either side to throw away your sins. Indeed, if you want to carry them along you are not on the right road. That bridge will break, those overhanging rocks will fall, the night will come down, leaving you at the mercy of the mountain bandits, and at the very next turn of the road you will perish. But if you are really on this clean road of which I have been speaking, then you will stop ever and anon to wash in the water that stands in the basin of the eternal Rock.

A PLAIN ROAD.

" The wayfaring man, though a fool, shall not err therein." That is, if a man is three-fourths an idiot, he can find this road just as well as if he were a philosopher. The imbecile boy, the laughing-stock of the street, and followed by a mob hooting at him, has only just to knock once at the gate of heaven, and it swings open; while there has been many a man who can lecture about pneumatics, and chemistry, and tell the story of Farraday's theory of electrical polarization, and yet has been shut out of heaven. But if one shall come in the right spirit, seeking the way to heaven, he will find it a plain way.

He who tries to get on the road to heaven through the New Testament teaching will get on beautifully. He who goes through philosophical discussion will not get on at all. If you wanted to go to Albany, and I pointed you out a highway thoroughly laid out, would I be wise in detaining you by a geological discussion about the gravel you will pass over, or a physiological discussion about the muscles you will have to bring into play ? No. After this Bible has pointed you the way to heaven, is it wise for me to detain you with any discussion about the nature of the human will,

or whether the atonement is limited or unlimited? There
is the road—go on it. It is a plain way.

A SAFE ROAD.

Sometimes the traveller in those ancient highways would
think himself perfectly secure, not knowing there was a lion
by the way, burying his head deep between his paws, and
then, when the right moment came, under the fearful spring
the man's life was gone, and there was a mauled carcass by
the roadside. But, says my text, " No lion shall be there."
The road spoken of is also

A PLEASANT ROAD.

God gives a bond of indemnity against all evil to every
man that treads it.

I pursue this subject only one step further. I do not care
how fine a road you may put me on, I want to know where
it comes out. My God declares it : " The redeemed of the
Lord come to Zion." You know what Zion was. That was
the King's palace. It was a mountain fastness. It was im-
pregnable. And so heaven is the fastness of the universe.
No howitzer has long enough range to shell those towers.
Let all the batteries of earth and hell blaze away; they
cannot break in those gates. Gibraltar was taken, Sebásto-
pol was taken, Babylon fell; but these walls of heaven shall
never surrender either to human or Satanic besiegement.
The Lord God Almighty is the defence of it. Great capital
of the Universe! Terminus of the King's highway!

VISIONS OF HEAVEN.

Ezekiel, with others, had been expatriated, and while
in foreign slavery, standing on the banks of the royal canal,
which he and other serfs had been condemned to dig, by the
order of Nebuchadnezzar—the royal canal called the river
Chebar—the illustrious exile had visions of heaven. In-

deed, it is almost always so that the brightest visions of
heaven come not to those who are on mountain-top of prosperity, but to some John on desolate Patmos, or to some
Paul in Mamertine dungeon, or to some Ezekiel standing on
the banks of a ditch he had been compelled to dig—yea, to
the weary, to the heart-broken, to those whom sorrow has
banished.

Oh, what a mercy it is that all up and down the Bible
God induces us to look out toward other worlds! Bible
astronomy in Genesis, in Joshua, in Job, in the Psalms, in
the prophets, major and minor, in St. John's apocalypse,
practically saying, "Worlds! worlds! worlds!" What a
fuss we make about this little bit of a world, its existence
only a short time between two spasms, the paroxysm by
which it was buried from chaos into order and the paroxysm
of its demolition!

And I am glad that so many texts call us to look off to
other worlds, many of them larger and grander and more
resplendent. "Look there," says Job, "at Mazaroth and
Arcturus and his sons!" "Look there," says St. John,
"at the moon under Christ's feet!" "Look there," says
Joshua, "at the sun standing still above Gibeon!" "Look
there," says Moses, "at the sparkling firmament!" "Look
there," says Amos, the herdsman, "at the Seven Stars and
Orion!" Don't let us be so sad about those who shove off
from this world under Christly pilotage. Don't let us be so
agitated about our own going off this little barge or sloop or
canal boat of a world to get on some Great Eastern of the
heavens. Don't let us persist in wanting to stay in this barn,
this shed, this out-house of a world, when all the king's
palaces already occupied by many of our best friends are
swinging wide open their gates to let us in.

Oh, how this widens and lifts and stimulates our expectation! How little it makes the present, and how stupendous
it makes the future!

O Lord God of the seven stars and Orion, how can I endure the transport, the ecstasy, of such a vision! I must
obey His word and seek Him. I will seek Him. I seek Him

now, for I call to mind that it is not the material universe that is most valuable, but the spiritual, and that each of us has a soul worth more than all the worlds which the inspired herdsmen saw from his booth on the hills of Tekoa.

LONGING FOR HOME.

An old Scotchman, who had been a soldier in one of the European wars, was sick and dying in one of our American hospitals. His one desire was to see Scotland and his old home, and once again walk the heather of the Highlands, and hear the bagpipes of the Scotch regiments. The night that the old Scotch soldier died, a young man, somewhat reckless, but kind-hearted, got a company of musicians to come and play under the old soldier's window, and among the instruments there was a bagpipe. The instant that the musicians began, the dying old man in delirium said: " What's that, what's that ? Why, it's the regiments coming home. That's the tune, yes, that's the tune. Thank God, I have got home once more!" " Bonny Scotland and Bonny Doon," were the last words he uttered as he passed up to the highlands of the better country.

Hundreds and thousands are homesick for heaven : some because you have so many bereavements, some because you have so many temptations, some because you have so many ailments, homesick, very homesick, for the fatherland of heaven. At our best estate we are only pilgrims and strangers here. " Heaven is our home " Death will never knock at the door of that mansion, and in all that country there is not a single grave. How glad parents are in holiday times to gather their children home again! But I have noticed that there is almost always a son or a daughter absent—absent from home, perhaps absent from the country, perhaps absent from the world. Oh, how glad our Heavenly Father will be when He gets all His children home with Him in heaven ! And how delightful it will be for brothers and sisters to meet after long separation ! Once they parted at the door of the tomb, now they meet at the door of immortality. Once they saw only through a glass darkly; now it is face to face; corruption, incorruption; mortality, immortality. Where are now all their sins and sorrows and troubles? Overwhelmed in the Red Sea of Death, while they passed through dry-shod.

Gates of pearl, cap-stones of amethyst, thrones of dominion, do not stir my soul so much as the thought of home. Once there, let earthly sorrows howl like storms and roll like seas. Home! Let thrones rot and empires wither. Home! Let the world die in earthquake-struggle, and be buried amid procession of planets and dirge of spheres. Home! Let everlasting ages roll irresistible sweep. Home! No sorrow, no crying, no tears, no death. But home, sweet home; home, beautiful home, everlasting home; home with each other, home with God.

A DREAM.

One night lying on my lounge, when very tired, my children all around about me in full romp, and hilarity, and laughter—on the lounge, half awake and half asleep, I dreamed this dream: I was in a far country. It was not Persia, although more than Oriental luxuriance crowned the cities. It was not the tropics, although more than tropical fruitfulness filled the gardens. It was not Italy, although more than Italian softness filled the air. And I wandered around looking for thorns and nettles, but I found that none of them grew there, and I saw the sun rise, and I watched to see it set, but it sank not. And I saw the people in holiday attire, and I said: "When will they put off this and put on workmen's garb, and again delve in the mine or swelter at the forge?" but they never put off the holiday attire.

And I wandered in the suburbs of the city to find the place where the dead sleep, and I looked all along the line of the beautiful hills, the place where the dead might most blissfully sleep, and I saw towers and castles, but not a mausoleum or a monument or a white slab could I see. I went into the chapel of the great town, and I said: "Where do the poor worship, and where are the hard benches on which they sit?" And the answer was made me, "We have no poor in this country." And then I wandered out to find the hovels of the destitute, and I found mansions of amber and ivory and gold; but not a tear could I see, not a sigh could I hear, and I was bewildered, and I sat down under the branches of a great tree, and I said, "Where am I? And whence comes all this scene?"

And then out from among the leaves, and up the flowery paths, and across the bright streams there came a beautiful group, thronging all about me, and as I saw them come I thought I knew their step, and as they shouted I thought I knew their voices; but then they were so gloriously arrayed in apparel such as I had never before witnessed that I bowed as stranger to stranger. But when again they clapped their hands and shouted " Welcome, welcome !" the mystery all vanished, and I found that time had gone and eternity had come, and we were all together again in our new home in heaven. And I looked around, and I said: "Are we all here?" and the voices of many generations responded " All here !" And while tears of gladness were raining down our cheeks, and the branches of the Lebanon cedars were clapping their hands, and the towers of the great city were chiming their welcome, we all together began to leap and shout and sing, " Home, home, home, home !"

REUNION: A SHIPWRECKED FATHER AND SON.

I heard of a father and son who, among others were shipwrecked at sea. The father and the son climbed into the rigging. The father held on, but the son after a while lost his hold in the rigging and was dashed down. The father supposed he had gone hopelessly under the wave. The next day the father was brought ashore from the rigging in an exhausted state, and laid in a bed in a fisherman's hut, and after many hours had passed he came to consciousness, and saw lying beside him on the same bed his boy. Oh my friends ! what a glorious thing it will be if we wake up at last to find our loved ones beside us! The one hundred and forty and four thousand, and the "great multitude that no man can number"—some of our best friends among them—we, after a while, to join the multitude. Blessed anticipation! The reunions of earth are anticipative. We are not always going to stay here. This is not our home. O the reunion of patriarchs, and apostles, and prophets, and all our glorified kindred, and that "great multitude that no man can number!"

Does it not seem that heaven comes very near to us, as though our friends, whom we thought a great way off, are not in the distance, but close by? You have sometimes come down to a river at nightfall, and you have been surprised how easily you could hear voices across the river. You shouted over to the other side of the river, and they shouted back. It is said that when George Whitefield preached in Third Street, Philadelphia, one evening time, his voice was heard clear across to the New Jersey shore. When I was a little while chaplain in the army, I remember how at even-tide we could easily hear the voices of the pickets across the Potomac, just when they were using ordinary tones. And as we stand by the Jordan that divides us from our friends who are gone, it seems to me we stand on one bank and they stand on the other; and it is only a narrow stream, and our voices go and their voices come.

GLORIES OF HEAVEN.

O that I might show you the glories with which **God** clothes His dear children in heaven! I wish I could swing back one of the twelve gates that there might dash upon your ear one shout of the triumph,—that there might flame, upon your eyes one blaze of the splendor. Oh, when I speak of that good land, you involuntarily think of some one there that you loved—father, mother, brother, sister, or dear little child garnered already. You want to know what they are doing this morning. I will tell you what they are doing. Singing. You want to know what they wear. I will tell you what they wear. Coronets of triumph. You wonder why oft they look to the gate of the temple, and watch and wait. I will tell you why they watch and wait and look to the gate of the temple. For your coming. I shout upward the news, for I am sure some of you will repent and start for heaven. Oh, ye bright ones before the throne, your earthly friends are coming. Angels, posing mid-air, cry up the name. Gate-keeper of heaven, send forward the tidings. Watchman on the battlements celestial, throw the signal.

If a soldier can afford to shout "Huzza!" when he goes into battle, how much more jubilantly he can afford to shout "Huzza!" when he has gained the victory! If religion is so good a thing to have here, how bright a thing it will be in heaven! I want to see that young man when the glories of heaven have robed and crowned him. I want to hear him sing when all huskiness of earthly colds is gone, and he rises up with the great doxology. I want to know what standard he will carry when marching under arches of pearl in the army of banners. I want to know what company he will keep in a land where they are all kings and queens forever and ever. If I have induced one of you to begin a better life, then I want to know it. I may not in this world clasp hands with you in friendship, I may not hear from your own lips the story of temptation and sorrow, but I will clasp hands with you when then the sea is passed and the gates are entered.

We can, in this world, get no just idea of the splendors of heaven John tries to describe them. He says "the twelve gates are twelve pearls," and that "the foundations of the wall are garnished with all manner of precious stones." As we stand looking through the telescope of St. John, we see a blaze of amethyst and pearl and emerald and sardonyx and chrysoprase and sapphire, a mountain of light, a cataract of color, a sea of glass, and a city like the sun.

John bids us look again, and we see thrones, thrones of the prophets, thrones of the patriarchs, thrones of the angels, thrones of the apostles, thrones of the martyrs, throne of

Jesus—throne of God. And we turn round to see the glory, and it is thrones! thrones! thrones!

Skim from the summer waters the brightest sparkles, and you will get no idea of the sheen of the everlasting sea. Pile up the splendors of earthly cities, and they would not make a stepping-stone by which you might mount to the city of God. Every house is a palace. Every step is a triumph. Every covering of the head a coronation. Every meal is a banquet. Every stroke from the tower is a wedding-bell. Every day is a jubilee, every hour a rapture, and every moment an ecstasy.

HEAVENLY HOSTS.

David cried out : "The chariots of God are twenty thousand." Elisha saw the mountains filled with celestial cavalry. St. John said : "The armies which are in heaven followed Him on white horses." There must be armed escort sent out, to bring up from earth to heaven those who were more than conquerors. There must be crusades ever being fitted out for some part of God's dominion—battles, bloodless, groanless, painless ; angels of evil to be fought down.

John bids us look, and we see the great procession of the redeemed passing ; Jesus, on a white horse, leads the march, and all the armies of heaven following on white horses. Infinite cavalcade passing, passing, empires pressing into line, ages following ages. Dispensation tramping on after dispensation. Glory in the track of glory. Europe, Asia, Africa, North and South America, pressing into lines. Islands of the seas shoulder to shoulder. Generations before the flood following generations after the flood, and as Jesus rises at the head of that great host, and waves His sword in signal of victory, all crowns are lifted, and all ensigns slung out, and all chimes rung, and all hallelujahs chanted, and some cry, "Glory to God most high!" and some, "Hosanna to the son of David!" and some, "Worthy is the Lamb that was slain"—till all exclamations of endearment and homage in the vocabulary of heaven are exhausted, and there comes up surge after surge of "Amen! Amen! and Amen!"

HEAVENLY AWARDS.

There are old estates in the celestial world that have been in the possession of its inhabitants for thousands of years. Many of the victors from earth have already got their palaces, and they are pointed out to those newly arrived. Soon after our getting there we will ask to be shown the Apostolic residences, and ask where does Paul live, and John, and ask to be shown the patriarchal residences, and shall say, " Where does Abraham live, or Jacob?" and shown the martyr residences, and say, " Where does John Huss live, and Ridley?" We will want to see the boulevards where the chariots of conquerors roll. I will want to see the gardens where the princes walk. We will want to see Music Row, where Handel, and Haydn, and Mozart, and Charles Wesley, and Thomas Hastings, and Bradbury have their homes; out of their windows, ever and anon, rolling some sonnet of an earthly oratorio or hymn transported with the composer. We will want to see Revival Terrace, where Whitefield, and Nettleton, and Payson, and Rowland Hill, and Charles Finney, and other giants of soul-reaping are resting from their almost supernatural labors, their doors thronged with converts just arrived, coming to report themselves.

But brilliant as the sunset, and like the leaves for number, are the celestial homes yet to be awarded, when Christ to you, and millions of others, shall divide the spoil. What do you want there? You shall have it. An orchard? There it is; twelve manner of fruit, and fruit every month. Do you want river scenery? Take your choice on the banks of the river, in longer, wider, deeper roll than Danube, or Amazon, or Mississippi if mingled in one, and emptying into the sea of glass, mingled with fire. Do you want your kindred back again? Go out and meet your father and mother without the staff or the stoop, and your children in a dance of immortal glee. Do you want a throne? Select it from the million burnished elevations. Do you want a crown? Pick it out of that mountain of diamonded coronets. Do you want your old church friends of earth around you? Begin to hum an old revival tune and they will flock from all quarters, to revel with you in sacred reminiscence. All the earth for those who are here on earth at the time of continental and planetary distribution, and all the heavens for those who are there.

That heavenly distribution of spoils will be a surprise to many. Here enters heaven the soul of a man who took up a great deal of room in the church on earth, but there forsooth he is put in an old house once occupied by an angel who was hurled out of heaven at the time of Satan's rebellion.

Right after him comes a soul that makes a great stir among the celestials, and the angels rush to the scene, each bringing to her a dazzling coronet. Who is she? Over what realm on earth was she queen? In what great Dusseldorf festival was she the cantatrice? Neither. She was an invalid who never left her room for twenty years; but she was strong in prayer, and she prayed down revival after revival, and pentecost after pentecost, upon the churches, and with her pale hands she knit many a mitten or tippet for the poor, and with her contrivances she added joy to many a holiday festival, and now, with those thin hands so strong for kindness, and with those white lips so strong for supplication, she has won coronation and enthronement and jubilee. And Christ says to the angels who have brought each a crown for the glorified invalid, "No, not these; they are not good enough. But in the jewelled vase at the right-hand side of my throne there is one that I have been preparing for her many a year, and for her every pang I have set an amethyst, and for her every good deed I have set a pearl. Fetch it now and fulfil the promise I gave her long ago in the sickroom, 'Be thou faithful unto death, and I will give thee a crown.'"

THE HEALTH OF HEAVEN.

Look at that soul standing before the throne. On earth she was a life-long invalid. See her step now, and hear her voice now. Catch, if you can, one breath of that celestial air. Health in all the pulses—health of vision; health of spirits; immortal health. No racking cough, no sharp pleurisies, no consuming fevers, no exhausting pains, no hospitals of wounded men. Health swinging in the air; health flowing in all the streams; health blooming on the banks. No headaches, no side-aches, no back-aches. That child that died in the agonies of croup, hear her voice now ringing in the anthem! That old man that was bowed down with the infirmities of age, see him walk now with the step of an immortal athlete—forever young again! That night when the needle-woman fainted away in the garret, a wave of the heavenly air resuscitated her forever—for everlasting years, to have neither ache nor pain nor weakness nor fatigue.

And then remember that all physical disadvantages will be exchanged for a better outfit. Either the unstrung, worn-out, blunted, and crippled organs will be so reconstructed that you will not know them, or an entire new set of eyes, and ears, and feet will be given you. Just what it means by corruption putting on incorruption we do not know, save that it will be glory ineffable, no limping in heaven, no straining of the eyesight to see things a little way off; no putting of the hand behind the ear to double the capacity of the tympanum; but faculties perfect, all the keys of the instrument attuned for the sweep of the fingers of ecstasy.

HEAVEN RIGHTS ALL WRONGS.

In the midst of the city of Paris stands a statue of the good but broken-hearted Josephine. I never imagined that marble could be smitten into such tenderness. It seems not lifeless. If the spirit of Josephine be disentabernacled, the soul of the Empress has taken possession of this figure. I am not yet satisfied that it is stone. The puff of the dress on the arm seems to need but the pressure of the finger to indent it. The figure at the bottom of the robe, the ruffle at the neck, the fur lining on the dress, the embroidery of the satin, the cluster of lily and and leaf and rose in her hand, the poise of her body as she seems to come sailing out of the sky, her face calm, humble, beautiful, but yet sad—attest the genius of the sculptor and the beauty of the heroine he celebrates. Looking up through the rifts of the coronet that encircles her brow, I could see the sky beyond, the great heavens where all the woman's wrongs shall be righted, and the story of endurance and resignation shall be told to all the ages. The rose and the lily in the hand of Josephine will never drop their petals. Beautiful symbol of the fact that heaven rights all wrongs.

NO SORROW THERE.

This is a planet of weeping we are living on. We enter upon life with a cry and leave it with a long sigh. But there God wipeth away all tears from all eyes. Oh, this is a world of sorrow! But, blessed be God! there will be no sorrow in Heaven. Not one black dress of mourning, but plenty of white robes of joy; hand-shaking of welcome, but none of separation. Why, if one trouble should attempt to enter Heaven, the shining police of the city would put it under everlasting arrest. If all the sorrows of life, mailed and sworded under Apollyon, should attempt to force that gate, one company from the tower would strike them back howling to the pit. Room in Heaven for all the raptures that ever knocked at the gate, but no room for the smallest annoyance, though slight as a summer insect. Doxology, but no dirge. Banqueting, but no "funeral-baked meats." No darkness at all. No grief at all. Our sorrows over. Our journey ended. It will be as when kings banquet. And just as the snow of winter melts, and the fields will brighten in the glorious springtime, so it will be with all these cold sorrows of earth; they shall be melted away at last before the warm sunshine of heaven. When the clock of Christian suffering has run down, it will never be wound up again. Amid the vineyards of the heavenly Engedi, that will be restoration without any relapse, that will be "The Saints' Everlasting Rest!"

THE BIBLE THE ONLY TRUE GUIDE-BOOK.

I have not heard yet one single intelligent account of the future world from anybody who does not believe in the Bible. They throw such a fog about the subject that I do not want to go to the sceptic's heaven, to the transcendentalist's heaven, to the worldly philosopher's heaven. I would not exchange the poorest room in your house for the finest heaven that Huxley or Stuart Mill or Darwin ever dreamed of. Their heaven has no Christ in it; and a heaven without Christ, though you could sweep the whole universe into it, would be no heaven. Oh, they tell us there are no songs there, there are no coronations in heaven. But that would not satisfy me. Give me Christ and my old friends—that is the Heaven I want, that is heaven enough for me. O garden of light, whose leaves never wither, and whose fruits never fail! O banquet of God, whose sweetness never palls the taste and whose guests are kings forever! O city of light, whose walls are salvation, and whose gates are praise! O palace of rest, where God is the monarch and everlasting ages the length of His reign!

> " When shall these eyes thy heaven-built walls
>   And pearly gates behold?
>   Thy bulwarks with salvation strong,
>   And streets of shining gold."

HISTORIC WONDERS.

We shall read there not the history of a few centuries of our planet only, but the history of the eternities—whole millenniums before Xenophon or Herodotus or Moses or Adam was born. History of one world, history of all worlds!

HIGHER MATHEMATICS.

What are our mathematical friends to do in the next world? They found their joy and their delight in mathematics. There was more poetry for them in Euclid than in John Milton. They were as passionately fond of mathematics as Plato, who wrote over his door, "Let no one enter here who is not acquainted with geometry." What are they doing now? They are busy with figures yet. No place in all the universe like heaven for figures. Numbers infinite, distances infinite, calculations infinite. The didactic Dr. Dick said he really thought that the redeemed in heaven spent some of their time with the higher branches of mathematics.

LAW STUDIES.

Studying law in a universe where everything is controlled by law, from flight of humming-bird to flight of world—law, not dry and hard and drudging, but righteous and magnificent law, before which man and cherub and seraph and archangel and God Himself bow. The chain of law long enough to wind around the immensities and infinity and eternity! Chain of law! What a place to study law, where all the links of the chain are visible!

ASTRONOMY.

Studying astronomy not through the dull lens of earthly observatory; with one stroke of wing going right out to Jupiter and Mars and Saturn and Orion and the Pleiades—overtaking and passing swiftest comets in their flight! Herschel died a Christian. Have you any doubt about what Herschel is doing? Isaac Newton died a Christian. Have you any doubt about what Isaac Newton is doing? Joseph Henry died a Christian. Have you any doubt about what Joseph Henry is doing? They were in discussion, all these astronomers of earth, about what the aurora borealis was, and none of them could guess. They know now; they have been to see for themselves.

THE SCIENCES.

Instead of a few thousand volumes on a few shelves, all the volumes of the universe open—geologic, ornithologic, conchologic, botanic, astronomic, philosophic. No more need of Leyden jars, or voltaic piles, or electric batteries, standing face to face with the facts of the universe. Scientists following out their own science, following out and following out forever. Since they died they have solved ten thousand questions which once defied the earthly laboratory. They stand on the other side of the thin wall of electricity, the wall that seems to divide the physical from the spiritual world; the thin wall of electricity, so thin the wall that ever and anon it seems to be almost broken through—broken through from our side by telephonic and telegraphic apparatus, broken through from the other side by strange influences which men in their ignorance call spiritualistic manifestations. All that matter cleared up. Agassiz standing amid his student explorers down in Brazil, coming across some great novelty in the rocks, taking off his hat and saying: "Gentlemen, let us pray; we must have divine illumination; we want wisdom from the Creator to study these rocks; He made them; let us pray"—Agassiz going right on with his studies forever.

EXPLORATIONS.

With lightning locomotion and with vision microscopic and telescopic at the same time. A continent at a glance. A world in a second. A planetary system in a day. Christian John Franklin no more in disabled *Erebus* pushing toward the North Pole; Christian De Long no more trying to free blockaded *Jeannette* from the ice; Christian Livingstone no more amid African malarias trying to make revelation of a dark continent; but all of them in the twinkling of an eye taking in that which was unapproachable. Mont Blanc scaled without alpenstock. The coral depths of the ocean explored without a diving-bell. The mountains opened without Sir Humphrey Davy's safety lamp.

THEOLOGY.

What are our departed Christian friends who found their chief joy in studying God, doing now? Studying God yet! No need of revelation now, for unblanched they are face to face. Now they can handle the omnipotent thunderbolts, just as a child handles the sword of a father come back from victorious battle. They have no sin, nor fear, consequently.

Studying Christ, not through a revelation, save the revelation of the scars—that deep lettering which brings it all up quick enough. Studying the Christ of the Bethlehem caravansary, the Christ of the awful massacre with its hemorrhage of head and hand, and foot and side—the Christ of the shattered mausoleum—Christ the sacrifice, the star, the sun, the man, the God.

SOCIETY.

What a place to visit in, where your next-door neighbors are kings and queens. You yourselves kingly and queenly. If they want to know more particularly about the first Paradise, they have only to go over and ask Adam. If they want to know how the sun and the moon halted, they have only to go over and ask Joshua. If they want to know how the storm pelted Sodom they have only to go over and ask Lot. If they want to know more about the arrogance of Haman, they have only to go over and ask Mordecai If they want to know how the Red Sea boiled when it was cloven, they have only to go over and ask Moses. If they want to know the particulars about the Bethlehem advent, they have only to go over and ask the serenading angels who stood that Christmas night in the balconies of crystal. If they want to know more of the particulars of the crucifixion, they have only to go over and ask those who were personal spectators while the mountains crouched and the Heavens got black in the face at the spectacle.

When I get to heaven I will come to all the people to whom I have administered in the Gospel, and to the millions of souls to whom, through the kindness of the printing-press, I am permitted to preach every week in this land and other lands—letters coming from New Zealand and Australia and the uttermost parts of earth, as well as from near nations, telling me of the souls I have helped—*I will visit them all. I give them fair notice.*

OCCUPATION.

Plenty of occupation in heaven! I suppose Broadway, New York, in the busiest season of the year, at noonday, is not so busy as heaven is all the time. Grand projects of mercy for other worlds! Victories to be celebrated! The downfall of despotisms on earth to be announced! Great songs to be learned and sung! Great expeditions on which God shall send forth His children! *Plenty to do, but no fatigue!*

NEW JERUSALEM CHURCH.

After a while our names will be taken off the church books, or there will be a mark in the margin, to indicate that we have gone up to a better church and to a higher communion—a perfect church, where all our preferences will be gratified. Great cathedral of eternity, with arches of amethysts, and pillars of sapphire, and floors of emerald, and windows aglow with the sunrise of heaven! What stupendous towers, with chimes angel-hoisted and angel-rung! What myriads of worshippers, white-robed and coroneted! What an officiator at the altar, even "the great High Priest of our profession"! What walls, hung with the captured shields and flags, by the church militant, passed up to be church triumphant!

Hark! the bell of the cathedral rings—the cathedral bell of heaven. There is going to be a great meeting in the temple. Worshippers all coming through the aisles Make room for the conqueror. Christ standing in the temple. All heaven gathering around Him. Those who loved the beautiful, come to look at the Rose of Sharon. Those who loved music, come to listen to His voice. Those who were mathematicians, come to count the years of His reign. Those who were explorers, come to discover the breadth of His love. Those who had the military spirit on earth sanctified, and the military spirit in heaven, come to look at the Captain of their salvation. The astronomers come to look at the Morning Star. The men of the law come to look at Him who is the Judge of quick and dead. The men who healed the sick, come to look at Him who was wounded for our transgressions.

All different, and different forever in many respects, yet all alike in admiration for Christ, in worship for Christ, and all alike in joining in the doxology: "Unto Him who washed us from our sins in His own blood, and made us kings and priests unto God, to Him be glory in the church throughout all ages, world without end!"

MUSIC.

The Bible says so much about the music of heaven that it cannot all be figurative. The Bible over and over again speaks of the songs of heaven. If heaven had no songs of its own, a vast number of those of earth would have been taken up by the earthly emigrants. Surely the Christian at death does not lose his memory. Then there must be millions of souls in heaven who know "Coronation," and "Antioch," and "Mount Pisgah," and "Old Hundred," and they can easily learn the "New Song." And the leader of the eternal orchestra need only once tap his baton, and all heaven will be ready for the hallelujah.

Cannot the soul sing? How often we compliment some exquisite singer by saying: "There was so much soul in her music." In heaven it will be all soul, until the body after a while comes up in the resurrection, and then there will be an additional heaven. Cannot the soul hear? If it can hear, then it can hear music.

Grand old Haydn, sick and worn out, was carried for the last time into the music hall, and there he heard his own oratorio of the "Creation." History says that as the orchestra came to that famous passage, "Let there be light!" the whole audience rose and cheered, and Haydn waved his hand toward heaven, and said: "It comes from there." Overwhelmed with his own music, he was carried out in his chair, and as he came to the door he spread his hand toward the orchestra as in benediction. Haydn was right when he waved his hand toward heaven and said: "It comes from there." Music was born in heaven, and it will ever have its highest throne in heaven; and I want you to understand that our departed friends who were passionately fond of music here, are now *at the headquarters of harmony.* I think that the grand old tunes that died when your grandfathers died, have gone with them to heaven.

SWEET SABBATH SONG.

When the redeemed of the Lord shall come to Zion, then let all the harpers take down their harps, and all the trumpeters take down their trumpets, and all across heaven let there be chorus of morning stars, chorus of white-robed victors, chorus of martyrs from under the throne, chorus of ages, chorus of worlds, and let there be but one song sung, and but one name spoken, and but one throne honored—that of Jesus only.

What doxologies of all nations! Cornet to cornet, cymbal to cymbal, harp to harp, organ to organ! Pull out the tremulant stop to recall the suffering past! Pull out the trumpet stop to celebrate the victory!

O song louder than the surf-beat of many waters, yet soft as the whisper of cherubim!

[Then shall be heard the great anthem of the ages, rolling out and rolling on, in tones "loud, as of numbers numberless, yet sweet, as of blest spirits uttering joy"—the oratorio of the skies, in full orchestra, swelling the praises of God and the Lamb, for ever and ever. Amen.—EDITOR.]

CHAPTER XXII.

Dr. Talmage in Palestine.

The following letter from the Rev. Dr. T. DeWitt Talmage was written from the Holy Land to Dr. H. A. Tucker, President of the Board of Trustees of the Brooklyn Tabernacle:

HOTEL VICTORIA, DAMAS (SYRIE),
DAMASCUS, Dec. 21, 1889

To the Officers and Congregation of the Brooklyn Tabernacle ·

DEAR FRIENDS: I greet you from this distant land. I have accomplished what I came for. Our journey in Italy, Greece, Egypt, and Palestine is completed. We have been blessed and prospered at every step. I will bring home with me for our new church a stone from the Jordan to be sculptured into a baptismal font, and for the corner-stone of our church a stone from Mount Calvary (I rolled it from the Hill Golgotha, or Place of a Skull, with my own hand); and a stone from Mount Sinai. These two will preach the Law and the Gospel from our church wall long after our lips have ceased to preach. The stone from Mount Calvary will of course be put on top of the one from Mount Sinai. I bring also from Mars Hill, Athens, where Paul preached, a stone for a pulpit table.

On the way to the Jordan we met an American who expressed the wish to be baptized by immersion in that sacred river. So, with a number of people from different countries standing on the bank and singing the old hymn, " On Jordan's stormy banks I stand," and after I had read of the baptism of old in the river, the candidate and myself waded into the swift stream, and the ordinance was more solemn and suggestive than I can describe.

From Damascus we start homeward. We will (D. V.) sail from Liverpool January 22, Wednesday, and arrive home the following

Wednesday, and I expect to preach to you the first Sabbath in February.*

Asking for a continuance of your prayers in our behalf, I am your pastor,

T. DeWitt Talmage.

On his way from Damascus, Dr. Talmage was honored with receptions by the American Ministers in Constantinople and Paris.

---

* Dr. Talmage took the S. S. *Aurania* from Liverpool on Saturday, January 25, and arrived in New York on Monday, February 3. A public reception was given to him on Thursday, February 6, at the Armory of the 13th regiment, Brooklyn.

ALPHABETICAL INDEX.

CPSIA information can be obtained
at www.ICGtesting.com
Printed in the USA
BVHW011135211221
624602BV00002B/26